The Challenge of the Prairie

About the Author

HIRAM M. DRACHE, native of the small farming village of Meriden, Minnesota, has spent his life as a resident in and student of rural America. He received his B.A. from Gustavus Adolphus College, M.A. from the University of Minnesota and Ph.D. from the University of North Dakota.

Dr. Drache has been a professor of history at Concordia College, Moorhead, Minnesota, since 1952. In addition to teaching, he has spent five years in the business world and since graduation from college he has been continuously involved in farming. Presently he is actively engaged in several farming operations. The family lives on a farm at Baker, Minnesota. A dozen articles about his farming activities have been published in regional and national farm periodicals. He developed one of the first completely personal computerized accounting systems for his feedlot operation.

Drache is known for his radio series, "Tales of Bonanzaland" and as a speaker in agricultural circles in the Dakotas and Minnesota. His first book, *The Day of the Bonanza*, published in 1964 and now in its sixteenth printing, is an account of large-scale farming activities of the late nineteenth century. He is listed in Who's Who in American Education, Who's Who in the Midwest, and the Directory of American Scholars.

The Challenge of the Prairie

Life and Times
Of Red River Pioneers

HIRAM M. DRACHE
Concordia College
Moorhead, Minnesota

HOBAR

HOBAR PUBLICATIONS
A Division of Finney Company
www.finney-hobar.com

The original publisher was the
NORTH DAKOTA INSTITUTE FOR
REGIONAL STUDIES, State University
Station, Fargo, North Dakota 58102.

Library of Congress Catalog Card No.:
70-632775

Second Printing—December 1970
Third Printing—November 1971
Fourth Printing—December 1974
Fifth Printing—November 1977
Sixth Printing—October 1979
Seventh Printing—November 1987
First Paperback Edition—August 2010

ISBN: 978-0-913163-45-0

Cover image (background):
Prairie Sky Landscape © Tyler Olson.
Image from BigStockPhoto.com.

Hobar Publications
An Imprint of Finney Company
8075 215th Street West
Lakeville, Minnesota 55044
www.finney-hobar.com

1 3 5 7 9 10 8 6 4 2
Printed in the United States of America

Dedication

TO MY WIFE ADA WHO HAS SHARED THESE
WORDS WITH ME AT LEAST FIVE TIMES.

Foreword

THERE was a time in this country's past when the vast mid-continent area was governed only by natural systems: the drainage system of a river basin, the flyway system of migratory waterfowl, the temperature system that created four seasons, the rainfall system that controlled the plant life, and the soil system laid down by grinding glaciers and their retreating lakes.

So the Red River Valley of the North was governed for centuries by natural systems—until the frontiersmen with their surveyor's rods arrived on the scene with man-made systems. They disrupted and reshaped nature's systems by overlaying them with section lines, townships, counties, and state boundaries. They laid out roads, railroads, and bridges. They broke sod, burned brush, and drained potholes. Some problems caused by nature were overcome, but many man-made problems were born. *The Challenge of the Prairie* is a recounting of the first skirmishes between the systems of man and nature as they took place in the drainage basin area of the Red River of the North.

The settlers' Red River Valley is relatively young—only about a century in age. It is so young that there are a few who still remember it in its infancy. But memories are fading, eyes are growing dim, and much is slipping away beyond the horizon. It is time to gather the events and conditions of the homesteaders into an historically accurate account as they are documented or remembered. It is time to record what went on in the Red River Valley as small ripples of settlement developed into waves of migration by people who had one thing in common—they were seeking! Dr. Drache's *The Challenge of the Prairie* tells of those

vii

seekers who did not always find, but in their efforts achieved or failed, rejoiced and suffered, stayed or left, lived or died.

In the beginning the Red River Valley was divided by the river itself, and then later it was subdivided by territorial boundaries and the boundary with Canada. Counties were laid out and cities were founded. Yet, the people of the Valley, regardless of boundaries to this day are given a separate identity. They are regarded with envy because of what they have, with respect for what they have achieved, and with suspicion for the political power their density of population controls.

The fertility of the Valley soil, the wealth of its farms, the progressiveness of its cities, the dependability of rainfall, the density of the population, and the development of its educational institutions and health services have given the people of the Valley social, economic, and political force which is at times admired, but at other times resented by people from less endowed areas.

Some things about the Valley as they were a century ago are hard to believe. That steamboats pulled barges from Breckenridge to Winnipeg and back in less than a week on a tree-choked, narrow, looping Red River does not seem possible. Tobacco growing year after year for generations on R. M. Probstfield's farm is a head-shaker. Incredible it is that there were strong women who would endure the months of loneliness; who would battle searing prairie fires; who would watch for children or husbands coming home through the white gloom of a three-day blizzard; who would nurse sick children, work their gardens, make the clothing, cook the meals, and make a home in a single-walled shack, a log cabin, or a sod hut.

To those who live in the Valley now, there is much in *The Challenge of the Prairie* which explains today. So much of what was true for the homesteader is still true for those who live in the Valley. The weather, floods, taxes, low wheat prices, large-scale farming, too many schools, towns too close together are still with us.

But the Valley has relented and softened in many respects. It now provides for more opportunities for a good life to those who seek it. There are investment opportunities unlimited. A full spectrum of educational facilities has been established. The complete system of health care services is available to all. Recreational and cultural opportunities ease mind and muscle from the never-ending quest for achievement through work. The social ills of older parts of the nation such as air and water pollution, intense poverty, crime, racism and congestion have not descended upon the Valley. Perhaps the heritage left by those sturdy first families will be strong enough in this generation to ward off the mistakes of other sections of the United States. History is not finished in the Valley. It is being made every day.

There are those who once thrilled to the harvest-time sight of twenty or more straw stacks burning around the horizon in the darkness of evening, their glow dancing against the low hanging clouds that threatened to dampen the countryside. Then came the combine and burning straw piles were gone.

We remember when the long, sleek, solid-looking railroad diesel engines replaced the big, black steam engines whose long plume of trailing smoke seemed an inseparable part of railroading.

We watched the one-room school disappear. We are amused that the vanished county courthouse spittoon is now in great demand as a collector's item. Drivers who could not have stayed on a horse a century ago are now blithely weaving in and out of traffic at 75 miles an hour, piloting two tons of automobile that is considered well on the way to obsolescence after its first year.

We can remember when sulpha and penicillin appeared on the scene to ease the burden of the small town doctor.

But we have cause to wonder how many Randolph Probstfields are still being produced. His meticulous and methodical records give us an exceptionally clear pane through which to view the past. Dr. Drache's use of Probstfield's records and those of many others has let us live with those pioneers and sense their determination and strength yet understand their pain and privation. *The Challenge of the Prairie* is a valued glimpse into a bygone era.

Perhaps this history of the Red River Valley settlement is dearer to me because I grew up in the small but neat town of Amenia, which was founded as the headquarters for the Amenia and Sharon Land Company's huge bonanza farm operation. My father managed a major segment of that land company known as the Carrie T. Chaffee estate. There was a proud esprit de corps around Amenia. We knew of its history and its founders. But we saw it change too, just as every community in the Valley has changed and will continue to do so.

The homesteader is gone, but *The Challenge of the Prairie* keeps alive a short, intense and robust period in the history of what was the beginning of the development of the Red River Valley and points west and north wherever the steamboat plied or the track was laid.

WILLIAM L. GUY
Governor of North Dakota

Preface

The valley of the Red River of the North in the heart of the North American continent is one of the richest agricultural regions of the world. The Valley proper is more than 300 miles long, and about 50 miles wide. It is almost perfectly flat. Originally it was the drainage area of a large receding glacier, and for a long period it was part of the post-glacial Lake Agassiz. Now it is the drainage basin of the Red River of the North which includes several tributaries that flow into the Red River from both east and west. Because all of these streams have their sources in the higher lands on both sides of the Valley, it has a basin-like appearance that is clearly visible when one enters the region from the east or the west.

The area is virtually treeless, stoneless, and flat as well as very fertile, making it ideal for farming. The major handicaps to maximum agricultural production are the relatively short growing season and the frequent periods of excessive moisture, especially in the spring. Water from melting snow and spring rains cause frequent floods that cover wide areas on both sides of the river. The flood problem is intensified by the fact that the Red River flows north and its mouth is still frozen while the source, farther south, is experiencing the spring thaw.

Although the soil structure varies, the soil is generally very fertile and has a high water holding capacity. This has prompted some to call the Valley "the land of the sure-crop." In the Valley's natural state, most trees were found along the streams and rivers. The thick, native prairie grass of the early days provided an abundant supply of food for the buffalo and other wild life.

In spite of its enticing characteristics, the Indians were never particularly attracted to the Valley. Periodic buffalo hunts were the only Indian activity in the area. The Indian was never a major obstacle to settlement in the Red River Valley because most of the white man's migrations into the area did not take place until the Indian was subdued.

Some of the earliest pioneers journeyed to the Valley by covered wagon. The great bulk of them, however, came in immigrant cars provided by the newly constructed railroads. Railroads made the land more accessible, brought markets within reach of the area, and also provided a source of work and cash income for many of the early farmers.

Generally, three types of settlers interested in farming came to the Red River area: (1) the settler who acquired from 160 to 480 acres from the government under the Homestead Act of 1862, and frequently additional acres under the Timber Act; (2) the settler who purchased railroad land or title rights from other homesteaders, giving him more land than could be secured under government programs; (3) the bonanza farmer who secured virtually all of his land from the railroad land grants. Most of the settlers who succeeded in the long run fell into the second category. The successful quarter section homesteader, with the exception of those who had sizeable livestock operations, was a rarity in Red River Land. The term "homesteader" is frequently applied to the small scale family farmer who either purchased his land or acquired it under the Homestead Act.

The purpose of this study is to provide a vivid illustration and a better understanding of the life of some of the pioneer farmers and their families in the Red River area. Some attempt has been made to include stories about pioneers from the fringe areas as well as those in the Valley proper. How they came to the area, how they spent their first years as struggling pioneers on the naked prairie, how many of them prospered, and how many of them failed are the central themes. Family, social, religious, and economic life are covered without any intent to emphasize one phase over the other. The story is intended to be about people, with other facets being incidental. The story is not intended to be complete, for that is virtually impossible. The social history of the bonanza farmers, the development of government, the agrarian discontent and resulting farmer organizations are some of the topics that will be told in another volume already in progress.

The maps on the inside covers locate all of the towns and villages in the area mentioned in the text. Farms of the more frequently mentioned families are also indicated. Tributaries of the Red River and rail lines most essential to the story are also included.

The inspiration to write this story came about when Mrs. Hugh Trowbridge and the late Mrs. Max Dahl, daughters of Red River Valley pioneers, pleaded with me to write a "real live history" about this area's past. *The Challenge of the Prairie* is a portion of the story and it is my hope that it is what they wanted.

HIRAM M. DRACHE
Professor of History
Concordia College
Moorhead, Minnesota

Table of Contents

The Challenge of the Prairie

CHAPTER I

Lure of the Land

Owning land has long been one of the great desires of man. Land ownership brought with it a certain prestige that could not be gained through possession of any other form of wealth. America's western frontier with its free land was an attraction to the disenchanted farmers of her own eastern states as well as to those of Europe. Others in Europe also looked to the American frontier as the one remaining great opportunity. Improved transportation made possible "the greatest movement of people that the world had known to that day." Between 1870 and 1900, 430 million acres were occupied and half of those acres were brought into production. The pioneers were not always practical and frequently added to their hardships in their great haste for land, but they all had one thing in common that enabled them to do battle with the elements—a vision for a greater life. The noted historian, Carl Becker, writing about the Kansas frontier, described that vision in this manner:

Idealism must always prevail on the frontier, for the frontier, whether geographical or intellectual, offers little hope to those who see things as they are. To venture into the wilderness one must see it not as it is, but as it will be. The frontier, being the possession of those only who see its future, is the promised land which cannot be entered save by those who have faith.[1]

First Settlers

The first permanent settlers in Red River Land searched for that vision in the area of the lower Red River Valley at the junction of the Assiniboine and Red Rivers. The location was called Fort Garry and later named Winnipeg. This region had been first explored in the 1670's and fur trading posts were established there as early as 1738. By the time the first agricultural settlers arrived, the fur trade was already on the decline. Buffalo, however, still blackened the neighboring plains; elk, deer, and bear abounded in the forested areas; and many

3

fish were found in the rivers. "Moschetoes" (mosquitoes) were found
around Georgetown (the site of a Hudson's Bay Company trading
post along the Red River) in "perfect swarms. . . . [They] will drive
any man out of the woods in five minutes unless he has the hide of a
rhinoceros and is toughened to their stings. They are the same on
the prairie. . . ." [2]

Between 1811 and 1815, Lord Selkirk, a Scotsman with substantial
holdings in the Hudson's Bay Company, sent four different groups,
totaling at least 363 persons, to his Canadian grant of 116,000 square
miles around the junction of the Assiniboine River and the Red River.
Most of these people had been laborers, farmers, and herdsmen in
Scotland and Ireland. After arriving, they had a continuous battle
with nature which climaxed with the flood of 1826. At that time all of
the people were forced from their homes and 243 deserted to Fort
Snelling in Minnesota.

Farther south in the upper Red River Valley, settlement followed
the anticipated establishment of military posts. Early explorers had
spotted an ideal townsite where the Otter Tail River flowing from the
east met the Bois de Sioux River from the south to form the Red
River. They were so impressed by the Red River that they envisioned
a town which would become a second Chicago controlling all the
American trade with western Canada. In October, 1856, several townsite groups were organized and financed in St. Paul for the purpose of
founding a town near this junction to provide better facilities for the
anticipated increase in trade along the Red River.

The townsite expedition which left St. Paul, January 1, 1857, consisted of three leaders, a cook, four teamsters, and two half-breed
French Chippewa Indian guides—Charles and Pierre Bottineau. Pierre
later became famous as a guide for many subsequent expeditions
throughout the region. Of the leaders, Daniel S. Johnstone was the
best known. The expedition required thirty days to travel the 203
miles from St. Paul to Breckenridge. It took them twenty-four hours
to cover the last twelve miles, but the sight of eighty buffalo at the
river junction made them forget the difficult journey. They had left
St. Paul with 159 pounds of pork, a keg of molasses, a barrel of flour,
a bushel of beans, and some salt. The buffalo provided their first
chance for fresh meat. After much effort and nearly a day and a half
of hunting, two calves, one cow, and one bull were killed and butchered, giving them a ton of fresh meat. The bull was shot as it walked
almost directly on top of two hidden hunters, both of whom fired at
once.

Winter was not kind to these founders of Breckenridge. By February 15, 1857, one of the oxen had to be shot and butchered because it had become too weak to get up. Snow was so deep that hunting for other food was virtually impossible. On March 4, the food inventory consisted of two quarts of beans, two pints of salt, and some meat. The weather was unseasonably warm and the early thaw gave them warning of an approaching flood. Between March 15 and April 12, the men were forced to work in water dismantling their cabin in order to rebuild it on higher ground. The warm weather caused the meat to spoil and they became desperate for food; however, rescue eventually came from St. Paul.

Progress in Breckenridge was slowed as the impact of the Panic of 1857 reached the frontier, and when the Sioux outbreak took place in 1862 all was destroyed but the sawmill.[8]

Early Transportation

No real progress could be forecast for a region as remote as the Red River Valley until some form of transpotation was perfected. The development of an organized transportation system in the Valley started in 1843 when the Red River carts, organized earlier by fur traders, provided the connecting link with the outside world. These carts with two high wooden wheels were pulled either by a single horse or by an ox, and they hauled loads of about 800 pounds. Sometimes one individual managed several carts by tying the animals and carts in tandem. Then in 1859, the *Anson Northup* became the first steamer to travel on the Red River. Finally, the Northern Pacific Railroad provided the greatest advance when it reached the Red in 1871. Dog teams were also a part of the transportation system and such prominent people as Walter J. S. Traill, an agent of the Hudson's Bay Company at Georgetown, and James J. Hill, who later founded the Great Northern Railroad, are reputed to have used them. They were used out of Moorhead as late as 1873, but primarily for sport by that date. Dog travel was fast and could function when all other means except men on snowshoes were stopped by storms.

Some early settlers complained that they were unable to deal with the Hudson's Bay Company at Georgtown. Retail sales, except to employees, were not part of the purpose of the Company and for that reason prices were kept extremely high. The post was to be used as a stage office and freight transfer point. If settlers objected to paying $14 a barrel (215 pounds) for flour at Georgetown, their alternative was a one hundred and ten-mile, two-week trip to Alexandria where the price was $7 to $10 a barrel. They also brought back salt, coffee, matches, tobacco, and windows for the houses. While in Alexandria, the men also filed claims for their homesteads.[4]

The records kept by R. M. Probstfield as manager of the Hudson's Bay Company post at Georgetown tell us much about the early settler's life and business. Hudson's Bay Company wagon trains, as large as 110 units, are known to have gone through Georgetown. A single consignment arriving at the post by ox team December 12, 1867, contained: 3 quarter casks of brandy weighing about 300 pounds each, 6 quarter casks of wine (one had a leak) averaging about 320 pounds each, 2 puncheons of rum containing 84 gallons, and a bale of bags which were to be used for shipping buffalo robes. Another consignment in transit from St. Cloud to Fort Garry weighed 4,512 pounds and consisted of: 31 boxes of foodstuffs (including a box of raisins that was broken open), 3 stoves, one of which had a piece broken in the rear of the pipe hole and a top plate cracked, a 38-pound can of Car C (kerosene) oil which leaked, a barrel of wrapping paper, 2 dozen brooms, 6 chairs, 3 barrels of Car C oil, a sack of rice, a bundle of boards, a 94-pound sack of nuts, a box of cranberries, and 3 barrels with contents unknown. It is interesting that the four men who signed the shipping bill all used "X"—"Goodwin *X* Mark; Baptist *X* Morris, Alexander *X* Parche', Enstoche *X* Rocette"—witnessed by E. R. Hutchinson, an associate of Probstfield for many years.

In that same shipment was another consignment destined for Fort Garry which weighed 3,404 pounds and contained: 2 stoves, 2 kegs of syrup, 2 kegs of white lead, a bundle of hay forks, a bundle of 12 brooms, 7 bundles of pails with 6 to a bundle, a nest of tubs (probably wash tubs), and 35 barrels with contents not identified. A third consignment consisted of 20 half barrels of sugar (3 of which had broken heads) and 25 half chests of tea.

No other shipments were recorded at Georgetown between December 12, 1867, and May 9, 1868, at which time the results of the winter's hunting became apparent. The first shipment upstream in the spring of 1868 was nine bales of furs weighing 1,100 pounds to F. E. Kew, London, England. That same shipment contained thirty-two cases of goods for the "Smithsonian Institution, Washington, D. C." On June 6, 133 bales of buffalo robes weighing 13,200 pounds were sent through Georgetown. A few days later the steamer *International* deposited 380 bales of buffalo robes weighing 38,000 pounds at Georgetown destined for J. C. Burbank and Company of St. Paul. Each bale contained about twelve hides. That shipment also had one deer head and horns valued at $100 for Cal Rowan, Clarendon Hotel, New York.

A cross section of other shipments through Georgetown in 1869 reveals the type of activity taking place downstream: 46 half chests of tea, 2 boxes of ammunition, 12 guns, 2 barrels of tents, 3 barrels of salt pork, 9 barrels of whiskey, 10 boxes of castor oil, 3 boxes of soap, 12 hay forks, 18 axes, 24 brooms, a keg of syrup, a barrel of pearl barley (for soup), 6 boxes of nails, a tool chest, a keg of rice, a bundle of shovels, 3 boxes of bacon which weighed nearly 400 pounds each, 8 barrels of crackers with a 5-pound box missing out of one barrel, 3 barrels of nuts, 6 boxes of candles, 5 cases of canned fruits and vegetables which weighed 320 pounds each, 8 cases of shoes and boots, 6 barrels of flour 215 pounds each, a 200-pound box of candy, a reaper shoe, a bundle of sickles for reapers, and a cook stove. There were some very sizeable shipments of household supplies later in the summer which comprised a total of 154 barrels of flour, 164 barrels of beef and pork, 2 boxes of dried apples, 11 boxes of matches, 13 kegs of salt, a single box of spices, and 10 nests of wash tubs. The survey of the shipping bills helps reveal what the pioneers most needed or desired to battle the elements. Liquor was an important commodity of trade, but food made up the bulk of the early shipments reflecting the settler's heavy dependence upon the established communities for survival. The population of the Hudson's Bay Company post at Georgetown, which carried on this remarkable trade, never surpassed forty-one, including employees and their families.[5]

In 1859 the steamer *Anson Northup* (later renamed the *Pioneer*) began its role on the river and in the following year the *International* was added. River transporation was a short-lived business but its impact was great. Moorhead and Fisher's Landing were two important river points. Fisher's Landing on the Red Lake River, a rail head for the line reaching north from Glyndon, boomed for about four years in the 1870's. During that time "it had all the characteristics of an open frontier town with its absence of law and order. It had . . . no little reputation along the river as a gambling place. . . ." Fisher's Landing at its peak had four hotels, two stores, four frame saloons, and sixteen tents which served as saloons or gambling places. Seven boats, all with barges, were needed to handle the traffic from that railend community. In the years 1875 to 1879, nearly all the immigrants into the interior of Canada traveled over this route. In 1878, however, when direct rail connections were finished to Winnipeg, Fisher's Landing lost much business. In 1879, when James J. Hill's railroad completed its bridge across the Red into Grand Forks, the tracks were torn up at Fisher's Landing and the boom for another town came to an end.

In 1880 all that was left of the booming river and rail terminus were two empty buildings.[6]

Moorhead, situated on the Red River, also boomed because of the river traffic. At least seven steamers and twenty barges were based at Moorhead in 1874. The smallest was 75 tons and the largest 175 tons. In that season twelve thousand sacks of flour alone were shipped to Fort Garry and more than ten thousand tons of goods were shipped in total. Traffic continued to increase until about 1878 and then it declined gradually until the last boat was sunk in 1909. The *Manitoba* and *Minnesota* were the first boats constructed in Moorhead. The *Northwest*, built there also, was over two hundred feet long and had the distinction of being the largest boat on the river. On its final voyage on the Red to Winnipeg, May 15, 1881, it carried forty carloads of lumber on its barges. On other trips it pulled as many as five barges. The *Northwest*, as was true of all steamers, carried passengers as well as freight. It had eighteen cabins and two staterooms, but more passengers were always welcome to quarter themselves on the deck. The round trip between Moorhead and Winnipeg normally took ten days. The *International* made the fastest recorded round trip in five days and eighteen hours.

The progress of these communities was tied to the transportation systems. In fact, Fisher's Landing failed partly because its residents demanded too high a price for railroad right-of-way at the river crossing which caused the surveyors to favor a crossing at Crookston. In another case in Moorhead, high priced lots and the Northern Pacific's preference for Fargo enabled Fargo to outgrow Moorhead during the same period.

Winnipeg, formerly Fort Garry, experienced a similar boom with the advent of river transportation, and later, of railroad transportation. It had grown from a village of one hundred in 1870 to five thousand in 1875. By the time the first railroad entered the city in 1879, land prices had gone up to $70 per acre.[7]

The Probstfield diary, belonging to pioneer settler R. M. Probstfield and spanning the years 1859 to 1962, gives us some little known sidelights about river shipping. Some idea of the amount of river traffic can be determined from the records he kept of steamboats as they passed his farm. Probstfield sold firewood to the steamers and he was always on the lookout for the boats because they frequently took on fuel without permission. It was his problem to prove that they had done so and to collect for the fuel. Scattered notes from the records gives samples of such activity: "September 5, 1873, *Selkirk* passed at 6 a.m.; September 18, 1873, *Selkirk* stopped going upstream, took five and one-fourth cords of wood; September 20, 1873, *Selkirk* passed downstream, 6 a.m., took five cords of wood; October 27, 1873, ice flowing on the Red. *Selkirk* passed going upstream, 12:30 p.m." On an average day the *J. L. Grandin*, which was about the size of the *Selkirk*, used eleven cords of wood. On April 18, 1874, the ice broke loose on the Red. The steamer *Dakota* traveled upstream at 4 p.m. on April 24. The next day the *Selkirk* went downstream at 6 a.m. Two days later the *Cheyenne* passed upstream at 6 a.m. On May 1 the *International* went upstream at noon. May 6 the *Alpha, Pance*, and *Selkirk* all passed by going upstream.

Probstfield made a journey on the *International* from Moorhead to Pembina and kept a record of its progress. It left Moorhead Sunday, August 30, 1874, at 10 a.m. He left Georgetown, only thirteen miles downstream, at 4 p.m. At 8 p.m. he was at the Elm River opposite Hendrum, just another thirteen miles downstream. Twelve hours later, at 8 a.m., he was another thirteen miles downstream at the Goose River. Then came the difficult part of the journey over Goose Rapids. Those eleven miles to Frog Point took until 7:45 p.m. Monday. Tuesday at 2 a.m. he was at Grand Forks, a trip of twenty-eight miles in six and one quarter hours. At 9:15 that same morning he left Turtle River (opposite Oslo) another twenty miles downstream. He arrived at Pembina the last stop, forty miles farther downstream, at 1:30 a.m. Wednesday. The total distance as the crow flies was 125 miles covered in a total elapsed time of 56 hours and 30 minutes. Actual distance traveled by the *International* was easily twice that and possibly exceeds three hundred miles because of the crookedness of the stream. Freight and passengers were discharged and loaded at each of the designated stops. The *International* continued her journey beyond Pembina to Winnipeg and returned while Probstfield did his business in the town. The return trip upstream from Pembina to Moorhead took exactly seventy-three hours. The total elapsed time for the round trip was eight days and three hours for what is today a 554-mile round trip by car. Probstfield made no comment about the trip in any manner, so apparently the slow pace was completely satisfactory to him.[8]

The river traveling season started later in 1875; it was not until April 26 that the *City of Moorhead* made the first trip downstream to Fort Garry. On May 10, 1875, the *Manitoba* passed down with a large crowd of passengers. On July 10 some people called at Probstfield's to board the *Manitoba* as it passed at 3 p.m. This incident implies that sometimes the riverboats did pick up passengers between scheduled stops. They were known to be quite independent, however, about picking up freight.

Probstfield made quite a business of supplying fuel for the riverboats. The boats of the Grandin Line were probably his biggest customer, but the *International*, the *Selkirk*, and others also stopped. The usual wood purchase was five cords which was enough for about twelve hours. The price of wood varied with the season of the year and also with the economic situation. At times Probstfield complained because the price was barely enough to pay labor. Late in 1874 he sold 109 cords for an average of $3.25 per cord.

Frequently, he had difficulty with riverboat crews who tried to avoid paying for the wood. On December 28, 1876, he received a letter from Norman Kittson containing $13.33 to settle a $40 bill for wood that the *International* had taken in the spring. His luck was not much better with the Grandin Line for on May 13, 1879, he "found out that captain . . . of steamer *Grandin* stole my rails and cordwood, can't say how much." He also supplied timber for boat construction at Moorhead. On April 15, 1875, he sold two logs that measured 23½ inches by 38 feet to the boat company to be used as timbers to support the steam boiler on a riverboat. The size of those trees indicates why Probstfield had so much wood to sell.[9]

Charles Gordon, an early settler in the Hillsboro area, reported on the many types of river craft used in the early days, including hundeds of large rafts of cut lumber which were floated downstream. Sometimes they were loaded with freight providing stiff competition for the steamboats. The river was so wide in most spots that boats could easily meet or pass. In Gordon's day there were about a dozen steamers in service which normally towed barges or lighters. Gordon worked on the *J. L. Grandin* which generally pulled two barges. It had an eleven-man crew with four men on each of the barges. Two men worked a five-hour shift steering the barge. Their wages were $35 a month. Later Gordon received $40 per month as second in command on the *Selkirk* which had a fourteen-man crew including some Negroes. Men generally liked working on the boats even though the work was hard and sometimes dangerous. The *International* lost two crew members who fell overboard on the voyage in which she set the round trip record between Moorhead and Winnipeg. Nevertheless, the pay was good and the food was excellent. There was always activity on board — boat races, Indian problems, explosions, and on one trip seven babies were born to Mennonite immigrants aboard the *Selkirk*. Travelers usually included immigrants, salesmen, land seekers, sightseers, hunters, honeymooners and soldiers.

Once the river days came to an end, many of the boats were dismantled and taken to Canada. A large number of them, however, never got out of the Red River for they met ill fate there. The best known case of an unhappy ending came to the *J. L. Grandin*. In 1882 she had broken loose from her moorings at Nobles in northeast Cass County (no longer in existence) and floated down the Red and into the Elm River where she was rescued at Kelso. In the great flood of 1897 the *Grandin* broke loose again. This time she floated downstream to a point just west of Halstad. When the waters receded the boat was left stranded. For many years it served as a reminder to all of the great days of Red River boating. Another riverboat, the *Grand Forks*, made a gala tourist excursion in June, 1909, but on April 10, 1912, while at anchor finally sank, formally closing an era.[10]

No longer is the Red River capable of supporting any sizeable craft on an economical basis. Up to 1874 the low water mark at Breckenridge was considered about 1,000 cubic feet per second. Until 1886 the lowest volume downstream at Moorhead was 500 cubic feet per second. At that time the water was so low in Breckenridge that there was "a regular meadow below the Breckenridge and Wahpeton bridge." In 1932 and again in 1936 the river went dry in places and there was no flow for eleven days at Wahpeton-Breckenridge. This dry situation was quite a contrast to the conditions of the first trip by the *Anson Northup* which cut across several bends in its maiden voyage to Georgetown. The chief concern then was avoiding floating timber.

After 1859 the next high water came in 1873 which was surpassed in 1897 by the greatest flood on record when the river reached a record 50.2 feet at Grand Forks. The estimated high volume at that location in 1897 was 80,000 cubic feet per second. From the cupola of the courthouse in Breckenridge one saw only water and a few knolls in every direction. Flood stage was 17.0 feet that year. The figure was higher than the 16.35 feet (and a flow of 9,400 cubic feet per second) reached in the great flood of 1969.[11]

Railroads

The river steamers brought a great deal of progress to the Valley, but the scope of their activity was, of course, limited to the proximity of the river and they did not provide a link with areas beyond. It was not until the entry of the railroad that travel from east to west as well as year round transportation became reality. Mrs. Kate Glaspell, a pioneer settler summed up what the railroad meant: "The Northern Pacific was the greatest asset this country [Dakota] ever had . . .

people flocked to the north who would never have considered it had not the railroad paved the way." The advent of the railroad changed the pattern of settlement and way of life for the residents of bonanzaland. The pre-railroad settlers preferred sites along streams and in wooded areas. After the railroad, locations along the railroad right-of-way were favored. Later railroad sidings were established about every seven or eight miles for the convenience of farmers. These sidings resulted in rapid settlement and rising land prices along the right-of-way. Before 1875 more pioneers had settled in the lower part of the Valley in Manitoba than in the American part, but with the construction of railroads in the upper Valley, the pattern was reversed.

The Northern Pacific, which entered in 1871, was the first railroad in bonanzaland. But it was James J. Hill of the Great Northern who proved to be the real spark in developing much of the area. About 1873 he began building railroads into the country northwest of St. Paul and Minneapolis after he had secured property from bankrupt firms. In his railroad adventure Hill was particularly successful because he correctly judged the market potential and built his railroads ahead of settlement. This practice assured him business almost at once. Hill also took soil samples and studied other conditions all along his railroad route to determine the best crops for any given area. To safeguard against crop failures, he encouraged farmers to practice diversified farming including livestock production.[12]

The progress of railroads was one of the chief topics of conversation on the frontier. As one pioneer put it:

When rumors of a railroad started, it was something like the discovery of oil. . . . It does something to one — brings out some sort of expectancy of great possibilities, soon or in the distant hazy future — keeps one going high. Everybody was wondering where the railroad would come, and when. One day the surveyors came through. Soon the . . . railroad was being built and people kept pretty well informed on how far it had come and how fast it was coming. As soon as they knew where the townsite was they began to build the church. They were selling townsite lots . . . for stores, a bank, lumberyard, post office, elevators, pool hall, of course, blacksmith shop, feed mill, implement store, livery barn, and meat market.[13]

The railroads had excellent relations with most of the local papers and appealed to settlers for cooperation. An article in the *Fargo Argus* of October, 1882, stated that the Fargo-Southwestern line was being completed into Sheldon and "hopes to reach Lisbon this fall. The engineer said that track laying will end soon, and if each farmer could help out for one day the track could reach Lisbon for sure. This would mean 10 cents to 15 cents more for wheat, fuel would cost less, and provisions and lumber would be cheaper." Two months later the paper reported: "All is commotion, excitement, and enthusiasm [in Lisbon because the railroad has entered]. To estimate the importance, the value and the influence that will be exerted on our country by the road that touches us today is beyond our limited power."

Not every community was as fortunate as Lisbon in having a railroad from its very beginning. The region around Alvarado, Minnesota, was first settled in 1879, a townsite was established in 1885, but it was not until 1905 that the Soo Line built tracks into town. "People came for miles to look" at the railroad cars and engines for many of them had never seen a train before. The most significant travel event in Christine Hagen Stafne's home area took place on July 4, 1884, when the first train of the Chicago, Milwaukee, St. Paul and Pacific Railroad entered Abercrombie on its way from Ortonville to Fargo. Great crowds appeared in every community along the line to celebrate and herald the coming train. Mrs. Emma Elton who homesteaded north of Williston, North Dakota, testified that even though she was located near a general store and post office, there was little optimism about the future of farming in that area until the railroad came.[14]

Because the settlers realized the railroad was the key to their economic well being, each farmer was more than willing to contribute time toward the construction by shoveling out snowbound trains, or by rebuilding washed out tracks. They were anxious to get service restored, but they were also happy to earn the cash, for in the area there were two common sources of non-farm cash income for the small farmer — the railroad and the big bonanza farms. During March, 1882, relief parties of settlers from around Larimore went out several times to shovel snow from a big cut so that the trains could get through. On March 23, 1875, at 1:30 p.m. the first train passed through Moorhead since the heavy storms of March 13. Storms that delayed trains caused some hardships because small communities often ran out of fuel. On one occasion 750 immigrants in twenty coaches and their sixty-five cars of luggage were stranded because the trains were blockaded.

The problem of snowblocked or otherwise stalled trains continued for several decades, resulting in irregular service. The *Warren Sheaf* of February, 1881, reported that mail had arrived only twice the previous week because of the snow blockade at Fergus Falls. On April 12, 1894, Probstfield's comment was brief, but meaningful "Trains not running — strike is on." This is a reference to the nationwide Pullman strike in action at that time. During the heavy storm of February 24,

1897, he recorded, "A.M. two men came over from train which had been stuck since midnight and got dinner for eighteen men." The railroad later paid $4.50 for the food furnished.[15]

Everything that happened on the railroad was big news. When R. M. Probstfield shipped fresh vegetables on the first train to travel out of Fargo to supply the railroad construction gangs, it was news. When the Northern Pacific decided that all passenger conductors should be uniformed in "handsome navy blue cloth" effective May 1, 1882, it was news. Whenever another immigrant house was added along the line, denoting progress of the frontier, it was news. Every time another passenger or freight train was added to the scheduled operations, it was news. When the first tramp to travel transcontinent over the Northern Pacific arrived in Oregon in September, 1883, it was news. He complained bitterly because his journey had been made difficult by the irregularity of the tie spacing — some were twelve inches apart, others were forty-two inches. By September, 1881, Fargo could boast of being a real rail center with two freights, one express, and one passenger train westbound daily, and a like number eastbound. In addition, salesmen could purchase passage in the caboose of the freight trains enabling them to work out of Fargo. An *Argus* reporter watched the activity of the railroad closely as a forecast of things that were to happen. In the spring of 1883 he predicted a big year for immigration because every passenger train was heavily loaded. "Every available inch of room seems occupied with something, even if nothing but the gentle scents of limburger cheese. The rush of immigration has commenced, and this will rapidly fill up all the unoccupied land in this territory."

Whenever there was a special occasion, such as a political convention, a county picnic, or a shopping tour, the railroad proved very accommodating. During the summer of 1882 the Northern Pacific announced a $2.00 round trip excursion for Saturday through Monday from Fargo to Detroit Lakes. The regular fare was $2.45. To please the large crowd of shoppers in Fargo from Jamestown, the Northern Pacific announced that it would delay departure time from 4:30 to 7:30 so the shoppers could enjoy the 1882 Fargo Fair.

The railroad fare per mile of travel was not much different from what it is today, but because of the difference in the value of the dollar, travel was expensive. In September, 1881, two of the Probstfield children, aged eighteen and nineteen, took a five-day trip to the Twin Cities to see the Minnesota State Fair. The total cost of the trip was $29.90 which represented the pay for at least twenty days work during harvest season. Rail fare from Moorhead to Barnesville or Crookston and back to Moorhead was $4.10, the price of three days labor. When Probstfield served as state senator, his expenses from January 6 to February 23, 1895, were $61.80 including $9.66 for round trip rail fare, and leaving him only $1.08 per day for food, hotel, and incidental expenses.

The trains were not particularly fast those days compared to present-day travel, yet they managed to do in one hour what the ox-drawn covered wagon could do in one day. When the Divet Brothers moved their farm equipment by rail from Byron, Minnesota, to Breckenridge in 1880, the trip required three days from Byron to St. Paul (75 miles) but only thirty-six hours from St. Paul to Breckenridge (210 miles). The Northern Pacific announced in the spring of 1882 that its fast freight from St. Paul to Fargo could make the 250-mile trip in twenty-four hours. The Jamestown Special traveled the 100 miles between Jamestown and Fargo in four and one-half hours. Probstfield was pleased to note that the forty-four mile trip from Moorhead to Detroit Lakes took only three hours. Railroad travel was great progress when compared to walking or by ox train, and few complained.

Although the railroads were in the area ahead of most of the settlers, the wagon train was the most commonly used method of travel for a majority of the earliest settlers. It was true, to a great extent, even a decade after the railroads arrived. R. D. Crawford's parents, who later settled in Richland County, were impressed by the many wagon trains that passed through their town, Rochester, Minnesota. One of these wagon trains contained thirty-three wagons. Another train had a wagon which carried the inscription, "Go west we must or Jimtown will Bust." Covered wagons were important, but the railroads were even more valuable. The real impact of the railroads on the economy was felt after the Northern Pacific went bankrupt in 1873 and "Fargo practically died" for train service was restricted to one train each direction each day.[16]

National Origins

However this decline did not last long for by 1874 conditions improved when wheat prices rose to $1.50 a bushel. As the wounds of the Panic of 1873 healed, Red River Land took on the appearance of a miniature Europe attracting immigrants from many countries who helped to develop a varied and stimulating society, based on multi-racial-cultural interchange. The debt owed to these pioneers must be remembered. As Carl Sandburg says in "Remembrance Rock":

If America forgets where she came from, if people lose sight of what brought them along, if she listens to the deniers and mockers, then will begin the rot and dissolution.

Red River Land opened rapidly between 1870 and 1890, not only because of the publicity created by bonanza farms, but also because of railroad construction, public land laws, immigration from foreign countries, land surveys, the availability of new agricultural implements, rapid establishment of governmental units, and wholesale efforts by the railroads and the government to colonize the land. In 1868 the State of Minnesota commissioned Paul Hjelm Hansen, a Norwegian-American journalist, to do a series of articles on the Valley which he referred to as "New Canaan." The articles, which were distributed in Norway, were influential; for of the 120,000 Norwegians who left their homeland between 1866 and 1874, a large portion of them came to Minnesota and Dakota. The movement into Red River Land started slowly, but from 1870 to 1878 settlers came in gradually increasing numbers. In the period from 1879 to 1884 the migration into the area was so overwhelming that it became known as the Great Dakota Boom.

Many Norwegians were reluctant to settle on the prairie and preferred to locate near wooded areas along streams which were more like their homeland. When those areas were all taken, newcomers were forced onto the open prairies where they endured considerable hardships because of the lack of water and wood. Even before the river woodlands were all taken, however, and before Hansen's articles were published, some Norwegians had settled on the prairies of bonanzaland. Probably the first Norwegian settlement in the upper Valley was established by Erick Hoel in Abercrombie Township, Richland County, in 1869. Hoel had learned of the Valley while working in Wisconsin lumber camps. In 1870 two more Norwegian settlements were established west of the Red River along the Wild Rice and Sheyenne Rivers in Cass County. Later friends and relatives arrived from Norway to enlarge these communities and establish new ones to the west and the north. Those who were unable to locate in the Valley went to the wood and swamp area of northern Minnesota; others went to the drier regions farther west.[17]

The 1870 census listed 627 persons on the Minnesota side of the Red River Valley and 2,405 on the North Dakota side. Of these 1,213 were in Pembina County. Included in these total figures were 808 Indians and Métis. The Métis were generally the offspring of French, Scottish, or English fathers and either Chippewa, Cree, or Assiniboin mothers. Clay County listed ninety-two people, all of whom resided in Kurtz, Oakport, and Georgetown. Two-thirds of these were Métis who had come from earlier settlements in Manitoba. After 1870 many people left eastern Canada to settle in the Canadian west. The Canadian prairie provinces provided the greatest competition to the American states and railroads in attracting settlers to the prairies. Melvin Morris, who farms (1969) at Wheatland, said that his parents, Mr. and Mrs. Peter Morris, were part of a large group who moved from Ontario into the Valley and the Dakotas in 1878. Peter Morris' parents had come from England and Mrs. Morris' parents had come from Scotland. The Peter Morrises decided to move to western Canada and traveled west through the United States. Impressed with Red River Country, they settled near Wheatland instead of continuing to the western Canadian prairie provinces.

Most early settlers did not regard the handicaps of the frontier as hardships, but they only looked forward to success in a new life. Difficulties strengthened their spirit of rugged individualism and they were willing to make temporary sacrifices for the long range goal of owning a farm. Their chief motive seemed to be to accumulate enough land so that they could leave a farm to each child.[18]

Some of the largest groups which came to the Red River Valley were tightly knit religious communities from southern Russia. In the 1700's Catherine the Great of Russia had invited large numbers of German Mennonites to occupy and settle on the fertile plains of the Ukraine. Within a century they founded some of the most prosperous communities of Russia and were envied by native Russians. As the military and the political situation became more intense in the late 19th century, the government was forced to adopt universal military service. In a spirit of reaction, the Czarist government decreed in June, 1871, the abolition of all guaranteed rights and privileges to former immigrants, giving them virtually the choice of either leaving Russia within ten years or becoming Russianized in language and religion.[19]

These prosperous and successful Mennonite communities arriving from Russia in the latter part of the Nineteenth century were the most desired of all American colonization groups. Their tightly organized colonies under religious leadership made it relatively easy to hold them together for mass migration. In 1873 Mennonite delegations from a dozen communities in Russia were sent to investigate unappropriated lands in Manitoba and in the Missouri Valley. These delegates were also invited to visit the Red River Valley where they opened negotiations with the Northern Pacific for a large block of land west of the Red River. At this time the Northern Pacific was hard pressed for settlers because individual farmers were not developing the area fast enough to be of much value to the railroad. The visiting Mennonites liked the Valley, particularly the land around the Maple and Rush Rivers in Cass County. The Northern Pacific agreed to set aside all of the land grant for the first fifty miles west of the Red River where the railroad had forty sections per mile for a total of two thousand sections (1,280,000 acres). The railroad offered this land for $3.00 an acre with ten per cent down and the balance to be paid in seven years. It also gave a ten per cent freight reduction for three years plus reduced passenger fare from New York.[20]

The Mennonites, interested in retaining solid communities, desired to obtain the even-numbered sections of public domain within the land grant in addition to the odd-numbered railroad sections, an exception which would have violated the popular Homestead Law. In addition, the Mennonites also wanted exemption from military service. The American Congress first considered granting the exemption because there was no great concern over war at that time. Pressure from state colonizing agencies and other railroads outside of the area, however, caused them to refuse both requests. The proposed legislation was never passed and so negotiations with the Mennonites came to an end, marking a low point in Northern Pacific colonization efforts. Soon after this the company closed its European agencies.

When negotiations with the Mennonites ended in the United States, the Canadian government willingly met their demands and offered them twenty-five townships of land in the lower Valley. Eight of these were in the Morris area and the remaining seventeen in the Altona region. They were also given solid blocks of free land, were guaranteed religious freedom, and exemption from military service, as well as "the right to live in closed communities with their own form of government, and sufficient financial aid to cover the cost of moving from Russia to Canada." The large movement of Mennonites into Manitoba for the next several years caused much excitement along the transportation routes of the Valley. Three of their contingents moving through Moorhead "consisted of more persons than lived in any county of the American part of the Red River region." By 1878 they had forty-four village units established in Manitoba with 9,000 acres in crops, but they were still receiving financial assistance from the Canadian government.

Some Mennonite groups settled near Yankton, Dakota Territory, in 1873. The following year Walter A. Burleigh made the largest land sale in the Dakotas up to that time when he sold 2,500 acres in southeastern South Dakota to a Hutterite group for $25,000.[21]

Red River Land newspapers gloated over the many large groups of immigrants coming to the area. Citations taken from the *Fargo Argus* of 1882 near the height of the boom tell much of this enthusiasm. "Several emigrant wagons from Kansas to Dakota are said to have borne the following inscription on ther [*sic*] covers: 'Good bye, Kansas, we bid you adieu. We may emigrate to h___, but never back to you.'" Kansas had suffered some dry years prior to 1882 and her loss was bonanzaland's gain. Little did some of those eager homesteaders realize that their new home would soon be faced with a similar extensive dry spell.

A few days later the same paper noted, "Some Illinois papers plaintively declare that it seems as if their state is to be depopulated by the 'Dakota fever.' Hundreds of people are leaving constantly for the world's great wheat fields and only genuine banana belt."

Settlers came from Maine, Vermont, Rhode Island, Massachusetts, Norway, Germany, and even Switzerland. The *Argus* noted, "All kinds of passenger cars are now brought into service to accommodate the great rush of settlers over the Northern Pacific. All the seats in the long trains are filled, and a good many have to be satisfied with standing room." [22]

Those who were locally defined as Americans (anyone who was "Americanized") made up a large portion of the immigrants including railroad employees, boomers, bonanza farm owners, lawyers, educators, clergy, and retail merchants. Railroad section hands, homesteaders, and bonanza farm employees were more likely to be foreigners. Many came, however, from the immediately adjacent states. A table in the footnotes indicates the cross section of nationalities found in Dakota. [23]

Early Settlements

Whenever newcomers came to Red River Country, if at all possible, they attempted to settle among others with similar backgrounds. Whether they came to the frontier alone or with a group, they seemed to find their "kind of people" and occupied land near them. Who were some of the earliest settlers and where did they locate?

Edward Connelly arrived in Wilkin County in 1859 and is believed to be one of the first settlers, but it was David McCauley who, after his arrival in 1861, made the most significant impact in that area. Like everyone else, McCauley was forced to vacate his first home because of the Sioux outbreak but he returned in 1864 to open a general merchandise store and trading post at McCauleyville, north of Breckenridge on the Red River. He seeded seventy-five acres of oats that

year which established him as one of the earliest farmers in the upper
Valley. On June 4, 1867, he was named postmaster, the second in the
upper Valley, and became a very influential man in Wilkin County.

An acquaintance of McCauley, Randolph M. Probstfield, is generally recognized as Clay County's first permanent settler. Born in
Coblenz, Germany, November 9, 1832, he was an exceptionally well
educated man who was graduated from college and was in training
for the priesthood when he decided to leave Germany. Probstfield
had an excellent command of English and German besides knowing
Latin, Spanish, French, and Indian dialects.

According to his diary, he "landed on the Red River in 1859,
April." He worked for the Hudson's Bay Company at Georgetown and
also established a farm at the same time. Probstfield returned to Europe in 1860 and brought three brothers and two cousins back with
him. These men brought five yoke of oxen, ten cows, and thirty young
cattle from St. Paul to Georgetown on June 22, 1861. On September
10 of the same year he married Catherine Goodman of South Bend,
Indiana. Their honeymoon consisted in part of an eighteen-day trip
covering 255 miles with an ox team and covered wagon from St. Paul
to Georgetown. On June 17, 1862, Mary Anne Elizabeth, the first of
eleven children, was born. In August the inhabitants of Georgetown
left for Winnipeg because of the Indian outbreak, but due to dissen-
sion within the group, the Probstfields and eight others returned to
Georgetown where they remained until March, 1863, when the military ordered them to Fort Abercrombie. They stayed there until
May, 1864, when they returned to Georgetown.

Probstfield took charge of the hotel at Georgetown and on May 20
he was named first postmaster in the Valley south of Pembina. The
following year he was made manager of the Hudson's Bay Company
trading post, a position he held until 1869. Then Probstfield left
Georgetown and settled in Oakport (north of present-day Moorhead)
where the Northern Pacific survey crew had their campsite. Although
his land borders the Red River his farmstead has never been flooded,
so apparently he made a wise choice.

One of the first settlers in the southwest corner of Clay County,
adjacent to the Red River, was Ole Thompson. After his father's
death, his mother left Norway in 1861 with her five children to come
to a relative's home in Mitchell County, Iowa. Young Ole Thompson
spent the next eight years in Iowa and Wisconsin working as a hired
man. In 1869 he set out for the Red River Valley and in the Com-
stock-Holy Cross area found land that he liked. Because his log house
was one of the first in that vicinity, it became a traveler's inn and a

common overnight spot. In 1872 he traveled to Benson, Minnesota, a distance of 120 miles, to secure lumber for a frame house. In 1885 he covered the wood with brick, making it the only brick house in the area until bonanza farmer David Askegaard built a large, solid brick house at Comstock in 1890.[24]

One of Thompson's first neighbors was the Bernhard Bernhardson family who arrived at Comstock, July 3, 1870. Bernhardson, who was born in Sweden in 1840, emigrated in 1868 with his wife and three children to Pope County, Minnesota. Because he did not like that area, he scouted the Red River Valley in 1869 and found land to his liking near Comstock. On his journey from Alexandria to Abercrombie, a distance of 100 miles, he did not see a single white man and many times he did not know in what direction he was walking because of the high prairie grass. On his return to Pope County he traveled through Ottertail City to file his claim. The family traveled to Comstock by ox-drawn covered wagon with the two boys, John and Lars, driving the sheep and cows behind. They were worried that the animals would be lost in the tall grass but fortunately they preferred to stay in the tracks made by the wagon. When the Bernhardsons crossed Whiskey Creek by ferry near Breckenridge they had only seventeen cents left. Unfortunately, shortly after their arrival they received a letter from relatives with fifteen cents postage due. The letter was a blow to Bernhardson for it took his last pennies and also contained a reprimand from an aunt protesting their going into the wilderness.

The covered wagon served as a home until fall when they built a log cabin. Because he had no money, Bernhardson was unable to purchase glass for a window so hay was stuffed into the window opening. Frequently a colt ate the hay at night and by morning cold winds were blowing into the cabin. The little one-room cabin with a packed earth floor was crowded with Bernhardson, his wife, three children, two of the neighboring Hicks boys, and a crate of chickens. The cows, sheep, and oxen were forced to find their own shelter in a nearby grove. The following year a second room was added to the house, but that soon became crowded also when three more children were born. The Bernhardsons prospered and by 1909 owned 3,315 acres in Holy Cross Township. At marriage each of the children was given a farm.

Bernhardson's good friend and neighbor, Haken Hicks, also acquired a sizeable family farm near present Hickson. He built a large log house, twenty-one by twenty-nine feet, for his family of ten children. The Hicks family had a narrow escape from death on their eight-day, 120-mile journey from Pope County with two ox-drawn wagons. During the last twenty-four hours they had to keep going continuously to avoid freezing to death in a blinding snow storm and fifteen degree below zero weather.[25]

Ole G. Thortvedt, who lived at Mound Prairie, Houston County, Minnesota, left on May 18, 1870, with his family together with the Torje Skrei and Gunder Weum families and the bachelors Ola G. Midgarden, Tarjie G. Muhle, Ole Amundson, and Halvor Findahlsvedt (Salveson). All were Norwegian and were looking for better land along the Red or Otter Tail Rivers. The Thortvedts had two covered wagons—one pulled by horses, the other by oxen—and four cows, a heifer, two yearling colts, and thirteen sheep, all of which were herded along with the wagons. Twenty-five chickens were crated in the wagon.

This small band reached Alexandria on June 15 having covered a distance of 275 miles in twenty-eight days. At Alexandria, the last sizeable community, they replenished their supplies. On June 29, 1870, they reached Moorhead where they met R. M. Probstfield and E. R. Hutchinson. The Thortvedt group crossed the Red River at Probstfield's farm to scout for land but returned via Hutchinson ferry at Georgetown determined to go back to Otter Tail County. They believed that the land west of the river was too low for farming. Probstfield commented that during high water periods the Hudson's Bay Company people in Georgetown usually moved their cattle east along the Buffalo River and he offered to help them look for land in that area. The short, stubby but nutritious buffalo grass, the elm, oak, ash, and basswood trees along the Buffalo, and the pleasant, clear, smooth-running river were all that was needed to change their minds. A meal of fat, boiled catfish quickly caught by the boys, along with some wild fruit, convinced them that they had made the right decision. They immediately staked out their claim on a spot about eight miles northeast of Moorhead. The Thortvedts and their neighbors were so enthusiastic about their new home along the Buffalo River that they wrote to old friends in Houston County encouraging them to come because there was "good, rich, level prairie ready to put a plow in without moving a stone or stump, plenty of timber right by to build houses, wood for burning, plenty of running water in the river and full of fish." [26]

Benedik Gunderson and family arrived in the spring of 1871. His brother, Ole Thortvedt, had reserved land for them in Section 21 within the bend of the river. Before their arrival, Knut Moraas, a drifter who had no intentions of either settling or farming, but knew that the Thortvedts were holding this land for relatives, had built a very crude, small, round log hut on the land and pretended to claim it. Benedick Thortvedt offered Knut $100 cash for the claim and Knut "was gone in minutes" with his easily earned money. Soon six other families from Houston County joined their friends along the Buffalo. The original intention to settle in Otter Tail County was soon forgotten. However, some of the Norwegians did not like the flat lands so they went east to settle in the hills. Other Norwegian farmers and their families from southern Minnesota moved farther north along the Red River and formed the communities of Vineland, Fisher, Roone, and Bygland. This region is an exceptionally fertile one which has escaped serious flooding, even in some of the worst years.[27]

One of the largest settlement efforts within the Northern Pacific land grant came under the leadership of Luman H. Tenney. Tenney, who was closely linked to a temperance group in the East, wanted to establish a secluded settlement, and received rights for twelve townships in the Glyndon, Minnesota, area in return for his promise to deliver 1,000 families by May 31, 1874. By the spring of 1872 Tenney had secured promises from about 600 persons wishing to move to the Valley. Glyndon boomed in 1872: a newspaper was established, a church and a school were under construction, and nearly 100 settlers had arrived.

Tenney received funds for his settlement project from the iron millionaire Charlemagne Tower of Pennsylvania. Failure of the Northern Pacific to have a reception house in Glyndon completed by the time the first colonists arrived proved to be a serious handicap for Tenney's plans. The reception house, when eventually completed, was a two-story, 32 x 160 foot building with a large kitchen annex which served Northern Pacific immigrants for many years. Other inconveniences encountered by the colonists were grasshoppers, mosquitoes, and the cold weather.

Financial problems caused by the collapse of the Northern Pacific made it impossible for Tenney to achieve his goal. He succeeded, however, in bringing a group of Congregationalists from the east coast. This encouraged the Reverend George Rodgers of England in his efforts to bring Congregationalism to the American frontier. Part of Rodger's objective was to help the English agricultural economy through emigration of farmers. Reverend Rodgers came to eastern Clay County in 1872 and laid the foundation for what was called the Yeovil Colony which included two settlements around Hawley and Muskoda. The first Englishmen arrived here in April, 1873, and hoped to bring their families over later. Even though the Yeovil Colony was not a success, the English were the second largest group in Clay County in 1875.

During the height of the Panic, Evald Wiedemann, one of Clay County's most successful settlers, arrived in Glyndon. He had left Saxony in 1866 for New York where he hoped to work as a skilled laborer. An accident, which forced him to give up his vocation, proved to be a boon for him for he was forced to work in a candy store and made $5.00 a day. He earned additional money selling sheet music and soon had enough saved to move to Glyndon. In 1874 he purchased a plow and horses and took jobs as a sodbuster. When not breaking sod he operated a blacksmith shop in Glyndon, a business which helped him considerably. He purchased his first land in 1881 and by good farm management along with his blacksmith income, he was able to acquire 4,400 acres by 1899.[28]

The hardships encountered by settlers enroute to the frontier in Red River Land were only minor in comparison to what would follow after settlement. These earlier hardships were reduced each decade with the advance of the railroad and other conveniences that followed it. For various reasons, during the early years many settlers became disillusioned and either returned east or went farther west. The records do not indicate how many failed, but one may reasonably assume that the failure rate was at least 50 per cent; however, in the post World War I era it reached 95 per cent among the successors to the Dalrymple bonanza. The total unpreparedness of some of the pioneers because of their lack of knowledge of the frontier and of farming caused them to give up the fight against the elements when their physical and financial resources were exhausted. Others came in order to capitalize on a financial boom, but when faced with the drudgery of frontier farming, quit and left the country. Those pioneers with the determination to stay and to conquer, however, have given their descendents in Red River Land a proud inheritance.

Indians

Among the many hazards encountered, the Indian was a problem only to a limited number of the early homesteaders in the Red River area. David McCauley of McCauleyville and Fort Abercrombie said that he had to be on guard against Indians at all times as the Indians were quite destitute because of poor crops in 1859, 1860, and 1861. Treaty violations and the Civil War gave them a welcome opportunity to revolt. In early August, 1862, they destroyed McCauley's grain and potato crop, a practice which they repeated again and again throughout a large area. On August 22, 1862, the news reached George-town that Fort Abercrombie was besieged. Two companies of troop had been withdrawn from Georgetown leaving it indefensible, but with the arrival of a large Hudson's Bay Company ammunition train at midnight, total manpower increased to forty-four men with a supply of thirty-three guns, including some old flint locks. Captain Norman W. Kittson waited with the *International* at Georgetown for two weeks in hopes that help would arrive from Fort Abercrombie, but in the meantime it had become surrounded by Indians and anyone who attempted to leave the fort was killed. The Georgetown settlers finally abandoned their quarters and possessions and headed north on the west side of the river. Near present-day Grand Forks they met fifteen well-armed horsemen including Joe Rolette, Hugh Donaldson, William Moorhead, and Pierre Bottineau who had been sent from Pembina to help against the Indians. Because of conflict within the George-town group, R. M. Probstfield and family returned to Georgetown and were later rescued by troops from Fort Abercrombie.[29]

By 1864 the white men who had vacated a twenty-three county area in western and northern Minnesota because of the uprising were returning, and except for isolated incidents, had no further trouble with the Indians. An extensive military campaign had finally subdued the Indians in the area. In general, most of the pioneer's anxiety concerning the Indian was caused by isolation and an ingrained fear.[30]

Most of the earliest white residents of Red River Land were hunters and trappers. One of the most interesting early events of the Indian problem concerns Marie Anne Lagimonière, who was the wife of a trapper and is credited with being the second white woman in the Red River Valley. Neither Marie nor her husband feared the Indian. The wife of an Indian chief visited their camp west of Pembina one day in either 1811 or 1812 and after the visit Marie noticed that her baby boy was gone. Marie gave chase, caught the Indian woman, and regained her son without a struggle. Later, while trapping in the same area, the chief appeared with a large string of horses and offered to trade them for the boy. As the bargaining progressed he not only offered to trade all of the horses but also included one of his own children. He was determined and only Marie's tears caused him to back down.[31]

The Lagimonières were here nearly a half century before farmers arrived in the area. These early settlers did not share the same feeling toward the Indians as the Lagimonières, but they had no major reason for concern until 1874. During the summer of 1874 Probstfield commented about localized Indian scares which he passed off with a final remark on July 7, "Indian outbreak exploded." In the summer of 1876, J. B. Power, land agent for the Northern Pacific, wrote company offices that "a senseless Indian panic" in parts of Otter Tail County was causing settlers to leave "by the scores." This panic, he thought, would have some effect on the Northern Pacific's colonizing campaign. On June 12, 1876, Probstfield "went to town to attend committee on history of town. Nobody attended. All excitement and scare about Sioux Indians." The following day the "Indian scare increased. Settlers around Georgetown contemplate gathering in Georgetown. Nothing definite heard so far—hope it will fizzle." Apparently his hope was fulfilled.

Christine Hagen Stafne, living near the Wild Rice River, noted that although members of her family heard of Indian massacres they never saw evidence of one and were never molested by Indians. An occasional Indian would canoe up the Wild Rice River to stop and beg for food. She remembered, however, that there was an Indian scare in the Fergus Falls area in 1876 when, according to rumors, about 300 Sioux attacked settlers in Otter Tail County. The Hagens later witnessed small bands of Sioux going west as they crossed the Sheyenne southwest of their farm. When Fort Abercrombie was abandoned in 1877 some of the settlers still felt a sense of loneliness and a degree of insecurity.[32]

During the winter of 1878 and 1879 Indian trouble occurred along the Northern Pacific west of Jamestown when the railroad company renewed construction after a lapse of six years. The Indians did not want to see the railroad completed and troops had to be called in to protect the work gangs. With completion of the tracks at Gold Creek, Montana, in September, 1883, several celebrations were held at major towns along the line. The greatest such event was held in St. Paul where the program committee felt it would be appropriate to have Sitting Bull, chief of the Sioux tribe, give one of the speeches. A soldier helped him with the speech and acted as interpreter:

When Sitting Bull was called upon, the soldier motioned to him and he rose clumsily, but to the astonishment and horror of the soldier said, "I hate you, I hate you. I hate all white people. You are thieves and liars. You have taken away our land and made us outcasts, so I hate you." The soldier, sure that there were very few in the audience with any knowledge of the language [Sioux], realized it was up to him to preserve peace. He sat quiet until Sitting Bull had finished, then . . . he rose smiling [and gave] as the interpretation, the friendly, courteous speech he had prepared, which met with applause and a disagreeable incident was ended. Later the truth was revealed, it caused considerable hilarity.[33]

The following year when Sitting Bull and One Bull, with an interpreter, passed through Fargo on their way to South St. Paul to make cattle contracts for the Sioux Indian reservation, Mrs. Mary Woodward living south of Mapleton was not very impressed. "His nose is hooked and is gradually protruding more and more toward his chin. His face is a mass of wrinkles, and in a greasy hunting suit, wolfskin cap, and calico shirt, he looks little like the great warrior history will portray."

Generally most Indians encountered by Red River Land settlers were docile and more concerned with the necessities of life than in taking scalps. Once, six Indian squaws entered the Narve Roen cabin at Comstock with some prairie chickens they had just caught. They haphazardly picked off the feathers and cooked the birds over the fire without removing the innards. When the squaws got out of the cabin they tore the prairie chickens apart and enjoyed the meal.

Edgar Olsen, who lived near Hannaford, reported that his family fed Indians frequently and they repaid the kindness by bringing the Olsens prairie chicken, venison, and gophers. Olsen commented that the Indians were always puzzled by the white man's refusal to accept gophers. Emma Elton, who lived in the timbered area east of Hawley on the edge of the Red River Valley, said that Indians stopped frequently to get food and were always friendly.[34]

Generally, women feared the Indians, but, as one pioneer woman said, "actually they never did any harm, and only wanted something to eat. Given salt pork or anything at hand they left after making known their thanks . . . they rubbed their noses on the door casing to express this."

One of the first times (ca. 1875) Indians came to the Ole Olson Hovde home near Hillsboro, their small son was frightened and hid behind the stove while Mrs. Hovde continued making lefse. First one Indian came in and received some food and he was followed by others in rapid succession. On another occasion two Indians who had begged for food and had received some, started down the road where they were met by others who took the food away from them. The two Indians then returned for more food and Mrs. Hovde gave them some flatbread. A few days after Mrs. Hovde had given birth to a child, three Indians approached the house. The hired girl saw the Indians coming down the path and without a word opened the trap door and climbed into the cellar. The Indians entered the house and when they saw Mrs. Hovde in bed indicated that all they wanted was salt.

Receiving that, they became interested in the new-born baby which they picked up, passed from one to another, carefully returned it to the crib, and left. Another time they wanted flour. When they were asked why they wanted it, they invited Mr. Hovde to join them for a meal of skunk stew. Hovde declined the invitation but gave them the flour. The Hovdes could often see the Indian campfire and tepees down by the river bank. The Indians normally arrived early in the evening, did a little hunting or begging, and broke camp by noon the following day. Once the Hovdes noticed Indian women chasing buffalo over a high bluff along the Goose River "near Nelson's farm." The squaws killed and butchered the bruised animals and carried the meat to camp. When Mrs. Hovde caught some Indians stealing a sheepskin she had brought over from Norway, she gave chase causing the Indians to drop the skin. At first the Hovdes owned the only shotgun in the entire vicinity and it was frequently borrowed by the neighbors. When they returned it they always "brought some of their game." Apparently none of the homesteaders in that Traill County community felt the need of a gun for protection.[35]

Reflections

There were serious obstacles to pioneering in Red River Land but not all of them were obvious. Probably the greatest of all obstacles was the daily drudgery, heartbreak, and self denial required in pioneer living. These hardships gradually broke the spirits of many, including some of the most determined. Guy Divet, son of Daniel Divet, was nine years old when his family moved to Richland County, and wrote in retrospect of his childhood experiences:

Pulling up the family roots, moving to a new land and attaching those roots in new ground, building a new life, fostering new friendships and releasing old ones, is an adventure that only one who has gone through it can fully appreciate. I believe mankind would be happier if less of this had been done and were still being done.

If I were a professional writer, I should like to write the romance of such change. I have furnished much of the story to others who have sought to put it into print, but they have missed the little things, the frayed ends of the little heartstrings broken in the process of uprooting never to be brought together again, the separation of a mother, as my own was, from her girlhood home, the shattering of her hopes, again and again, to revisit that home, which my mother never did.[36]

R. D. Crawford was one of those who was not willing to pay the price of hardships and self denial required of the pioneers. His father had purchased sections 1 and 17 in Brandenburg Township, Richland County, but never developed section 17. This land was secured from the Northern Pacific Railroad for $2.87 per acre. After meeting some of the settlement options the price was reduced to $1.90.[37] R. D. Crawford farmed for his father until his early twenties. He became bitter about his boyhood experiences and wrote in retrospect in his eighties:

I have never felt satisfied that pioneer life paid. Certainly not from an income standpoint. The low prices robbed me of the education I should have had. By the end of 1894, I had lost all interest in farming and left the state for good in January, 1895. . . . October 23, 1895, found me in a factory where electrical machinery was made working as an apprentice at seven cents an hour. Ten hours a day for five days, nine hours on Saturday.[38]

Guy Divet, in years later, distinguished between the "workers" and the "shirkers":

I am impressed with the thought that the workers and stickers on one hand, and the shirkers and quitters on the other, were present in about a proportion of fifty-fifty. . . . They [the quitters] would sell out for a few hundred dollars and leave. There were the Backus family, the Glanders, . . . possibly a dozen in all whose names have been forgotten, and few now know they even existed.

I remember the Bohns, Belings, Ziegelmans, Hoefs, Holthusens, Lubenows, Seidlers, and Talls . . . [and many others] who came to stay, to work, and to stick; their descendants are with you today, monuments to lifelong industry and thrift, and examples to future generations . . . the quitters are gone and forgotten; the stickers and workers have left their indelible mark upon the welfare of our country.[39]

Divet was rather harsh on those he called the shirkers and quitters. The Divets had an advantage in that they had income from their Minnesota farm during the early stages of farming in the Valley. In Guy's own words, they "occupied a position between the [small] homesteaders and the big [bonanza] farmers. Our farming operations were just large enough to attract the attention of these larger operators [such as Miller, Dwight, Hugh Moore, and W. P. Adams, all bonanza farmers]." Even with such a start, Guy tired of the long hours and left the farm to become a school teacher by the time he was seventeen. He eventually became a successful lawyer and spent most of his life in Washington, D.C.

Red River Land was not a typical American farm frontier area because most of the homesteaders were not satisfied to confine themselves to a quarter section. From the beginning, without considering the bonanza farms, the farms were larger than in the previous farm frontiers to the east. One of the chief factors was psychological (and also practical) for there were no obstructions to the plow or the seeder, so why stop at the half-mile line? Farther west or to the south, more land was needed because of the lack of adequate rainfall and lower gross crop per acre. Short growing season and not lack of moisture was the initial limiting factor on income per acre because far more crops have been destroyed from too much water than too little in the Valley proper. In the counties on both sides and immediately adjacent to the Red River, the farms averaged 242 acres in 1880 and 306 acres in 1900. This compares to the United States average of 134 and 146 respectively. Only one of the farms used in this study, the Overbys of Wolverton, did not exceed the 160-acre size. The others varied from 240 to 1,920 acres or more and yet have to be considered strictly family farm operations—i.e., a farm where the family labor input is greater than the hired labor input.[40] The quarter section was not generally considered a standard unit for farming as it was in the areas directly to the east and south. There were probably several reasons for these larger homesteads: the attractiveness of the unobstructed prairie, the great amount of low priced land because of railroad land grants, the timing of settlement in relation to the agricultural revolution that was providing horse powered machinery to the farmer, the desire of farmers from established areas to relocate on a frontier where they could acquire enough land to leave a quarter section as a start for each child, the timing of settlement relative to improved transportation creating a world market for American farm products, and the influence of the giant bonanza farms on the traditional concept of farm size and efficiency of operation.

FOOTNOTES

[1] Ray Allen Billington, "Preface," *The Farmer's Frontier, 1865-1900*, Gilbert C. Fite (New York, 1966), vi; Carl Becker, "Kansas," *America is West: An Anthology of Middlewestern Life and Literature*, ed. John T. Flanagan (Minneapolis, 1945), p. 633.

[2] Lewis Henry Morgan, *The Indian Journals 1859-62*, ed. Leslie A. White (Ann Arbor, 1959), p. 130; for more on early travels in the area see Joseph James Hargrave, *Red River* (Montreal, 1871); Stanley Norman Murray, *The Valley Comes of Age* (Fargo, 1967), pp. 12-17, 29-31.

[3] Chet Gewalt, *Breckenridge 100 Years of Progress* (Breckenridge, Minn., 1951), pp. 3-9, 11-12, 16-23; Mrs. L. E. Jones, "Our Town in Early Days," a typed manuscript in the files of the Wilkin County Historical Society, written before 1936; Randolph M. Probstfield, Family Diary 1859 to 1962. (Hereafter cited as Probstfield.) Much of the material for this book comes from the Probstfield family diary, a many-volume set that was faithfully kept by Mr. Probstfield and by the members of the family in his absence. It contains detailed accounts of the family's personal life, weather conditions during adverse periods, and economic conditions of the farming operations and the area especially during the 1870's, '80's, and '90's. The diary is in excellent condition, written in ink, easy to read and to understand. Professionally, I con-

sider this my greatest find in research, for Probstfield was not only one of the first settlers in the area but he also made many significant contributions to the area. The Probstfield Elementary School in Moorhead is named in his honor. Research in this thorough primary source was enhanced by the many conversations with Raymond and Evelyn Gesell, grandchildren of R. M. Probstfield, who were well versed in the family history. The Gesells have preserved the original family home, built in 1868, with many of the original fixtures, for future generations to view. Those weeks of research spent with Raymond and Evelyn Gesell were rewarding and exciting—for that I am most grateful.

[4] Arthur Overby, "David McCauley," an unpublished manuscript in the files of the Wilkin County Historical Society; Glenn E. Johnson, "Here, There, Everywhere," *Valley Times* (Moorhead, Minn., 1967-68), in the files of the Clay County Historical Society; Probstfield; Alexander Ross, *The Red River Settlement: Its Rise, Progress and Present State* (London, 1856), pp. 11-13.

[5] Probstfield; *Moorhead Independent*, Jan. 5, 1900, pp. 1-3; Ross, pp. 11-13; Gewalt, Breckenridge historian, offers three suggestions on how the Red River got its name— one is because of Indian bloodshed from the many battles along its banks, second is because of the red willows, and third because vegetation caused the river to be red at times; Glenn E. Johnson, "Here, There, and Everywhere."

[6] Alfred Torrison, "Fisher's Landing, Minnesota," *North Dakota Historical Quarterly*, IX (Oct., 1941), pp. 27-34. (Hereafter cited as *NDHQ.*); Murray, p. 61. Fisher's Landing was named after I. B. Fisher, superintendent of the railroad division at that time.

[7] Helen R. Euren, "Moorhead Highlights During the 1800's," a fact sheet on early Moorhead; Murray, p. 157; Roy Johnson, "They Carried It All," *Dakota Territorial Centennial, Fargo Forum*, Feb. 29, 1961, p. 18; On one trip the *Pluck* had two barges loaded with three carloads of threshing machines, two and one-half carloads of wagons, a carload each of portable engines, salt, and plows, two carloads of pork and five carloads of miscellaneous freight; C. K. Semling and John Turner, *A History of Clay and Norman Counties*, I (Indianapolis, 1918); the *Selkirk, Dakota, Cheyenne* (or *Sheyenne), International, Alpha, Pance, J. L. Grandin, Pluck, Alsop, Omega, Grand Forks, City of Moorhead, Anson Northup* (sometimes *Northrup,* later the *Pioneer*), *Northwestern, Manitoba,* and *Minnesota* are riverboats listed in that article.

[8] Probstfield; *The Hillsboro Banner, Diamond Jubilee Edition,* June 28, 1956, p. 16.

[9] Probstfield.

[10] Roy Johnson, "Indian Attacks in the Red River Valley," ed. Father Louis Pfaller, *Red River Valley Historian,* II (March, 1968), p. 14. (Hereafter cited as *RRVH.*); *Hillsboro Banner,* June 28, 1956, pp. 8, 9, 16.

[11] G. W. Chestney, "The Red River of the North" (W.P.A. Project Feb. 21, 1939), on file at Wilkin County Historical Society.

[12] Murray, p. 110; Joseph G. Pyle, "James J. Hill," Minnesota History Bulletin, II (Feb., 1918), 301-320. (Hereafter cited as *MHB*); *Pioneers: A Look Into the Past,* Old Settler's Memorial Movement Association, Inc. (Hillsboro, N.D., 1963), pp. 40-41. While Jim Hill did much for the people of bonanzaland, he was also highly sensitive to community reaction as is shown by the story related by Nina Hermanna Morgan, daughter of Peter Herbrandson, early settler at Caledonia and personal friend of James J. Hill:

One cold, stormy winter evening a fur-clad man driving a team of dogs stopped at the American House in Caledonia and asked for food and shelter for himself and team.

A nattily dressed clerk in the hotel said they had no room for the weary stranger and his "dirty dogs," though the man said he was able to pay and pay well.

The man got into his sleigh and drove down the ice covered bed of the Goose River and after several miles travel saw the light from a lamp in the cabin of a homesteader. It was the home of a widow named Johnson and she kindly asked him in.

While he fed the dogs frozen meat from her scanty store and sheltered them under the roof that was over her wood supply, she got him a good hot meal and steaming coffee. Then she gave him her bed and she crawled into the loft to sleep with the children.

The next day before he departed, he paid her generously and ever after he remembered her with gifts of money. The stranger was James J. Hill.

He was on a hurried trip from Winnipeg to Minneapolis, scouting out a line for his road from Fargo to Grand Forks. He vowed then and there that as long as he lived his railroad should never be built to Caledonia.

[13] Sena Amdahl Rendahl, "Rendahl Family Records" (Fillmore, N.D., 1955) a typed manuscript on file at Concordia Library.

[14] *Fargo Argus*, Oct. 16, 1882, Dec. 2, 1882; *Alvarado Golden Jubilee, 1905-1955*, Alvarado Jubilee Committee, copy loaned by Alfred Sands; Emma Erickson Elton, *History of the Vaalhovd Family 1857-1957* (Hawley, Minn., 1960), p. 38; Anna Stafne, "Christine Hagen Stafne: Pioneering in the Red River Valley," unpublished manuscript on file with Professor Thomas K. Ostenson (North Dakota State University, Fargo, 1943), p. 36.

[15] *Larimore, North Dakota, 1881 Diamond Jubilee 1956*, Larimore Diamond Jubilee Booklet Committee, p. 4; *Warren Sheaf*, Feb. 9, 1881, March 9, 1881; Probstfield.

[16] Probstfield; *Fargo Argus*, Nov. 22, 1881, Feb. 28, 1882, March 13, 1882, Aug. 2, 1882, Sept. 20, 1882, Sept. 13, 1883; Conversations with Sam Syvertson, Great Northern agent; Mrs. H. E. Crofford, "Pioneer Days in North Dakota: Ida C. Hall, a Pioneer Teacher of North Dakota," *NDHQ*, II (Jan., 1928), 132.

[17] Murray, pp. 57-62; Carlton C. Qualey, "Pioneer Norwegian Settlement in North Dakota," *NDHQ*, V (Oct., 1930), 18-28; Mrs. Ann Olson, interview by the author, Crookston, Feb., 1966. Qualey traces the Norwegian settlement to the west and north and establishes the period and areas where Norwegian groups settled.

[18] Ray Allen Billington, "How the Frontier Shaped the American Character," *American Heritage*, IX (April, 1958), 87; Fred A. Shannon, "The Homestead Act and the Labor Surplus," *The American Historical Review*, XLI (July, 1936), 649; Murray, pp. 79 and 93; Dora J. Gunderson, "The Settlement of Clay County, Minnesota 1870-1900," unpublished Master's Thesis (University of Minnesota, Minneapolis, Minn., 1929), pp. 19-26; Melvin Morris, interview by the author, Wheatland, May 2, 1968; Usher L. Burdick, "Recollections and Reminiscences of Graham's Island," *NDHQ*, XVI (Jan., 1949), 5-30. The parents of Usher Burdick, long time congressman from North Dakota (his son, Quentin, later became a senator), came to North Dakota during the Great Dakota Boom. Usher was born Feb. 21, 1879, at Owatonna, Minn. The family moved to a claim northwest of Carrington in 1882. In Canada as elsewhere, the immigrant was optimistic, as indicated by one son who wrote back to his father in Ontario: "Don't fear us starving in Manitoba; we are doing better here than we could in Ontario, despite the ravages of grasshoppers. Two of us have cleared $160 per month all summer, burning lime and selling it for $.45 per bushel; another has averaged $5 per day with his team, sometimes teaming to the new penitentiary, and sometimes working on the railroad. The fourth works at his trade, wagon making, in Winnipeg for $60 per month, steady employment. Our potato crop is splendid, our peas are excellent, and one field suffered no intrusion from the pest. The weather is excellent, prairie chickens are numerous, and our anticipations as regard a good time next year are big"; Murray, p. 110.

[19] Herbert S. Schell, "Official Immigration Activities of Dakota Territory," *NDHQ*, VII (Oct., 1932), 12; John Warkentin, "Mennonite Agricultural Settlements of Southern Manitoba," *The Geographical Review*, XLIV (July, 1959), 343-345.

[20] Murray, p. 70; Schell, p. 13.

[21] L. H. Dewey, "The Russian Thistle: Its History as a Weed in the United States," United States Department of Agriculture Bulletin No. 15 (Washington, 1894), pp. 7-12; Schell, pp. 13-16; Murray, pp. 70-87; Warkentin, p. 346.

[22] *Fargo Daily Argus*, March 24, April 6, April 26, 1882; Wendelyn Vetter, "A Brief History of German-Russian Migration: Viewed in the Light of Land Tenure," a typed manuscript (Department of Agricultural Economics, North Dakota State University,

1952), p. 11; H. V. Arnold, *The Early History of Ransom County: Including References to Sargent County, 1835-1883* (Larimore, N.D., 1918), p. 49.

[23] Harold E. Briggs, "The Great Dakota Boom, 1879-1886," *NDHQ*, IV (Jan., 1930), 88-94; Elwyn B. Robinson, *History of North Dakota* (Lincoln, 1966), various pages; J. B. Hedges, "Colonization Activities of the Northern Pacific," *Mississippi Valley Historical Review*, XIII (Dec., 1926), 314-321.

NATIONAL ORIGINS OF NORTH DAKOTANS IN 1890

Nationality	Number	Location
Norwegian	44,698	Cass, Traill, Walsh, Nelson, Grand Forks counties had heavy numbers
German	17,541	Cass, Richland, and Barnes counties
Canadian-English	13,079	Scattered
Irish	8,554	Pembina and Grand Forks counties
Swedish	7,650	Scattered
English	5,226	Scattered
Russian	5,130	Scattered
Scotch	4,354	Chiefly in counties bordering Canada
Canadian-French	4,251	Scattered
Danish	3,915	Scattered
Bohemian	2,103	Scattered

[24] Jon Evert, "A History of Comstock, Clay County, Minnesota," an unpublished manuscript (History Department, Concordia College, Moorhead, Minn., 1968), Ch. II, pp. 13-16.

[25] Evert, Ch. II, pp. 19-24.

[26] *Moorhead Independent*, Jan. 5, 1900, p. 18; Levi Thortvedt, "The Early History of the Red River Valley," a manuscript on file at the North Dakota Institute of Regional Studies, File 332. (Hereafter cited as NDIRS.)

[27] Thortvedt, NDIRS, File 332; Torrison, p. 28.

[28] Murray, pp. 67-69; Tenney Papers, NDIRS, Files 515 and 519; *Moorhead Independent*, Jan. 5, 1900, pp. 37, 41, and 46; Gunderson, pp. 40-42.

[29] *Moorhead Independent*, Jan. 5, 1900, pp. 1-2; Arthur Overby, "Sod House Days in the Red River Valley: A Biography of Mrs. Andrew Overby," a typed family history on file at the Wilkin County Historical Society, p. 17.

[30] Briggs, "The Great Dakota Boom, 1879-1886," pp. 101-103.

[31] W. J. Healy, *Woman of Red River* (Winnipeg, 1923), p. 8.

[32] James B. Power letter to Frederick Billings, July 15, 1876 (Power Letterbooks, Vol. I-XIV), NDIRS, File 309; Probstfield; Stafne, pp. 24-25.

[33] Mrs. Kate Eldridge Glaspell, "Incidents in the Life of a Pioneer," *NDHQ*, VIII (April, 1941), 187-188.

[34] Evert, Ch. III, p. 8; Edgar I. Olsen, interview by Donald Berg, July, 1966. Mr. Olsen for many years was a county agent in North Dakota, and served as deputy commissioner of Agriculture and Labor for North Dakota. His wife was the former Alice Flaten, niece of prominent early Moorhead photographer; Elton, *Vaalhovd*, p. 35; Mary Dodge Woodward, *The Checkered Years* (Caldwell, Idaho, 1937), p. 120.

[35] Mrs. Ole Olson Hovde, "A Family History of Mr. and Mrs. Ole Olson Hovde" (1937), pp. 12-13; Doris Eastman, "Pioneer Women—The Lonely Ones," *Fargo Forum*, Feb. 28, 1961, p. 25; *Hillsboro Banner*, June 28, 1956, p. 2. On another occasion skunk meat was consumed accidentally by some settlers in eastern Montana. A housewife had a skunk in the oven to bake out the fat which was commonly used as an ointment for croup. Some friends stopped in while the housewife was out in the field. They helped themselves to the good looking and pleasant smelling roast. One of the visitors later told the housewife that the roast "was so good we just about cleaned it all up. My I never ate such tender sweet meat in my life."

[36] Guy Divet, "The Divet Story," NDIRS, File 69, pp. 4-5. (Also in the *Fargo Forum* and *Richland County Farmer-Globe*.)

[37] R. D. Crawford, "The First Pioneer Years in Dakota Territory, 1881-1882," a manuscript written in 1954, NDIRS, File 290.

[38] Crawford, NDIRS, File 290, pp. 5, 27.

[39] Divet, NDIRS, File 69.

[40] Alva H. Benton, "Large Land Holdings in North Dakota," *Journal of Land and Public Utilities Economics*, I (1925), 411; Murray, pp. 134-135.

CHAPTER II

Be It Ever So Humble

T HE MOST pressing task that the pioneer family faced after arriving on the frontier was the erection of a shelter. These homes reflected the social, economic, and cultural development of each community. They were far from "palaces" and many times more than people "resided" in them as O. A. Olson testifies from personal experience:

> The field mouse that lives in my mattress
> Finds bunch grass a nesting delight.
> I have not the heart to evict her
> Though my fondness for her is slight.

Sod, Log, and Frame Houses

Many of the shortcomings of pioneer life could have been more easily endured if the housing had been satisfactory. The pioneers, however, made few complaints about the homes, and if they did complain, it was out of amusement rather than because of any discomfort that they suffered. On the midwestern frontier where trees were readily available, log cabins were built at a cost of from $25 to $100. A typical log cabin consisted of one large room with sleeping space in the loft. When a frame house could be constructed and financed in southern Minnesota and northern Iowa, it was normally one and one-half stories, measuring 24 x 24 feet with four rooms and cost between $300 and $350. In Red River Land, where trees were not so plentiful, the average house was 16 x 16 feet and the prices were higher. The standard size for the more primitive claim shanties was 12 feet square. Some of these temporary homes cost only a few dollars and this was spent for hardware on doors and windows. "A sod house was 'made without mortar, square, plumb, or greenbacks.'"

During their first winter in the area, some pioneers were forced to make their homes in dugouts or earth mounds. Because there were no hills, they dug into the river banks just far enough to protect their livestock and themselves. On the present site of Fargo, during the winter of 1871-72 railroad construction workers made their homes in holes they had dug in the ground. Jorgen Johnson, a bachelor who settled in the Comstock area in 1872, lived for many years in a carved out, man-made mound of earth that had a log front and a log roof covered with sod. Fingal Enger, the first settler in present Steele County, shared a dugout with another bachelor during his first summer. Later he built a 16 x 16 foot log house that was still standing in 1969. In general, frame houses appeared relatively early on the Valley frontier because logs for log houses were scarce and sod houses were only considered to be temporary dwellings. Also, cut lumber was available at an early date from the mill at Frazee. Charles Hobart of Cummings recalled that when he first moved into the Goose River country there were only a few settlers ahead of him, most of whom had frame houses, but there was one sod and one log house. A bachelor near Hope turned a triple wagon box upside down, covered it with sod, and used it as a dwelling because he had arrived too late in the season to build any other type of house.

One of the few pictures available of a sod house in the southern part of the Valley is the one from the Andrew Overby farm near Wolverton. The Overbys lived in their wood-framed sod house for over a decade. They brightened the interior by using lime that had been fired making it suitable for whitewashing. The lime came from a lime pit on the Tansem farm near Rollag. When fired lime was not used, they papered the walls with copies of the *Youth's Companion* and other magazines. Each spring the walls were repapered with new issues. Pegs were driven deep into the sod walls to hang clothes and kitchen utensils. "Outwardly they appeared to be crude and primitive, but on the inside many were cozy and clean." [1]

The Fuglestad family, like many others in the area, lived in three types of houses—sod, log, and frame. The first winter they lived with relatives rather than in the claim shanty that they had obtained along with a pair of bib overalls in a trade for a Meerschaum pipe. (Fuglestad had been informed that he should bring hand carved pipes with him from Norway because they were valuable in America). In the spring they built a semi-sod house with the walls and roof framed of rough boards. The sod for the walls was cut about four inches thick and had long grass roots which made it tough and flexible. In the construction of the house, sand was spread upon each layer of sod and allowed to fill all the irregular spots, eliminating any openings in the walls. The walls were eight to twelve inches thick. The roof boards were covered with tarpaper over which sod was laid in strips that were at least three feet or more in length. These longer strips of sod were laid lengthwise on the roof with the top strip overlapping the lower one about half way providing a double thickness of sod with no open seams exposed. This roof leaked only once in its eight years of use and that was during a cloudburst. When the roof was finished, a second sod wall was built on the inside of the wooden frame. This sod was made smooth by sweeping, and whitewashed annually with white clay from a nearby slough. The double thick sod wall made a comfortable home that was cool in summer and warm in winter. Even when fire went out at night during the winter, the water in the pail never froze. The house had two windows, one facing the south and the other the east, while the door opened to the north.

Most sod roofs were not as tight and successful as that of the Fuglestads. The Hagens of Abercrombie had what might be considered the more normal experiences with sod roofs. After heavy rains bedding, clothing, and linen had to be hung out to dry. On one such occasion grasshoppers attacked and consumed Mrs. Hagen's "silken finery that she had brought from Norway." When Fort Abercrombie was abandoned, Hagen purchased the shingles from the roof of one of the buildings and relaid them on his house which made a "great improvement."

The Fuglestads lived in their sod house from 1883 to 1891 when they built a log house that was their home until 1905 when a modern wood frame house was constructed. It was common practice as the family grew to add leans onto the original sod and log houses. The Fuglestads added to their log house three times. Just as the Fuglestads had spent their first year with relatives, the Hagens lived with a neighbor, Einar Hoel, while their log cabin and farm buildings were being erected. In the spring of 1874, Jens Hagen, his wife, and six children moved into a two-room log cabin that had a dirt floor and two windows with hanging shutters that could be closed during cold weather. The furniture was homemade from native lumber, and if possible, built into the wall. Hagen later enlarged his log house by annexing the first schoolhouse in their area, which had become too small for school purposes, to provide extra bedrooms for his growing family and laborers. When his daughter, Christine, married in 1883 she moved into a new house that was built partially of logs and partially of sawed lumber. All of their out-buildings, however, including the barn were still built of sod. The new house had a bedroom and a combination kitchen-living room downstairs and a bedroom and small storeroom upstairs.[2] The Thortvedts built a 12 x 14 foot log house with a thatched roof. One year later the walls were supplemented with 14 x 14 inch squares of sod. They were unable to add the sod walls the first summer because they also had to spend time building a stable. Thatched roofs instead of sod were common, especially among the Mennonites living in the lower Valley.

As indicated, the log cabin was never extremely popular in the Valley because good logs were scarce, and if either logs or lumber had to be shipped in, it was more practical to import the lumber, which was cheaper to haul and easier to work with. Northern Minnesota mills were the nearest source of supply, but in 1883 when the Pehrssons built their house located along the Northern Pacific only a mile east of Buffalo, the lumber was shipped in from St. Paul. When the Madsens of Wheatland built their first house in 1877, they obtained their lumber from mills in northern Minnesota; however, when they built their second house in 1892, the lumber came from the Pacific Northwest.

Because lumber was scarce and expensive, most early homes were not overly large or luxurious. According to C. L. Pratt, one of the original settlers in Steele County, "Lumber for the first homes was usually hauled quite a distance and, as you know, everybody isn't a carpenter and some of the first homestead shanties were rather crude. These people were brave, courageous, and hopeful, busy establishing their new home and there was not much time for frills." Martin Johnson of Petersburg started with a 7 x 9 foot claim shanty and added to it whenever the need arose. Mrs. Henry Woell, daughter of Casselton farmer, Frank Langer, said that all six children in their family, including her illustrious brother, the late Senator "Bill" Langer, slept in a single upstairs room. Because the house was of typical "A" frame construction, the ceiling in the upstairs room came down to the floor on two sides. The walls and roof were plastered, but not insulated. The room was heated only by a register in the floor directly above the space heater in the living room. After their marriage, the Woells lived in a 14 x 16 foot, one and one-half story house where they remained until they had three children.

For added protection against the cold, it was practical to dig a log cabin into the ground, but this was possible only if the building site was high enough to avoid moisture problems. In the Cummings area one log cabin was set into the ground so that only four feet of wall was exposed to the elements. This reduced the amount of banking and made the log cabin more comfortable than if it were standing out on open prairie. The Hovdes, who settled west of Hillsboro, built a 10 x 12 foot log cabin that was "comfortable because [it was] dug well down into the ground." In their second year they added another room to the house. By 1874 they had increased their homestead to 240 acres, and because by this time there were three children in the family, they built a new house. This one-room, story and one-half, 18 x 14 foot house was "considered roomy." Ten years later, when hauling grain to Fargo, Hovde purchased flooring lumber to cover the original single boarded floor. That original rough floor had been an improvement over the dirt floor they had in their first dwelling.

When the Ole Overbys first came to the Sheyenne Valley in 1883 they made their "temporary" home with a young bachelor in a 12 x 14 foot log cabin, and before they moved into a home of their own, they had five sons. There was sleeping room in the loft. The cabin contained a total of 336 square feet of floor space or 42 square feet per person. Many times during those first years any guest, including the traveling preacher, was put up for the night because "there was always room for one more. The shelves under the eaves were handy supports for improvised beds." The preacher was content and the Overbys were anxious to have him. Ten years later Overby concluded that eight people in a 12 x 14 foot house was too crowded and he built a new home three miles west, away from the Sheyenne in open country. "The house was conspicuous because it was one of the first homes in the region to be built exclusively of lumber. It had three rooms and a dirt cellar; a few years later an extra room was added." With the birth of three daughters, Alma, Mabel, and Klara, the family increased to eight children during the ten years they lived in their second home. Mrs. Overby was happy with the girls and "claimed that girls were not produced in the valley." Later, when the family moved back to the Sheyenne Valley, another boy was born.

As the children grew older and were able to help with the farming, Overby increased his holdings. When he decided that they needed new and larger buildings, Overby moved back to the Sheyenne Valley to be more centrally located. He spent many evenings "by lamplight drawing pencil sketches" of prospective houses. In 1902 a new home was built—a full two-story house, 32 x 34 feet with five bedrooms. For the first time the boys and girls had separate rooms in the four bedrooms upstairs. Later, a summer kitchen and a washroom were built against the main structure. The house had a full basement walled with boulders that had been dynamited to smaller size for hauling and then hand chiseled to make a smooth interior wall. This was the first full basement in the community and contained the first hot air furnace in the entire Finley-Sheyenne-Cooperstown rural area. He also completed a set of out-buildings, including a 40 x 60 foot barn. These elaborate buildings were proof of Overby's prosperity. In their progression through three new homes in nineteen years, living space per person had increased from 42 square feet to 198 square feet, certainly a measure of their affluence.

In 1890 Erik Stafne, like many other successful pioneers, had to build a new set of buildings to keep up with his growing family and his expanding farm operation. He built a ten-room frame house with an extra bedroom that was always being used by some "minister, missionary, or fund raiser" passing through the country. By 1902 the Stafnes had to add four more rooms to accommodate their ten children and two hired men. While remodeling, they also installed a telephone. In 1908 they added a steam heat furnace, running water, septic tank, and a Delco electric plant. Those "modern conveniences" brought "endless trouble" with frozen water pipes, clogged sewage lines, and broken water pumps.

After living in a claim shack their first summer, the Madsens built a 26 x 28 foot house, half of which had two stories. It was the only two-story house in the Wheatland area in 1878. The wall of the second floor went up three feet where it joined the roof. The Madsens hung a lantern in the upstairs window when anyone from the family was out for the evening. By 1892, when the family had increased to ten children, they built a new 32 x 42 foot, two-story house. Total cost was $1,600 for the 2,688 square foot house—$800 for lumber shipped in from the west coast and the remainder paid for hired labor, windows, furnace, and all other fixtures. The Madsen family did much of the rough work in the construction, but they hired carpenters who did the finishing and supervisory work. In 1969 this house was still in good repair and was the residence for one of the Madsen grandsons.

Because of illness and less satisfactory crops, Charles Hobart was unable to make as rapid progress in house building as the Overbys, Stafnes, and Madsens. His original house, built in 1882, was the third frame house in the Cummings area and measured 12 x 18 feet with twelve-foot walls. A partition of matched boards divided the house into two rooms—a kitchen 10 by 12 feet and a bedroom 8 x 12 feet. The bedroom had one window and the kitchen two, and there were two outside doors. The upstairs contained one room with four-foot side walls where the room came to a peak in the center. The three-foot slant in the gable gave a seven-foot ceiling at the peak. The upstairs had a full length window on each end of the house which "made a good sleeping room." Access to the upstairs room was provided by a stairway hinged at the top in order to pull it up under the kitchen ceiling during the day. The opening to the upstairs was a simple trap door in the floor. Charles Hobart and his wife slept upstairs because his father, who lived with them, had to sleep downstairs because he was crippled and could not climb the ladder. A trap door in the kitchen floor opened to a very small cellar which one entered by a ladder. Hobart was quite proud of his house, but he soon discovered that without either plaster or clapboard it was impossible to keep it warm during cold weather; consequently, during the first winter his wife had to move to Fargo to live with relatives. After Lizzie left, Hobart boarded up one of the doors to the kitchen and built a small lean-to-porch to protect the other door and to store coal. He used horse manure to bank the house solidly, leaving only the windows exposed. The second year they were better prepared to cope with the winter and Mrs. Hobart remained on the farm.

After living in the original house for two years, Hobart added a 10 x 18 foot lean-to on the north side making the house 22 x 18. Hobart and his hired man, Hans Devald, worked on the lean-to for two years, finishing it in the fall of 1886. Unlike the original building, which was of single wall, the lean-to had a double wall with an inside wall made of lath and plaster. The hinged ladder to the upstairs was moved from the kitchen to the lean-to, and instead of a trap door in the floor, a four-foot door now provided a "walk-in" opening to the upstairs. The stove pipe was removed and a chimney was built, one of the first in the area. The Hobarts had not intended to build at this time, but they had received news that relatives were coming from the East and being a proud eastern family, they did not want to let the relatives see the crude house in which they lived. "Aunt Stella" had suggested the plastered walls.

The heavy snows of the winter of 1896-97 piled snow against the house so high that Hobart could walk directly up to the chimney and look down into it. This deep snow prompted him to move the house the next spring about ten rods south to take better advantage of the trees he had planted. At this time a six-foot addition was made, making the house 18 x 28 feet. The roof was raised and outside walls were heightened to sixteen feet permitting an eight-foot ceiling upstairs. The upper story had four rooms with closets and a hall. Later, Hobart regretted having spent so much money on the house for he had to borrow most of it because of poor crops, leaving him somewhat embittered by this experience.

Single-walled houses were not unusual at this time, for the first home of the Freys of southern Cass County was a single-walled, one-room shack with a lean against one side for the horses and cows. Several years later they built a new three-room, double-walled house. The Crawford's house was considered to be of the best construction. The outside wall was shiplap covered with heavy building paper and finished with lap siding. On the inside of the studs there was back plaster (lath and plaster) finished with wall paper. This made five layers of material and a dead air space between the studs, which was the standard house construction for many years to come until modern insulation material became a recognized building material. The Woodwards had one of the warmest and best built houses in east central Cass County. They used two layers of building paper, clapboard, siding, an air space in the studding, shiplap, plaster, and wall paper. But in spite of this, the weather was so cold at times that Mrs. Woodward was forced to make breakfast in the living room. "I cooked with my hood, shawl, and mittens on . . . The Lord help those who have no warm houses . . ." Their house, which was considered very sizeable in 1886, consisted of a sitting room, dining room, kitchen, large pantry, and three bedrooms. Chris Nelson, Hobart's neighbor, had a two-room, sixteen foot square log house that was set into the ground four feet with the additional luxury of shingles on the roof. It had a single opening for a window that contained no glass, and a single door. The room, which served as the kitchen and living room, was 8 x 10 feet and the other room was just large enough for a bed. In 1906, when Emma Erickson Elton homesteaded in western North Dakota, she built a 10 x 14 foot tar paper shack and banked it with sod which was still the standard in that vicinity.

Mike McMahon, who worked as an independent contractor for James J. Hill, built his first shanty in the fall of 1881 near McCanna. It "was well built with a shingled roof. It had a heater and a cook stove." But it still had its heating problems as Mrs. McMahon recalled about May 20, 1882:

[I] woke up to hear the wind blowing and when I stepped out of bed I found the floor covered with snow and snow on the pillow . . . Our shanty was a good one but it . . . [had been rebuilt] so a few nail holes were there that had not been covered with the new shingles. The snow and the wind found these nail holes. . . . It wasn't long before Tom Forbes was frozen out so he came to my place. He could not build a fire in his house because everything was covered with snow. Then Mr. Willett got frozen out of his shanty and he came along.

Even though Mike McMahon wanted to continue his contracting work with the railroad, his wife Ellen wanted to homestead so "they" decided to build a permanent home. McMahon had done well as a contractor and had better equipment and more cash than most beginning farmers so that they could build a substantial house. They moved into it on November 2, 1882. "The house had four rooms and I thought it was the most wonderful house that had ever been built. No one else had a house with four rooms. We had no paint to put over the plaster but even having it plastered was something." A few years later they painted the plaster and in the early 1890's purchased rugs for the bedroom and living room. Next came a dresser, a wash stand, lace curtains, and finally a second bed.

When John Webb settled in Hamilton, Pembina County, in September, 1881, he built a house at once for it was too late to do any farm work. He traveled twenty-two miles to Pembina for supplies and lumber that cost $25 a thousand and shingles were $4.00 a square. Total cost for felt paper that was used over the entire house, including the roof, was $8.00. This proved to be a "very comfortable house" and cost only "about $400." It must have been "quite luxurious" when compared to many others in the area, for $400 was far beyond what the average farm home cost at that time. When Charles Hobart built a 16 x 16 foot house for "Aunt Hannah" in 1892, he spent only $125. Hobart was particularly pleased because that year "Aunt Hannah" sold the standing hay crop from her quarter for $100.

Probstfield, who stayed in Grand Forks in 1871-72, in an attempt to establish a second homestead claim, built a house there and rented it to another person afterwards. Houses traditionally were rented for 1 per cent of the cost price per month so that the $3.00 a month rent he received for the house in 1875, just when Grand Forks was starting to grow, indicates that the house did not cost him over $300. The W. J. Peets had one of the most elaborate rural homes in Wilkin County. Built in 1902, it measured 34 x 60 feet, and had six rooms upstairs, five on the main floor, and a full basement. The original contracted amount for the building itself was $3,455 but for an additional $75 maple flooring was installed. A bathroom was included in the price but the Peets paid an additional $380 for a complete hot air heating system.

Generally all kinds of buildings were less pretentious in those early years. Chapin's Hotel, which was one of the first buildings in Moorhead, had board floors with the roof and the walls made of canvas. The building did not last very long because, like many other frontier stores, hotels, and saloons, it was taken down and sent to another frontier town. John Kurtz, a prominent Moorhead doctor, had two "firsts" to his credit in house building—in 1875 he built the first brick house and in 1894 the first stucco house. The Lamb Brothers, who had a brick factory in Moorhead, built Dr. Kurtz's house. In the

1890's some very pretentious houses, still standing today, were built by merchants and bonanza farmers, but it was not until about World War I that the average homesteader's family was able to afford a fine house.[3]

The Probstfield house, first built in 1868, was constructed of oak logs and tar paper. In 1875 it was sided by William Burger and his brother. It took them nine and one-half days to do the job and cost Probstfield $23.75 or $1.25 per man per day. These figures are proof that skilled labor was well paid on the frontier. A contemporary farm magazine pointed out that "the immigrant who stops in a city as a day laborer will always be that, but he who hastens to the country and hires out upon a farm will in a few years be able to purchase and stock a farm in the west, with skill to work it profitably." Farm laborers and handymen in frontier towns both received proportionately better pay on the average than did the factory worker in the East.

The cost of building material varied from community to community. Lumber yards that controlled a trade area without much competition sold lumber for $25 to $30 a thousand board feet while in areas where there was competition, common lumber sold for $17 to $21 a thousand. Nails of all varieties averaged about eight cents a pound. These prices remained fairly constant from the early 1870's through the 1890's. A lumber bill from the John S. Jonnson Lumber and Implement Company of Christine, North Dakota, dated June 20, 1892, and another dated July 11, 1893, of the Gull River Lumber Company, Wolverton, Minnesota, give a good sampling of comparative prices. These bills were taken to a local lumber yard, only twenty miles from Wolverton, in 1969 for comparison and showed the results of inflation in those eight decades. Judging from the dimensions of the materials purchased, they must have been used to build a bridge, but the comparison of price is still valid. Fifteen 2" x 10" x 18' timbers which cost $9.45 in 1892 were priced at $112.50 in 1969; five 6" x 8" x 20' timbers increased in cost from $8.40 to $104.00; two 6" x 6" x 14' timbers jumped in a similar ratio from $.84 to $10.92; one 2" x 6" x 16' timber was valued at only $.32 in 1892 but cost $3.68 eight decades later; ten 3" x 12" x 16' timbers made the greatest jump in price from $9.12 to $132.00. The total bill increased from a mere $28.13 in 1892 to a sizeable $363.10 in 1969.

Furnishings

The pioneer's dwelling was not only small and inexpensive by contemporary standards, but it was also meagerly furnished. There were few appliances and only the absolutely essential pieces of furniture, generally homemade. Emma Elton's homesteader's shack was perhaps typical of pioneer homes of that time and region. The table was a large box that had been used to ship some of her belongings. A large wooden cracker box was her cupboard. Two other boxes served as combination storage and lounges. The old laundry stove "with an oven built in the stove pipe" provided cooking and heating facilities. An old "American sewing machine" was in use constantly not only because it was necessary to make clothes, but also because it provided the chief means of passing time during the long winter days.

Mrs. Elton's bed was attached to a spring and hinged lengthwise on the wall to fold up making more room during the day. The trundle bed was as common as the wall type bed that flipped up sideways. Trundle beds were slipped under the parents' bed in order to make more room in the daytime. Girls generally had first choice of a bed, and if the family could afford it, the boys had beds too. The Thortvedts built double-deck beds against the walls with the bottom bunk serving as a lounge during the day. Some homes, especially log cabins, had the beds suspended directly from the rafters. Sometimes there were triple-decked bunks, but it was not uncommon to have no beds at all in the early years. In that case, sheep pelts, buffalo robes, horse or cow hides were placed on top of the straw-filled mattresses. They softened the impact of sleeping on the floor and also served as insulators. "Then there was the double blanket—we laid on the lower half and had the upper half over us. The fold at the bottom [of the bed] kept us from getting our feet uncovered. Besides this big blanket we had, as I remember it, three or four blankets and heavy quilts."

Straw-filled ticks were the common mattresses. When threshing season came the flattened-down straw was removed from the tick which was turned inside out and washed. Ticks were refilled as quickly as possible after threshing in order to avoid wet straw. The fresh straw, either oats or wheat, but never barley, was stuffed into the ticks, which varied in thickness from twelve to twenty-four inches. "Ticks were so much fun when they were first filled with fresh straw because you had to climb up on them. As time passed they flattened right down to the slats and were not much comfort to the sleeper." Cleaning out the ticks and refilling them was the job of the mother and the children, but on a few of the larger farms the stable or chore men also helped. "Often the ticks in the bunkhouse where the hired men slept had mice in them. [There were] few mice in our own house because of the many traps but this didn't seem to work in the bunkhouse because the men were not as careful about keeping the traps set." The children had fun catching the mice as they came out of the ticks. However, the grown-ups did not think mice were so much fun. "We are tormented with mice which gnaw everything in the house. One even built a nest in the sleeve of Katie's cloak." [4]

Pioneer homes left much to be desired as far as keeping warm was concerned. A person's attitude, of course, made the difference, for "in Iowa the cold penetrates into one's marrow, but in Dakota it only sharply nips the surface." Some early pioneers were proud to brave the cold. "Twenty-eight below and John froze his nose but Walter won't freeze because he is bound to think Dakota a very warm country. I am afraid he will get left some of these warm days when the mercury is fifty below zero."

The absence of storm windows not only caused the houses to be colder, but also made it difficult to see out when they were covered with ice. The children commonly defrosted the windows by holding their hands against them but one family "used to keep a flat iron on the back of [the] big base burner in the living room and when we especially wanted to see out, we held it close to the [frosty window panes] and we could see beautifully for a few minutes." Sometimes it got so cold in Glaspell's bedroom (Jamestown) that the bed was brought to the living room next to the stove and the big double sliding doors were drawn shut to keep the heat inside. However, during one cold spell when the temperature dropped so low that the water in a glass by the children's bed froze, Mrs. Glaspell commented, "We should have slept in the cellar." When the temperature dropped to twenty below zero on March 16, Mrs. Woodward's rose geranium near the stove was chilled and "the ink jug, blueing bottle, and other things in the kitchen and pantry froze solid." The Probstfields who had two heating stoves in addition to the kitchen cook stove felt the cold too and "sat shivering in the house all day . . . could not keep the house warm, too cold to cook in the kitchen."

The Grand Forks County community of Bachelor's Grove got its name from seven bachelor farmers who had moved up from Iowa and southern Minnesota and, rather than fight the winter individually, built one good cabin and lived together until they had time and funds to build satisfactory individual homes. Many young married couples lived with their families on the "home farm" for a year or two until they could build a comfortable permanent home. Frequently, they lived on their own claim during the summer in a temporary shack with only a room for cooking and sleeping and in the fall moved back to the home farm.

Cold weather and inadequate housing made heavy clothing a winter necessity. A typical pioneer man wore the heaviest woolen underwear he could get under a pair of mackinaw trousers that most likely were made of "thick red cloth, almost like felt." Over that came a pair of lighter trousers, and on top of that a heavy flannel shirt and a pair of bibbed overalls. This was standard gear for cold days. Men often wore muskrat caps with earlaps that reached down to the chin and muskrat mittens. If muskrats were hard to get, cat skins made "especially good mittens." Toboggan caps and high fur collars, when they came into fashion, were worn by all the women and children.

Cold houses were very discouraging to personal cleanliness as R. D. Crawford wrote:

Mrs. Woodward says she hears that there are people who do not undress all winter. I will not try to dispute it. In homes where the only heat was from the cook stove, it took a lot of courage to completely undress and put on a night shirt. . . . It was easy to change one's habits under such circumstances. We boys were required to change underwear once a week—Sunday. Didn't remove it for any purpose till the next Sunday. . . . Bathing? In warm weather there was the tub. From about the first of December through April or May, we boys were required to strip to the waist and wash good under the arms.

On many farms the nearby creek or swimming hole was the most commonly used bath tub. The first bath tub Edgar Olsen ever used was "a make shift one an agent sold us, a rubber contraption that set in a wooden frame. I still remember the urgings we received from our different teachers to take a bath more often." Most pioneers relied on the wash tub, which was placed in front of the open oven door for the winter Saturday night bath. Few families were as fortunate as the Henry Schroeders of Sabin who not only had a seven-bedroom house, but also two 200-gallon water tanks in the attic to supply water for household needs, including a porcelain bath tub.

In 1897 the citizens of Warren, Minnesota, were happy at the news that "the boys at the mill have fitted up an elegant bathroom in a corner of the [steam] engine room, where a nice bath in soft water, hot or cold, may be obtained by anyone for a small sum of 25 cents. For a luxuriant bath in a warm, cozy place, call at the mill bath parlors." It can only be assumed that ladies were also welcome to use these facilities and very likely the boiler man made them comfortable.

Toothbrushes were not commonplace articles in the pioneer's household. The Lockharts, of Grandin, rolled up pieces of cloth and sprinkled salt or soda on the roll which they rubbed over the teeth. Salt and soda were the accepted tooth cleaners although there was a period when charcoal also was used. That fad did not last long, but "apparently the gritty substance did scour the teeth." Some towns had drug stores where toothbrushes were available, but the general store apparently did not have much call for them.

Public facilities were no more comfortable than private homes. When Probstfield arrived by train in Moorhead at 4:50 a.m. on September 27, 1890, and was unable to get a room in the Jay Cooke House, he remained in the lobby where he "sat around shivering until 7 a.m. when a fire was started." When Guy Divet taught country school near Hankinson, North Dakota, he slept at the local hotel that had initially been a livery barn. The converted hay loft contained thirty homemade beds. "The rule of the house was that two people must occupy each bed, and any guest must accept as a bed partner anyone who was assigned to a bed with him, unless two permanent guests would pair off together as permanent bedfellows, which an engineer of the water pumps and I did." Divet observed that the "two in a bed" rule was probably necessary to keep the guests from freezing to death.[5]

Many homes built in the period from 1890 to 1920 had elaborate woodwork and other frills, including stained glass windows. These elaborations tended to give a false picture of overall prosperity. By contrast, the average settler's home had only one or two small, four-pane windows, making the rooms dark and dismal. Most of the early homes had no paint, either inside or outside, but annual coats of white-washing with either white clay or burned lime helped to lighten the interior. It was not until 1883, fifteen years after their house was first built, that Probstfields abandoned whitewashing and used paint. Mrs. Probstfield and her daughters did most of the interior painting. The $15.05 that was spent for enough paint to paint the exterior of the house in 1881 placed the Probstfields far ahead of most pioneers in home beautification. Even though the house was small, the job took three months for it was done in spare time. In 1883 they applied a second coat to the exterior using two gallons of paint that cost $1.75 each.

Furniture items were held to a bare minimum in cost and wherever possible built directly into the walls to conserve both money and room. Initially the settlers built much of their furniture themselves. It was not until 1883, twelve years after settlement, that the Jens Hagens had their first piece of purchased wooden furniture. Halvor and Christine had spent the winter working in Fargo and decided to bring gifts home to their parents. They purchased a black walnut marble topped dresser with a plate glass mirror and a rocking chair.

As time passed and people prospered, more furniture was purchased and only a few pieces were homemade. O. W. Flaten, prominent Moorhead photographer, purchased a complete line of furniture in September and November of 1897. The original bills are in possession of Flaten's niece, Mrs. Edgar I. Olsen. The differences in prices in a little more than seven decades would astound even the most avid antique collector. The Flaten's bedroom suite was purchased for $28.00, a center table for the living room cost $4.00, six dining room chairs were priced at a total of $9.00, a sideboard for the dining room bordered the luxury class at $25.00. The most expensive piece of furniture was the kitchen stove complete with pipes, elbow pipe and damper, which was $35.25. The living room proved to be expensive also for three large chairs cost a total of $26.75 and the divan was $12.00. The clock shelf added a mere $.45 and a fine mahogany table was purchased for $4.00. Other essential furniture brought the entire furniture bill to $175.05 for one of the finest homes in Moorhead.

Mrs. Flaten still needed miscellaneous kitchen and laundry room items to make her house complete. A dust pan, toaster, and egg beater were billed at a combined price of $.75. A large dish pan, iron kettle, and the giant-sized bread pan increased the bill $1.60. The ever-common coffee pot, two dripping pans, a cast iron spider (frying pan) added another $1.45, while the tea kettle, another frying pan, and a large iron kettle sold for $2.15. Two yellow bowls, a flour sifter, and two kettles cost only $1.00. The laundry room was furnished with two wash tubs, a clothes basket, a washboard, a clothes wringer, and a wash boiler for the meager sum of $5.00. The drinking pail and dipper added another $.45 to kitchen costs. Miscellaneous items totalled $18.30 bringing the entire cost for furnishing the house to $193.35.

Many of the above items would not have been found in the average pioneer home for the pioneers did not have room to haul these types of goods in their covered wagons and they certainly did not have the money to buy them. The total assortment of cooking utensils in the Andrew Overby household, besides the personal eating dishes, was a cast iron kettle, cast iron skillet (or spider), a tea kettle, a coffee pot, and a large iron soap kettle. Boxes and wall racks for chairs and furniture were commonplace.[6]

Lighting and Telephones

Technical changes came about rapidly during the later years of the nineteenth century. Some of these transformations did much to lighten the burden of everyday living as well as to add to the productive capacity of the farmer. Probably no other single change aided the farmer as much as the improvement from candlelight to electric light.

Many pioneers lived through four or five phases of household lighting. Artificial lighting in any form was expensive in the early days in terms of money and labor involved. The tallow candle provided the first light in those tiny pioneer homes. Tallow candles, a by-product of home butchering, were commonly made by tying twisted cotton rags between two legs of a chair and slowly pouring warm tallow over the rags. After the first layer of tallow hardened another layer was poured and allowed to harden. The process was repeated until the candle attained its desired size. For those who could afford them, candle molds were available. The mold was placed upside down with only a hole large enough for the string wick to stick through. A little of the wick was left sticking out of the mold on the open end to pull the hardened candle out of the mold. Making candles was a slow task and, therefore, they were used as sparingly as possible. They gave a dim yellow light, smoked, and smelled bad while burning.

The second form of lighting used in the homes was the kerosene lamp that used a wick and was no less smoky and smelly than the tallow candles. It was, however, much cheaper because kerosene, or "car oil," was relatively inexpensive. A United States Department of Agriculture survey in 1920 revealed that eight out of ten farmers' wives were spending at least one-half hour each day to clean and refill the lamps used in their households. Their common complaint— "Oh, washing those chimneys every day." The earliest pioneers who had experienced using and making tallow candles did not complain quite as much about the job of cleaning the kerosene lamps. Much later, improved refining processes of kerosene reduced the smoke problem and a brighter light was secured through the use of a mantle. The most popular of these mantle lamps was the Aladdin lamp.

After the periods of the homemade tallow candles and the kerosene lamps came the calcium carbide gas light. The carbide came in ten-gallon drums with a water dripper attached. As the water dripped into the drum, the carbide released gas that burned to supply light. Galvanized tubes were used to run the gas to the various rooms of the house. Some of the out-buildings had gas light, too, but this was an extreme fire hazard. The light instrument itself looked much like the Bunsen burner used in science laboratories. The cost of such light was advertised at $1.60 per thousand cubic feet, or about one-half cent per hour.

The next step in lighting was the gas lamp that produced the first virtually smokeless "white light." Gas lamps used mantles and were much simpler in construction and required only fuel and a match to light them. One brand, made by Coleman of Kansas, proudly bore its trade mark on the bottom: "The sunshine of the night."

Around the turn of the century some of the more progressive farmers quickly adopted the Delco system that provided electricity through the use of storage batteries kept charged by wind operated generators. The Delco system "could even pump water and elevate grain" but most farmers used lanterns for lights and gasoline engines for portable power until the advent of rural electrification in the late 1930's. The advent of REA at that time possibly marked the most decisive change in American agricultural progress, and also marked the beginning of the second agricultural revolution.

The cities and villages were ahead of the farmer in securing electric lighting. By November, 1881, Fargo had a water works, a light plant, and a telephone exchange. One utility firm, which was the result of the merger of several companies, was called the Union Light Heat and Power Company. Union secured a franchise from the city of Fargo in 1881 and remained in business until purchased by the Northern States Power Company in the early 1900's. Subscriptions to telephones rose so rapidly that after a first signup no additional phones could be installed in Fargo until a second switchboard arrived. "This was shipped some two months ago, which proves that freight is nearly as slow as the Western Union Telegraph."

The April 13, 1882, edition of the *Argus* related the joyous news: "Last night Fargo was radiant" for electric lights were turned on for the first time. The presence of the lights in the distance helped overcome the feeling of isolation for those on the prairie who could see them. "Last night was so clear that the electric lights of Fargo fairly shone into my [Mrs. Woodward's] bedroom window. Who would suppose the town was eight miles away as the crow flies." In Moorhead the Grand Pacific Hotel opened in 1881 and boasted of gas lighting furnished by the hotel's private gas plant. It was not until 1895 that the city of Moorhead installed an electrical system and a water works.

In April, 1886, the booming village of Hillsboro, North Dakota, got its first street lights—gasoline lamps. The gas lamps were used until Hillsboro converted to electricity and the lamps then were sold to Michigan, North Dakota. Hillsboro had fire protection before any type of public lighting was installed. In 1881 it boasted of four 1,000-barrel cisterns that were located at various points in the village. At first each of these cisterns had a supply of buckets to fight fires. Later, a hand pump machine was added. However, fire protection for rural people in general was unknown in the country at large until the 1930's.

The village of Arthur, North Dakota, received lights much earlier than did most communities of that size. The Burgums, land owners in the area who operated the local elevator, decided that electric power would be much safer and more practical in the elevator. They installed an electric generator in 1912 and sold electricity for street lights because power was not needed during the night at the elevator. There was a big celebration in town when the street lights were turned on for the first time. Other communities received their first electric power in a similar manner. In Hope, North Dakota, electricity came shortly before World War I when the Hope House, "the center of all activity," secured its own generator. Between 1909 and 1925 Otter Tail Power and Northern States Power brought electricity into the towns and villages along the Red River. In 1898 Casselton had a steam operated electric generator that was operated each evening. Later, it operated on Monday mornings so that the ladies could use electricity to wash clothes. Tuesday afternoons, when the ladies wanted to iron, soon became a second daytime period of operation. When Hallock, Minnesota, first operated its electric plant, the hours were from dusk until 11 p.m. except on Saturday when lights were on until midnight. At Amenia, North Dakota, the Amenia and Sharon Land Company installed a calcium carbide acetylene gas plant for lighting shortly after 1900 and street lights were installed there about 1905. In 1919 the company installed a Fairbanks-Morse electrical system that was operated in conjunction with its elevator. Local municipal plants charged as high as $.30 per kilowatt hour on a part-time service. When Otter Tail Power entered on a twenty-four hour basis, electricity was offered at $.16 per KWH for lights and $.04 for cooking in contrast to present rates of about $.025 per KWH. Many youngsters such as Oscar Overby, who lived during pioneer times, also lived through all five phases of lighting.[7]

Except for a few privately built telephone lines on the bonanza farms, there was no telephone service in the rural areas. No doubt this was a decided handicap, even though the business conducted on telephones in the early days was not nearly as urgent and voluminous as today. People expected others to "rubber" as listening in was called. The first residential telephone installed in Fargo was in the home of James Holes, Sr. in 1881. In 1895 H. F. Miller's Glendale Farms, ten miles from Fargo, had both a water closet and a telephone. But it was not until 1900 that rural telephone service became quite widespread in the area. Typical of such a line was the one established at Wolverton in 1902. These rural circuits had about twelve homes on each party line with a different ring for each residence. All rings were heard in every home on the line so that whenever anyone got a call, it was a signal to "rubber in." The W. J. Peet home was used as a "relay station" between Barnesville and Wolverton. The Peets had a phonograph and an organ and quite frequently gave a "general ring" (an extra long ring) which meant everyone was to listen in. The Peets would then play music over the phone to all of their neighbors. Numbers were played by request for as long as three hours in a single evening. Quite a number of old timers on this telephone line had the experience of hearing telephoned music.[8]

FOOTNOTES

[1] Clarence Danhof, "Farm Making Costs and the Safety Value, 1850-1860," *The Journal of Political Economy*, XLIX (June, 1941), 341; Gilbert Fite, *The Farmer's Frontier, 1865-1890*, p. 43; Robinson, p. 129; Evert, Ch. II, p. 31; *Fingal Enger Family History* (Fargo, 1961), p. 5, copy obtained from Mrs. Delmer Nystadt, granddaughter of Fingal Enger; Stephen Sargent Visher, *The Geography of South Dakota* (United States Geological Survey, 1915), p. 147; Torkel Fuglestad, "A Fuglestad History," a typed manuscript (Concordia College, 1937), p. 14; A. Overby, "Sod House Days," pp. 1-3; Charles A. Hobart, "Pioneering in North Dakota," *NDHQ*, VII, 196; *Hope of the Prairie, 1882-1957: 75th Anniversary Booklet*, Hope Anniversary Committee (Fargo, 1957), p. 10; Stafne, pp. 19, 25; Arnold, *Ransom County*, p. 57. Torkel Fuglestad was born in Norway in 1856 and attended a school where twelve subjects were taught and all males were required to spend some time in military training. When his education was completed, he was expected to take over his father's farm, which was a medium-sized operation with thirteen milk cows, two horses, and sixty sheep. Instead he went to Stavanger where he worked at a foundry making parts for steamships until he was laid off in 1882 at age twenty-seven. In 1883 he secured tickets to America for himself and Mrs. Fuglestad. During their month-long journey to America, the Fuglestads lived on sour vegetables and half baked bread and were very anxious for better food. At Ellis Island, Fuglestad purchased a loaf of rye bread to eat with some butter they still had from Norway. "We were sitting on a bench with our backs to the wall and eating. The bread lay on the bench between us. I was about to cut another slice—and reached out and felt the empty bench. We got up and looked about but the bread was stolen." Fuglestad described a second unpleasant incident that occurred on Ellis Island: "My wife has always been a worker. She sat knitting . . . and had a large ball of yarn beside her on the bench. Suddenly she held the end of the yarn in her hand. The ball of yarn had been stolen, disappearing just as had the rye bread. Later I began to think that the thief was apparently a reckless female who was loafing there. She spoke Norwegian and sat for a while beside my wife. She followed us to a restaurant . . ." Those two experiences were "a warning about what I could expect in the new land where heartless money men with the law in their hands could rob settlers of millions." During the two-week trip to Duluth on a Great Lakes freighter, Finnish, Norwegian, and Swedish immigrants slept wherever they could find a place between the freight. The Fuglestads' sleeping place was next to fourteen cows but every time freight was moved they had to move their bedding. One Swede slept on top of a pile of steel pipes but one night at midnight he was forced to move his bed when the pipes were being unloaded. The first year in Dakota was hard on Mrs. Fu-

glestad who had come from a home of plenty and position in Norway. When she saw their prairie land in Dakota she sat on a stone and cried and vowed that if they had had the money she would have returned to Norway.

² Stafne, pp. 2-12.

³ Fuglestad; *The Record* (Fargo, Sept., 1895), p. 8; Thortvedt, NDIRS, File 332; Daniel F. Pehrsson, letter Aug., 1965, and interview by the author Nov. 30, 1966; Iver A. Madsen Jr., interview by the author March 10, 1967; *Hope of the Prairie*, p. 4; Mrs. Henry Woell, interview by the author May 18, 1968; Hovde, pp. 11-15; Hobart "Pioneering," VII, 196-221, VIII, 130-131; Oscar R. Overby, *The Years in Retrospect* (Northfield, Minn., 1963), pp. 10-21; C. H. Frey, letter July 10, 1966; Mrs. Michael (Ellen) McMahon, interview by Leonard Sackett, 1937, NDIRS, File 195; Crawford, NDIRS, File 290; Webb, *NDH*, XVIII, 243; *Moorhead Independent*, Jan. 5, 1900, p. 49; Stafne, pp. 31, 34, 42, 52, 61; Woodward, pp. 27, 114, 133; David Peet, interview by the author Aug. 24, 1968. The Woodward house has been preserved by the recent owner, Leo Murphy, who donated it to Bonanzaville U.S.A. Located at West Fargo it can be visited in a pioneer setting.

⁴ O. A. Olson, "Christmas Eve in the Eighties," a typed story of an early Christmas in the Olson family; Woodward, p. 103; Elton, *Vaalhovd*, p. 38; Crawford, NDIRS, File 290; Probstfield; A. Overby, "Sod House Days," p. 3; Thortvedt, NDIRS, File 332; Mrs. R. F. Gunkelman, interview by Donald Berg, Aug. 1, 1966, NDIRS, File 569.

⁵ Glaspell, p. 188; Crawford, NDIRS, File 290; Edgar I. Olsen, interview by Donald Berg, July 10, 1966; Hobart, "Pioneering," VIII, 196; McMahon, interview, NDIRS, File 195; Probstfield; *Warren Sheaf*, Jan. 21, 1897; Divet, NDIRS, File 69; Woodward, pp. 66 and 72; *The Record*, Aug. 10, 1895, p. 29; Mrs. Robert Pratt, interview by Donald Berg, July 14, 1966; Gunkelman interview; Ernest Schroeder, interview by the author July 24, 1968.

⁶ Probstfield; Danhof, "Farm Making Costs," p. 323; *Warren Sheaf*, Jan. 5, 1881; A. Overby, Collection of Wolverton Township Official Papers; Edgar I. Olsen interview; A. Overby, "Sod House Days," p. 15; Stafne, p. 30.

⁷ O. Overby, *Retrospect*, p. 34; *World's Work*, XL (Sept., 1920), 435; *The Fargo Argus*, Nov. 17, 1881, April 13, 1882; *Hillsboro Banner*, June 28, 1956, pp. 6 and 11; Euren; Louis Bettschen, interview by Donald Berg, Aug. 3, 1966; *Hope of the Prairie*, p. 20; Woodward, p. 54; E. F. Krabbenhoft, interview by the author Aug. 19, 1968; Russell Slotten and Douglas Anderson of Northern States Power Company, interview by the author Oct., 1968, and Jan. 10, 1969; Pat Goggins, letter Feb. 3, 1969; Thomas C. Wright, *Otter Tail Power Company: From Its Origins Through 1954* (Fergus Falls, Minn., 1955), p. 15; Albert V. Hartl, letter Aug. 23, 1968.

⁸ David Peet interview; Mrs. Bernard Holes, interview by Donald Berg, July 15, 1966; *The Record*, I (Aug., 1895), 29; Henning Rheder, interview by the author, Aug. 11, 1968; Schroeder interview.

CHAPTER III

Bones to Bushels

T HERE is a saying among historians of agriculture and economics: if a man who had farmed during the days of Elijah (nine centuries before Christ) could have reappeared on earth in 1830 he would have recognized every implement in use on the farm. But if he had visited American farms in 1930, he would not have recognized a single farm implement. The first agricultural revolution, which introduced horse powered machinery, had brought more progress in that one century than in all previous history. This rate of progress—in mechanization as well as in theory of agriculture—has compounded ever since and those who have kept up with it have prospered.

Mechanical Progress

It was during the advance stages of this first agricultural revolution that farming started in Red River Land. The stony hillsides, forest lands, and small fields of the eastern areas of the United States were not suitable for large-scale mechanization; but the vast, fertile, treeless, stoneless prairies of this area, combined with growing markets and transportation, stimulated mechanical agriculture. Prior to mechanization (1830), it took over three hours at a labor cost of eighteen cents to produce one bushel of wheat, but by the late 1880's the labor cost was seven cents and the time forty minutes for Valley farmers. It was capital investment in machinery that made the big difference.

The length of time used by the old and the new methods of farming in the 1890's is best illustrated in a table found in footnote 1 for this chapter. Total time required to produce fifteen bushels from an acre of wheat in the pre-reaper, pre-thresher period (ca 1830), was sixty-four and one-fourth hours. Only sixty years later a mechanized farm in the Valley using a grain drill, binder, and thresher could produce the same volume of wheat in ten hours and twenty-six minutes. On homesteads in the Red River Valley, the working time was about two hours more per acre than on the bonanza farms because smaller equipment was used. In some eastern states in 1893 total harvest time was still twenty-five hours per acre, while in New England and other states, because of their refusal to mechanize, it was still forty-two hours. This time saving gave Red River Land farmers a great advantage over those of the older wheat-producing areas. The Red River farmers were also less bothered by weeds, by insects, and by disease, and because they were less tradition bound, they were more willing to adopt new methods.

Agricultural periodicals indicated that there was a smugness of success among the farmers of America as people began to talk about a "new agriculture" which would become the nucleus for the nation's prosperity sweeping the farmer along with it. The invention of the self-binding reaper caused one agricultural writer to boast, "Perfection by human means may be said to have been about reached." Others were writing in great terms about some new source of power for agriculture. There was a time when the Devon ox crossed with the Shorthorn had proven to be the ultimate in ox power. When the first machines were used, oxen could draw them. But soon machines demanded faster motion for smoother operation and so horses were used to replace the oxen. The adoption of large-scale machinery by bonanza farmers introduced factory methods to agriculture simply by multiplying the number of machines in each field. The average American farmer was content with the traditional rule-of-thumb methods and was naturally prejudiced against "book" farming and against new machinery. Only a few read the new farm magazines and tried new ways. But in the Red River Valley, homesteaders saw the examples established by the bonanza farms and "spent much time talking with superintendents and foremen from the [bonanzas] because they wanted to find out the latest in farming and also what the bonanzas were experimenting with." Homesteaders visited the bonanza farms frequently to get new ideas. The wide interests of R. M. Probstfield and the rapid rise of John W. Scott of Gilby are further proof that not all homesteaders were tradition bound. Although the 1880's and early 1890's were not exceedingly prosperous years in American agriculture and caused the farmers to hesitate in making scientific or mechanical advances, the Red River region was soon recognized for its innovators. Only in California where grain matured uniformly under dry conditions was there any advancement over bonanzaland techniques. Because the horse was such an uneconomical source of power, progressive farmers hoped that the steam engine would be more practical. However, they were very disappointed in its use and the big progress in power had to wait until the gasoline engine and later the electric motor provided the breakthrough.

The great parades of new machinery on the bonanza farms encouraged the homesteaders to keep up with their illustrious neighbors. Salesmen and crews of experts brought machinery to the bonanzas for experimentation and demonstrations, thus creating much publicity and influencing other farmers to buy machines too. Homesteads in this area were much larger than the average and they had a greater need for labor-saving machinery. The deciding factor in the sales talks was usually the explanation of the liberal financial terms provided by the salesmen: a down payment of one-third of the price, another one-third to be paid after each of the next two harvests, with interest at a "very attractive" 8 to 12 per cent. Members of the J. I. Case Company of Racine founded the First National Bank at Crookston in order to help farmers purchase new equipment. The national census of 1890 demonstrated the impact which mechanization had on area farmers. The average investment in machinery was $287 per farm in the Valley as compared to $143 in Illinois and $181 in Iowa. The large amount of machinery which these Valley farmers used enabled them to increase the total acres under cultivation from 350,000 in 1880 to 3,488,000 in 1890.[1]

Surveying and Plowing

In some respects Red River Land was settled in a more organized manner than previous frontiers. Only a few settlers arrived in the area before the government surveys took place so pre-emption by squatters was not very commonplace. The cultivation of the prairie, however, presented a unique problem; for example, with its vastness and lack of markers, there was little to guide the plowman to keep him within the proper bounds of his own farm. Iver Madsen, who became an experienced surveyor, started his career by laying out fields and plowing the sod for other farmers at $4.00 an acre. Madsen privately surveyed several farms in the Page area where the sections had been designated by laying four rocks in a row in each direction from the survey stake. Half section lines were indicated by a stake set with two rocks in a row on only two sides to indicate the direction of the half section line.

Surveying, which had to be completed before legal settlement could take place, was done in three stages. The initial government survey, which was made in 1858, laid out parallels every twenty-four miles with corrections to adjust for the earth's curvature. The second survey, completed in 1870 (1872 for Ransom County) or later, laid out the townships. In the third survey, which came just ahead of settlement (1880 for Ransom County), the sections were identified. This final survey was done by a team of eight or nine men who had all of their camping equipment with them in three covered wagons. The assistant surveyor, who was in charge of the camp and who ran the compass, took his orders from the contract surveyor who had several survey teams out at one time. The assistant surveyor operated from a cart pulled by a single horse but a saddle horse was brought along when faster trips were necessary. Although the lines were shot by the assistant with a compass, the actual distance was measured off by a team of men using a 100-foot length of "number ten" chain manufactured at Troy, New York. Since only one team of men marked off the sections and since no double checking was provided, it was possible for a section to be one or two "chains" off in the official survey.

A typical survey team required one week to lay out a township to the half mile lines. The marking of the center of the sections was left to the individual farmers. The corners of the sections were identified by oak stakes about four feet long and three inches square. At the half mile line stakes two by three inches were used. Each stake was marked with the section, township, and range numbers on the evening before it was placed in position. This marking was done in a manner so that the number pointed toward the proper section. Yet it was often impossible to find the stakes later because they might have been broken off by animals, burned off by prairie fires, or simply stolen. To avoid loss of the survey results because of the absence of the stakes, a standardized mound of dirt four feet square, easily recognizable as a survey mound, was placed around each stake. The dirt for the mound came from trenches three feet long and eight to ten inches deep dug to indicate the four points of the compass. The trenches and mounds lasted many years in this tough prairie sod. Survey department instructions stated that pieces of charcoal were to be placed in the trenches but apparently this was seldom done for no old timers remember finding them. At each of the half mile marks, which identified quarter section lines, two diamond shaped trenches five feet long were dug; these pointed in the direction of the quarter line.

Despite the difficulties of correct land markings, progress on the prairie continued. A primary breakthrough toward greater agricultural production was the development of the chilled cast iron, three-piece-lay walking plow in the 1830's. This plow could turn the tough prairie sod and scoured well, thereby greatly reducing power needs. Although the riding sulky plow was introduced in 1864, many farmers thought that riding while plowing was a sign of poor health or even of laziness and thus were reluctant to adopt it. Others did not have the third horse necessary for the efficient operation of such a sulky. Within a few years, the larger "gang plow" was produced and was first used in great numbers on the bonanza farms.

Plows were expensive in relation to the price of land. In May, 1878, Probstfield purchased a gang plow from Whitmans in Fargo and signed a note for it for $99.00, interest free until November 1 after which the interest was to be 12 per cent. In 1881 he purchased a new sulky plow for $60.00 and two years later a walking plow for $24.50. The difference in price between the two was certainly enough to discourage the purchase of the sulky type. Charles Hobart purchased a used sulky from the blacksmith in Mayville for $50.00 in 1883 and later that year secured a new gang plow from Horton and Company in Mayville for $125.00, which was a large cash outlay for the average homesteader.[2]

Bones, Sod Breaking, and Backsetting

But even with the new equipment, the farmer encountered difficulties. One such difficulty was the abundance of buffalo bones. In the days before the settler, Red River Land had supported large herds of buffalo which thrived on the rich grass of the area. When the white man entered the Valley, some of the largest buffalo hunts on the North American continent took place here. Buffalo bones virtually covered the ground around watering holes and favorite resting sites. In O. A. Olson's words:

> The bleaching bones of the buffalo
> Were gathered and bartered for "eats,"
> Like flour, coffee, and potatoes,
> And once in a while for meats.

The great number of buffalo bones scattered over the prairie presented a problem to the man who broke the sod. Twelve year old Guy Divet was supposed to gather up bones but could not do it fast enough to keep ahead of the two oncoming plows, so a teen-age neighbor boy was hired at $1.50 a week to help him. The bones were large and bothered the plows, but they were also a source of income. It took about thirteen buffalo to make up a ton of bones and thousands of tons of bones were sold for cash—$6.00 to $10.00 a ton. A few aggressive farmers ground buffalo bones for garden fertilizer.

The sod breaker had to turn the sod in such a manner that it would rot and be fit for cultivation the following year. All he had in the way of implements to break the sod was the plow—no pulverizers, vibrators, field cultivators, harrows or discs—and no chemicals to kill the grass. The prairie sod had roots that extended into the soil at least twelve to fifteen inches and were so thick that it took a sharp plowshare to cut them. Without a steel plowshare it would have been impossible to break this sod. The heavy prairie soil would never have scoured in a second or third plowing without the polished steel moldboard. The plowman carried a file and after every round or two had to hand file the lay to keep it sharp. Each evening the lays had to be pounded out on an anvil with a hammer and then ground to sharpness. For a few farmers like the Divets who had their own anvil and grindstone, this job was not considered serious, even though it had to be "done each evening by lantern light after [the day's] plowing was finished." Many of the farmers did not possess even this limited equipment and they had to rely on local blacksmiths. Fortunately, however, much of the sod was stoneless.

Although the prairie soil was well matted, it contained soft spots where a horse, an ox, or even the plow could suddenly sink "out of sight." The stuck animal had to be unhitched and other animals used to pull it out. If the plow went down too, the horses were hooked to the back of the plow to pull it out. There seemed to be "no bottom" to these places but after the land had been plowed a few times it became firm. These soft spots were not explained but they occurred even in areas where hay had been cut for many years.

Prairie sod was not only thick in itself, but also supported very tall grass making it difficult to plow. For a proper job, the first breaking could not be more than three inches deep—just enough to turn the grass under the sod—and it was then left this way for a few months so that the grass could rot. The breaking share was replaced with a cross share and "backsetting" commenced. "Backsetting" meant plowing the area an inch to three inches deeper than the original breaking in order to throw up fresh dirt which would "chink" the cracks between the clumps of sod and thus seal off the air to hasten decomposition. It also made the field smoother for the following year's seeding. If time permitted, the original breaking was dragged several times before backsetting took place. Not until backsetting took place did the farmer find out whether or not he had done a good job of breaking. If he had not turned the sod over properly it would not be well rotted. If he had plowed too deeply he would not be able to get under the sod to break it up. Charles Hobart made the mistake of plowing eight inches deep in some of his original breaking and then could not turn it back in the backsetting process. But he was so proud of his three oxen "which he drove like horses [meaning fast] and plowed eight [inches] deep, because the oxen were so strong" that he paid the price for his mistake during seeding, for the seeder teeth caught pieces of sod three and four feet long which slowed down his seeding and left the field very rough.[3]

Breaking and backsetting were slow and costly jobs. Having to do those jobs, the homesteader was not only deprived of a crop in his first year, but also he had to spend most of his time plowing and thus could not earn any cash by doing other work. If he hired the plowing done, it cost him $2.50 per acre for the breaking and $1.50 for backsetting. Some homesteaders hired professional sod breakers to plow ten acres the year before they arrived. This plan enabled them to seed a crop and to start plowing more land as soon as they came. Other homesteaders, like Divet and Hobart, came out a year earlier without their families to open some land. Whenever possible homesteaders worked on the railroad section, or worked for other farmers and plowed their own land whenever they found time during their first years on their new places.

The typical quarter section homesteader did not get much more than ten to twenty acres plowed in his first year. Fuglestad had only two oxen but by devoting every possible free hour to plowing his first year he was able to break fourteen acres. The Overbys of Wolverton said their main concern that first year was to make enough money to be able to eat and to pay the taxes, which were eight cents an acre, and the interest; however, no payment on the principal was due until after the first crop was harvested. They plowed about twenty-five acres a year and managed to get their entire 160 acres plowed in six years. In a long day, if it were cool and there were no flies, Overby could plow two acres, but in hot weather and in fly season the oxen would lie down and refuse to work. No amount of coaxing or beating could get them to move. On hot days the oxen would quit at about 11 a.m. and refuse to work until about 4 p.m. Then they were willing to work until dark. In warm weather one homesteader fed his oxen ground corn about 3 a.m., worked them until 6 a.m. and then let the oxen graze while he fed and harnessed the horses, milked the cow, and got the family up for breakfast. He then returned to the oxen and plowed until 11 a.m. Whenever the oxen let their tongues hang out they were allowed to remain right in the field to graze and rest until 3 or 4 p.m., when plowing again commenced and continued until dark. Even though they were slow, one yoke of oxen broke a record 130 acres in a single season. Hobart, who used three big mules on a walking plow in his first year, claimed that he could do twenty rounds a day with a twelve-inch plow—a total of two and eight-tenths acres. A twenty-mile day was a long day of work. The Crawfords, for example, on third plowing, were satisfied to accomplish eighteen miles (or rounds) a day with five horses on a fourteen-inch gang which meant thirty acres in a six-day week. Sixteen year old Mary Probstfield, with just four horses on a new double gang plow, averaged only eight rounds a day. However, she and her fifteen year old brother broke a total of seventy-five acres in 1878 by working steadily. They averaged ten hours a day and on some days plowed as much as two acres. The previous fall the weather had been exceptionally mild and Probstfield had been able to plow until December 27 giving an optimistically false impression of local temperatures to many future homesteaders.

The Divets used five horses on a double gang plow which made twenty miles (or rounds) and plowed five and six-tenths acres per day. In their first year the Divets had two plows devoted full time to plowing and were able to break and backset only 250 acres. At that rate it is understandable why a busy homesteader by himself could not do more than ten to twenty acres per year. In the second year after seeding, the Divets opened another 250 acres using four plows which were operated by a crew of six men and twelve year old Guy on rotating shifts. In the third year seven men using thirty-seven horses broke an additional 500 acres, giving them 1,000 acres for crops in the fourth year. The ability to break so many acres in one year set the Divets apart from the average homesteader.

For that first summer on the prairie some homesteaders got along with very little comfort. Charles Hobart had left his family in New Hampshire and camped out-of-doors while he broke his land. His camping equipment consisted of a sheet-iron stove, a small flat iron kettle, a tin plate, a knife, a fork, a spoon, and a few other miscellaneous items. He had pancakes for breakfast "cooked in my flatbottomed kettle on my little stove." He ate one pancake while he prepared the second and subsequent servings. "For other meals sometimes I cut up breakfast bacon [side pork] into cubes half an inch square or smaller and cooked it. Then I poured in water and made hasty pudding—very simple and good. And there were no dishes to wash except the kettle and the spoon." He slept under his wagon for he needed no claim shanty because he had purchased railroad land for cash. He did not build a house until the spring of 1882.[4]

Tools

One of the greatest handicaps to the pioneer was the almost complete lack of tools. Even the simplest tools, now found in every home, were not readily available then. The lack of tools was a particular handicap because so much of the machinery used on the farms and the furniture used in the home had to be made by the settler. Sharing necessary tools was taken for granted as in the case of the Thortvedts who were asked by their fellow settlers to take the middle farm in the Buffalo River settlement because they possessed the only grindstone for sharpening scythes, sickles, and axes. The central location would be more convenient for the neighbors who needed to use the stone.

The tools usually used for building a log house and making repairs on the farms consisted of a hammer, an auger and one or two bits, a saw, an axe, and a chisel. Whipple trees, eveners, neckyokes, wagon tongues, and wagon boxes were nearly always homemade as were most early horse-drawn sleds. Probstfield made his own sleds until 1883 when he purchased a new factory-made bobsled for $27.50. Many pioneers even made the sash work for the windows and the doors for their early log or frame houses.

Haying

In the days before horse-powered machinery, farmers found it nearly impossible to make a living by cropping alone; therefore they were forced to have livestock for additional income. Early farming in the Valley was no exception, but, fortunately, there was an abundance of native prairie grass. To maintain his livestock, one of the first tasks confronting the pioneer when he reached his new home was the stockpiling of hay for the winter. When the Buffalo River settlers reached their destination in late June, 1870, it was too late to raise a crop but it was imperative that the settlement stockpile hay. They did not even take time to build houses but placed a stove under an elm tree and lived in their wagons until fall. Fuglestad at Hannaford did nothing but plow and make hay during the first year on his homestead. All of the hay was cut with a scythe and put up with a fork. To make the task somewhat easier, he exchanged haying labor with his neighbor, Elling Froiland.

The native prairie grass was the only hay which was put up until the early 1880's when progressive men like R. M. Probstfield, J. B. Power, and Pierre Wibaux introduced alfalfa and clover into the Valley and into the cattle country to the west. Probstfield was probably one of the first in Red River Land to seed tame hay. In 1881, and again in 1883, he seeded Hungarian grass. Probstfield was even ahead of James B. Power whose seeding of alfalfa in 1887 marked the next earliest tame hay seeding to take place in the Valley.

Haying machinery was being developed about the same time that this area was being opened. A man with a scythe could not cut more than one and one-fourth acres of hay a day and a total of thirty-five and one-half man hours were required to harvest and stack just one ton of hay, but by the end of the 1800's with the use of a mower, a dump rake, and a stacker, the total time to do the same work was reduced to eleven and one-half hours. Haying equipment was relatively expensive, however. A mower-reaper combination and a hand rake cost Narve Roen $135.11 in 1874 when ordered through the State Grange which sold machinery to its members. Pitch forks and hand rakes cost about $5.00 each. A dump rake, or what was called a one-horse sulky rake, cost Ole Gunderson of Buffalo River $45.00 in 1873.

Besides its price, the new haying machinery presented other problems which hindered its adoption. Hobart claimed that the $75.00 hay loader which he bought in 1892 was "the poorest piece of machinery that I ever owned." A part broke after only a few days' use and the replacement ordered from the factory did not arrive until after haying season was over. Hobart was so disgusted that he pulled the loader into the grove on his farm. He never used it again. Instead he went back to loading hay by hand.

All things considered, haying consumed more time than any other process except plowing on the average farm and it was in progress from mid-July through early fall. It was often hard to hire men for haying because, by comparison, it took longer to hay than to do any other farm task. It was more monotonous and also harder work. "Men claimed they were hired for threshing—did not want to work in hay. Too hard work—hence quit. Walter [Probstfield] drove to town and hired two men who promised to be here in the morning to work. They did not come."

Winter or summer there was always hay to be hauled. All hay was stacked in the fields to save time during haying and also as a precaution against fires. In winter, the snow had to be removed to get at the stacks and in the spring the hay had to be moved to the yard before the fields got too soft for the wagon. The more people who could help in haying, the more efficient it was; therefore, women and children necessarily became involved in that work.[5]

Flail Threshing

Even though the reaper had been invented in 1831 and the threshing machine a few years later, many of the first farmers in the Valley used the cradle scythe to harvest their grain and the flail to thresh it. The beginning farmer operated on such a small scale and with such limited funds that often he found it virtually impossible to purchase sizeable horsepowered equipment. In 1871 the Thortvedts and the others who settled on the Buffalo River in 1870 harvested an average of ten acres of grain per farm with a cradle scythe. During the winter the bundles were placed on the frozen Buffalo River and threshed with a flail. The Reverend James Ostlund, a "moonlighting" minister, harvested eight acres in Traill County in 1872 with a cradle scythe and in the winter flail threshed it on the frozen stable floor.

Prior to 1875, Probstfield was unable to realize a profit from raising and harvesting wheat by hand; consequently, he raised only oats and barley for his chickens and livestock during this period. His diary notes that on August 2, 1875, he "cradled one-half acre of barley. Mrs. P. bound over half of it." That year he raised his first wheat and cradled a swath through the field to open it for John Bergquist's new self rake reaper which he had hired. Mr. Thomas drove the reaper and in one full day and three hours of the second day, he had cut fourteen acres of a thin stand of wheat. John Bergquist, Jacob Wamback, Catherine Wamback, and Mr. and Mrs. Probstfield required two and one-half days to bind and to shock it. It took four men two and one-half days to haul and to stack the twenty-nine loads grown on those fourteen acres. The workers were paid $2.00 per day. That same year Helmuth Schultz raised the first wheat in Ransom County. After he and John A. McCusker had threshed it by tramping it with oxen, they hauled the wheat forty miles to Fargo by wagon. Certainly the economics of such production were doubtful even under the best of conditions, for the product was too far away from the market.[6]

Power

The wide open spaces of the Valley made the farmer more vigorous in his search for some form of power that would more effectively aid him in conquering these vast stretches of prairie. Fields stretched out to the horizon and there were few obstacles such as rocks, trees, and hills to handicap the use of large-scale animal-powered implements. This opportunity made the settler more determined than ever to substitute animal power for man power. The first homesteaders had brought horses and oxen with them in about equal numbers. Oxen were less expensive and could maintain themselves more easily than horses, but when machinery became popular horses replaced oxen primarily because horses worked faster and were more readily obtainable. Oxen outnumbered horses in Minnesota by 10,000 head in 1860 but by 1870 horses outnumbered oxen by 50,000. However, sometimes even horses were not fast enough for efficient operation of the new implements. "Edmund [Probstfield] quit cutting wheat after making a few rounds because horses would not move fast enough to *cut* as he had no whip." Oxen disappeared slowly, nevertheless, and some were used as late as 1925. In 1893 Hans Kloster of Wolverton listed a seven year old 1,600-pound brown ox with a white spot in the forehead as collateral on a mortgage for a new McCormick harvester. That same year he purchased one ox for $60.00, giving an eight percent note to Peter Erickson. In 1893 Ole Storseth gave a note to Haugen Brothers of Northwood for $68.20 at ten percent interest with two oxen named Thor and Sven as collateral.

Oxen were never as important as a source of power here as they had been to previous frontiers. Many of the "old timers," however, insist that oxen were far more important than most people realize today. Because they could be butchered when their work days were over, many homesteaders continued to use oxen even after they had horses. R. M. Probstfield took advantage of this dual purpose and on October 27, 1873, started feeding corn meal to Bright, one of his oxen, which he butchered on November 6. Just how much good it did to fatten an ox on corn meal for only eleven days is debatable, but at least, if he had planned to sell the meat, he could have said that it had been corn fed. On December 30, 1873, he butchered two oxen which weighed a total of 1,689 pounds. One would have to assume this to be dressed weight because oxen were usually quite old before they were butchered. In this case the live weight of each animal would have been between 1,300 or 1,400 pounds—not exceptionally large by present standards—but judging from the pictures of many oxen they would have been large animals for those days. The condition of their flesh obviously was dependent on how hard they had worked and how well they were fed.

Charles Hobart was used to oxen from his previous farming experience in New Hampshire. In the spring of 1885 he purchased a pair of big red oxen for 200 bushels of wheat. The pair had a market value of about $120, and he also bought a pair of smaller ones for $90. The big red ones worked fine in cool weather but they "played out" when it got warm; therefore, Hobart "left the big one loaf until fall and then made beef out of him." "Big Red" dressed out to 250 pounds for each quarter which meant that he must have weighed between 1,400 and 1,650 pounds when alive. The survivor of this pair, the smaller of the two oxen, was harnessed between two horses "and he made the best horse in the team." [7]

Among the larger homesteaders and the bonanza farmers oxen never played a major role, and even horses were not efficient enough as a source of power. The great horse-drawn machinery parades across the fields were dramatic, to be sure, but nearly one-fourth of the land farmed had to be used to feed the horses. As one early settler said, "The feed question was a nightmare [the first year]. We bought when we could get the money, paying as high as ninety cents a bushel for some oats. When we could not get the money we borrowed and borrowed until it took all but a few sacks of my share of oats raised on Mr. Shattergaard's place to pay up in the fall." Yet, for a short period, horse power seemed to be adapted to mechanical functions, such as threshing machines, grain elevators, feed grinders, fanning mills, well diggers, stump pullers, and winches which used tread mills or sweep power. When Charles Hobart threshed in 1892 he used Lewis Wright's three-horsepower tread mill as power. At least it was supposed to be three horsepower, but as soon as the platform began to move, one horse named "Gypsy" jumped out of the chute, leaving two horses to do the work.

In the 1880's the Ericksons at Hawley used a four-horsepower sweep for threshing and for pulling stumps, but most horsepower sweeps for threshing used from eight to sixteen horses. The Hovdes used a ten-horsepower sweep on their thresher and the Freys used a fourteen-horsepower sweep with their Nichols and Shephard thresher. The biggest problem was that there were seldom enough horses available to provide all the power necessary to run the machines efficiently. Some tried to use oxen with horses, but the oxen were slower and soon became dizzy from walking in a circle and lay down. Horses got dizzy too. Once when Oscar Overby unhitched a team of horses from a sweep on an elevator which they had been pulling most of the day, instead of going in a straight line to the water tank, they continued walking in a circle. It was comon practice to blind the one eye of the inside horse so it could not see the machinery in action.

In agriculture in general, tradition-bound thinking retarded the adoption of mechanical power. National farm magazines, agricultural societies, and government leaders had been discussing the possibilities of steam power since the 1850's and if there had been a demand for steam traction engines at that time they would have been manufactured. When a large steam engine sank nearly "out of sight" on a midwest prairie in 1858, Illinois, Iowa, and southern Minnesota farmers were almost delighted because "they knew all the time it would never work." Steam traction engines were being used successfully on the Pacific coast, but this made little impression on farmers elsewhere who were satisfied to use stationary steam engines which they pulled around with horses. Progressive thinkers such as Horace Greeley wrote in the 1850's that what the farmer really needed was a steam engine that did not weigh more than a ton—a machine that could work steadily for half an hour without stopping for refueling, and that could travel on plowed fields. Beside threshing, this machine should be able to pull wagons, harrows, stumps, plows, and pumps, and to dig cellars and ditches. Farmers laughed at such dreams. Later writers in farm magazines stated that such a tractor might enable the family farms to continue in operation, but the farms would become "fewer, larger, and costlier, forcing the farmers into some kind of effective combination of producers among the major commodities." Such prophecy of corporate farming and collective bargaining must have sounded like heresy to farmers of the nineteenth century.

Although the first steam traction engine was developed in 1855, it was not manufactured for the market until 1873 because of the lack of demand. In the early 1880's experiments with steam power plowing were conducted on bonanza farms but, except for threshing purposes, there were few buyers. The reason was that farmers had to have a full line of horses on the place for seeding and harvesting anyway and they could not afford to buy a second source of power for just plowing and threshing. Although steam power was not adopted for field use, the bonanza farms found that steam traction engines were practical for moving the threshing rigs from one field to another because a great amount of labor was always wasted in the long periods (down time) it took to move the tractionless engines. By 1885 all bonanza farms used steam traction engines for their threshing. Their movement was at first a novelty. "It is queer," Mrs. Woodward said, "to see an engine moving about the yard with no horses to pull it."

Among the first to adapt to steam power in Red River Land were the Pazandak Brothers at Fullerton. By 1909 they had completely switched to mechanical power and claimed to have had the first horseless farming operation in North Dakota. However, the steam engine was never completely satisfactory to either the large or the small farmer because it was cumbersome and because of the fire hazard. Fire insurance rates were very high on farms where steam power was used. In 1908 Iver Madsen purchased a twenty-horsepower I.H.C. Mogul tractor that could pull a plow with four sixteen-inch bottoms on light soil. Madsen did not claim to have the first gas tractor in the area, but thus far no earlier purchases have been established.

In 1922 Ernest F. Krabbenhoft, in search of more economical power, purchased a twenty-horsepower, three-phase electric motor which was mounted on a wagon chassis and was used to run his twenty-two-inch threshing machine. His appraisal of this setup was that it was "safe, very efficient, and we did not need a man to attend it." A group of farmers had formed a company and had built a power line from Watts Siding to Sabin, a distance of seven miles, to obtain their power from Northern States Power Company.[8]

Fencing

Farm income is generally derived from three sources—livestock, vegetables, or grain. Many of those who came to the Red River Land hoped to make a living by raising only wheat. Historically, however, the frontier farmer had seldom succeeded without some form of livestock production. He was so limited in his capacity to produce enough grain or other products by his own effort that he was compelled to rely upon the natural increase of livestock for additional sustenance and income. But livestock production and wheat raising together on the wide, open prairies created an inevitable conflict. The farmer had either to herd his cattle or to build fences for them.

In the decades just before this area was settled, fencing had proved to be one of the greatest sources of dissatisfaction in agriculture because it was expensive. It was estimated that fences cost $2.00 per acre for a section, $4.00 per acre for a quarter, and $8.00 per acre on forty acres, an obvious hardship for those who needed fencing most—the small farmers. These farmers complained that fencing exceeded all forms of taxation, and a lack of fencing materials prevented many livestock farmers from entering treeless areas. The *Rural New Yorker* of 1857 described the problem well:

We never realized so fully the expense and difficulty of fencing as when standing on those broad plains . . . land could be bought . . . on so favorable terms that the poorest man could possess himself a home; but the cost of fencing was so great, many were compelled to seek a home in the timber. . . . Fencing costs more than land . . . and fencing must be paid for in cash while the land can be bought on such terms that the money for the payments of both principal and interest can be realized from the land.

Pioneers in Red River Land were resourceful when it came to fence building and they used whatever material was available, but even so the cheapest fences were expensive and time consuming. In 1874 R. M. Probstfield hired a neighbor, Jacob Wamback, and four other men to set posts and build a fence for him at the rate of three cents per post plus meals. In 1881 he made rails for his hog pasture. Rail fences were exceedingly wasteful of timber and were slow to build. After the trees had been cut down and trimmed, the average man could split only about 100 ten-foot rails in one day. A typical rail fence took five lengths of ten-foot rails to make seven lineal feet of fence. No wonder the farmers preferred either keeping the hogs indoors or letting them run wild in the woods.

After Torkel Fuglestad burned off his claim to make plowing easier, he noted that it was covered with stones. He used the stones to build confines for his livestock just as was done in Norway. Not only were they the best and the cheapest fencing material available to him, but also his fields were cleared in the process. Even though stone fences took time to build they were extremely durable. Some of Fuglestad's stone wall fences are still intact after more than eighty-five years.

Stray Livestock

Rounding up animals after they had strayed was a nuisance and a very time consuming job. Like the farmers in older sections of America, pioneers here were at first perfectly willing to let their cattle roam, but as settlers became more numerous, unoccupied land became scarce and crops were damaged by the stray animals. The time for freedom of livestock, or what might be called "open range," was short lived. The day-to-day tribulations of fencing problems and stray animals are hard to document because no one bothered to record them and they were so commonplace that they were not mentioned in the local papers. R. M. Probstfield was frequently frustrated over the problem of stray cattle and as early as July 13, 1875, noted a "lot of strange cattle mixed with ours." A few days later his pet horse, Fancy, could not be found and he assumed that she must have fallen into the river. The next day Fancy was found in the woods all tangled up in grapevines. On September 19, 1875, Mr. Burke from Cass County appeared at the Probstfield farm in search of a pig he had lost. The pig had swum the Red River and had been on the Probstfield farm since September 10. Burke paid a Probstfield boy thirty cents for keeping it.

During 1876 when farm and animal numbers in the area had increased, Probstfield recorded several instances regarding stray livestock. April 21: "Strange bull came to the yard with my cattle"; May 18: "Stray cow appeared on the yard"; May 22: "Man from Moorhead called to find his drove of hogs"; July 29: "Cattle and horses all gone"; (They were found late in the day about three miles southeast of Moorhead, at least six miles from the Probstfield farm.) August 7, just nine days later: "All cows and horses gone again." Before he began looking for them, Mr. Probstfield went to Moorhead and bought cowbells to put on all his animals. On one occasion the Probstfield children did not bother to see that the sheep were fenced for the night, and the next morning the sheep could not be found. Six days later they were discovered at the Wiedemanns, five miles southeast of Moorhead and more than eight miles from the Probstfield farm. They were brought home two days later. This type of problem continued into the 1890's.

At one time in the late 1880's when everything seemed to be going wrong, the Probstfield's "hogs [were] out all week . . . cannot hold them in fence . . . if they are out much longer there will be no need to harvest wheat. Peter Lamb's cattle in our wheat too—drove them into the river." A few days later Peter Lamb notified the Probstfields that their boar was at his place. No doubt a great deal of time was spent looking for strays. All of this bother combined with the loss of good condition in the roaming animals amounted to a great economic burden for the farmer.

At least one enterprising person took advantage of the problem of confining animals and offered his services as a herder. James Steader of Warren advertised that he would herd cattle and give them proper care. Steader wanted the cattle to be branded and he would care for them for $1.00 per head for the season, an extra charge of $.10 if salt was desired. The charge for horses and colts was $1.00 per head per month.[9]

Barbed Wire

In 1870, before barbed wire came into use, the United States Department of Agriculture made a study of fencing and determined that it represented the greatest single form of capital investment in the nation. Fences represented nearly a third of the total value of all farms and were valued at 50 per cent more than all livestock. Total investment in fences was nearly equal to the gross national debt of the federal government. This study did much to set off a wave of research and experimentation that led to the invention of barbed wire in 1874 which helped to revolutionize land values on the plains. In 1886 R. M. Probstfield and Charles Hobart used barbed wire for the first time. Hobart went to great lengths to explain how he built his first wire fence. First, posts were sharpened and then driven into the ground with a maul. Then a wagon was jacked up so that one rear wheel could be used as a winch to tighten the wire, but as soon as the wire fastened to the corner post was pulled taut, the post came up out of the ground. Hobart and his neighbor learned that the corner post had to be well anchored first and he hung a heavy stone on it beside bracing it with stakes and tension wires.[10]

Another lesson had been learned and with it one of the greatest problems of pioneer agriculture was reduced to a simple mechanical chore.

FOOTNOTES

[1] Earle D. Ross, "Retardation in Farm Technology Before the Power Age," *Agricultural History*, XXX (Jan., 1956), 13; *Fargo Argus*, March 24, 1882; Frank H. Spearman, "The Great American Desert," *Harpers*, LXXVII (July, 1888), 233-235; Gunkelman interview; Murray, pp. 139, 141, 149; Merril E. Jarchow, "Farm Machinery in Frontier Minnesota," *Minnesota History Bulletin*, XXIII (St. Paul, 1942), 324; Thortvedt, NDIRS, File 332; Woodward, p. 135;

HOURLY REQUIREMENTS TO PRODUCE ONE ACRE OF FIFTEEN BUSHEL WHEAT

Pre-Mechanization	Hours	1893 Mechanized Valley Farm	Hours
Plowing	6:40	Plowing	2:30
Sowing	1:35	Drilling	0:30
Brush harrow,		Cutting	1:00
sickle, binding	2:50	Shocking	1:40
Shocking	20:00	Threshing and storing	3:06
Haul to barn	4:00		8:46
Flailing	13:20		
Winnowing with sheet	12:00	Not included in above is five draggings	
Measuring and sacking	4:00	which were not always performed ...	1:40
	64:15		10:26

[2] Wayne D. Rasmussen, "History of Mechanization of American Agriculture," United States Department of Agriculture, a mimeographed copy in my possession received from Dr. Rasmussen; Probstfield; Hobart, "Pioneering," VII, 208; Madsen interview; Arnold, *Ransom County*, pp. 49-52; letter from John Reber, Foxhome, Minn., to Arthur Overby, June 23, 1968. Mr. Reber's father did surveying for road building in Wilkin County. John Reber, born in 1883, worked for his father in that business. He claims to have dug up the last recognizable original stake in 1914 in an undisturbed swamp on the borders of Akron and Tanberg Townships in Wilkin County. The mound and pits were still in evidence; Holes interview, Mrs. Bernard Holes has a survey chain used by her father-in-law's brother, Andrew Holes, Moorhead pioneer. It has little tags on it marking off every two feet in the hundred-foot length.

[3] Divet, NDIRS, File 69; Steward Holbrook, *Machines of Plenty, Pioneering in American Agriculture* (New York, 1955), p. 180; Hobart, "Pioneering," VII, 198-202, 219; Crawford, NDIRS, File 290; Murray, pp. 112, 163.

[4] A. Overby, "Sod House Days," p. 4; Probstfield; Hobart, "Pioneering," VII, 195; Fuglestad, p. 11; Divet, NDIRS, File 69; *The Record*, June, 1896, p. 10; Crawford, NDIRS, File 290. Hobart's father had established a homestead claim near his son's half section of railroad land. He was a partial invalid and it soon became obvious that he would not be able to "live up the claim"; therefore, he relinquished his right to his son who filed a tree claim on it. This land was covered with stone that Hobart called "drift boulders." Many of the stones were removed and used as underpinning (foundation) for buildings. People from Mayville and vicinity also came to haul away stones for building purposes. Hobart hired a sod buster to plow ten acres for the tree claim. After turning a few furrows in the stony ground the plowman quit because he had already broken $24 worth of plow shares and eveners. After that the hired man, Lewis Wright, tackled the job of plowing in his spare time. "He never worked a full day but came home with something broken." Wright kept at it much of the summer but it was fall before the ten acres were finally plowed. After the grain was stacked Hobart took his "four steadiest horses and we both went up. Lewis held the plow and I drove and finished up without breaking anything. The trouble was that the horses were not used to stone; as soon as the plow

touched [a stone] one of them would jump ahead while horses that are used to stones will ease up."

⁵ W. B. Thornton, "The Revolution by Farm Machinery," *World's Work*, VI (Aug., 1903), 3770; William H. Brewer, "Agricultural Progress," *Harper's The New Monthly Magazine*, I (Dec., 1874-May, 1875), p. 883; Thortvedt, NDIRS, File 332; Madsen interview; Probstfield; Donald Welsh, letter Aug. 7, 1967 (Dr. Welsh is an authority on Pierre Wibaux); Jarchow, p. 326; Hobart, "Pioneering," VIII, 128.

⁶ Leo Rogin, *The Introduction of Farm Machinery in its Relation to the Productivity of Labor in the Agriculture of the United States*, IX (Berkeley, 1931), pp. 218-228; Rasmussen, p. 15; Murray, p. 90; Danhof, "Farm Making Costs," p. 341; Thornton, p. 3771; Brewer, p. 885; Thortvedt, NDIRS, File 332; *Hillsboro Banner*, June 28, 1956, Sec. V, p. 2; Probstfield.

⁷ Probstfield; Hobart, "Pioneering," VII, 218.

⁸ Arnold, *Ransom County*, p. 47; *Historical Statistics of the United States from Colonial Times to 1957*, pp. 289-290; Harold E. Pinches, "Revolution in Agriculture," *Yearbook of Agriculture, 1960, The Power to Produce*, ed. Alfred Stefferud (Washington, 1960), pp. 1-10; Ross, pp. 12-14; Holbrook, pp. 176-187; Jarchow, p. 318; Ferd Pazandak, interview by the author Sept., 1964; Madsen interview; A. Overby, Township records of Wolverton Township; Mrs. Cedric Onan, letter April 20, 1969. Horse powered stump pullers and ditchers for drainage purposes became commonplace as the area developed and were generally owned by custom operators or by several farmers cooperatively. The horse powered stump puller was a winch anchored to a large tree and made use of cables to pull out the desired stumps. The ditcher required four horses working around a winch which wrapped up forty rods of cable pulling the plow with it which pushed the dirt out on both sides and left a flat bottom ditch. It provided the only effective means of digging drainage ditches until steam powered draglines were adapted just before World War I. A ditch up to four feet in depth could be dug with the horse powered implement. Two men were required to do the job—one to drive the horses, the other rode on the plow and partly controlled its movement which was extremely slow, but ditches of a mile in length were dug by individual farmers to improve drainage on their land.

⁹ Clarence Danhof, "The Fencing Problem in the 1850's," *Agricultural History*, XVIII (Oct., 1944), 168-173; Walter Prescott Webb, *The Great Plains* (Boston, 1931), pp. 145-51; Fuglestad, p. 14; Probstfield; Hobart, "Pioneering," VII, 217, 220; Danhof, "Farm Making Costs," p. 330.

¹⁰ Danhof, "The Fencing Problem," p. 174; Probstfield; Hobart, "Pioneering," VII, 220.

CHAPTER IV

More than Wheat

BECAUSE it is flat and treeless, the Valley frequently gives the impression of a monotonous landscape, but to many it provides a view that cannot be equalled. Even those who are not amazed by the beauty of the flat land cannot avoid the feeling that this is a land of great wealth. When entering the area from any direction one feels not unlike a desert traveler coming to an oasis. The historian for the exploring party of Joseph N. Nicollett recorded his impressions and those of the advance scout upon their approach to the Valley from the west in 1841:

When we reached him, we found him in the most ecstatic contemplation before the vast and magnificent valley of the Red River . . . spreading itself in an almost insensible slope to the east, to the north, and to the south, and bounded only by the horizon. It is difficult to express by words the varied impressions which their [the prairie] spectacle produces. Their sight never wearies. . . . In the summer season, especially, everything upon the prairies is cheerful, graceful, and animated. The Indians, with herds of deer, antelope, and buffalo, give life and motion to them. It is then they should be visited; and I pity the man whose soul could remain unmoved under such a scene of excitement.

Wild Life

Those who know the Red River Valley in its present state may have difficulty realizing that it once was a paradise of wild life. The early settlers depended very much upon these gifts of nature for their food supply as well as the yields from farming. Charles Cavileer, who was one of the first permanent white settlers in North Dakota, came to Pembina as a customs collector in 1851. Addressing an old settlers' reunion at Grand Forks in December, 1891, he recalled seeing his first buffalo on a trip west of Pembina while traveling in the Turtle Mountains. "[I] could see for miles and miles, and the prairie was black with them, and only here and there I could see spots of snow. . . . there were simply millions upon millions of them." Cavileer continued by stating that the Red River Valley was "one vast immense waste . . . the home of the Indian and the Halfbreed . . . buffalo, elk, antelope, bear, wolf, and fox and other fur bearing animals."

Cavileer's impressions of 1851 compare well with those of Alexander Henry who traveled through the area in 1800 and 1804. Of the Pembina River area he wrote: "We found immense herds of buffalo which appeared to touch the river and extend westward on the plains as far as the eye could reach. The meadows were alive with them." Eleven days later in the Park River region he noted: "Buffalo continue very numerous; from the top of my oak, or ladder, I counted 15 herds." Later Henry "bought a beautiful white buffalo skin" which had long soft hair that resembled a sheep's fleece.

Mrs. H. Crofford, an early settler, who traveled by covered wagon, remembered that buffalo bones were very thick on the prairie as did Guy Divet who felt that their farm must have been a gathering point or a hunting grounds for buffalo because the ground was covered with "skeletons of thousands of buffalo." Early settlers collected buffalo bones to be sold for cash. This money frequently proved to be a very important part of their first year's income. These bones were later made into carbon black used in sugar processing. Many merchants in the area accepted bones in payment for merchandise sold. Both the Northern Pacific and the Great Northern Railroads had facilities to handle the huge piles of bones which, in the early days of settlement, appeared in the railroad yards. At least one yard received over 100 wagonloads of buffalo bones a day for several months.

Torkel Fuglestad's farm was covered with buffalo bones—"Some were old and imbedded in the sod, others were quite fresh." He and his neighbors gathered bones by the wagonload and "sold them in town." The price of bones varied from $6.00 to $10.00 a ton. A double wagon box could hold about two tons. The average full grown buffalo produced about 150 pounds of bones. Some of the earliest pioneers ate buffalo meat, but most of the buffaloes had been killed before the area was settled. Probstfield often commented about buffalo but never about buffalo bones because he disliked the idea that these animals had been killed in such large numbers by hunters who did it for the sport alone.

Theodore Peet, a Wilkin County farmer, opened eighty acres of virgin land in 1946 that still contained many buffalo bones. He also detected the "buffalo ring" made by buffalo bulls running in circles to protect the calves and the cows from danger. It was in that area where the buffalo bones were most numerous.[1]

Trapping, hunting, and fishing were also important as sources of material for clothing, for food, and for the cash income of the average pioneer farmer. Raccoons were apparently plentiful in the woods adjacent to the Probstfield farm and during the winter of the late 1870's and early 1880's, members of the family went hunting many days in succession. On the first day they "cut down four trees and did not even get a smell of coon." The next day they "got four coons out of one tree plus a dead one." Another day, when the temperature was thirty-one degrees below zero, they "caught six coons—two alive and four dead." It is probably safe to assume that raccoon meat graced their table just as it did the tables of many of the other pioneers. A day or two after each hunting trek Mrs. Probstfield "and girls tanned coon skins and worked on coon robes."

Emma Elton, who grew up in the wooded land just on the east edge of the Red River Valley, felt that "there was security on the farm in those days" because wild life was so plentiful that it overcame the deficiencies of small farm income. On her home farm "there were plenty of wild berries—strawberries, raspberries, grapes. There was a great variety of nuts—particularly hazelnuts and walnuts." Beside that, "prairie chickens, ducks, rabbits, and fish were plentiful." The entire Probstfield family frequently spent "all day in the woods picking enormous quantities of raspberries" or whatever else was ripe. Ida Hall Crofford's comments about the abundance of prairie chicken might appear somewhat exaggerated, but nonetheless picturesque: "Grass was thick and two feet tall and prairie chickens so thick that whenever a wheel rolled through the grass it would come up dripping egg yolks." Prairie chickens were also thick around the Overby farm along the Sheyenne. "In spring [they] would hold noisy mating rallies in our front yard. [Father] had a convenient peek hole in the door through which he projected his gun barrel, took aim and fired into the merry flock. The bang of the gun . . . [in the house] went off with a terrifying explosion and we had prairie chicken for dinner." The Ankerfeldts who lived in the sand hills region of Cass and Ransom Counties had "a good many meals of prairie chicken and grouse." The birds reportedly were so thick around the farm yard and so unafraid of people that the Ankerfeldts "didn't even shoot them" but caught them with snares because they did not like to use their shotguns around the yard. The birds were especially thick around straw and hay stacks.

In the early 1880's at the Woodwards, southwest of Fargo, ducks and geese were "extremely plentiful, but they are so wild that one can seldom get a shot at them." However, Walter always had his gun ready. In general, hunters killed large numbers of them. Two of the Woodwards' neighbors hunted for six hours and killed sixty ducks— thirty mallards and thirty pintails and teals. Mrs. Woodward objected to the taking of so many. "I think they should be protected by law."

For many years Probstfield recorded when the first geese and ducks were sighted. The significant point is that his "first sightings" were all between March 27 and April 8 which, even today, may be of some value to a study of migratory habits of the birds. The Probstfields hunted throughout the year and nearly always brought something home. Even large and prosperous farmers like the Divets did not overlook the availability of wild geese to supplement their meat supply. In the early years it was possible to drive very close to the large flocks of geese resting on the water and several men could shoot many of them before they flew away. As time passed trickery had to be used because they were harder to get and quite obviously "wild geese became less important as a food supply after the first few years." [2]

Fish

Few people associate Red River Land with fishing, but there was a time when fish were abundant in the rivers and creeks and were an important part of the food supply. The rivers of the Valley region were stocked with large catfish, white fish, pike, pickerel, crappies, and sturgeon. "In the winter there were many fish houses placed on the Red River to protect the fishermen who were after the abundance of fish which included "catfish that weighed up to 40 pounds and sturgeon as much as 200." At times catfish was the sole diet for many of the early settlers living along the Red. Catfish fat was also used as a lubricant for farm machinery.

The Crawfords had access to four rivers, each of which apparently had its own variety of fish. The Bois de Sioux was good for pickerel; the Red seemed full of pike and catfish; the Otter Tail was filled with a "good lively silvery" colored fish that weighed a pound to a pound and one-half, but no mention was made of what species was most abundant in the Wild Rice, the river nearest to them. "Mother would tell us to go down and fish for supper. It never failed to produce. Fishing was very good." The Thortvedts, living along the Buffalo River in central Clay County, had the same results. When Levi Thortvedt was a boy, it was his duty to fish regularly in hopes of obtaining the meat supply for the next meal. The Thortvedts caught pickerel weighing from four to six pounds and catfish up to seventeen pounds.

The Probstfields apparently did not do much fishing prior to the winter of 1873-74 because he made purchases of fish in lots of fifty pounds or more at a price from three to five cents a pound. By the mid-1870's the children were old enough to go fishing in order to help provide food. Whenever the supply was large enough they sold the surplus on the market at Moorhead. On February 11, 1874, Probstfield sold ninety-five pounds of fish at four cents a pound and on the same day he sold dressed beef for eight cents a pound. The Probstfields did some line fishing but when they wanted a larger supply they used a net which they set by their fish dam. In preparation for the fishing season in the winter of 1874-75, they spent one day in December, 1874, "working on fish dam. Put net in—had fish for supper," and on the following day thirty-two fish were trapped in the net and served for supper.

Probstfield commonly reported the number of fish that were caught each day during the winter season by use of the net. Exciting catches were reported throughout the winter fishing season of 1877. On January 9 he recorded that thirty-one gold eyes weighing three-quarters to two pounds were caught and prepared for smoking; three suckers and four dogfish completed the day's catch. Similar catches were made each of the following days but on January 17 the total increased to three hundred gold eyes, three red horse, and forty-nine dogfish. The biggest single day's catch for that year came on the twenty-first when eighty dogfish were taken and "gold eyes too numerous to count." The next day a diary notation stated that the Probstfields had twenty gallons of salted fish in storage.

In the following year one of the big days was January 27, 1878, when "265 gold eyes, 63 dogfish and a dozen other kinds" were caught. Two days later 350 pounds of fish were caught. The Probstfields, however, were not alone in having a dam and a fish net out. In December, 1883, "Dr. Wilson called and we helped set out his fish net." In 1888 fishing became a necessity for the Probstfields. "The first real summer day this year. Boys were fishing all day. It is necessary as we are almost entirely out of *crop*, out of money, and out of anything to realize money on."

The Ankerfeldts lived only a short distance from the Sheyenne River. In the spring of 1888 the flood brought fish up to their yard where they speared them with hay forks. When the river went down many suckers, carp, and other fish were left stranded. The Ankerfeldt boys frequently went to the Colton Mill at Lisbon to fish where "they caught fish by the barrels. There was no limit in them [sic] days, you know. They were mostly suckers and red horse and they sure was [sic] [full] of bones as the dickens but they tasted good." Ankerfeldt stated in 1966 that in his opinion there has been a greater variety of fish in the Sheyenne in recent times than there was in the 1880's and 1890's. This change is probably caused through the periodic stocking by the game and fish departments.

Since the Madsens lived quite a distance from any body of water, they were unable to obtain fish except those they purchased from the "frozen fish man" who made his rounds in the winter. They supplemented their meat diet in another way by encouraging pigeons to nest in their barn and then trapping them. In this manner they would catch a hundred or more each winter and freeze them for pigeon pie. No doubt many others did the same.[3]

Cows

Most pioneers coming to the Valley knew that either the horse or the ox were absolutely necessary to farming, but the farmer could get by without the cow, especially if he did not have any children or was not very concerned about the family's diet. Many pioneers in this area, probably more so than on previous frontiers, did try to establish a farm without having a cow. This practice increased the element of risk because the cow served the dual purpose of providing milk and meat and for this reason helped reduce the reliance on cash from wheat alone. The sale of surplus milk or butter also provided a good income for many of the household needs of the pioneers. Because of the shortage of dairy animals in the area and the poor quality of dairy products that came from most of the farms, those who produced high quality butter and cheese received a premium for goods sold. The Ericksons, who had brought their cow with them from Iowa, were soon exchanging butter for groceries and dry goods at the rate of ten cents a pound in trade. Mrs. Erickson "made very good butter and later sold it all at a premium to private customers in Moorhead."

Mrs. Charles Hobart was able to provide additional income for her family in the early years because in 1883 her husband purchased a cow and a calf which provided the foundation stock for a small herd. When the local cream buyer stopped collecting cream, Mrs. Hobart turned to making butter. Most farmers' wives received ten cents to fifteen cents a pound for their butter traded at the store, but because Lizzie Hobart was a good butter maker, she had all the customers she could supply for twenty-five cents a pound. A neighbor, Fred Turell, purchased Hobart's cattle after Lizzie Hobart had a heart attack. He also acquired Mrs. Hobart's butter customers but soon lost them because Turell's wife "was a village girl and perhaps never made a pound of butter before in her life."

Mrs. Woodward was equally grateful for the cow on their farm. "Our cow Daisey, gives a pailful of milk and, what do you think, we have cream in our coffee!! I have made a little milk room of the closet off the sitting room. The coal stove heats it night and day, and I have a splendid chance to make butter there this cold weather. I have already churned six pounds. The price in town is thirty cents a pound." At another time she expressed joy when their cow had a calf and could produce milk again for they had to walk a mile to the neighbors to buy milk at eight cents a quart. That price, she thought, was more than they could afford with wheat at only fifty cents a bushel.

In 1871 O. O. Hovde had purchased a cow for $30 at Ottertail on his way to the Valley. When a prairie fire threatened her home a year or two later, the first thing Mrs. Hovde did was make sure of the safety of the cow by tying it to the family clothes trunk placed on the plowed sod. Then she prepared to fight the fire. In 1884, in his second year of farming, Torkel Fuglestad purchased a cow and a calf in the spring and later bought a second calf for $5 "from a bachelor who did not want to bother with a calf." This was the beginning of a small herd that supplied the sizeable family raised by the Fuglestads. One of the big jobs for the Hagen children was to build smudge fires in order to drive flies and mosquitoes from the cows so they would stand still while being milked.

When the Thortvedt's cows wandered away for eight days, it caused a "near food panic in the household" for dairy products provided one of the two staples in their diet; the other was flour. The McMahons had two bachelor neighbors, "and how Ole and Christ enjoyed milking our cow. She sometimes wandered away from our place so they would milk her because milk was such a treat to them. Dr. Turnblem and his wife and his girl would milk the cow when she went near their place. Willetts had no cow either so they would come for milk too. I thanked God we always had plenty of milk and butter." The McMahons did not object to the neighbors milking their cow when it strayed to their places because they realized how much everyone craved having fresh milk.

Iver Madsen's father "got a cow as quick as they could get a building ready because he knew how important it was for the children." The Madsens had ten children. They eventually milked fourteen cows and made all of their butter for personal use and for trading. After they got a windmill the Madsens purchased a big butter churn and used the windmill to power it. They could always tell from the house when the butter was ready because the churn would turn so hard that it would force the belt off the pulley and the windmill would speed up. The Madsens sold butter and milk in their neighborhood and George Stanley, a merchant in Casselton, paid a top price of fifteen cents a pound for guaranteed uniform quality and a steady supply. After the Wheatland Creamery was organized, Madsen took the cream to town every other day and used the skim milk on the farm for the calves and the hogs. Most of the farmers did not have as many milk cows as the Madsens who eventually developed one of the largest commercial dairy herds in North Dakota. Most of them probably did not have more than one or two milk cows until after the turn of the century, although the census figures indicate that there were about ten head of livestock per farm in the 1880's. Even then most herds never became large. During the "boom" of the early 1880's cows sold for from $35 to $50 each, but with the following dry years and the exodus of farmers, the price dropped to $25 or less by 1890 and cows were hard to sell.

For ease of reference and also because of the rather close attachment, most farmers named their cows. Probstfield gave the cows in his stables on January 1, 1875, such fancy names as Jenny, Lily, Brindle, and Bessy. Six heifers being raised to keep the milking herd at strength were Bossy, Molly, Daisy, Pansy, Pink, and Polly. The king of the Probstfield herd was Bolus. Probstfield took advange of the dual purpose of the cow and had a ready market for fresh meat in Fargo-Moorhead. As early as 1873 he sold beef to railroad employees for eight cents a pound, dressed. From that date on he made continuous sales of meat. In the fall of 1875 he sold veal for ten cents a pound and tallow at the same price. Apparently the demand for tallow for candles made it as valuable as the meat. Probstfield frequently traded meat for articles of clothing at Moorhead stores. In the spring of 1877 he sold the 1,064-pound cow, Lily, to Jack Eastwood for $37 live weight.

Ten years later R. D. Crawford reported that stall fed steers were selling at three and a half cents a pound, live weight, and dressed hogs on the farm were four and half cents. By 1886 Probstfield had developed a market at the Fargo-Moorhead hotels and restaurants. He delivered dressed veal to the Jay Cooke House in Moorhead for ten cents a pound, exactly what he had received a decade earlier. Ironically, he sold a cow hide in January, 1886, for $4.15 which is more than the cow hides sold for during much of 1967. In the late 1880's Probstfield's meat business expanded when he became involved with the Czizek butcher shop in Moorhead which the Probstfield family operated for several years. Six children were old enough to be active in the business which provided an outlet for all the meat that could be produced on their farm and more besides. In general, the settlers along the Red River had a meat deficit in the early years, and they had to rely primarily on livestock that was shipped in from southern Minnesota and Iowa for butchering purposes. All hoped that they could live by wheat alone and with only a few exceptions none of them raised beef animals. This local shortage became even more pronounced when the bonanza farms imported their large labor forces. Even with their own supply produced on the farm, the Divets still bought heavily from the traveling fresh meat wagon that went to the small towns and the larger farms in their area.

James J. Hill did much to overcome this meat deficiency by encouraging farmers to diversify their farming operations by adding livestock. He and James B. Power, the father of North Dakota agriculture, brought many valuable animals into the region to be used as foundation stock. During the Great Dakota Boom, Hill provided, at his own expense, 151 blooded bulls to area farmers. They had cost him an average of $666 each. Hill's and Power's efforts suffered many setbacks because of the shortsightedness of the pioneers who butchered valuable breeding animals before their intended purpose could be fulfilled. Many farmers, however, did appreciate the efforts of these two men. When the McMahons learned that Hill and three of his friends were at McCanna hunting prairie chickens in the fall of 1884, they invited them to dinner. The next spring Hill thanked the McMahons by giving them a Polled purebred Angus bull and two purebred Berkshire pigs. These animals became foundation stock for a sizeable livestock enterprise on the McMahon farm.[4]

Sheep

Sheep were introduced to upper Red River Land in 1862 when R. M. Probstfield purchased twenty-four animals at Fort Garry for $24 in gold. The freight charge for transporting them to Georgetown via the *International* was $40. Within eighteen hours after their arrival twenty-three of these sheep were killed by sled dogs owned by the Hudson's Bay Company. The last sheep of that flock was killed when Georgetown was evacuated that fall. This misfortune did not put Probstfield out of the sheep business however, for after he became established at Oakport in 1870 he purchased more. He maintained constant activity in the sheep business, buying and selling and shearing. By August, 1878, his flock was large enough that he could sell ten ewes and eleven lambs to Moorhead butchers for a total of $34. In 1896 he sheared ninety-one sheep for a total fleece of 482 pounds. A woman was hired to help prepare the wool for family use.

Charles Hobart, who had raised sheep in New Hampshire, started with a small flock as soon as he had facilities, and by 1889 he had twenty head. He purchased another forty head for $160 and built a separate sheep shed. He had a crop of fifty lambs in 1891. Hobart was a good sheep man. He purchased ear tags that bore his name and a separate number for each sheep so that he could keep individual records on them. Hobart, with his 100 sheep, and a neighbor, Crane, who had 300 head, hired Charlie, a young boy, to herd them. Charlie herded the sheep each day and brought them back to either Hobart's or Crane's yard each night. After threshing, the sheep were allowed to run on stubble fields until spring without a herder. They "had the run of the whole country" and only once in twenty-five years did the flock fail to come home. On that occasion Hobart found them the next morning, three miles from his farm on a piece of clover and defended them by saying, "I think they got there just at night and hated to leave it."

George F. Thayer of Aneta favored sheep too. He purchased fifty-three sheep in 1887 for $225 and by 1891 he had sold $1,000 worth of mutton and wool and had increased his flock to 220 head. Thayer felt that North Dakota was "an Eldorado for the sheep industry." Just as enthusiastic, but more reserved about his comments, was Frank Liebenow of Chaffee who said that sheep were a real life saver for him. He grazed a small flock from the middle of May to sometime in November each year on a ten-acre tree claim and during the winter fed them roughage that the cattle refused to eat. In spite of this limited input, sheep grossed Liebenow an average of $1,000 per year. Since his parents had not been farmers, he learned sheep management from watching how the Chaffees handled sheep on their bonanza farm. His father, Karl Liebenow, had come over from Germany in the 1870's and was a blacksmith at Everest, about four miles south of Casselton.[5]

Swine

Hog raising was never a major commercial enterprise in the Valley. In many parts of the country hogs could support themselves with little extra feed because they were such good scroungers. Scrounging was not so easy in this area where all a hog could find outside of its pen were crops which it could ruin. After the advent of the cream separator in the 1880's hogs were commonly fed skim milk and soaked ground oats or barley. Hogs were raised because pork could be easily preserved by smoking and salting. Enough were raised so that pork became a staple in the diet. The Madsen's large cow herd provided an adequate supply of skim milk for many hogs so that they "were heavy on pork and butchered several hogs each fall." Charles Hobart and the Divets also raised hogs, selling only those that were in excess of normal household needs. The Divets, with five children and two to four hired men at all times, had an average of ten people eating at the table and, according to Guy Divet, were heavy on pork.

Not until the 1890's did beef and chicken become commonplace in the Divet family diet. Hobart's farm crew and family were not as large as the Divets but Hobart was always careful to have a diversified homegrown meat supply on hand. In addition to sheep and cows, which he raised for subsistence and commercial purposes, he had hogs and chickens for domestic needs only. He purchased a ninety-pound black sow for $9 and then traded wheat for two male pigs.

Obviously, Probstfield's commercial hog operation was not typical of the average homesteader for he was more interested in livestock production than in raising wheat and he took advantage of the active demand for pork in Moorhead. As early as March 19, 1874, he sold his first meat—a 14½-pound ham for $2.15. From 1884 through the late 1880's, the Probstfields supplied pork for a butcher shop which they owned in Moorhead. As many as sixteen hogs were butchered in one day. Because of the commercial aspect of his operation, Probsfield kept a close record of when pigs were to be born and how many were produced from each litter. In March, 1885, there were thirteen litters of pigs with an average of 7.4 pigs born per litter and 6.8 pigs raised per litter. His average would have been considered very respectable down through the period up to World War II. The hard times of the late 1880's are reflected in his note of November 20, 1888: "Killed a sow in P.M. so we have *some* meat again." [6]

Chickens

It is interesting to note that originally chickens were raised on nearly every farm. It is difficult, however, to obtain figures on the actual chicken population of early days for even the agricultural census gives only limited information about it. The pioneers, whether village dwellers or farmers, took chickens with them when they traveled to the frontier. Apparently chickens got "seasick" for there are comments that the chickens acted sick when the covered wagon moved. Crates of chickens were hauled in the immigrant railroad cars along with other supplies and livestock. Some women brought hatching eggs with them and at least one had them destroyed when they were exposed to a cold rain.

In the late 1960's the area produced less than a third of the chickens that were produced at their peak period prior to World War I. And now the per capita production of chickens is much less than in pioneer days. Red River Land is a seriously deficit poultry and egg region and evidence indicates that there never were enough chickens raised locally to supply the market adequately.[7]

Chickens were not as hardy as other forms of domestic animals introduced into the area by the pioneer. Until good facilities were erected to protect them against the rigors of the winter, many farmers limited their number of chickens and in the cold season let them run loose in the barns to take advantage of the heat produced by the hogs, cows, and horses. Obviously, this plan was undesirable but the economics of the situation dictated it as the most sensible solution. The Andrew Overbys had about a dozen chickens that ran loose in their small sod barn and it was not uncommon to see them sitting on the backs of the four oxen or the cow. As soon as farming became more profitable, most of the farmers built separate structures for chickens. Mrs. Elton noted that chickens were left to take care of themselves in the summer and eggs were plentiful, if they could be found. With an average egg production of not more than twelve eggs per day throughout the year, Probstfield's forty-nine hens had all they could do to keep the household of eleven children and one or two hired men supplied with eggs.

Newspapers occasionally noted the shortage of eggs and the editor of the *Warren Sheaf* complained that he had been unable to get any eggs for Easter. He added that there were no eggs and that none had been available in the community and he lamented the lack of foresight of the settlers. The Probstfields, the Madsens, and the Divets substituted eggs for meat when meat was not readily available, especially in the summer. Their large families, plus extra hired men, could consume a goodly number of eggs in the absence of any regular meat supply. There were times, however, when chickens had to be sacrificed to provide meat as Probstfield noted in April, 1889: "Out of meat—had to kill some hens for dinner." Charles Hobart "planned it that way," and traded one of his cows for six hens. When he lost two of those hens during the first winter because they were allowed to run loose in his cattle and horse barn, his trade appeared to be a bad one. Luckily for Hobart, eggs from the remaining four hens produced seventy-five chickens. His flock increased by about that number during the next four years.

Hobart may have paid too much for his first chickens, but eventually he profited more from them than he would have from one more cow. As soon as too many chickens made a nuisance of themselves in the cattle barn, Hobart built a separate chicken house. His hens did not lay in the winter, but in summer they "laid eggs all over the farm." Normally Hobart picked eggs "every day or two but got too busy in harvest and did not pick for ten days—had two large pails full. Tested them in water and twelve dozen of them would float," indicating they were rotten. After the flock became large enough "there was never a day that we could not have chicken for dinner, but after we got the sheep we depended mostly on them for fresh meat during the summer."

Mrs. Woodward also had hardships raising chickens but she saw the economic wisdom in keeping them:

The horses have killed about half of my chickens. I have decided there is no use trying to raise them without a hen house. We have such quantities of screenings that I wish I had a hundred hens. There is no better market for eggs in America. I think some enterprising people might get rich in this business. Now that wheat is so low, farmers should turn their attention to some other industry.

Chickens were relatively high priced when compared to hogs, sheep, or cattle. In January, 1886, Probstfield paid Charles Schroeder $1.50 for a rooster, while during the same period he was paying $1.00 per head for sheep and sold forty-pound pigs for $3.00, and $30.00 for cows.[8]

Animal Problems

Poultry and livestock operations were not always profitable to the homesteader because of the labor and the investment involved in owning and caring for them. Even though land was cheap, not enough land could be properly farmed to enable the homesteader to make a living without some form of livestock enterprise. Winters were too long and rigorous to expect the animals to pull through on their own as it is the case in a more temperate climate. Providing roughage and grain for feed as well as shelter took time and capital and often created problems. Such problems were particularly serious in the first years when the settlers were not fully aware of the total feed requirements for the long winter and, more often than not, they underestimated rather than overestimated the needs.

In March, 1871, the Thortvedts ran out of hay but were able to "borrow some" from Torje Skrei to keep the cows in production. However, their horses were turned out to live on prairie grass and wormwood. Probstfield learned from experience and always guarded his supply of roughage insuring adequate feed for his cattle. Thanks to a large wood lot on his farm, his cattle were protected from the elements in late fall and early winter so he kept them on prairie grass and in the woodland as late as possible. Many times Probstfield did not feed hay to his cattle until November. Cattle left out to depend on nature that late could not have been highly productive unless the weather was exceptionally mild and the native grasses abundant.

Predators—Man and Beast

Predators also added to the hazards of keeping livestock and poultry. Probstfield probably had more than the normal amount of trouble with predators, both two-legged and four-legged, because his farm was located near a sizeable community and also near a large wooded area. Thieves not only stole wood from his lot and meat from his grain bins but also made repeated trips to his farmstead for chickens and livestock. These occasions were so frequent that he merely noted in his diary, "thieves in the chicken coop 9 p.m." When Probstfield's neighbor, Nils Larson, had his team of mules stolen in 1874, Larson borrowed Probstfield's horse, Nelly, to hunt them down. Two weeks later Probstfield was called to Fargo as a witness for Larson and to identify a man named Stickney as the culprit in the mule-stealing case.

Probstfield was not always satisfied with the workings of justice. A man who had been stealing wood from his land was tracked by "F. Remeley, W. J. Bodkin, Alexander [Probstfield], and recognized as J. Thomas." Three days later on January 6, 1878, Probstfield "walked to town to attend trespass suit against Thomas. The less said about—the better. Before or by the time I got through I ought to have been under the impression that I was the criminal. Mr. Thomas an innocent martyred victim and justice and lawyer, for charitys sake will not mention their names here—the heroes; that secure right to the innocent and oppressed and nonplus the wicked like myself for instance."

On another occasion he did not appeal to justice. Noticing that a Holstein heifer was missing, he picked up its tracks and then remembered seeing some men go off in that same direction earlier in the day. After returning to the house for his shotgun and horse and buggy, he followed the tracks to a farm place and discovered the men butchering the animal in the barn. The animal was already hanging and skinned by the time Probstfield arrived. He saw the hide and had no doubt it was his heifer. He sat down in the barn and chatted with the men while they butchered the animal. After it was completely dressed, he went to his buggy and got his shotgun, returned to the barn, and demanded that the men place the dressed carcass in his buggy. After they had done so he thanked them for preparing his meat and drove off.

Farmers in the Abercrombie area were victims of organized crime in the 1880's when Jans Hagen and seven of his neighbors had all their oxen stolen the same night. A posse was organized, without the help of the sheriff, and the men had no trouble following the tracks for about seventeen miles to a grove south of Wahpeton where all of the animals were found. However, there were no clues as to the identity of the thieves.

Nearness to civilization did not keep other "predators" from preying on the Probstfield farm. In January, 1880, Probstfield commented that "wolves were howling around" to the extent that it was "dangerous to go out at night." Wolves were a severe menace to all forms of animal life. In the winter of 1891 the Probstfield boys were out hunting and they killed foxes for "eggs, poultry, and guineas were nearly all gone." In either form these predators proved to be costly to the farmer who lost poultry or livestock to them.[9]

Animal Sicknesses

Sickness in animals, always a serious problem to livestock farmers, was more serious then than it is now; for in those days veterinary medicine was no more advanced than any other branch of the medical sciences. Little could be done to prevent or to cure animal diseases. Veterinarians were handicapped by farmers who were reluctant to call upon their services because they had no faith in "new fangled" scientific ideas and because they objected to the professional fees. Losses caused by sickness and death were expected to occur and little or no record was kept of them. However, Probstfield meticulously noted injuries, sicknesses, and other aspects of animal husbandry including the records of small pigs lost at farrowing. In January, 1874, a British Boundary Commissioner left a horse at Probstfields that had a ruptured vein on one hind leg caused by a kick from another horse. Probstfield purchased 100 pounds of bran for $1.25 for the horse and called the veterinarian out to look at it. On February 6, an employee of the Commission stopped to pick up the healed horse and paid Probstfield $14.75 to cover expenses incurred during the seventeen days. At nearly $1.00 per day to care for and heal a horse, veterinary cost was high and avoided by a farmer who could not make that much money in an average day.

In September, 1875, "Nellie's colt [became] sick, having nothing at hand [Probstfield] gave it a dose of horseradish and water. Prospects for recovery not very good." Three days later the colt seemed better Obviously some disease had hit Probstfield's horses for he lost one horse early in September and on the seventh all the horses were too sick to work and the ox team had to be used to do bridge work on the coulee. On the thirteenth a second mare died. Charles Brown, who did a post mortem, "found an inflamed spot in the heart cavity." Probstfield reasoned death was caused from exposure to a heavy rain storm on September 2. But that did not explain the death of the animal which had died before the storm. The next day a third mare was very sick. "It looks decidedly blue for me this fall. No plowing done, nor any prospect of any. Scarcely no hay made. Everything behind hand." Other neighbors, including Leveretts, were over to see if they could borrow horses indicating that Probstfield was not alone in his plight. Aleck Halett, who called at the farm, had horse trouble of a different nature, for during supper his mare got away and he was forced to stay overnight.

In early April, 1887, Probstfield purchased an ox which later got a turnip caught in its throat. Not wishing to take a total loss, he decided to get the butcher and slaughter the animal. While Alexander Probstfield ran to town to get the butcher, some of the other Probstfield boys rammed the turnip down the ox's throat which caused bloating. No slaughter took place, but for two days and nights they had to keep stabbing the ox in the side with a knife to open a hole in the paunch to let the gas escape. If they had not kept up the stabbing, the animal would have quickly died from bloating. After the turnip was digested the ox got better.

Usher Burdick, who immigrated to Carrington from Owatonna, Minnesota, in 1882, remembered how shocked the family was when the veterinarian told them their horses had glanders, an ulcer condition in the respiratory tract or lungs, and would have to be shot. They were "a beautiful team of grey mares, perfectly matched, fat and sleek. I remember how much I liked them." Horses were selling for $500 a team and in order to save money Burdick's father purchased a team of 1,800-pound oxen called Buck and Bright. According to one area farm magazine fifty-three "glandered" horses were killed in Minnesota in the last four months of 1885. When another outbreak was feared in 1886 after a man had died from the disease at Red Wing, all suspected horses were ordered shot at once. Glanders is a very severe disease of horses and mules which can also affect dogs, goats, sheep, and man. It spreads through nasal discharge and breaks in the skin. An affected animal develops bunches in the veins over the eyes and on the inside of the legs and also festers on the membrane of the nose. Even today there is little immunity or chance of cure for glanders, and destruction of infected animals is still required.

Charles Hobart commented on an all too frequent animal killer— overeating. A young colt named Kit got loose in the barn one night and located the barrel where wheat was soaking to be fed to the hogs. The soaked wheat was such a treat that Kit consumed all twenty quarts Hobart had measured out. Dr. Taylor, the local veterinarian, was called and stayed "two days but saved her."

A great number of the remedies for sicknesses in animals were based on nothing more than pure superstition, but some were based on simple but sound scientific knowledge. An illustration of some science and some superstition is noted in the following incident. The Woodwards had a Hereford cow which became very sick after calving. The cow was given a dose of nitre oil, salts, and linseed tea. Her udder was packed with a compound of bran, salt, and flaxseed. Farm magazines of that day often gave remedies and cures. The standard cure for lice was kerosene. One editor warned that it was not the most effective remedy but it was as safe as any and it generally got results. On the other hand, farmers were warned not to apply too much kerosene because it would take off the hair. A half pound of tobacco in a gallon of water was supposed to be an effective delouser for cattle. A little lime and water mixed with milk and fed to calves occasionally was recommended as a good preventative for scours. George Roff of Dickey submitted an article on the growing of pearl barley which, he said, if fed freely to hogs would, to a large extent prevent hog cholera—a good example of superstition—but the editor of the farm magazine apparently thought the idea was valid. To make a horse's mane and tail grow, the farmer was advised to use warm, soft water, Castile soap, and sal soda. He was to wash and thoroughly clean the mane and tail three or four times a day, but he was told not to card it out.

Probstfield, who was far better educated and trained than most of the pioneers, had several remedies for animal health problems incorporated in his diary. The following remedies were recorded in September, 1884, and give a good idea of the simplicity of veterinary medicine of those days: "Remedy for Bone Spavin [bone spavin is basically a lameness in the bones of the hock joint.]: Use ½ ounce oil of Vitriol [nitric acid] and mix with 2 ounces sweet oil. Use every other day. Mix muriatic acid and Seneca oil in equal moneys worth, say 10¢ or 15¢ of each, apply two or three times a day until cracks open, then stop." Such casual use of dangerous acids would certainly not be a recommended practice.

Probstfield's recipe for colic contained one ounce of balsam capsule, one ounce of "spirits of nitse," an ounce of oil of juniper, a like amount of peppermint, which were to be well mixed before using. A dose of one ounce of the mixture was to be given daily with one-half pint of lukewarm water.[10]

For livestock farmers who have come to understand the powers of penicillin, streptomycin, and sulfamethazine, the cures described above would create doubts about the economics of nineteenth century livestock enterprises.

FOOTNOTES

[1] Charles Cavileer, "The Red River Valley in 1851," *NDH*, XII (Oct., 1945), 212-213; Russell Reid and Clell G. Gannon. "Natural History Notes on the Journals of Alexander Henry," *NDHQ*, II (April, 1928), 174-175; Crofford, p. 130; Divet, NDIRS, File 69; Fuglestad, p. 15; *Hillsboro Banner*, June 28, 1956; Theodore Peet, interview by the author May 20, 1968; Robinson, pp. 161, 186; Probstfield; Joseph Nicolas Nicollet, *Report Intended to Illustrate a Map of the Hydrographical Basin of the Upper Mississippi River* (Washington, 1843), p. 52.

[2] Thortvedt, NDIRS, File 332; Probstfield; Elton, *Vaalhovd*, p. 36; Crofford, p. 130, O. Overby, *Retrospect*, p. 10; Divet, NDIRS, File 69; Woodward, p. 33; Emil Ankerfeldt, interview by Donald Berg June 13, 1966.

[3] Murray, p. 12; Chestney, p. 2; *Hillsboro Banner*, June 28, 1956, p. 16; Crawford, NDIRS, File 290; Thortvedt, NDIRS, File 332; Probstfield; Madsen interview; Edwin Ankerfeldt, interview by Donald Berg June 21, 1966.

[4] Elton, *Vaalhovd*, p. 35; Murray, p. 100; Hobart, "Pioneering," VII, 208, VIII, 127; Hovde, pp. 10, 12; A. Overby, "Sod House Days," p. 4; Fuglestad, p. 11; Thortvedt, NDIRS, File 332; McMahon, NDIRS, File 195; Madsen interview; Stafne, pp. 19, 63; Woodward, p. 64; Probstfield; *The Dakota Farmer*, IV (Sept., 1895); *The Record*, I (Aug. 1895).

[5] *Moorhead Independent*, Jan. 5, 1900, p. 1; Hobart, "Pioneering," VIII, 120-124; *The Record*, I (June, 1895), p. 13; Probstfield; Frank Liebenow, interview by the author May 12, 1967. Liebenow is a retired farmer living at Chaffee, North Dakota, where he had farmed all his life. He was born at Everest in 1883.

[6] Madsen interview; Probstfield; Divet, NDIRS, File 69; Hobart, "Pioneering," VII, 214.

[7] R. F. Engelking, C. J. Heltemes, Fred R. Taylor, *North Dakota Agricultural Statistics*, North Dakota Agricultural Experiment Station Bulletin 408 Revised (Fargo, 1962), pp. 52-56. (Hereafter cited as *N. D. Ag. Stat.*); *Minnesota Agricultural Statistics, 1967*, Minnesota Department of Agriculture and United States Department of Agriculture (St. Paul, 1967), pp. 64-67. (Hereafter cited as *Minn. Ag. Statistics*.)

[8] Gunkelman interview; Elton, *Vaalhovd*, p. 36; *Warren Sheaf*, April 2, 1891; A. Overby, "Sod House Days," p. 4; Madsen interview; Probstfield; Hobart, "Pioneering," VIII, 129-130; Woodward, p. 70.

[9] Thortvedt, NDIRS, File 332; Probstfield; Conversations with Ray Gesell relative to the Probstfield files; Stafne, p. 30.

[10] Probstfield; Burdick, p. 9; *The Merck Veterinary Manual* (Rahway, N.J., 1961), pp. 419-421; Hobart, "Pioneering," VIII, 118; Woodward, p. 241; *Dakota Farmer*, V (Feb., 1882), 5, V (April, 1886), 3-5, V (June, 1886), 16, V (Sept., 1886), 8.

CHAPTER V

The Housewife's Dilemma

MANY of the ordinary chores of the pioneer farm home were extremely time consuming in contrast to modern day routines. The simple mechanics of living consumed much time in the pre-electric era. Getting groceries was not a matter of pushing a shopping cart and paying the bill. The pioneer farmer and his family not only raised the necessities of life, but they also processed them for use. One of the most difficult problems was keeping a supply of meat on hand. Acquiring and preparing meat took much time, and it was not always easy as O. A. Olson implied:

> A plover, misjudging the distance,
> Was something delicious to eat.
> Without any "critters" to butcher
> We rarely enjoyed fresh meat.

Butchering

Those who had livestock were more fortunate for once an animal's most productive years were past it was fattened to be butchered. Most butchered animals were for family use and they had to be consumed quickly. During warm weather Hobart let his neighbors know whenever he was ready to butcher. Hobarts slaughtered and dressed a sheep every few days, kept some for themselves, and sold the rest to the neighbors who were glad to get it. In the threshing season when larger crews of farm workers were around, several neighbors usually went together and butchered a beef. Then they sold the meat to each other for "five cents or six cents a pound" dressed weight. In that manner all the meat was consumed while it was still fresh. Otherwise-except for a very few fortunate ones who had a supply of ice, most settlers could not enjoy fresh meat for more than a day or two at a time in the warm seasons.

It became the custom for neighbors to work together in late November and December to butcher beef and hogs when the weather was cold enough so that the carcasses would not spoil. In this way as many as two cattle and five hogs might be butchered in one day. All the work, from killing to the final sausage stuffing or meat canning, was done on the farm. The first step in butchering a hog (after it had been killed and bled) was to dunk it in a fifty-gallon barrel filled with scalding water. This step required several men and large amounts of boiling water. The intestines were then turned inside out and washed to be ready for use as sausage casings. The cattle hides were saved to be tanned and made into robes or mittens. All the fat from the animals was saved and rendered into lard which was an ingredient in lye soap. A thirty-gallon iron kettle was the standard container for that job. After butchering, many days were spent smoking the meat. Smoking involved a pre-curing with special salts before the meat was hung in a smoke house where a constant smoke fire was maintained for a period of one, two, or even three weeks, depending upon the type of meat being smoked and the intensity of the smoking. The common smoke house was about 4 x 6 feet wide, 6 to 8 feet long, and about 6 feet high—only large enough to hold all the hams, side pork, and sausages that the family would eat during the winter, unless they butchered more than once a year. As one pioneer woman remarked about the constant diet of smoked meat, "My oldest boy doesn't like ham and much prefers beef because of an almost steady diet of ham, sidepork, and smoked meats when he was young. I don't blame him." Many pioneers kept chickens just for "incidental home use" to provide variety in the diet. Later, when the canning of meat became more popular, small chunks of beef or small steaks were preserved in two-quart glass jars.

The processing of the meat had to be done as quickly as possible after butchering because no refrigeration was available. Consequently, many of the work days stretched to midnight during the butchering season. The total butchering season for the housewife could easily last two weeks with something cooking constantly on the stove, and all the pots and pans of the household filled to capacity.

During the winter the carcass was frozen as it hung from the rafters of the machine shed or the hay track in the barn, or from the nearest satisfactory tree. The hay track was the most desirable spot for hanging because the carcass could then be pulled up out of the reach of dogs and cats. The frozen carcass was then sawed into chunks and buried deep in the grain bins. The grain acted as an insulator and kept the meat frozen "late into May." Sometimes mice got to the meat but this apparently was not too common. One night thieves attempted to steal meat that R. M. Probstfield had stored in his grain. Had it not been for that event, he would not have recorded his use of the "granary deep freeze." Many used large twenty-gallon crocks to store salted meats.[1]

Butter Making

Making butter was as steady and as monotonous as any task which the housewife had to perform. The average farmer had only enough cows to supply his own family with butter, but if there were any surplus it was traded at the local store. For Ada Lockhart Gunkelman "the job I hated most was turning the butter churn. The first churn we had was the plunger type and that was even harder than the later style roll churn." The Lockharts made butter about every three days during the summer, but in the winter only when they needed it. It was part of the average housewife's routine to make the butter. The Department of Agriculture reported that sixty percent of the farmers' wives were still making their own butter in 1920 despite the fact that most of those who had milk cows were patrons of a local creamery which produced butter available to them at a special price. Twice a day, seven days a week, the housewife also had to wash the milking utensils—the milk pails, the milk or cream cans, and the cream separator.

Although the Madsens were the only ones who used their windmill as power for churning the butter, many others wondered why they had not thought of it. When a sixteen-mile-an-hour wind was blowing, the average windmill could generate as much power as a one-fifth horsepower electric motor. After 1905, Henry Schroeder of Sabin even installed a gasoline engine in the basement of his house to churn butter, to separate milk and cream, and to run the washing machine, but his was not a typical farm home. According to the United States Department of Agriculture, as late as 1920 only twenty-two percent of the butter churns on the farms were being operated by some power device in spite of the fact that over half of the farms had some kind of power available which could have easily been applied.[2]

Ice Making and Cooling

The lack of refrigeration or cooling of any kind caused a constant struggle to keep foods fresh. Meat, dairy products, and eggs were difficult to keep fresh. Even keeping cream sweet from one day to the next was a difficult problem. One means of keeping products cool was by storing them in a cellar which, in many homes, was no more than a dugout under the kitchen. The cellar was entered by a ladder through a trap door in the kitchen floor. The foods in the cellar were subject to freezing during a long cold winter, but in the summer the temperature often rose into the fifties. Food was frequently packed into pails and lowered into wells where the pails floated on the water. Here it was cooled to the ground water temperature which averages forty degrees in the Moorhead-Fargo latitude. Those who did not have wells on their property were at a slight disadvantage. When John O. Tansem in eastern Clay County shot a deer during warm weather he divided most of the meat among neighbors. Salt was used in preserving meat, but it was scarce. In order to avoid using it, pieces of meat were put instead into containers and lowered into the cool spring water where the meat remained fresh for a few days.

When hand pumps, and later windmills, became common, a double tank system was adopted. The water was pumped into a tank, usually made of cement, which stood in the pump house or milk house as it was variously called. Water flowed through this tank into the stock tank outside providing a constant supply of cool water in a clean tank in which cans of cream, watertight cans with food in them, and even homemade root beer or "home brew" were kept cool. This efficient system worked with little extra labor or expense for six or seven months of the year. Of course, every time the housewife wanted butter, milk, cream, or other items kept in her "cooler," she had to make a trip to the well house which was usually located from forty to one hundred and fifty feet from her kitchen door.

Harvesting ice for personal needs was done only by a few "bonanza" farmers and by those settlers who were fortunate enough to live near a large enough body of water for the harvesting of ice. Probstfield did not refer to harvesting of ice until the 1890's. To profit from the ice harvest, an ice house and a supply of sawdust were necessary for preserving the ice through the summer. Mrs. Woodward termed the ice gathered by sawing and hauling from the Sheyenne River a "hard earned luxury," but she enjoyed using it.[3]

Milling Wheat

Wheat, a staple in the diet of the pioneer farmer, had to be milled into flour locally by custom millers. This milling was a common practice as late as World War I. In the earliest years prior to 1872 residents had to travel to Alexandria to obtain flour because they had difficulty obtaining it locally. It was many years before flour mills were numerous in the area and they were never in over-supply because capital requirements were too large to make them profitable in an area of sparse population.

Henry A. Bruns established the first flour mill in the Valley at Moorhead in 1872. It prospered from the beginning and in 1878 he installed the first steam powered elevator. But the shortage of grist mills is reflected in the fact that in 1881 when a mill was established at Colfax it received a $1,000 bonus from the village. Before 1881, settlers west of the Red River had to go about twenty-seven miles to Elizabeth or to Pelican Rapids for their milling. The Woodwards went to those towns until the Colfax mill was constructed. The Overbys at Wolverton also went to Elizabeth until mills were built at Rothsay and at Barnesville. A community was built around a flour mill at Norman, about four miles northeast of present-day Kindred along the Sheyenne River. When the railroad bypassed Norman, most of its business moved to Kindred. A modern steam powered mill was built in Sheldon in the late 1880's. This mill was serious competition for those mills that relied on water power, especially the one at Kindred.

Probstfield lived only about three miles from the Bruns mill, but it was always so busy that he patronized other mills in the area instead. There was the Oak Grove mill in Fargo, the Robert's Mill in Fargo, Jacobsen's at Hawley, and one at Muskoda, eighteen miles east of Moorhead on the Buffalo River. Probstfield patronized them all and an experience in October, 1887, clearly demonstrates the time involved in this one task so vital to the settler's daily living. At 8 a.m. October 31, Probstfield left with a load of wheat for Jacobsen's mill at Hawley twenty-five miles away. He arrived there at 4:45 p.m. His travel time with a load was about normal, assuming good road conditions. There were twelve teams ahead of him waiting so he left his team in charge of another man in the line and walked home that evening to save the cost of lodging and meals. The next day he walked the twenty-five miles back to Hawley. Despite the fact that the mill operated on a twenty-four hour basis, Probstfield did not get his wheat milled until 4 a.m. on November 2. He returned home at noon on that day after he had spent fifty-two hours to get one batch of wheat milled. He paid Mrs. Jacobsen, the miller's wife, $1.50 for five meals, lodging for himself, and hay for the horses.

Probstfield had 854 pounds of flour for dark bread because milling processes were not yet available to enable production of flour for white bread. He also had 175 pounds of graham flour (unsifted flour), 294 pounds of bran, and 166 pounds of shorts. The bran was used as cow feed and the shorts were soaked for hog feed. The miller took 331 pounds of wheat as his pay for the grinding. Probstfield justified the economics of this practice: he had 1,820 pounds, or roughly thirty bushels of wheat, which would not have sold for more than $21. He received just over 1,000 pounds of flour which would have cost about $37.50 retail. The bran and the shorts offset the cash expenses of his trip for lodging and meals. He had a net savings, then, of $16.50 for two and one-half days of driving and waiting, or $6.60 a day. These figures represented excellent savings if one remembers that a man could be hired for winter work at fifty cents a day, plus room and board. The miller, if he sold his wheat at retail, received more than sixty cents per 100 pounds for the milling he did for Probstfield. Probstfield recorded at other times that cash milling rate was thirty-five cents per hundred. This price reflects the premium for cash payments.

Apparently the charge was not excessive or Probstfield would have made a remark in his diary as he often did when he felt he had been "taken." The charges made by Jacobsen were the same as those of the other mills which he patronized. In November, 1877, Probstfield took to Hawley thirty-four bushels of wheat which, according to his figures, he could have sold for $.85 a bushel, or $28.90. From these thirty-four bushels he received 1,063 pounds of flour which he valued at $2.75 a hundred, or $29.80, 104 pounds of shorts worth $1.04, 189 pounds of middlings at $2.85, and 345 pounds of bran at $2.60. His products at retail were worth $36.29, or $7.39 more than if he had sold his wheat on the market and purchased the products instead. The miller received 339 pounds of wheat for his services. Probstfield always had his own wheat milled after that with the exception of small purchases when he ran out of it or did not have time. Several families reported that sometimes their children ground wheat with the coffee grinder when the father was too busy to go to the mill to have some ground for flour.

Grain had to be ground for feed for the livestock and this proved to be as time consuming and difficult as was the securing of flour for household purposes. In 1884, Hobart purchased a feed mill which was operated by four horses walking in a circle. In order to refill the mill and to take the ground feed away, the operator had to dodge in and out of the teams as they walked. For many years it was the only mill in Hobart's township and all the neighbors came with their teams and their grain to use it. Hobart proudly added that not a single farmer ever failed to pay for using it.[4]

Gardening

Most people have the impression that the pioneer family had an extensive garden to help provide food; however, contrary to that popular belief, only a few pioneers did a good job of gardening. Many did not have the necessary time to do a good job with a garden, but some did have excellent gardens. Frequently, the only crop planted the first year was potatoes. A furrow was opened and the potatoes were hand planted in the rough plowed sod. Even in hard times of the 1930's when many wheat farmers were failing to make a living they still would not plant gardens. In those years the Farmers Home Administration advised farm wives to can garden produce, but few did it. Far too many were still living in the image of the bonanza farmer who never bothered to raise a garden because he proudly raised only wheat.

Local newspapers lamented that not even eggs could be purchased during certain seasons of the year. They pointed out that many farmers had poor diets because they did not have vegetables, even in season, because of the absence of gardens. Newspapers, farm magazines, and farm authorities had long encouraged farmers in the Valley to diversify their crops, but a real movement in that direction did not take place until after World War I.

Of course, there were some farmers, especially those who had immigrated from Germany, Norway, Sweden, and the British Isles, or those living near the larger settlements, who did have sizeable gardens. Gardening, and the storing or canning of the garden products, was primarily the job of the women and the children for it was one of the best ways to utilize child labor. The Lockharts always had a large garden. When produce was ripe and there was much to be canned all at once, even the stable man would help Mrs. Lockhart and the children with it. The Lockharts had a root cellar where carrots, potatoes, and cabbage kept well, but they also canned great quantities of beans, corn, beets, peas, and pickles, mostly in two-quart jars.

The Woodward family had a successful garden in 1884 and their turnips averaged nearly five pounds each. That same fall a twelve-pound turnip, thirty inches in circumference, and a thirty-four pound head of cabbage, four feet six inches in circumference, were displayed in a Fargo store window before they were shipped to an exposition in New Orleans. Even with such proof Mrs. Woodward expressed doubt that any other crop in a country where the mercury drops out of sight so frequently could ever compete with wheat "for all time." The 1920 agricultural census figures indicated that most of America's farmers were raising gardens and they also revealed that 56 per cent of all farm women took complete care of their large gardens themselves.

Without a doubt, R. M. Probstfield was the most outstanding early large-scale gardener in the area. His approach was scientific; he held membership in the Minnesota State Horticultural Society dating from January, 1880 and in 1909 he received an honorary life membership. His diary not only describes the extensive variety of garden products with which he experimented, but it also reflects the economics of gardening in a frontier region. He was one of the few real students of agriculture among area pioneers, and it is satisfying to note that the truck garden business which he established in the 1870's was still being conducted by the family in 1968, making it the oldest continuous family-owned truck gardening operation in the Valley. In later years produce has been sold from a family-operated vegetable stand known as The Old Trail Market on old Highway 75 north of Moorhead.

The garden was a training school for hard work for every member of his large family. In his first years of farming Probstfield had the advantage of his location next to the largest commercial vegetable market in the area—the colony of Northern Pacific construction gangs. After the Northern Pacific reached Bismarck that place became a secondary market for him. Two sales give a sample of his Bismarck transactions: on November 14, 1874, he sold red cabbage there for $.15 a head for a total sale of $20.00. On September 12, 1875, he delivered five bushels of tomatoes to the Headquarters Hotel (the depot) in Fargo. From there they were sent by express to Bismarck, and sold for $1.50 a bushel. It is interesting that prices charged for the cabbage and tomatoes on a wholesale basis at that time are comparable to rural retail prices charged for them in the 1960's.

The prices which Probstfield received for his produce reflected two basic conditions: one was that at times there was an obvious oversupply of vegetables on the Fargo-Moorhead market because many farmers traded whatever they could at the stores for the products that they needed; the other was that prevailing economic conditions caused the market to be so depressed at times that even vegetables were difficult to sell. On June 24, 1873, at a time of year when supply is normally low, Probstfield sold nine bushels (540 pounds) of potatoes for $1.00, or roughly $.20 a hundredweight. In October, 1873, he sold cabbage in Moorhead for $1.60 per hundred pounds, or about $.10 per head. Rutabagas brought $.35 a bushel; beets and carrots $1.00. The prices on this date represent one of the two lowest periods in the economic history of this region. The Panic of 1873 brought activity to a complete standstill. The other low point came when a prolonged dry period combined with the depressed prices of the late 1880's. Both of these depressions were more serious than the one of the 1930's.

Prices had revived somewhat after October, 1873, probably because of the oncoming winter season, and Probstfield received $.35 a bushel for potatoes that he delivered on contract to Rushmans in Moorhead. He also peddled onions to individual households and sold twenty bushels this way for $1.75 per bushel. One of the hotels purchased nearly a ton of cabbage for sauerkraut from him at $1.75 per hundred. Ole Gunderson, who farmed near Glyndon, brought two lambs to Probstfield which he exchanged for four bushels of onions.

Throughout most of 1876 Probstfield was quite dissatisfield with the sale price of vegetables. On June 30 he noted: "Had new peas and potatoes for dinner. Picked a bushel of peas *for the great Moorhead and Fargo Market*." Total sales for potatoes, onions, lettuce, and peas, he noted unhappily, were only $7.55. A few days later he "took up about $3.90 worth [of vegetables]—brought back more than half—prosperous times!" Conditions had not improved greatly by July 29 when "Mary and Alexander drove to town with $4 worth of vegetables, brought back nearly all."

Apparently there was an adequate supply of vegetables locally and commercial activity had not yet revived because land sales and the railroad business were still very slow. Ironically, eggs sold for twenty-five cents a dozen in 1876, which was the same price received for eggs during several months in the late 1960's, but Probstfield could get a haircut for the price of a dozen eggs.

In the early 1880's good wheat prices, bumper crops, and bustling activity on both railroads changed the economy of the area. On October 18, 1881, Probstfield was pleased when he had disposed of a wagon load of cabbage at twelve and a half cents per head for a total of $13.35. By 1890, however, the bottom of a cycle had appeared once again; after dry years with low prices for wheat, vegetable prices again were low. Then he sold thirteen cabbages to the Jay Cooke Hotel for fifty-cents or just one-third of what he had received for cabbages in 1881. On another day he delivered one dozen cabbage, one quart of string beans, and four dozen ears of sweet corn to a customer—all for $1.20, "a new low for vegetable prices."

In the fall of 1890 he had an abundant supply of raspberries which he attempted to dispose of in Moorhead but lamented, "cannot sell them so must put them up for our own use." In the mid-1890's he sold potatoes to neighbor, Kassenborg, for eight cents a bushel, which was again less than on any previous date.

One sideline of Probstfield's garden business was the production of sauerkraut. He developed a steady market for this product at the hotels and the Kiefer and the Hannaher families and many others were also regular customers. Sauerkraut was sold by the gallon or by the barrel and averaged about thirty-four cents a gallon (1960 prices averaged about $1.00 a gallon). This was obviously a profitable business and one in which a great amount of family labor could be utilized. On September 29, 1875, the Probstfield family cut up one ton of early cabbage to be made into sauerkraut.

R. M. Probstfield was an imaginative, experimental-minded man who contributed greatly to the agriculture of the area. He planted a tremendous variety of vegetables, fruits, berries, and trees. Some of his work was known and appreciated by the state agricultural institutions, but much of it was known only to local residents and to his personal correspondents. His plantings included the following: horseradish, rutabagas, pumpkins, parsley, lettuce, sweet corn, carrots, salsify (sometimes called oyster plant), cucumbers, watermelon, bassano beets, celery, rhubarb, muskmelon (canteloupe), wax beans, green beans, cauliflower, sage, coriander (spice), winter thyme; peas such as Early Philadelphia, Champion of England, Black and White Marrowfat; several varieties of cabbage including Fettlers Improved Brunswick, Little Pixie, and Burpees #1 Premium, Winnigstadt, Late Dutch, Marble Head, and Calahrica; Hubbard and regular squash. He also planted at least four different varieties of tomatoes; several kinds of beans such as Dwarf Golden Wax, Early Valentine, White Kidney, and Red Kidney; several varieties of radishes and onions; many varieties of potatoes; several varieties of peppers; Kohlrabi, egg plant, strawberries, and raspberries. Many of these seeds came from University of Minnesota experimental farms. He also planted turnips, red beets, and mangels as livestock fodder as well as sunflowers, corn, oats, and two types of wheat—Defiance and Champlain.

This volume of his garden production was great, for in 1875 he planted 4,000 cabbage plants and even more in later years. That same year by May 28, he had transplanted 496 tomato plants from his hot bed. He even raised peanuts but after 1876 discontinued planting them because he found them "not profitable." Probstfield's garden and yard also contained a large number of flowers of many varieties. No comment is made on whether any of these were ever sold or if they were planted purely for home beautification. Between 1876 and

1882 Probstfield planted thirteen peony plants, one for each member of his family. That row of thirteen plants was still thriving in 1969.

It was possible for Probstfield to grow many long-season plants because he had an extensive hot house operation. On March 14, 1874, he sowed tomato seeds in boxes in his residence which he transplanted to the hot house in early April and then to the garden in May. This gave him a chance to sell many products on the local market well in advance of the other truck gardeners in the area. Eggplant, cabbage, cauliflower, peppers, and many other plants were all handled in this manner. He carefully nursed the hot bed starting in March until all plants were transplanted to the garden. Several times he recorded temperatures of the hot bed as on April 8, 1874, when it reached 122 degrees, but on the same date in 1876 he recorded that the manure had "not started heating yet."

Except for purely experimental purposes, the Probstfields probably had the distinction of raising tobacco farther north for a longer period of time than any other family in the United States. The first reference to tobacco in the family diary came September 10, 1875, when Probstfield noted, "first frost—tobacco not injured." Six days later a heavy frost appeared and the following day the family cut the tobacco and put it up for curing. In 1876 the first hard frost did not arrive until September 26, but three days later a second frost forced them to cut their crop for curing. Probstfield's grandson, Ray Gesell, said the family raised three-fourths of an acre of Ornico and Havana tobacco continuously until World War II. Those in the family who smoked always used the home grown product and sold some of it to friends. Tobacco was also fed to the horses. "They were crazy about it. Besides, it was supposed to be good for worming them." The family was satisfied with the return on their tobacco acreage and Gesell said that "it did very well."

In addition to the sizeable natural grove on their farm, Probstfields also planted an orchard starting in 1873 and added to it each year. When Probstfield purchased his first box of apple trees from Dr. T. E. Ernies of Clinton, Iowa, he was disgusted with the nineteen-day shipping time and especially with the discrepancy in freight charges. For example, charges from Clinton, Iowa, to St. Paul, a distance of about 320 miles, was $4.50, while from St. Paul to Moorhead, a distance of only 240 miles, but with only one railroad serving the area, the charges were $11.45. He planted thirty more year-old apple trees and large numbers of willows and cottonwoods in 1874. In 1877 he planted 150 black walnut and 700 butternut trees. In 1878 and 1879 he planted an additional 600 apple trees of the following varieties: Wealthy, Whitney #20, Duchess of Oldenburg, Powers Large Red, Early Strawberry, and Beeches Red. In 1886 he planted twenty-one other varieties of apples. There were also at least seven varieties of grapes in the 1880's. He apparently did some experimental work, for on several occasions his neighbor, Charlie Brendemuehle (now spelled Brendemuhl) was hired not only to trim but also to graft apple trees. Unfortunately, no mention was ever made of the results. He had at least one pear tree in his orchard, planted June 13, 1878. In 1880 the *Warren Sheaf* reported that he had raised twenty-three barrels of several different varieties of apples and the article concluded: "Proof that Red River Valley soil can be successfully cultivated to something besides wheat." [5]

Chickens

The chores that went with the raising of chickens were generally considered another of the wife's or the children's duties. Before the days of chicken coops, chickens were permitted to lay eggs anywhere on the farm which made egg collecting a time consuming job. To guarantee the supply of chickens, hens had to be placed on nests for the hatching of eggs. It was not easy to keep the clucks (setting hens) on the nests for the twenty-one days necessary to hatch chicken eggs, and for ducks, geese, or turkeys, it took even longer. Not all hens started to set on the same day which spread out the hatching season.

Probstfield set thirty-five hens on nests in 1876, starting on April 15 and ending on July 3. Because he was more of a businessman than most, he knew the date when each hen was set and the number of eggs under it. Most farmers' wives kept either a mental note of the settings or marked them on a calendar that contained dates of breeding and other farm items. Later on when incubators were introduced the job of hatching was somewhat simplified.

Clothes Making

The frontier farmer's wife also had to make and to mend clothes —a continuous job, for many households virtually produced all their own clothing, especially for the feminine members and the children. The complete process of carding, spinning, and knitting was still performed by many of the women. Some children never had a piece of purchased clothing until they started school. Socks, stockings, booties, and mittens were generally homemade until much later. Mrs. Probstfield continued making clothes all her life and used the spinning wheel as late as 1894 when her youngest child was twelve. As the family increased she often hired a woman to sew for her at $2.50 per week. Her husband, even after he became state senator, wore some homemade clothing throughout his life. In 1876 the Hutchinsons, good friends of the Probstfields, purchased a sewing machine called "The Wilson." Probstfield noted that it "worked fine." Michel Berseth, a widower with eight children who lived near the Hagens at Abercrombie, had the first hand operated sewing machine in that area. He had brought it with him from Goodhue County, Minnesota, in 1878.

Mrs. Andrew Holes had the first sewing machine in Moorhead and possibly in all of the area. Many of the neighborhood women brought some of their sewing over to her house so that they could use the machine. At the first Clay County Exposition, which was held in the Northern Pacific Reception House at Glyndon in 1872, she exhibited a silk patchwork bedspread containing 7,600 pieces. A sewing machine was a fairly expensive but an essential piece of furniture. In 1894 prices for foot operated Singers ranged from $12 for the plain model with no cover or drawers to $20 for the deluxe machine with a cover and six drawers.

Sena Rendahl, who lived from pioneer times to the Golden Jubilee of Esmond in 1955, commented on women's clothes and manners in this way: "At the celebration [in 1955] many women were dressed in long dresses. They thought they looked like the women of pioneer times, but they didn't. The women of the nineties were prim and neat and very particular about their apparel, not slouchy and careless like they are now."

"Store-bought" clothes were always available but they were too expensive for the homesteader. In smaller communities overalls, work dresses, shoes, and most work clothes could be purchased at the one store in the community, but finer clothing or anything out of the ordinary had to be ordered from eastern stores. A 1920 government survey indicated that the average farm wife still spent most of her afternoons sewing and mending, unless she was helping in the fields, working in the garden, butchering, baking, washing clothes, or perhaps making her bimonthly shopping trip to town which took well over half a day. After Sears, Roebuck and Montgomery Ward and Company were founded, they provided "dream books" for the farmer's wife and provided her with a much improved selection of goods.

Washing Clothes

Washing clothes was also a woman's chore. Cisterns were built to store a supply of soft water for washing clothes and for bathing.

Often the early cisterns consisted of merely a barrel or two set at each corner of the house or nearby buildings to collect the water as it ran down from the shingled roof. In the winter time snow was melted in large tubs to provide the soft water for laundry work. When the second generation of houses were built they were larger and they had cisterns in the basement which could hold enough water to last for several months. If the family was not too large this water supply possibly lasted for the year, if not, the laundry water had to come out of the regular well or from melted snow. It was not until the 1890's that storage tanks were placed in attics to provide homes with "pressure" water systems. The W. J. Peet's of Wolverton had running water in 1903, Henry Schroeder in 1905, and the Stafnes in 1908.

Those lucky homesteaders who were located near a river, such as the Probstfields, could haul their water and thus refill their cisterns. On January 4, 1885, the temperature was forty degrees below zero but on the next day it was twenty degrees above zero, so Mrs. Woodward and Katie melted snow and washed. They had ten sheets, "innumerable other things" and twenty-two towels. The clothes were dried around "the kitchen fire—everybody knows what a delightful job that is." Later she noted that "everybody in Dakota should have a covered place in which to hang clothes in winter. It would pay a man as well as anything he could build. It would save the wear and tear on clothes, besides the health of the ones who hang them out." Many women froze fingers hanging clothes out on the line and taking in overalls, dresses, and union suits that were frozen stiff as a board.

Hard water, homemade lye soap, and the scrub board made washing clothes a hard and unpleasant chore. Not all pioneers wanted to spend forty cents for a scrub board so they rubbed the clothes on stones placed in a barrel of water. Is it any wonder there was a bit of tattle-tale gray? Mrs. Henry Woell remembered what a joyous day it was in 1895 in the Langer household when her father brought home a hand-powered washing machine. "Mother was so thrilled not to have to use the scrub board." The children took turns providing the power leaving their mother free to do other jobs. It takes only a little imagination to realize that the hand-powered machine was a great labor saver in contrast to the scrub board.

The next advancement in washing in the Langer family came "about World War I when they got a gas-powered washer . . . it was another great blessing" for no one was required to stand at the machine. Mrs. Woell added that in her lifetime she had seen the change from scrub board to automatic washer and she ended with the query, "What will be next?" [paper clothes.] The United States Department of Agriculture study of 1920 noted that sixty percent of the farms had automobiles, but motor driven washing machines, vacuum cleaners, gas or electric irons were still almost non-existent on these same farms.

General Housework

In pioneer days it was almost impossible for a single man or a single woman to farm alone, for farming had to be a family affair with women and children needed to do much of the routine work. By the 1920's it was obvious to the professional economists that the then apparent prosperity in American agriculture had resulted chiefly from two causes—the steady rise in land prices and the "unpaid service of women and children." The study concluded that if there were any prosperity in agriculture, it rested "squarely on the backs of the women and children who worked without pay, and unless prices of farm crops advance greatly there it will continue to rest." As recently as 1929 Mary Atkeson, an authority on women in agriculture, wrote, "The woman on the American farm has been considered, by those who have studied the position of farm women the world over, to be in a very happy situation." The farmer's wife did not rebel because she liked the idea of the family working together; she took great pride in being a real help to her husband and for these great ends she was willing to take a somewhat lower standard of living than did her counterparts in town.

In contrast to Europe, where most women and children were expected to do every type of field work, the American farm woman only worked in the field during the peak harvest season and by 1920 in some communities she did no field work at all. It was not uncommon for a farm woman in Europe to be yoked with the family cow to pull a drag or plow. The 1920 census revealed that the lowest ratio of women who worked in fields in America was in the wheat country and the corn belt where it was about twelve percent. Nationwide, one-fourth of the farmers' wives worked in the fields six weeks or more each year. The figure reached as high as fifty-five percent in the truck gardening, cotton, tobacco, dairy, and poultry states. The predictions at that time were that unless the farmer's income rose, the farmer, his wife, and older children would seek off-the-farm work. This prediction was correct and between 1920 and 1969 the total number of farms was reduced by more than sixty percent and at the later date farmers' off-the-farm income equalled net income from farming.

The low percentage of farmers' wives who worked in the fields should not mislead the reader into thinking that the farm woman had an easy time of it. Even though she was not expected to do regular field work, she was not saved from cranking the washing machine, the butter churn, or the cream separator, pumping water for the livestock, cleaning the chicken house, "slopping" the hogs, or milking the cows. One farm authority of the 1920's wrote that when a farmer's wife was asked what convenience she most needed on the farm she replied, "A new hired man." She probably spoke for the majority of her contemporaries and her predecessors. That 1920 study by the United States Department of Agriculture indicated that the farmer's wife's average work day was thirteen hours. Half of all the farm women rose at about 5 a.m. to build a fire; six out of ten carried their own water from a well which was at least forty feet from the kitchen door; eight out of ten fed the poultry; and four out of ten milked cows. The wife seldom saw any money from the sale of wheat or livestock, and a good deal of the money from butter, eggs, or garden produce, which were considered the "women's enterprises," went for mortgage payments.

The heavy work day of the farmer's wife was caused by three things; the limited number of manufactured products that she could afford to buy, the almost total lack of labor saving appliances, and the large families and many laborers for whom she was required to provide. Mrs. Mike McMahon, who had seven children, summed it up this way: "For one with such poor health, I had quite a family. [Besides the seven children] we always had about three men in the winter and four or five in the summer and ten to twenty during harvesting and threshing. How I did all that work, I do not know."

Mrs. Overby of Cooperstown cooked for several hired men as well as her nine children. One summer, when the Overbys built a complete set of new farm buildings three miles from their old homestead, it was her duty to feed the large crew of carpenters too. The laborers were usually new immigrants from Norway who were working to repay the expense of their journey to America. Besides the normal household duties she also took care of a large garden, the chickens, and the cream for marketing. However, "she did have a hired girl," which may or may not have been an asset. The situation was not much different at either the Lockhart or the Pratt farms.

The Lockharts kept a few hired men during the winter, but their regular crew swelled to twelve when spring work came and it increased to thirty during threshing. They always had a hired girl and, because of the large numbers of livestock, they also employed one full-time stableman who helped in the garden, took care of the lawn, and helped with heavy work around the house. Mrs. Lockhart was fortunate in that her oldest child was a girl, Ada, who helped her mother with the house and yard work. During harvest season Ada enjoyed taking meals to the men out in the fields. "With a crew of thirty it was always like a big picnic." The big pans and kettles were wrapped in sacks and quilts to keep the heat in.

Mrs. Pratt said about her life as a farmer's wife that it was "hard work but in those days everybody had to work harder. When I look back on it, I feel that it was a nice life." When asked what were the best years of her life, Mrs. Andrew Overby at age 100 firmly insisted that the days in the 1880's in the sod house were "the most pleasant of her life even if they did have to work hard." Mrs. Overby and her husband had cooked for 200 men at a Wisconsin lumber camp before they came here, consequently, she was accustomed to heavy household duties. The Overbys never had as many men on their place as did the Pratts of Grandin who had two year-round hired men. The threshing season was Mrs. Pratt's biggest headache. "Invariably it would rain at harvest time. It used to irk me so . . . we had about twenty men in the bunkhouse—well they would either go to town and get drunk or something else or else they would sit in the bunkhouse and play cards. They had to have something to do, but as I always said to my husband, work or not, they *never* missed a meal."

The Woodward household was as modern as could be expected for that day. Although the Woodward children were fully grown, Mrs. Woodward liked her busy life which she characterized as always having had "plenty of work and . . . no time to sew except in the winter. I cannot see to sew in the evening." About mid-November of each year the last of the field hands left and now her work load lightened. "I shall not get up until six any more this fall. I have been getting out of bed at five all summer, and sometimes earlier than that. But now we have only one man, there is no use getting up and stirring the animals before daylight."

In July, 1887, when she was sixty-one years old, she was still cooking for twelve men. Every day she baked nine loaves of bread, biscuits, and pie or pudding. "Some days I get very tired and have to lie down and rest which I never used to do." About that same time she was overjoyed when the boys built a slopbarrel cart using seeder wheels. "The ground is too level to pour slops near the door." There were no garbage disposals in those days.

The Probstfield farm, which was never more than a couple of hundred acres, nearly always had two full-time laborers and several children who worked. As early as the threshing season of 1876, there were twelve extra men to feed three to five times each day. Preparing meals for such large numbers on the old fashioned cook stove without the benefit of running water, food grinders, mixers, refrigerators, or freezers was a giant sized task. Only those who have worked with the large threshing crews that continued up to World War II really understand the problems involved. Because of the long work day, two lunches were served in addition to the regular meals. Morning lunch was at 9:00 to 9:30 and afternoon lunch from 3:30 to 4:00. Today, two men with a combine and trucks can thresh many more bushels per day than a thirty-man crew could in the 1880's.[6]

Prior to the advent of Rural Free Delivery, Ada Lockhart was able to get away from the drudgery of housework and perform one of her favorite jobs—making messenger trips to Kelso where she purchased small items and the usual supply of tobacco for the men and picked up the mail. The trip was usually made weekly and took about two hours. She said that her "little jenny mule was stubborn until Dad got it off the place and on the road, then I had no trouble with her." Jenny knew the way to town and back and never gave her small rider any trouble. Obviously, the young lady did the trip in fair weather only. Most housewives would have enjoyed a leisurely trip to town, but they could not spare the time except for major shopping which was not more than every two weeks.[7]

Fuel and Banking

One of the many extra chores which kept the pioneer farmer busy was the time consuming task of preparing fire wood and the collection of fuel. The fuel was especially important in a country where the winter was severe and lasted such a long time. More than one prospective settler coming to the area turned back when he saw the treeless prairies and located instead in the semi-wooded areas on the edge of the prairie and along the rivers. A large number of early settlers had to resort to the collecting of buffalo and cow chips for fuel, a task explained by O. A. Olson, who did the job many times:

> If no hay could be supplied
> You fired with cow-chips, turned and dried.

The prospect of having to use a wheel barrow to collect this "fuel of the prairie" (sometimes called oxoline), did not appeal to many people. Others used twisted prairie hay, corn cobs, and sometimes ears of corn for their fuel. Corn cobs, often collected from the hog yard, were only good for quick fires for cooking purposes in the sum-

mertime. Nevertheless, the *Warren Sheaf*, in 1881, advised farmers
to raise corn as a substitute for wood or coal. The article suggested
that three acres of corn would provide the average house with fuel
for the year and that two bushels of ear corn would heat a house on
the coldest day. The article cautioned: "Selling the corn to buy wood
will not begin to do." This suggestion, however, does not seem to
have been practical in an area where corn was obviously a very mar-
ginal crop.

The straw burner attachment to the cook stove, an oblong tube
twelve to eighteen inches in diameter and twenty-eight inches in
height, was one way of using a fuel which was always available on
the farms. This covered tube was placed over the stove holes and
filled with straw, hay, or corn stalks. The draft was regulated by
moving the tube off, or over the stove holes as was necessary to keep
the fire going. If properly packed, one of these tubes had enough
straw to burn for an hour. Other models were attached to the rear of
the stove and had much larger containers, but they were more expensive. Advertisements claimed that these straw and hay attach-
ments reduced the farmer's coal bill by half. The Mennonites in the
lower Valley used "Mist" which was a mixture of animal manure and
straw for fuel. But none of these fuel substitutes proved to be efficient
and useful in the long run.

Even those who had access to timber found that preparing it for
heating and cooking purposes was a big job. The Lockharts, living
near the Elm and Red Rivers, secured wood from the banks of either
of those rivers, wherever it could be secured most easily. Just before
1900, when wood became too scarce to be a reliable source of fuel,
they switched to coal. The Hobarts had no trees on their land or
near their farm; consequently, they were forced to buy imported wood
or coal. For the first two years the Divets secured their free wood
from the Sand Hills region ten to thirty miles northwest of their
farm.

Frequently friction arose among the settlers over the free timber
on government or railroad lands, which nearly was "up for grabs."
Some farmers built private bridges and prevented others, who were
after timber, from crossing them. After two years of driving to the
Sand Hills, the Divets concluded that the labor and the time involved
made the cost of "free" timber prohibitive and they began hauling
their wood purchased at the railroad siding in Wahpeton. When the
railroad was extended west they secured it from the yards at Mooreton and Farmington. The wood came in eight-foot lengths because
that was the best size for hauling it on flatcars and it sold for $3.75

to $4.00 a cord. Eight-foot lengths were also handy for fence posts, straw sheds, and other buildings. For the stoves, however, they had to be sawed and split into smaller pieces. Most of the wood used by the Divets was shipped in from Underwood, east of Fergus Falls.

The Woodwards, who also lived on treeless land, imported their wood in carload lots from northern Minnesota via the Northern Pacific. A carload held nine cords and cost them $49.50 at Mapleton siding from where they had to haul it. Mrs. Woodward said that they burned more wood in the summer than in the winter. When they had a large crew to feed, the cookstove was fired from 5 a.m. to 9 p.m. daily. Andrew Overby of Wolverton had to drive about seven miles to the banks of the Red to get his wood. Ole Overby of Cooperstown had a three-mile walk to the nearest stand of timber along the Sheyenne. Carrying his saw and axe with him each day, he cut and piled wood on the John Hogenson farm and received half of it for his labor. He hauled the wood home as he needed it.

Chopping, hauling, and stacking wood was a constant task. On some days Probstfield hauled four loads to the house, probably using a triple wagon box. On September 27, 1873, besides hauling in wood, he set up the box stove in the "big room." A box stove is a tub-like affair, not unlike an oblong barrel, with four legs and a fire door on the front end. Each fall Probstfield "banked wood" which meant that he stacked it next to the house or in a wood shed to have it available for immediate use. This was a sizeable job for it took several days each fall to stack an adequate supply for the winter.

In the winter of 1874-75 Probstfield hauled in sixteen and one-half cords of wood for household use alone. The rule of thumb was that two cords of mixed native wood, such as elm, oak, or box elder, were equal to one ton of coal in heating value and wood was priced accordingly. An average sized home used at least fifteen cords of wood each winter. Probstfield's house was larger than the average house so he had to use more firewood. Although the Probstfield house is the oldest in Clay County that is still occupied, it has never had a furnace in it. At first it was heated by a cookstove and one or two space heaters were needed. Because they had a ready supply of wood on the farm, they continued to use it until just before World War II when they converted to fuel oil, and in 1968 electric heat was installed. (The house is destined to become a state historical site.)

Preparing trees for fuel was a difficult task in the days before mechanical saws had been introduced. Most pioneers used only an axe and a buck saw, but some also used crosscut saws. Sawing down a tree, trimming it, and cutting it into four-foot lengths, and hauling it to the yard took an average of one man-day's work per cord. Later the wood was sawed in stove length pieces, split, and stacked for use. This process took nearly another half day of work per cord. Men were commonly paid $1.25 per cord which included chopping down a tree and stacking it into one-cord piles. Only wood used for the cook stove had to be split—the heating stove could handle larger pieces. The Henry J. Schroeder home used a boiler-type furnace that took four-foot lengths of cord wood. At least twenty-two days each year were spent in preparing wood for an average sized house. There were very few settlers who used coal in the early years.

To stop the chill of winter from consuming fuel too rapidly and to make rooms more comfortable, it was customary to "bank" the houses which was done by putting paper and dirt, leaves, straw, or manure against the foundation and lower part of the house to stop the cold air from getting under the floor or through the walls. Most farmers used horse manure because it was the driest and was the best insulator. Few went to the extreme of Charles Hobart who banked his house up to the eaves. Most pioneer homes did not have storm windows to slow down the loss of heat in winter because many of them did not understand the value of a dead air space as an insulator. In the early days sacks and robes were often placed over the windows; glass was expensive because it had to be transported great distances at a considerable risk. Each year Probstfield made a few storm windows for his house and it took him several years before he had done the job for all the windows.

After the house was banked, the well house, the water hole, the chicken coop, and, if possible, the barn were also banked. Some farmers even covered the roofs of their chicken coops and hog barns with straw to keep the heat in. This gave them the idea for the straw shed that served as an excellent structure for hogs and beef cattle and remained in use until the threshing machine was replaced by the combine. Banking the buildings, which took several days' work each fall, required a like amount of time each spring when it was removed.[8]

Water Supply

One of the most immediate tasks for the pioneer was to locate a supply of water. As soon as possible he dug a well, but in many cases much time elapsed before a well was dug and frequently it went dry. O. A. Olson illustrates the plight of the homesteader:

> Out there is my wheelless windmill
> Over a waterless well.
> A mile or more to water
> Makes cooking a sample of hell.

Frontier standards of hygiene were not the same as today, and what was a perfectly satisfactory water supply in those days would not do for today. Contrary to popular opinion, some water scientists contend that fresh water bodies were only slightly less polluted in pioneer times than they are today. One pioneer expressed the belief that if water passed between two stones and a person drank from the downstream side he would be getting pure water.

Most of the first settlers relied on getting their water from nearby streams. As the land became more occupied, the later settlers were forced to walk long distances to the streams, dig their own wells, or make watering ponds. Throughout the year, the Crawfords and the Woodwards drove cattle one and three-fourths miles to the nearest river for watering. For family drinking purposes the Crawfords secured water from a neighbor's well a mile away. Mrs. L. A. Schultz of Chaffee stated that they did not have a well on their farm for many years because they were located along the Maple River and secured water from it.

Torkel Fuglestad drove his cattle two miles to the Sheyenne River for the first few years that he farmed. On one such watering trip in January, 1884, he had his first experience with a blizzard. While the cattle were drinking he noticed how quiet and clear the day was for he could hear the axe blows of the people who were chopping trees downstream. Everyone was working in shirtsleeves. Suddenly he noticed a big black cloud in the northwest and before he got the cattle back to the barn a full scale blizzard was in process. It raged for three days and during that entire time the cattle were neither fed nor watered. Charles Hobart did not like the idea of getting his cattle out of the barn during storms or carrying water to them; therefore, he enlarged his barn so that it covered the nearby well and the cattle could be watered in the barn.[9]

Securing an adequate water supply in the Red River Valley has always been an uncertain proposition and remains so to the present. In many areas the water table is extremely high, but to guarantee a year-round water supply deep wells have to be dug, for shallow ones frequently dry up. The Woodwards had three wells on their farm, but they were shallow, and in dry seasons they had to haul water in barrels from the Sheyenne River. In 1886 they dug a fourth well eighty feet deep. The well driller was paid $260 in cash and the farm workers' wages brought the cost of the well to $9.00 a foot. At that time they also had a rain water cistern for wash water. One of their neighbors dug sixteen wells before he abandoned his farm for one that had water.

Hobart had one well for the house, another in the corner of his pasture for his cattle and sheep, and a third one in his stable. In his area an adequate water supply was available at twelve feet. The Divets, west of Wahpeton, said that digging a well was the first job they did after establishing the boundary of their farm. Although they only had to dig ten feet, they were fortunate enough to hit a flow that supplied their farm with water for the first few years.

H. V. Arnold, an early area historian, reported that there were hundreds of artesian (flowing) wells west of the Red that were from 500 to 800 feet deep. The Hovdes were very lucky to hit a strong flowing well which was reputed to be 500 feet deep. This well was opened in 1883 and, except for several cleanings, was still providing water in 1937 when the family history was written. That well was generally used to supply livestock needs. Later, a smaller open well with ropes, pulley, and bucket, was dug near the Hovde house. A little shed was built over it and it was used until 1921 when a new sealed well, with a pump, was installed.

Wells were established by three methods—hand digging, augering, or driving with cable tool rigs. A few lucky settlers hit deep veins which had more than adequate flow, especially in the Dakota sandstone area just west of the Red River. But this water was highly mineralized and not very desirable for drinking purposes. The Andrew Overbys dug their first well with a horsepowered auger well machine, striking water at forty feet. The auger was quite large and as it went down curbing was built to keep the well from caving in. Madsens used the same system and curbed their four feet by four feet well for the first forty feet but tapered the curbing down to three feet square for the remaining ten feet. To get a well larger than the auger, the side of the well was shaved down by hand and the dirt pulled out by buckets and a horsepower winch. The Madsen well maintained a stand of water about twelve feet deep except in extremely dry periods when it dropped a little.

Open wells had serious drawbacks—they were unsanitary, hard to draw water from, and hazardous. Because they were open to the elements and all forms of small animal life, these wells were certainly contaminated and how many people died from drinking this water is impossible to determine. Pumps were not common on the frontier, so water was drawn by rope and bucket. Most people associate open wells with the relatively small "old oaken bucket," but when larger amounts of water were needed for watering livestock, a larger bucket with a bottom paddle valve was often used. It opened from the bottom when lowered into the water and closed by water pressure when full and raised. The Overby's bucket was about three feet long and the Woodwards had one that held eight pailfulls of water.

Many accidents happened when people or animals fell into these open wells. A typical experience occurred when Charles Hobart dropped his pail into the well one evening while watering stock. He climbed down into the well to retrieve the pail and a small platform just above the water gave way. The well was four feet square and it was nine feet down to the water which was covered with a sheet of ice. Fortunately, as a precaution he always left a twelve-foot pole in the well and used it to climb out. On another such occasion Martin Monahan, south of Hallock, was watering his horses when his bucket dropped in. He went down after it and as he was climbing back out on the rope, the rope broke just before he reached the top. Because he had drawn a large amount of water, there was only a foot of water left in the well when he first fell into it, but it slowly refilled once he stopped drawing water. Monahan was a bachelor and there was no one else around the farm until the next day when a neighbor came by to borrow a fork. When he found no one in the house and noted that the animals were uncared for, he began to look around. He found Monahan in the well with water up to his waist. It was February and the outside temperature was twenty degrees below zero. When the neighbor found him he had been in the well for twenty-four hours and his feet and legs "were black but he was expected to recover."

Charles Hobart had a second experience with his open well. One day, while he was watering cattle, a yearling steer slipped and fell into the well by the house. Unlike Hobart, the steer was unable to climb out. Getting a yearling steer out of a twelve-foot well called for some skillful engineering in the days before hydraulic lifts. Hobart took the rear axle and wheel assembly from a wagon and rolled it over the well. Then he carefully blocked the wheels so that they could not move. A rope was let down over the axle and tied around the steer. When the horses pulled on the rope, the axle turned and the steer was lifted out of the well. Mrs. Hobart and her father-in-law removed the blocks from the wheels when the steer was at ground level and the axle assembly rolled away with the steer free and un-hurt.[10]

Many of the children of homesteaders spent seemingly endless hours pumping water for household and livestock needs. Quite likely most animals did not get all the water that they required for max-imum efficiency and health. The same probably was true of the peo-ple, for if the water pail was empty, many were inclined to go thirsty until someone was sent out to fill it. Mrs. Overby "complained about the back-strain she suffered while carrying heavy buckets [of water] up the steep hill to our cabin" from the Sheyenne which was a quarter mile from the house, or from the neighbors who were a half mile away.

James Power was one of the first in the entire area to have a windmill when he started his large-scale cattle operation in the Sand Hills along the Sheyenne in 1880. The only known windmills in the area at the time were at the stockyards and water towers located along the railroad. Ada Lockhard Gunkelman said it was many years before they had a windmill and the choreman or one of the children "were always pumping water to keep the tanks full for the cattle and horses," besides the hogs, chickens, and household. She added, "and it was alkali water at that. . . . What a day of excitement when a windmill arrived and was erected, and took over the water pumping job. The entire family was relieved." Likely the livestock was relieved too for they were probably never adequately watered before that time. In the winter time "the boys try to get a bucket of water a piece to the horses each day." Whether that was sufficient for a healthy animal was not the major concern; there just was not enough time to carry water for twenty horses. Fortunately, the horses were generally idle in the winter for no working horse could have lived on one bucket of water daily.[11]

FOOTNOTES

[1] Probstfield; McMahon, NDIRS, File 195; Hobart, "Pioneering," VIII, 120-124; Divet, NDIRS, File 69; Madsen interview.

[2] David Peet interview; Mary M. Atkeson, "Women in Farm Life and Rural Economy," *The American Academy of Political and Social Sciences, Women in the Modern World, CXLIII* (May, 1929), 188-189; *World's Work*, XL (Sept., 1920), 435; McMahon, NDIRS, File 195; O. Overby, *Retrospect*, pp. 10-21; Gunkelman interview; Pratt interview; Probstfield; Interview with Arthur Overby about his mother's biography; A. Overby, "Sod House Days," p. 13; Woell interview; D. J. McLellan, Jr., Associate Extension Agricultural Engineer, letter June 13, 1968, relative to well digging and windmills; Woodward, pp. 57, 64, 102, 134, 147, 150, 181; Schroeder interview; Stafne, p. 61; Mary M. Atkeson, *The Women on the Farm* (New York, 1924), p. 120.

[3] *Dakota Farmer*, V (Jan. 1886), 10; See Fite, p. 41, Robinson and Billington for more details on fuel used by the pioneers; Gunkelman interview; A. Overby, "Sod House Days," p. 13; O. Overby, *Retrospect*, p. 10; Probstfield; Divet, NDIRS, File 69; Nelson interview; Madsen interview; *Warren Sheaf*, Feb. 9, 1881; Schroeder interview; Woodward, pp. 124, 151, 152.

[4] Probstfield; Harold E. Briggs, *Frontier of the Northwest: A History of the Upper Missouri Valley* (New York, 1950), pp. 510-511; F. G. Callan, "A History of Richland County and the City of Wahpeton, North Dakota," Federal Writer's Project, WPA (Wahpeton, 1937), p. 19; A. Overby, "Sod House Days," p. 9; Edwin Ankerfeldt interview; Emil Ankerfeldt interview; Stafne, p. 18; Woodward, p. 151; Hobart, "Pioneering," VII, 217-220.

[5] Percy W. Bidwell, "Pioneer Agriculture: The Northeast," *Readings in Economic History of American Agriculture*, ed. Earl D. Ross and Louis B. Schmidt (New York,

1925), pp. 172-192 (see other articles in same volume for various areas of pioneer agricultural development); Murray, pp. 204-205 (also see for additional information on use of potatoes, vegetables, and wheat by the initial settlers at Fort Garry and Pembina); *Moorhead Independent*, Jan. 5, 1900, p. 32; Wilkin County Publicity Club, "The Truth About Wilkin County" (Breckenridge, 1910), pp. 26-27; See Drache, *Bonanza*, Chap. IX for the impact of wheat monoculture on the area; *Warren Sheaf*, April 2, 1891; Gunkelman interview; C. W. Thompson, "The Movement of Wheat Growing: A Study of a Leading State," *The Quarterly Journal of Economics*, XVIII (1904), 573; Schroeder interview; *World's Work*, XL (Sept., 1920), 435; Probstfield; Woodward, pp. 51, 59; Conversations with Raymond Gesell; *Warren Sheaf*, Feb. 9, 1881.

⁶ Probstfield; David Peet interview; Woodward, pp. 134-50; Woell interview; Mary M. Atkeson, *The Women on the Farm*, p. 120; Rendahl, p. 5; McMahon, NDIRS, File 195; O. Overby, *Retrospect*, pp. 10-21; Gunkelman interview; Pratt interview.

⁷ *World's Work*, XL (Sept., 1920), 435; Probstfield; A. Overby, "Sod House Days," p. 13; Pratt interview; *Hope of the Prairie*, p. 12; Gunkelman interview; Glenn E. Johnson, "Here, There and Everywhere," p. 12; Stafne, pp. 15, 27; Thortvedt, NDIRS, File 332; Schroeder interview; Mrs. Bernard Holes interview; *Warren Sheaf*, Nov. 6, 1890; David Peet interview; Rheder interview; *The Record*, I (Aug., 1895), 29; Rendahl, p. 11.

⁸ *Dakota Farmer*, V (Jan., 1886), 10; Fite, p. 41; Gunkelman interview; A. Overby, "Sod House Days," p. 13; O. Overby, *Retrospect*, p. 10; Probstfield; Divet, NDIRS, File 69; Nelson interview; Madsen interview; *Warren Sheaf*, Feb. 9, 1881; Schroeder interview; Woodward, pp. 124, 151, 152; See also Robinson and Billington for more details on fuel used by pioneers.

⁹ Crawford, NDIRS, File 290; "Give the Farmers Wife a Chance," *World's Work*, XL (Sept., 1920), 435; Mrs. L. A. Schultz, letter July 20, 1966; Fuglestad, pp. 8-9; Hobart, "Pioneering," VII, 214.

¹⁰ O. Overby, *Retrospect*, pp. 17, 27; Woodward, pp. 28, 135; Hobart, "Pioneering," VII, pp. 211-212, 225; *Warren Sheaf*, Feb. 4, 1895; A. Overby, "Sod House Days," p. 4.

¹¹ Woodward, p. 86; O. Overby, *Retrospect*, p. 15; Gunkelman interview.

CHAPTER VI

Homemade

A TRADITIONAL concept of the pioneer is that he always carried a gun, a hatchet, and a fishline and whenever he had the opportunity to kill an animal, to pick a few berries, to chop down a tree for honey, or to catch a fish, he did so. In this manner he provided food for himself and his family. This common impression suggests that the pioneer was nearly self-sufficient. Self-sufficiency may have been characteristic in some areas, but not in Red River Land because the pioneer's productive capacity and time were so limited during his first years that he could not live from nature alone; hence, he was forced to purchase many processed foodstuffs.

Groceries—Charge Accounts

In the first year that Charles Hobart farmed in the area, he slept under a wagon and usually ate side pork and pancakes. However, when his wife and father came one year later, demands of the household increased. "With the beginning of housekeeping . . . came the question of how to get groceries," he wrote. "I solved the problem by giving Mr. Clayton, in Mayville, a note and mortgage for $75 at twelve percent to be taken in groceries as we needed during the summer. Later I traded with a Mr. Little, in Buxton, who trusted us." Hobart was not alone in having to pay interest on his grocery account. On January 4, 1881, Probstfield purchased $60 worth of groceries from the Stephen Brothers in Chicago for which he gave a note at ten percent and on April 4, 1881, he settled the account for $62.85. Paying interest irked the thrifty farmer but little else could be done about it because cash was scarce.

The most common procedure in buying groceries at that time was to charge them at the local store. Then when the crop was sold in the fall, the bill was paid. If there were no harvest, the grocery bill had to run for another year or until the grocer refused to extend any more credit. The size of farm made little difference when it came to charging grocery items, and farmers who owned several sections of land charged just as freely as did the owners of a quarter section. The average farmer extended his credit as far as he could in order to avoid going to the bank to borrow money at the customary rate of ten and twelve percent. Records of the Bettschen store at Arthur indicate that charge accounts of $200 to $500 per family were common. The Bettschens were lucky to live in a good community where most farmers paid their accounts every fall or signed notes for them if they could not pay.

Grocery bills of this size, accumulated by farmers whose total assets might not exceed $1,000, meant that the store operators were taking a big risk. Losses on such accounts could be overcome only by operating a grocery store on a sizeable margin. Eventually, the successful homesteader indirectly paid the bills of those who could not pay. The G. C. Winchester store in Warren, however, boasted that its customers did not pay for losses because of credit sales and it was proud of the low net cash prices it could offer because it extended "no credit, no time" and suffered no losses. Because there were several stores in Warren which gave credit, it was possible to have one "cash and carry" firm, but in the smaller communities which had only one store, "strictly cash" would have been virtually impossible. Farmers in those days did not have ready cash.[1]

Food and Its Cost

The daily fare in pioneer days was much less elaborate than today. This limited selection was caused in part by the scarcity of home grown foods and by the difficulty in securing commercial supplies. Mrs. Hovde said, "Housekeeping was not complicated with the simple diet of salt pork and whatever could be made of flour—bread, biscuits, flatbread, and the like . . . in our first year [we had a picnic] and everyone enjoyed the only food available—bread and milk." Because the Hudson's Bay Company post at Georgetown was reluctant to sell to the general public, the earliest settlers were forced to make a two-week trip to Alexandria for provisions until the railroad entered the area.

In their first year the Thortvedts, for example, twice experienced what it meant to be without staple food products—once during the summer when the cows were lost for eight days and a second time in the fall when they ran out of flour two days before the men returned from Alexandria with provisions. During those two days the Thort-vedts had only milk, fish, and berries to eat. Pioneers exhibited great ingenuity in adapting substitutes to stretch their own meager supplies. When the Bernhardsons of Comstock realized that they were running low on flour, they scraped the inside of tree bark and ground it into "a kind of bran" which was mixed with the wheat flour.

Coffee, although a staple in the daily menu, was so expensive that it had to be stretched by adding other materials. It was common to purchase unroasted green coffee to which barley or wheat was added prior to roasting it in the oven. The grain picked up flavor from the coffee in the roasting and blended with the coffee bean when ground in the standard home coffee grinder. Some suggested that this mixture tasted like Postum and they preferred it to straight coffee. In Mrs. August Hoppe's childhood home the mixing of grain with coffee became standard procedure and was not considered a substitute. Others liked tea which was as common as coffee.

Saffron was used as a substitute for tea or blended with tea to prolong the purchased product. C. H. Frey's father attempted to find a substitute for sugar to avoid having to purchase it. Those settlers who lived near the woods frequently collected honey from bee hives. The Posey family of Otter Tail County, and most of the other settlers in their community, raised a few acres of cane sorghum each year. They cut it and hauled it to the store at Phelps Mills to be made into sorghum. Mrs. Posey heated the sorghum and strained out the impurities after which it was stored in a fifty-gallon barrel in the cellar. Sorghum was the major sweetening used in that household until World War I and some of their neighbors continued this practice until well into the 1920's.

Salt pork, flour, beans, bread, syrup, and some kind of jelly, which came in many flavors, were the standard fare in the Divet household. On the east side of the Valley the Ericksons had potatoes, fresh or salted meats, milk gravy, and some kind of vegetable for a standard dinner menu. "Mush was a common supper dish made either with milk or water. Corn meal mush was relished by some. Then there was the 'fillebank' [fillebunk] or whole milk. This was left to turn sour and thick in a pan. Sugar was scattered on top of the cream and was eaten with bread. Good! This was a delicious supper dish and usually the whole family ate out of the same pan."

Milk was a product that could be served in several ways. Besides "fillebank," milk mush, or as the Norwegians called it, "gröt" [rome-gröt and flote-gröt], was very common. Milk soup, another standard, was milk with dumplings in it. Potato soup, which contained milk, potatoes, and onions, was an economical standard dish. In some communities goat cheese too was a popular specialty dish. In the Hannaford area goats were raised partly for fresh milk but more often for the cheese, which had a "sort of brownish color."

Emma Erickson Elton contrasted the difference in the foods in her Red River Valley home and her later homestead in Williams County. Nature there was not so bountiful and there were no products from the woods to supplement the wheat and vegetable diet; dairy cows were also scarce. From 1905 to 1912 her standard fare was bacon, beans, bread, butter, and coffee. Of course, some garden produce was canned for winter use, but wheat, the major crop of the area, was consumed in many different forms.

Among Norwegian settlers lefse was made whenever there was leftover mashed potatoes and on holidays when it was specially prepared. "Lutefisk," another Norwegian dish, was often on hand at Christmas, even though it came all the way from Norway in a "dry form and had to be watered out by the consumer." Flatbread (flot brod) was nearly always available because it kept well. Christmas was always a special feast. The Olsen household provides an example of the customary schedule at that time. The standard procedure on Christmas Eve "was to have a bath right after chores before supper. Then we had Christmas Eve supper which was always spare ribs, lutefisk, and rice pudding (ris grod) with an almond for good luck." The Jens Hagens, who were a bit more prosperous, had spare ribs as the standard main dish for the Christmas holidays, but they also had steak, roasts, pigs feet, headcheese, sylte, rull, and rome-gröt. The yeast-raised Jule Kage and pastries like fattigmand and sandbakkelse were also on the menu. All this was capped with home made wine made of wild chokecherries, plums, or grapes that had been picked in the fall along the Sheyenne River. Sometimes there was home-brewed "beer" made from home grown barley and from wild hops which were plentiful along the Sheyenne and Wild Rice Rivers.

Salt pork, the standard meat for the great majority of the homesteaders, was the complete cross section cut of the hog including fat, ribs, and loin. Salt pork, in ten-pound slabs, was packed twenty to a barrel, and sold in Moorhead stores in the 1880's for from ten cents to twelve and a half cents per pound or somewhat less in barrel lots. It was a good, substantial, safe food, and the most easily preserved meat. Most people liked it and it could be served in many different ways. Sometimes the entire ten-pound slab was boiled and then sliced and eaten cold or reheated. Much of the time it was boiled with beans and served either as bean soup or as bean and bacon "hot dish."

For breakfast the pork was sliced and fried like bacon. Some people parboiled it and then rolled it in flour and fried it that way and sometimes it was parboiled and then roasted. For a handy meal that did not take many dishes and could be heated on a small fire, salt pork was cubed into small pieces and mixed into biscuit dough. Hobart called this "hasty pudding." The fat that was left over from frying salt pork was mixed with onion, garlic, or other seasoning and frequently used as a substitute for butter. It was kept in a sealed jar and at each meal the proper amount was melted and served over boiled potatoes or biscuits. It was also used for frying potatoes and other foods.

In the summer time, when the housewife had to help with the work out-of-doors, pork and beans were mixed in an iron pot which held from two to four gallons and placed on the stove and left there for several days. Each time the stove was fired up for a meal, the big pot was heated to a near boil. After about three days of this procedure the beans and pork were thoroughly cooked and could be eaten without additional heating. This procedure gave the housewife freedom from cooking a few meals over a hot stove during the summer season.

Making bread and biscuits using yeast or sour dough as a leavening agent was a big job in the pioneer home. After the dough was mixed and allowed to rise overnight, it was ready for baking. A hot fire of several hours' duration was necessary to bake the many loaves that had to be prepared each time. Some pioneer women preferred the sour dough method because it required less heat and labor. According to Guy Divet, "a little of the sourings [starter] were saved after each baking, when pancakes or biscuits were wanted water and flour was added and left in a pan to sour." It was then ready to be made into pancakes or biscuits. This was especially handy for travelers, or in the summer when a light fire was preferred.

Many families liked the sour dough taste and texture in contrast to dough that had been raised by saleratus or similar products. One of the old recipes still in use for sour dough pancakes calls for flour, scalded milk, and salt added to the small hold-over of yeast starter. These are mixed and allowed to stand for several hours or overnight to rise. Then egg, sugar, and soda are added. Water may be substituted for the scalded milk and the egg can be omitted but in this case it is less tasty. This batter makes a smooth, moist, "rubbery" pancake in contrast to the drier, fluffy pancake made by other methods. Jelly, syrup, or fat from salt pork were used in pancakes and biscuits. The syrup was the heavy, dark type (possibly molasses) and it was commonly purchased in five or ten gallon containers.

There were few deviations from the above diets. If there were it was only due to good luck or because of strong dislikes on the part of the family. Some farmers who raised potatoes had to eat them three times a day. Others did not grow them and purchased them if they were available. In October, 1870, the men of the Buffalo River settlement went to Jimmy Rice's place near Comstock to buy potatoes. Although the Rice farm was twenty miles away from the Buffalo River settlement, it was the nearest source of potatoes. Potatoes had not been available to them since they left Houston County in May and they were unable to plant any during the first season because their time was taken in building a house, making prairie hay, and breaking sod.

As previously mentioned some settlers had gardens that provided them with vegetables which were canned to be eaten throughout the year. Others used gardens only to supply fresh vegetables to be eaten in season. In most of the communities a farmer or two, such as Probstfield and the McFarlans of Grandin, would provide vegetables in season for local markets.

Because flour was such a vital commodity in the total diet, its price was important. The first flour available for sale in the area was sold reluctantly at the Hudson's Bay Company post at Georgetown for $14.00 a barrel or $7.00 a hundred. After the Northern Pacific entered the Valley, flour sold in Moorhead for $3.50 a hundred pounds. However, in April, 1877, it temporarily spurted to $5.00 a hundred when the wheat price jumped to $1.75 a bushel. Wheat maintained a high average annual price of $.95 to $1.16 a bushel through 1883. Flour prices ranged from a low of $2.65 to a high of $3.50 retail in Moorhead during the early 1880's. All figures were for hundred-pound sacks because no housewife wanted to bother with smaller quantities.

In 1874, prior to milling his own wheat, Probstfield purchased about 1,500 pounds of flour for his family of eight children and three adults (one hired man). Allowing for company and for extra help, this represents one-third of a pound of flour per person per day—the equivalent of more than one loaf of bread. Flour was a bargain when compared to other food items and has become even more so in the twentieth century, although packaging in small containers has forced the price up per unit of weight.[2]

Butter and eggs were not necessarily staple items on the daily menu. Those who had dairy cows made their own butter and any surplus was traded at local stores. Thus, it came in as many flavors as there were women who had made it. Because of the lack of uniform quality, many people turned to butter substitutes, particularly margarine, but some women received a premium if they delivered a high grade butter product at the store. An interesting sidelight to the butter story occurred in the late 1890's at the Gunness Brothers store in Barnesville. A farmer's wife, who had a reputation for making good butter, appeared in the store and wanted to exchange her butter for some from the store. D. F. Gunness thought this odd so pressed for a reason. The farmer's wife said that her butter was perfectly fine, but a mouse had fallen into the cream and, "knowing this, it is difficult to feed this butter to my family." Mr. Gunness agreed to make the exchange. He took the butter into the back room, removed it from the woman's container, and rewrapped it in the store butter wrapper. He returned the butter that the woman had brought in to her with the same thought in mind, "what you don't know won't hurt you."

After 1879, when the DeLaval cream separator became available, cream was more easily separated from the milk. Turning the separator was a job for young boys who disliked it as much as their mothers disliked washing the utensils. Butter cost from twenty-five cents to thirty cents a pound retail. Eggs, a similar product in so many respects, retailed from fifteen cents to twenty-five cents a dozen with the farmer's price being ten cents to fifteen cents. Probstfield peddled fresh eggs for twenty-five cents a dozen.

Salt, molasses, syrup, coffee, and sugar headed the list of foods purchased and fruits came next. It was not uncommon for a family to purchase two or three barrels of apples for the winter's supply if they had a good root cellar in which to keep them. If not, dried fruits were second choice; the chief kinds were apples, peaches, apricots, currants, figs, and prunes. They were purchased in case lots of fifty pounds or more. In one order sent to Griggs and Company, a St. Paul wholesale grocery firm, in March, 1888, Probstfield purchased twenty-five pounds of tea, twenty-five pounds of currants, and fifty pounds of dry apples at a cost of $6.60, including freight.

Dried fruits were scare enough so that they were considered a treat by the children. Fresh oranges and bananas were available for a very short season, while lemons could be secured most of the time, but all were a real delicacy. Some people remembered the July 4 picnic mainly because of its lemonade. Lemons were sold in Moorhead in 1875 at three for twenty-five cents. In August, 1881, the *Warren Sheaf* advertised that a fresh supply of lemons had arrived and were on sale for sixty cents a dozen. In season, most families made annual expeditions along the rivers to pick grapes, plums, juneberries, chokecherries, and many other wild fruits, besides gathering hops.

Even though most farmers butchered their own cattle, occasionally they had to buy fresh meat, usually beef steak or boiling beef. Much of the meat consumed in early Fargo-Moorhead was imported live from South St. Paul or stock yards in northern Iowa and butchered by local retailers because there was no means of refrigeration. James B. Power had a large livestock operation and Probstfield supplied local butchers with hogs, sheep, and cattle. By the 1890's there were a few traveling meat wagons which sold their wares from farm to farm.

Other items appeared occasionally on the homesteader's grocery list, but they were expensive and were considered luxuries. Probstfield liked oysters and frequently spent fifty cents for them. An oyster dinner at Chapins, an early Moorhead restaurant, was $1.00. In 1884, herring could be purchased in two-gallon wooden pails in Moorhead for $1.50. Settlers close to Glyndon were fortunate because a cheese factory was in operation there as early as 1876. Probstfield purchased his cheese in forty-pound lots. Vinegar was $1.00 a gallon in 1875 and came in fifty-gallon wooden barrels with a discount for those who brought their own container. To break the steady flour diet, corn meal was used, especially for breakfast. It sold for about three cents a pound in ten-pound lots. Ginger and other spices were purchased to enhance the food.

No matter how hard up the settlers were, few of them returned home from a shopping trip without some candy. This treat was carefully hoarded by the mothers and a small sack lasted a long time, even in large families.

The old reliable item on the combined grocery and medicine list was castor oil which was considered by some a "mainstay" of the diet. Sulphur and molasses was the standard spring tonic.

Farmers were notoriously poor bookkeepers, even for business purposes. Most of them would have thought it ridiculous to keep a record of household and family expenses so there are none available except those of Probstfield and of some of the bonanza farms. Probstfield's itemized expenses for 1874, at a time when there were eight children in his family ranging in age from eight months to fourteen years, shed some light on the amount of goods purchased. The largest item on the list was meat, totalling $97.98, which represents about 500 pounds of the purchased product. This meat was used in addition to home butchered meats which provided all the meat needs except during the hottest weather or peak labor season. About eighty pounds of butter were purchased at a cost of $12.43, in addition to the butter made by the family. Flour was the third largest item purchased in 1874 when $47.50 was spent for 1,500 pounds of flour. The following year Probstfield started milling his own wheat.

Of those items which had to be obtained from commercial sources, sugar headed the list at a cost of $36.50, followed closely by coffee at $30.50. The coffee was supplemented with $9.00 worth of tea. His orchard was not producing at this early date so he had to buy $4.45 worth of apples. Another $4.00 was spent on salt, very likely 200 pounds or more. Vinegar used in canning and in other cooking cost $2.50. A considerable amount of soap was made at home, a byproduct of butchering, but the family still spent $4.05 for store-bought soap. Sundries was the catch-all word in the Probstfield budget and $9.35 of groceries fell into this column in 1874. In all, $258.16 were spent for purchased food during the year to provide for ten members of the family and hired help who might have eaten with them.[3]

Shopping Services

As recently as the 1920's it was still being said that one of the chief hindrances to good farm living, as the farmer's wife saw it, was the inability to get a dollar's worth of goods for the limited number of dollars she had to spend. At that time there were 39,000 small communities in the United States serving 20,000,000 rural people, an average of only 500 customers per town. The large number of these towns that have died since 1920, and an equal or greater number that are dying today, are testimony not only of overexpansion in rural America but also of improved transportation.

Too many small towns have spent their energies competing with each other rather than in serving their customers. These small towns, which tried to be all things to all people, had to charge about twenty-five percent more for their services than did the chain stores in the larger cities. In addition, the farm family was forced to select items from the limited variety of goods available. The mail order house could not serve as a complete substitute for the larger stores in the big centers, but they were very important to the farm families. The farm wife never had the privilege of window shopping and, moreover, she did not have a chance to learn about differences in goods. This lack was disadvantageous enough when shopping for food products, but it became a real calamity when it came to clothes, furniture, and appliances. For many years the lack of attractive clothing and furniture made the farm family feel somewhat inferior to the city folk.

Many farmers circumvented the local stores by ordering from wholesale houses in Minneapolis or St. Paul. The bonanza farmers had an advantage because they were well known and could readily charge their groceries and other items at Twin City firms from year to year if crops did not do well. The smaller sized farm operator could not easily obtain credit with these firms and was required either to send money with his order or to order C.O.D. Homesteaders resented the fact that the catalog houses insisted on cash because most of them were in the habit of charging from fall to fall at the local stores and wanted to do the same with mail order goods. One homesteader said that they later learned to trust the mail order house when they discovered that the "catalog houses always made good; they would back up their guarantees. Back in them [sic] days if you did not like the product they would give you your money back."

Butler Brothers of Minneapolis was favored by many because the homesteaders thought that they had the most complete line of farm and home needs. They were more popular than even Sears Roebuck or Montgomery Ward. Another favorite mail order house was T. M. Roberts of Minneapolis. The mail order houses cut heavily into retail sales of merchants in Fargo-Moorhead and Grand Forks. The presence of this competition forced the local merchant to become more aggressive in merchandising and the farmer profited from this. As an interesting sidelight, the increased use of mail order houses helped create a demand for rural free delivery.[4]

Many of the small town stores made an earnest attempt to serve the basic needs of the community. Several of the older folks who were interviewed felt that they liked the "old" stores better than those of today because there seemed to be so much more in them. No doubt it was one-stop service and the customer took what they had or went without, for even though they had a large number of items in stock, there was still comparatively little selection. Many were pleased with the "real department stores" which had not only groceries but also hardware, a ready-to-wear, a clothing, and a "dry goods" department. A "department" may have been nothing more than a different counter, but sometimes there were walls to separate them. It was not uncommon to have a post office or even a bank in one corner of the store.

Stores were much the same in all of the small communities of the Valley, except those established by some of the large bonanza farms in conjunction with their farming operations. The country store tried to fulfill the every day needs of the community and as the Askegaard-Halland store advertised, it "sold a complete line of goods down to your last need—the coffin." In 1881 Wahpeton had only two small stores which sold groceries, rough clothing, and boots, but "hardly any shoes" for Guy Divet said, "Anyone seen outside of town wearing shoes was a marked man." On one occasion the Bettschens of Arthur got in a shipment of "real expensive fur lined coats for men at $65 each." They considered themselves fortunate to find them very popular and were not left with any of these "luxury" coats in stock.

Each fall entire families made their annual trip to the community store to prepare the children for the school year. It was an all day trip to go to "Hope with Mother and Dad to get our winter clothes, shoes, overshoes, mittens, caps, etc." Each child was supplied with "two suits of underwear, a new pair of pants, a new pair of shoes, stockings, a shirt and a sweater,—this was just school stuff. All the clothes they wore at home was [*sic*] homemade." Although the Halland-Askegaard store at Comstock was originally established to serve the Askegaard bonanza, it evolved into a full-service community store which sold a full line of groceries and dry goods as well as drugs, paints, oils, harnesses, and even caskets.

A full line of machinery and other large items was available. If not in stock, they could be ordered. Steamship tickets were sold to all ports. Because David Askegaard was active on the grain futures market, the store also became a "brokerage center" for the Comstock area residents. Lunches were served to the general public and to the bonanza labor force. The Dalrymple bonanza, which had its own store and received regular shipments from a wholesale house, occasionally had to buy from the local store. When small items were needed to replenish the stock of the cook car, the cooks were allowed to go and make the purchase themselves. But when major items were required, Oliver Dalrymple himself went. On one occasion, when the hired men had forgotten to bring their blankets with them, Dalrymple purchased six dozen at the Bettschen store at Arthur.

In addition to the general store, the settlers were also served by the peddler who went from door to door. He added variety to country life for he was a contact with the outside world. The farm family waited for his appearance as much for his visit as to buy his goods. It was a big event for the children, too, for sometimes he had a stick of gum for each of them, not unlike the Watkins, Raleigh, or Jewel Tea man of a later date.

Some peddlers worked on such a limited scale that they went from farm to farm on foot carrying two suitcases of goods. Others used a horse and buggy and had a wide variety of goods, even though they only had one or two items of each. They sold pencils, writing paper, blackboard slates, tinware (pots and pans), cutlery, cheap jewelry, cloth, some tools, and any other commodity that they thought they would be able to sell. If the farmer did not have cash, he could trade old rubber, rags, brass, copper, and other items that the two might agree upon for exchange. The peddler or "road agent" was quite likely to trade some item for lodging, supper, and breakfast. Many had regular places where they stayed on their rounds.

Some farms, like those of the Probstfields and the Woodwards who lived close to a large center, were constantly bothered by peddlers. During January, February, and March the Woodwards experienced "a book agent covering Dakota on foot . . . a traveling agent selling broadcast seeders for wagon boxes . . . a book agent . . . a machine agent from Racine, Wisconsin [who] wanted to stay night. We could not refuse although we do not like to keep strangers. . . . Two Dutch peddlers . . . we traded a little just to encourage them to go on breaking roads." Appreciated by some and a nuisance to others, the peddler filled a need in his day, even though the price of his service was high.[5]

Illustrated Costs

Even with computerized checking accounts, few families today know what their actual living costs are. In this respect we have made little progress over our ancestors who kept even fewer records. Probstfield was an exception, but even he left limited records of personal expenses. In 1874 the total expense for his family including eight children was $469.18, broken down as follows:

Previously itemized $258.16 for foods, followed by assorted products such as lye, car oil (kerosene), garden seeds, matches, drugs, brooms, chickens, Grange dues, and machine oil, which totalled $69.65. Clothing, thread, needles, paper collars, towels, table cloth, and other cloth items cost $43.90. Books, stationery, postage, and newspaper subcriptions added another $15.77. More books, shoes, and mending material cost an additional $18.80. Tobacco and pipes, in addition to home grown tobacco, which cost another $6.80 was a small item when compared to "saloon expenses" at $56.10, which brought the total to $469.18.

These expenses were probably above average for a family of eight children even though the Probstfields relied heavily on home butchering and gardening. Homesteaders were warned that they should allow at least $100 for food expenses for their family from the time they arrived at their homestead until the first year's crop was produced. But this amount probably was not adequate for the mid-1870's in the Valley. Those who came later did not have to bring all the necessities of life with them as their predecessors had done, for they could expect to buy hardware, seed, lumber, machinery, livestock, clothing, and food in stores on the frontier.

H. D. Hurley, manager of the Kingman farm and director of the

First National Bank in Fargo, listed his family expenses for 1891 as $976.58 and in 1895 as $986.51. His total annual household expenses for nine people, including the hired labor, were $1,806.65 and $2,195.65 respectively. The Hurleys were prominent people, and it can be presumed that their personal expenses would be higher than those of other families of similar size.

For the initial pioneers even the services of a professional barber, which society takes for granted today, were not available. The wearing of long hair was not their way of reacting to society; it was the result of the inconvenience of getting it cut. Parents served as barbers for their children and grownups exchanged these services with each other. On February 18, 1877, Probstfield's neighbor, Mr. Harris, came over to cut Probstfield's hair and to have his hair cut by Probstfield.[6]

Obviously, life was more simple in those days. Services were limited and the pioneer farmer was generally too isolated to take advantage of even the few that were available. Although prices of both goods and services seem low by comparison to prices nine decades later, dollars were limited and the farm family was forced to produce many of its goods or go without.

FOOTNOTES

[1] Hobart, "Pioneering," VII, 203; Probstfield; Bettschen interview; *Warren Sheaf*, July 15, 1891; C. H. Frey, letter July 10, 1966; Mrs. Fay Purdy Pruett, interview by Donald Berg July 21, 1966.

[2] Hovde, p. 10; Evert, Ch. III, p. 4; A. Overby, "Sod House Days," p. 9; Frey letter; Mrs. August Hoppe, interview by the author May 23, 1968; Mrs. Erwin Tweton, interview by the author July 28, 1968; Divet, NDIRS, File 69; Elton, *Vaalhovd*, pp. 36, 38; Olsen interview; Pratt interview; Thortvedt, NDIRS, File 332; *Moorhead Independent*, Jan. 5, 1900, p. 45; Probstfield; Stafne, p. 27; Woodward, p. 82.

[3] Probstfield; *Hope of the Prairie*, p. 12; Gunkelman interview; Pratt interview; Pruett interview; *Warren Sheaf*, Aug. 6, 1881; O. Overby, *Retrospect*, p. 24; Divet, NDIRS, File 69; Woodward, p. 82.

[4] Probstfield; Atkeson, "Women in Farm Life," p. 189; Power letter to Allen, Moon, and Co., St. Paul, Minn., Jan. 13, 1891; NDIRS, File 309; Pratt interview; Emil Ankerfeldt interview; Edwin Ankerfeldt interview; Frey letter; Hobart, "Pioneering," VII, 196. Charles Hobart noted that when he was plowing sod during the early 1880's he seldom wore his cowhide boots. He took them off for two reasons—he liked walking in the freshly plowed earth, but more importantly, he was interested in saving his expensive boots.

[5] Pratt interview; Bettschen interview; A. Overby, "Sod House Days," pp. 10-14; Woodward, pp. 68, 72, 102; *Hope of the Prairie*, p. 12.

[6] Probstfield; All information on price of goods contained in this section came from the Probstfield diary between 1873 and 1896. All purchases were made in Moorhead with the exception of a few specifically named items which were secured in Fargo; O. Overby, *Retrospect*, p. 24; Crawford, NDIRS, File 290; Murray, pp. 94-99; Clarence H. Danhof, "Farm Making Costs," p. 350; *The Record*, Jan. 1896, p. 16; Woodward, p. 88. The Probstfield photographs were taken at the Flaten Studios in Moorhead, Flaten's part as a photographer in the area is most significant for he took large numbers of area pictures. These are the best collection outside of those taken by Haynes, the official Northern

Pacific photographer. For a history of the country store see Gerald Carson, *The Old Country Store* (New York, 1954). This book follows the store across the nation into the midwest. What might have been true of any store in the area was a typical frontier country store on display at the World's Fair exhibition at Philadelphia in 1876. The *Philadelphia Merchant* carried an article on it entitled, "The Omnibus Store." These stores covered the countryside in those days. Carson described them as follows:

It is a country store, continues this contemporary account of the little store, that seemed to have everything with tea, sugar, coffee, spices, molasses, dried fruits, etc.

It is a hardware store, with cutlery in variety, axes, rifles, divers mechanics tools, kitchen utensils, agricultural implement, bar iron, nails, etc.

It is a shoe store, and men, women, and children can alike be accommodated with foot wear.

It is a confectionary store, and there's a goodly row of glass jars of candies for the sweet tooth.

It is a drug store, and medicines, dyestuffs, paints, varnish, putty, tar, etc., are at your service.

It is a trimming store, and pins, needles, thread, tapes, ribbons, etc. await your call.

It is a jewelry store, with adjuncts of clocks, watches, violins, and jews harps.

It is a hat store, and you must not be positive that bonnets are not on hand.

It is a brush store, and bristles and broom corn are in readiness for a customer.

It is a crockery store, and you may buy queensware, earthenware, glassware, and stoneware.

It is a book and stationery store, equal to the ordinary requirements of the vicinity.

It is a tobacco store, and smokers, chewers, and snuffers can be supplied.

It is also the postoffice, and the merchant is the postmaster. He will have almost any article you can call for, the trade paper said, and will most agreeably make a note to get what he is just out of. Carson, pp. 192-193.

To give a better picture of the cost of living of those days, the following list, taken directly from the Probstfield diaries, provides actual cost and quantity of goods purchased in Moorhead by the Probstfields. When making comparisons with today's prices, the purchasing power of the dollar and the amount of labor it took to earn that dollar must be taken into consideration:

January 1873	lamp chimney ....$	.30
August	8 yards of calico shirting	1.00
September	Probstfield boots	6.50
	Mrs. Probstfield shoes	2.00
	table cloth	3.30
	baby chair	1.50
October	2½ yards of cloth for pants $1.35 per yard [probably wool]	3.35
November	10 yards gingham [women preferred gingham to calico for dresses because it was much more durable. One woman claimed that a calico dress would wear out in four weeks.]	1.70
December 1874	10 yards muslin	1.60
	9 yards of unbleached muslin, 16¢ per yd.	1.44
	5 yards cloth for boys pants, 45¢ per yd.	2.25
	2 yards flannel, 40¢ per yd.	.80
	6 yards calico, 12½¢ per yd.	.75
December 1874	Purchase of $9 worth of Christmas toys at Bergquists to be paid for with two cords of dry wood. Included were:	
	2 toy books	.30
	4 ABC books	.50
	5 tops	1.00
	1 doll	.50
Christmas foods:	1 pound candy	.40
	1 pound filberts	.30
	1 pound chestnuts	.30
	1 pound peanuts	.30
	3¼ pounds cheese	.65
	2 pounds peaches (dried)	.50

	2 quarts cranberries	.50
	1 pound raisins	.25
	4 cans oysters	2.20
	Traded beef on the bill at $.08 per pound.	
February 1875	3 pairs ladies white hose	.90
April 1874	4 yards print goods	.50
	2 yards wash goods	.40
	5 yards denim	1.00
September 1875	Contracted with Tailor Leems for a suit of clothes to be paid for in vegetables and wood. $40. Wood to be delivered at $4.50 a cord. Sixteen days later the suit was picked up.	
September	Purchased a set of plates, cups and saucers	2.00
October	2 skirts	2.75
May 1876	3 straw hats for boys	.75
June	12½ yards calico	1.00
August	Ten music lessons, one hour each, for Mary from Mrs. Partridge	5.00
November	shoes for Mary (age 14)	5.50
	Also $5.50 worth of cloth to be paid for by cord wood delivered at $4.50 a cord.	
December 1880	bed and chair from Luger Bros.	
	14 yards dress goods at 25¢	3.50
	10 yards of goods	.90
	1 skirt	4.00
	spittoon	.65
	6 pair ladies white hose	2.25
	2 suits of clothes for boys (ages 12 and 14)	16.50
June 1881	Five volume History of England	2.50
July 1880	Purchased set of Britannica, 21 volumes at $6 per volume to be paid for as they are produced and sent. Four years later to the month the final volume was sent paid for. [The History of England and the set of Britannica were still intact in the Probstfield house in 1969]	
August 1881	10 yards crash [coarse linen for toweling]	1.20
	10 yards Cheviot [wool cloth]	1.50
April 1883	violin string	.15
	cigars	.15
	2 pair overalls	2.00
	pair of suspenders	.25
May	large iron kettle	4.00
	buttons	.15
	thread	.10
June	2 gallons interior house paint	3.50
July	suit of clothes and suspenders	10.50
	tea pot	.65
	pen	.05
July 1886	14 yards skirting at $.12½	1.75
	4 yards oil cloth at $.25	1.00
August	pair of spectacles	2.00
	[Oscar Overby recalled when a man in his neighborhood purchased a pair of "store glasses" and was so amazed at the things that he saw that he became lost on his way home from Cooperstown.]	
November 1886	41 yards of muslin	3.15
	26 yards of calico at $.07 per yd.	1.82
	51⅕ yards of muslin at $.06	3.36
	17 yards cotton flannel	1.95
December 1886	10 yards of dress goods $.07 per yd.	.70
	Christmas expenses	.80
December 1887	pair of spectacles	1.00
February 1889	Probstfield was elected to serve in the state senate. He	

suited himself for the trip to St. Paul by purchasing a pair of boots, cap, overcoat, underwear, socks, shirt, collar, necktie, 2 linen handkerchiefs, muffler, watch for $41.75.

November 1889	shipment from Plymouth Clothing Company, St. Paul, express	.70
	suit for Walter, age 12	6.00
	overcoat	5.00
	suit for Arthur, age 10	5.00
March 1890	overalls for Walter, age 13	.75
February 1890	dress hat and shoes for Probstfield	4.25

On three different occasions, once in 1883, another time in 1890, and again in 1896, Probstfields had family pictures taken. In 1883 a picture frame for every member of the family of eleven children and one for the parents was $10 for all twelve frames. These were large, heavy, fancy frames. The family picture of 1890 was 18 inches by 24 inches. They had twenty-four prints made for $18.

CHAPTER VII

Trails to Rails

ALTHOUGH nearly everyone in the Valley proper was within ten miles of a railroad after 1882, transportation, or the lack of it, proved to be one of the most trying phases of pioneer life. The settler was not only isolated from civilization and markets, but even where transportation was available, it proved to be very costly. E. V. Smalley, writing in the *Atlantic Monthly* in 1893, discussed the problem of transportation and what it meant to the pioneer on the isolated prairie. After ten years of study and travel on the Great Plains, he concluded that "in no civilized country have the cultivators of the soil adapted their home life so badly to the conditions of nature as have the people of our great Northwestern prairies."

Smalley criticized the American system of settling on isolated individual farmsteads instead of following the traditional European and Asiatic pattern of residing in agricultural villages. Smalley contended, and correctly so, that isolated farmsteads proved to be a great burden to each individual farmer, for even if the land were completely settled with a farm on each quarter section, neighbors, on the average, were a half-mile distant. It was his opinion that even the Russian *mir* (communal farm village) was well advanced over the American way of scattered farms.[1]

Early Travel Conditions

A striking feature of transportation within this system of isolated farmsteads is the amount of travel that was done on foot. Because it was the quickest and most economical method, it was very common for early settlers in the Valley prior to 1872 to walk the 100 miles to Alexandria for flour and mail. A sack of flour was divided into two fifty-pound bags and one carried over each shoulder. People walked great distances even in winter. During the first winter (1871-72) everyone in the Buffalo River settlement was busy making oak skis. Hudson's Bay employees did not use skis but snowshoes made out of twigs and roots. The Norwegians used skis which they made in their homes. Soon the Hudson's Bay men realized the advantages of skis and began to use them.

To save on travel, the six men in the settlement on the Buffalo River agreed that one man should get all the mail each week from the post office at Georgetown, seventeen miles away. At the Woodwards, who were isolated, one of them walked the eight miles cross country to Fargo once a week to get the mail. On January 9, 1888, between blizzards, Walter Woodward set out to get the mail even though it was thirty-eight degrees below zero at the time. When he had not returned by late afternoon his mother became worried because there was a six-mile stretch between farms. She watched for him through her "spy glasses" until he appeared. After the railroad came through, distances to the "outside" were shortened considerably and Narve Roen recorded that he had to carry a 100-pound keg of nails only seventeen miles from Moorhead to his home at Comstock instead of going to Alexandria for them.[2]

There was a constant flow of men walking past the Probstfield farm three miles north of Moorhead because the Red River trail which most people followed in their journey to the northern end of the Valley was nearby. On November 19, 1873, Probstfield wrote, "Pete Genon from Frog Point stopped to stay overnight—wrote some letters for him." On January 5, 1875, "two Norwegians stopped overnight— lodging and breakfast 50¢."

Many pioneers stopped at the farm and asked Probstfield for advice about a place to settle. Because he was the first settler there he had seen the Valley in its completely natural state and knew areas that were subjected to flooding and other conditions. For example, on June 11, 1877, he "took [an] immigrant out to look at S. E. ¼ Section 10 Twp. 140 R. 149., he was well pleased," Probstfield was a well educated man and often wrote letters for others in the community. He was well aware of the need for such good deeds, for as former manager of the Hudson's Bay post at Georgetown both he and Mrs. Probstfield had witnessed many signatures which were only an *X*.

For several days in succession in the fall of 1873 Probstfield reported that individuals had spent the night at his place, some with teams, others on foot. All of these were not exactly welcomed. "A lousy Norwegian tramp imposed himself for lodging on us last night. *Found lice on floor.*" On May 17, 1875, "Lousy customer called again and I put him out." On November 29, 1877, "Man and half-breed woman stopped overnight. On their way to Pembina on foot." The number of complete strangers who stopped by, especially in the spring and fall, became excessive at times and on April 16, 1878, Probstfield "denied lodging and supper for the first time tonight. This thing is getting too thick to stand it."

Some of those who stopped were quite brazen. On one occasion "a tramp came boldly into the kitchen and stole a loaf of bread while we were in the front room. Edmund got on a horse and caught up with him at the culvert above here." However, travelers continued to impose upon the Probstfields for at least another two decades. On January 25, 1887, when the temperature was twenty-one degrees below zero, "a man with a double rig [two teams and wagons tied in tandem] called, his feet were frost bitten. He left at noon." While the teamster was still there "a pedlar [*sic*] stopped for dinner and oats for horse, traded 30¢ worth of towels." During the summer people stopped for another reason. On June 30, 1896, "temperature 92°. Very hot. More than 20 people stopped to get a drink of water." [3]

Although it was customary on the frontier to be charitable to travelers, so many came to the Probstfield's that they were forced to charge for their services. On November 21, 1873, two men from "H. B. Co." with six yoke of oxen stopped for supper, lodging, and breakfast. They had their own hay for oxen. Apparently he had an open account with Hudson's Bay Company and billed them periodically for aid to their employees. On another day a company teamster with two teams stopped. He had supper, lodging, breakfast, and dinner plus a place for his teams for $2.

Occasionally Probstfield was "taken in" on good will missions which left him somewhat bitter, as, for example, on April 30, 1878, when he "spent an hour with 2 yokes of cattle to haul some Cannuchs wagon out of mud in coolie [*sic*]—broke a chain—was paid liberally with 10 cents to mend chain—Thanks!" February 9, 1874, "W. Chaney and Mary stopped with mule team, drunk as a lord. Charged $1.50 to stable mules and dinner for Chaney and Mary." On March 11, 1874, Lou Parant, who stopped by many times, arrived with his team and "was intoxicated. Charged $1.50 for supper, lodging, breakfast, stable and hay for horses." For many years this was the standard charge for such accommodations and the Probstfield home remained a popular overnight stop. Later, when the Moorhead-Northern branch of the Great Northern was built near their farm, many people used the railroad tracks as the easiest passageway across the otherwise nearly trackless prairie.

Because of the lack of improved roads, stage coach drivers frequently appeared at Probstfield's farm to ask for a "pull." A coulee near the farm was a bottleneck, and not until the railroad was built could travelers cross that low spot with ease. At 11 p.m. on April 5, 1875, a stage stopped when the driver, who had been going in circles, was unable to find the "road" to Moorhead. These "roads" were nothing more than trails across the prairie, and even those familiar with the area had trouble following them in the dark.

One night, when the Crawfords were returning to their farm from Wahpeton, "the intersection was hard to find. Father had to get out of the sled and creep on hands and knees to find the track by the lumps that stuck up above the snow that had been blown in and covered all other trace of track. Once started on the road the horse kept it. How that was done, I don't know." "At night there are many areas in this boundless sea of undulating land where there are no lights visible. . . . Mr. McAuliffe got lost coming from Fargo last night. He has lived here for seven years. He wandered around until he found a [hay] stack with a path leading from it to a house where he remained until morning." On a foggy, dark, November night the Woodwards heard someone lost on the prairie "haloo for two hours." They assumed he was closer to their neighbors because of the volume and the direction of his calls and because of the fact that he apparently could not see the lights they had hung out. Therefore, they did not do anything.

Christine Hagen Stafne remembered that when they first crossed the Red River on Rich's Ferry at Wahpeton there were nothing but military trails west of the river. When the Hagens went to Fort Abercrombie to exchange eggs, butter, and cheese for groceries, they walked along the military road which ran from Abercrombie to Fort Totten. The children were always impressed by the prairie grass which stood high on both sides of them as they walked down the trail. Ox cart trails and river crossings made of logs remained the standard until about the time that Erik Stafne became county commissioner in Richland County in 1892 when some of the first township roads and bridges were built. One of the bridge crews roomed and boarded at the Stafne home while constructing a bridge over the Wild Rice River in the late 1890's.[4]

In the spring of 1876 "Peter Wilson and wife called [at Probstfields] on their way from Goose River to Moorhead [and] left 8 sacks of wheat on account of bridges being rare and bad roads generally." There were many days each spring when travel was possible only on foot or on horseback. After winters of excessive snowfall, such as in the springs of 1888 and 1897, conditions were so bad that at times foot travel was prohibitive.

On April 12, 1888, Edmund Probstfield "tried to drive to Andrews place but had to return on account of bad roads." On March 30, 1897, "Tom Keelan and wife stayed night [at Probstfields]—could not stay on the road. Roads impossible. Sabin all under water—stock suffering. No trains leaving on account of wash outs. Fills all washed out. Boys had to leave sled at Bosshards and ride horses home." Probstfield, at still another time, vented his feelings about the roads: "Land all dry as dust where not kept wet by the *Blessing* of Roads through the farm." When conditions were good, walking to town was taken for granted. On February 12, 1889, Probstfield "walked to town for Alliance meeting—no meeting. Yet a most beautiful day—mild and pleasant and roads good. Attended I.O.O.F. meeting . . . Fargo . . . meeting over at 12 midnight. Walked home in storm—arrived 1:30 a.m."

Probstfield was not the only one to comment about roads or the necessity of providing for travelers. Many farmers living near Mayville and Portland stopped at the O. O. Hovde farm while hauling wheat to Fargo where the price for it was a few cents higher. Most of them had food for themselves and for their oxen or horses, but they used Hovde's stove to heat their coffee.

Charles Hobart frequently hauled his wheat to Mayville, Buxton, or Hillsboro in order to obtain a few extra cents for it. In 1891, while hauling wheat the twelve miles to Mayville, he found that the road near his farm was fine because it was frozen. However, where the road ended, it became necessary to cross fields making travel difficult because the plowed ground thawed out faster than the packed road and "the loaded wagon sunk into the gumbo." ("Gumbo" was the local term used to describe the heavy, sticky soil of the Valley, especially the Fargo Clay soil along the Red River). It clogged the wheels so badly that they would not turn. Hobart had to use a spade frequently to clean out the wheels as he continued to Mayville. In the spring of 1894 Probstfield commented that the "wagon wheels [are] *solid* mud, cannot turn. Roads were never worse." [5]

R. D. Crawford noted that the thirteen-mile trip from their farm to Wahpeton "was no pleasure ride." There were four farms along the road with a stretch of ten miles between the Webers and the Matuffins. When they went to town they generally had a load both ways—grain on the way in and provisions on the return trip. With four horses hitched to a load of wheat the trip took at least three and a half hours in each direction, if conditions were good. Crawford said that in his first year on the frontier (1882) he got to town twice, both times in the summer. He complained that besides the rigors of climate, poor living quarters, and low wheat prices, all members of his family suffered from isolation because they were located "in a no man's land between two trails, no cross travel, and no nearby congenial families. The Germans and Norwegians who gathered in settlements were far better off."

Iver Madsen, who was born near Wheatland in 1891, got to Wheatland frequently when he was young for it was only about four miles from his house and he could ride with the cream wagon. However, he was eleven years old before he made his first trip to Fargo, forty miles away. Over sixty years later he remembered distinctly the morning the family drove to Wheatland in a buggy in order to catch the train for Fargo and then returned late on the same day.

In spite of the isolation and the poor transportation, news on the frontier spread surprisingly fast, according to Guy Divet. News was spread by "volunteer courier"—whoever was in town reported news of any great event that had come by telegraph. Divet reported that news of President Garfield's assassination reached their home less than twenty-four hours after it happened. Whenever such important news was learned, settlers took it upon themselves to inform their neighbors who lived within a two or three-mile radius. A few miles was nothing to walk, winter or summer.[6]

There were times when it was more practical to use horses rather than walking. Riding often presented problems too, for those who have used horses know that they can act rather peculiar at times. Horses with sore shoulders, itchy necks, or those that were just "temperamental" and knew how to "throw" the collar or the harness, were all part of the horse age. Charles Hobart's patience was tried by a balky horse named Doll. "Once when Lizzie [Mrs. Hobart] started to church . . . the pony stopped and after a while threw herself down and would . . . not get up. Crane and Fred came and got her up and then Fred went into church with Lizzie. She did not balk with him." On the following Sunday "Lizzie started to church and got down to the corner and Doll would go no further. I went down . . . and gave Doll a lesson that she never forgot; at least she never balked again."

On another occasion Hobart had a close call when he was hauling wheat to Mayville with his two most reliable horses, Gypsy and Norma. Hobart was walking beside the wagon to keep warm, and to avoid losing the reins he had tied them together and put them around his back. As the wagon was going down into a coulee he slipped and fell. The lines went under the wagon and Hobart was dragged, face down in the snow, at the rear of the wagon all the way downhill before he could get the horses stopped.

Once when Walter Woodward's horses became frightened by immigrant wagons in Fargo and tipped the buggy, he "hung on to the lines and was dragged on his stomach. When he let go of the reins the horses stopped to look around." Fortunately, there were no mud holes on the Fargo dirt streets at that date. A few years later, when the streets were of wooden blocks, the belly ride would have been much more painful.[7]

Even the slow, plodding oxen used for transportation were occasionally responsible for excitement. Dennis Carpenter left Minneapolis in 1872 with his ox team, his wife, and their six children. Late one afternoon they came upon a body of water with a beautiful grove on the opposite side that looked like an ideal campsite. In crossing on a narrow beaver dam one of the oxen reached down to drink and stepped off the dam, nearly tipping the covered wagon, with the mother and six children aboard, into the water.

Oxen were extremely hard to handle when they were hungry, thirsty, or warm, but for farm work and overland travel they were popular because they were much cheaper than horses and were more resistant to disease. The ox could travel all day and eat all night, something the horse could not endure. The ox could provide for itself by grazing while the horse needed grain and dry hay when doing hard work. However, oxen were so slow that unless there was a load to be transported, the pioneer was likely to walk rather than to ride the ox cart.[8]

Besides poor roads and temperamental animals, highway robbers occasionally interfered with frontier travel. Stories, that are difficult to document, indicate that a favorite "hold up" spot for robbers was under railroad bridges. At the end of the season farm laborers, who were paid in cash, usually walked along the tracks to town or to the nearest train depot. It was then easy for the robber to appear and take money from a single man walking along the tracks. However, local residents occasionally had similar encounters.

By the late 1880's the Probstfields made daily trips to town to sell produce from their garden. Since everyone knew that they would be returning to the farm with cash, it was only logical to expect that they would be held up for the day's vegetable receipts. These holdups did occur and nearly always at the same spot—at a bridge near a cemetery about half way between Moorhead and the Probstfield farm. On October 12, 1889, second son Justus Probstfield was held up and robbed of $5.40. On October 18, 1890, Mrs. Probstfield was returning from Moorhead at about 10 p.m. and "was held up by 2 road pads at bridge close to cemetery—but they let her go, saying it was a mistake—so it was if they wanted money. It was undoubtedly meant for me [Probstfield]." A few days later Justus, who had been working on a threshing rig near Davenport, was returning home and noticed that he was being followed. He had deposited "his money with Nordberg who was in the restaurant in Fargo" and was not bothered after that on the way home because the "tramps" knew what he had done.

Highway robbers were not the only ones to bother Probstfield. Because his farm had such a fine timber stand and was close to Moorhead, it became a target for lumber thieves. As early as January 5, 1873, his third year in Oakport, he stopped a stranger with a team of horses hauling a load of logs out of his woods. Later that year he "found Striebel [a neighbor] cutting wood on our land." In February, 1878, Probstfield noted that he finally caught the man who was stealing cord wood, but others took his place and thefts continued through the years.

Later Modes of Travel

As the pioneer farmer prospered he was no longer content to use the heavy work horse and the lumber wagon for both his business and his social trips. However, it was not until well into the 1880's that the light road buggy and driving horses were common in rural Red River Land. Buggies, to the early settler, were a luxury he could ill afford; furthermore, he needed a heavier wagon for farm work. Even though the Hobarts were familiar with buggies from their experience in farming in New England, they did not possess one of their own until the 1890's when Hobart purchased a second hand rig in Mayville for $50. Lizzie "was pretty well pleased for now she had a buggy as well as a pony."

Bicycles were not used extensively in the area until the late 1880's because they were very expensive and their use was limited to the harder surfaces of streets in town. There was an almost complete lack of good rural roads until the turn of the century. The *Warren Sheaf* advertised standard sized bicycles with twenty-four or twenty-six inch rear wheel and a twenty-four inch front wheel. They were all equipped with molded rubber tires. Fancy bicycles, as advertised in the *Sheaf*, were priced from $85 to $145 each—obviously a luxury item for the "local dandy" comparable to present-day sports cars.

Though quite expensive, in later years the bicycle provided much enjoyment. By the summer of 1891 the Probstfield family had four of them. "Bicycles were popular, it seemed as though every man, woman, and child had one. For two summers at least, I almost lived in my bicycle suit and high boots." Mrs. Glaspell, wife of a Jamestown attorney, felt that any little excuse served its purpose to make a bicycle trip down town. Not all cyclists had special suits and boots. In the 1890's bike racing was as commonplace as baseball and horse racing. Bicycles were frequently rented out by local livery stables. Fargo had the Sycamore Cycle Club that was very active from 1895 through 1916. The same was true for many of the smaller communities.

Before bridges were built across the Red River and some of the other larger streams in the area, river crossings were few and hazardous. The standard fee for one person to cross the Red River at Georgetown by ferry was twenty-five cents. At a few places, where the ferry did not have an operator, the potential passenger could use the ferry only when he happened to find it on his side of the river. Because stones were scarce, it was not always possible to build stone paths across the river beds for solid footing. Sometimes a combination of manure and logs was laid on the river bed to make temporary crossings. Fortunately for most travelers, rivers in this area were a serious obstacle for only a short season each year, usually in early spring.

After the ferry service at Halstad was discontinued, there was a period of about five years when a barge was used as a "floating bridge." After the *J. L. Grandin* went aground in the flood of 1897, one of its barges was anchored west of Halstad until the first permanent bridge was erected in 1902. Because this early bridge could not be economically built high enough over the river to avoid the ice and spring floods, it was dismantled each spring to permit the ice flow to pass. During such periods a standby ferry service was provided.

The livery stable was common to every community in the days of horse travel and often it was housed in the largest building in the village. It was natural for the livery stable operator to become engaged in the "taxi" business for people who arrived by train. As the town grew, the livery operator found it profitable to have a few wagons on hand to provide dray service from the depot to the local stores. Mr. Cook of Warren, who originally opened a livery stable in the late 1870's, found that public demand for dray service was sufficient to make it profitable to hire a man just to take care of that business. He also supplied horses as well as buggies or bicycles for those who wanted to do their own driving—a forerunner of the car rental service. When the automobile became more popular, many of the more alert livery operators transformed their businesses into auto-liveries.

Eventually the automobile competed with the horse and with the railroad as the chief means of travel. It was several years, however, before adequate roads were constructed for automobiles. The first graded road with bridges in Clay County was built in 1883 and stretched from Moorhead to Glyndon. Moorhead and Fargo did not eliminate dirt streets in the business area until the early 1890's when they installed treated cedar blocks. The blocks were laid in a smooth sand foundation, sprayed with hot asphalt to seal them, and then covered with a light sprinkling of sand.

It looked as if transportation would be much improved, but eighty inches of snow in the winter of 1896-97 created an unequaled flood condition. Much of Northern Pacific Avenue, up to Broadway, actually floated away for the wooden blocks were seen going downstream. The area most seriously affected by the flood was the southeast portion of Moorhead because of the extensive flooding of the Buffalo River. All the land from Sabin to Moorhead was under water. After that flood the streets were gradually rebuilt with more permanent materials. In 1904 electric street cars were adopted in both Moorhead and Fargo and in 1910 Wahpeton and Breckenridge had them. About 1918 Wahpeton also covered the surface of the streets in its business area with a form of asphalt.

E. V. Sarles, banker and prominent Traill County citizen, had the first steam driven automobile in Hillsboro—a Stanley Steamer. O. A. Pearce, a bank cashier, had the first car in Page. In April, 1905, the local paper reported that "O. A. Pearce ran over Will Berry's greyhound with his automobile last night. That's going some." In 1909 when Pearce took over the Ford agency in Page, new Model T's were selling for $850. By 1912 Model T prices had climbed to $1,025 for a "five passenger car fully equipped with nickel trimmings, electric lights, storage batteries, electric horn, a windshield, speedometer, and a top."

Pearce, however, was not the pioneer in the auto business in Page; the Murphys had established a Buick dealership in 1908 using the livery barn for their place of business. Later that year Murphy opened a garage where he employed an "expert mechanic from Minneapolis" after adding the Maxwell, E.M.F. 30, and Studebaker cars to his agency. Their first automobiles were sold to Fargo customers. The Murphys were early agitators for better roads after an experience in 1913 when they were forced to follow a Model T Ford in their Dodge for a distance of fifteen miles from Casselton to Buffalo.

The Model T driver was unable to get his car out of the ruts, hence the Dodge could not pass. After similar experiences people agitated for a road fund and better roads.

In 1912 the Ernest Krabbenhofts drove their E.M.F. (later called Studebaker) from Sabin to Raleigh, North Dakota, about fifty miles south of Mandan, a total of 260 miles. There were no sign posts to aid them in the three-day trip across the roadless prairie. Since there were no service stations, they had to purchase gas at hardware stores. It was also in 1912 that the citizens of Halstad organized a twelve-car motor caravan to Mayville. There were no graded roads, so one "pilot" car was sent out ahead, with six men in it, to mark the road. A "pathfinder" car, which led the caravan, followed the confetti trail of the pilot car. Reos, Buicks, Metzes, and Fords were in the tour promoted by the two Halstad auto liveries. There were several flat tires and each time the entire caravan stopped to help change the tire.

James Holes, Sr., a pioneer citizen, had such distrust for these new roads that he always called the weather bureau in Fargo before he left by car to make sure no rains were predicted. He made regular trips from his home in Fargo to his farms at Hunter. The Bernard Holes' first car in 1916 was a "real sporty one with side curtains." Their second car was enclosed. Mrs. Holes also drove the car and traveled the two and one-half miles to school to get the children during rain showers. One of her experiences was that every time there was a heavy rain she had to take off her shoes and stockings and pull the mud out from between the fenders and wheels otherwise the car was unable to move. When asked what kind of car they had in 1916, Mrs. Holes replied, "A Ford, of course."

John McGrath was one of the first car owners in Barnesville. On a trip home from Minneapolis where he had purchased the car, he had to back up several of the hills because reverse gear was lower than first gear and hence had more power. He sent several postcards home from towns along the way and as a joke mailed the last one at Rothsay, only fourteen miles from his destination of Barnesville.

All of the discomforts of early automobile travel were not caused by poor roads. Christine Hagen Stafne felt that "these machines were powerful and noisy sounding affairs whose tires were constantly having blowouts and even the shortest trips necessitated [pumping up] . . . the tires at least twice. No, the early cars were never a joy to me. I could always plan on something happening." In 1910 Stafne traded eleven horses for an Overland and later switched to Chandlers and to Fords. At Gunhild Stafne's wedding in 1908, fourteen automobiles were counted. Some had traveled as far as thirty miles.

The Overbys pioneered in automobiles in the rural Cooperstown area where they purchased a "Black Company motor buggy with a crank on the running board. . . . I remember the day Pete and I [Oscar Overby] went to Cooperstown to claim the strange horseless carriage. With an instruction book and a short lesson in driving, Pete started out for the farm; I followed with the road team and buggy. All horses were tremendously afraid [of the car], so I had my weak moments enroute, especially when Pete's motor stopped puffing."

Later when cars became more numerous, lines of Model T's stranded in the mud were not unusual. "A common sight was that of a man in his Sunday suit on his back in hub-deep gumbo, under his car trying to shovel out a path for his mud pan." Even though cars were troublesome, they were an improvement over "a buggy-full of people in their Sunday best splashed and soaked by a sudden shower." In one last nostalgic reflection, the thing Overby liked most about the buggy was the "gentle softness of the colorful robes with their romantic fringes . . . an indispensable piece of equipment for the gallant suitor." [9]

FOOTNOTES

[1] E. V. Smalley, "The Isolation of Life on Prairie Farms," *The Atlantic Monthly*, LXXII (Sept., 1893), 379.

[2] Evert, Ch. III, p. 4; Glaspell, "Incidents in the Life of a Pioneer; p. 184; Tweton interview; Probstfield; *Hope of the Prairie*, p. 10. Many people are not sure about the real difference between an ox and a steer. A steer is a bull calf that is castrated at a young age to be quickly fattened for beef. An ox is a bull that was left to grow into a full sized animal to develop a big body and power before it was castrated. On the average it weighed at least 900 pounds or was three years old before it was castrated.

[3] Probstfield; The Probstfield farm was not far from the Red River cart trail. Many of the Hudson's Bay Company teams crossed over the Red River at Georgetown and then swung northwest crossing the Goose River at Portland. This was sometimes called the Hudson's Bay trail from St. Paul to Pembina. Robert Stanley, a teamster on a thirty-five wagon freighting train that made this journey, reported that each wagon was drawn by six mules. This is one of the few references to mules used in wagon trains in the Valley. The train that Stanley worked with on his first journey hauled lumber for government fortifications. On Stanley's second trip the wagon train followed what he called the Kittson Trail which stayed closer to the Red River and crossed the Goose River near Caledonia. The trip from St. Paul to Pembina and return took two months and teamsters were paid $25 for the trip. After making a few trips as a teamster, Stanley became a stage coach driver out of Breckenridge. In 1875 he filed a homestead claim in Caledonia Township, Traill County, and became a farmer. Although Stanley reported using mules, horses and oxen were standard power for the Red River Carts and later freighting trains. Arthur Overby, president of the Wilkin County Historical Society, has established that English owners of the Red River Carts almost always used horses while the Scottish owners used the less expensive oxen; *Hillsboro Banner*, June 28, 1956.

[4] Probstfield; Crawford, NDIRS, File 290; Stafne, pp. 9, 23, 41, 44; Woodward, pp. 29, 89, 195.

[5] Hovde, p. 21; Hobart, "Pioneering," VIII, 126; Probstfield.

[6] Crawford, NDIRS, File 290; Divet, NDIRS, File 69; Madsen interview.

[7] Hobart, "Pioneering," VIII, 119-122; Woodward, p. 89.

[8] *The Warren Sheaf*, May 8, 1968, a story written by Mrs. Henry Dipple about her grandfather, Dennis Carpenter; Glaspell, p. 186; Hobart, "Pioneering," VIII, 210.

[9] *Pioneers*, pp. 40-41; A. Overby, "Sod House Days," p. 18; Thortvedt, NDIRS, File 332; McMahon, NDIRS, File 195; Woodward, pp. 24, 34, 54, 89, 124, 153, 195, 209; Crawford, NDIRS, File 290; Probstfield; O. Overby, *Retrospect*, pp. 20-24; Pratt interview; Gunkelman interview; Frey letter; Conversation with Sam Syvertson, Great Northern Agent, Barnesville, Minnesota, Dec., 1968; Glaspell, p. 16; *Moorhead Independent*, Jan. 3, 1900, p. 5; Henry Reitan and Johanna Opgrande, interview by the author July 2, 1969; *Hillsboro Banner*, Sec. III, June 28, 1956, pp. 6-7; Elton, *Vaalhovd*, p. 35; Hobart, "Pioneering," VIII, 222; *Warren Sheaf*, Nov. 6, 1890, Aug. 20, 1881; James Fay, interview by Donald Berg, Aug. 11-12, 1966; *Our Page 1882-1957*, A. A. A. Schmirler and Page Community Committee (Fargo, 1958), pp. 93-95; Holes interview; Goggins letter; E. F. Krabbenhoft interview; Stafne, p. 60.

CHAPTER VIII

Storms, Stems, and Stamina

Wᴵᴅᴇʟʏ circulated stories about flat, wind-swept lands, flooding and droughts, lack of trees, grasshoppers, and long, hard winters may have prevented prospective settlers from coming to Red River Land. Many people in those days thought that this region was no different from the rest of what was then called the Great American Desert. Still, many came, and soon found that one of their big problems was snow. O. A. Olson describes what probably was the typical reaction of the homesteader when he awoke to find his shelter covered with snow:

> The snow made a mound of my shanty,
> So that day was no different than night,
> I added a length to my stove pipe,
> For the drifts had obscured it from sight.

While the Valley proper is not an area of particularly heavy snowfall, in some years it does have excessive amounts of it. This phenomenon is especially likely when snow comes early and accumulates during the long season. When excessively heavy snowfall does occur, another hazard accompanies it; often, especially after winters of deep frost, there is extensive flooding in the spring because the ground cannot absorb moisture from the melting snow.

The winter of 1874-75 was so severe that Congress appropriated $150,000 for relief purposes in the area. In spite of that significant amount of help, however, over one-third of the homesteaders in Polk County abandoned their claims before 1876 because the winter was too long and cold and the spring season too wet. This undesirable weather retarded settlement in the Valley until 1879. Probstfield's first report of serious prolonged storms was in January, 1874, when strong northeast winds, heavy snowfalls, and intense sub-zero weather set in. The winter continued in this way until March 14: "Storm—stables filled with snow all through about four feet," he wrote. "Shoveled snow out of stables all day. Uncovered 6 head of cattle completely buried in the snow in stable. Shoveled snow [on the yard] for 3 days. Took little calf into the house." While most farmsteads were located on the open prairie, Probstfield's buildings were quite well sheltered from all directions by a natural grove. During the severe winter of 1874-75 he also recorded the temperatures: "January 3, 1875, 7 a.m. −24°, noon −12°, 8 p.m. −18°; January 8, 1875, 7 a.m. −34°, noon −27°, 8 p.m. −33°—very strong wind from N.W." On January 19, 1875, he noted that from the first of that month to the nineteenth the temperature had never gone above zero.

The winter of 1875-76 was both severe and long, for the weather was consistently bad from late November through January. The Red River, from which Probstfield watered his livestock, was completely frozen over on November 15. On November 29 it was twenty-nine degrees below zero and the river froze another four inches. Mrs. Probstfield was quite ill during this cold period, but no one dared to go for the doctor because of the severe weather. Probstfield himself attended his sick wife and sat up until 1:30 a.m. to keep the "fires roaring but could not keep warm alongside of the two red hot stoves." The strong southeast wind penetrated Probstfield's house in spite of storm windows and double walls.

It is little wonder that many other settlers who were living in single boarded shanties covered with tar paper could not withstand the winter and had to move in with others or abandon their claims. By January of 1876 the ice on the river was thick enough to be cut and stored. The last day of the cold spell that had started in November was January 31 when the recorded temperatures were: '7 a.m. −23°, noon −18°, 8 p.m. −23°." It was so cold that Probstfield once again had to take "Brindle's calf" into the house to keep it from freezing in the stable during the night.[1]

The winter of 1876-77 started much like the two previous ones and caused fourteen deaths in the Moorhead area. However, after a few severe December storms the weather turned deceptively mild. A large number of men and teams of horses overtaken by severe storms while on the road were forced to stop for shelter at the Probstfield farm and sometimes they had to spend several days there before they could move on.

The early settlers who had experienced the severe winters of the 1870's had learned what to expect of Dakota weather, but those settlers who came after 1877 were unprepared for the harsh winter of

1881-82 with its exceptionally early and heavy snowfall. By that time people had come to rely on the railroads and blamed them if they did not bring needed supplies during storm periods. But even with great effort it was not always possible for the trains to get through. The following winter the settlers along the Fargo and Southwestern Branch of the Northern Pacific learned that storms could stop the trains. The Northern Pacific had finished construction of a line to Lisbon on December 22, 1882, but in early January, 1883, a snowstorm blocked the road so completely that it remained closed until April 9. The effect of this closure was disastrous for the early settlers in this region.

An editorial in the *Barnes County Record* that was not as friendly to the Northern Pacific as was the *Fargo Argus*, criticized the railroad. The editorial, as reprinted in the *Argus*, read:

Somebody sharpen a stick and punch it into the ribs of the Northern Pacific railway officials, and see if we can't get some wood and coal hauled in. They have been sending out circulars telling the people what they are going to do, and as yet that is all they have done. Mr. McDonald our station agent, informs us that he has written the state of affairs here to headquarters every day for two weeks, and as yet has received no satisfactory reply. If we cannot have fire let us have war!

In an article in the *Argus* captioned, "General Manager Haupt Dislikes Having the Northern Pacific Blamed as Being Cruel to the Settlers," the road's defense was stated in this manner:

We want to see that the stations through Dakota are all supplied. My object in issuing circulars was to induce the people to look out for themselves in advance. Settlers are very apt to be improvident and not lay in their supplies of fuel until winter has set in, and the road is obstructed by snow blockades; they will be very importunate in their demands for fuel, when the company is not in a condition to respond immediately to such appeals.[2]

Dakota settlers soon discovered that it was more economical to buy coal or to import cordwood from the forested areas of Minnesota rather than to cut and to haul their own from the scattered groves along the rivers and streams in this area. But this easier way of getting fuel also had its disadvantages, for once they started to buy fuel, they often neglected to put in an adequate supply to last them throughout the winter. To aid the farmers in their dilemma, the Northern Pacific, and later the Great Northern, developed extensive nursery operations. The purpose of growing those trees locally was multifold: first to use them to establish snow catches along the railroad tracks; second, to prove the fertility of the soil; third, to encourage the farmers to plant trees around their homes for more comfortable and attractive living conditions; and, fourth, to enable the farmers to eventually develop their own fuel supply.

In 1872 the Northern Pacific started planting trees along their tracks to serve as snow fences in hopes that enough trees would break the wind and thus modify the climate. The railroad set an example and established nurseries about every twenty miles along its lines with Colonel Mike Smith in charge of the entire tree planting operation. Colonel Smith was also appointed nurseryman at the Casselton operation and was fairly successful in his endeavor. However, much of the initial $80,000 appropriated by the road for this project was spent in vain because most of the cuttings died in shipping before they were planted. Another reason for the failure of the project was the fact that there was still "too much Indian in the soil," meaning that the native sod was not properly broken and prepared so that trees could grow in it.

In spite of those early failures, the railroads persisted in their tree planting projects and by the 1880's many of the trees they had planted were growing. Once the Northern Pacific was refinanced in the early 1880's and construction was renewed west of Bismarck, tree plantings became a part of the overall plan of railroad development. Over two million trees were planted in 1882 alone. Individual farmers followed the example set by the railroad. Torkel Fuglestad, who had worked in the forests in Norway and knew the value of trees, planted his own trees because all the wooded claims were already taken by the time he arrived at Hannaford. He gathered seedlings from the woods along the Sheyenne River and temporarily planted them in freshly broken ground where they remained until he could prepare a more permanent seed bed for them. Now, more than eighty years later, a fine grove stands on the farmstead as evidence of his wise planning.

Charles Hobart came from New Hampshire where he had to clear away trees in order to prepare fields for farming and was delighted to find virgin prairie where no trees interfered with the plowing. However, after a few winters of shoveling his way out of the snow that barricaded his house at Cummings, he decided that trees were a necessity on a farmstead after all—at least as a snow break. He ordered 1,000 box elders and 1,000 cottonwoods, but when the letter notifying him of shipment came, he found that the ordered cuttings had arrived at the station in Buxton two weeks before! All of the cottonwoods had died in the meantime, but the box elders did very well and it was not many years before he had protection from the storms and snow.

Iver Madsen was forced to buy coal and wood in Wheatland for fuel because there were no trees available to him near his farm. To economize, he bought his coal in carload lots and sold what he did not need to his neighbors. The carload price in the 1880's was $4.20 a ton, about $1.00 a ton savings over ton lot purchases. But even with the economy of carload buying, Madsen worried over the excessive cost of fuel. He secured additional land for a tree claim, planted seventeen acres of trees to satisfy government requirements, and in time acquired an adequate fuel supply. Madsen used about fourteen cords of wood each year for winter heating.

The heavy snow of October 15, 1880, came so early that the settlers were not prepared for winter. Most of them had not even stored an adequate supply of food or fuel and "many were forced to use hay and corn for fuel." An article in the *Warren Sheaf* stated that "never in the history of Minnesota have we heard of it being so cold for so long a time, as it has been this winter. It froze the water in the reservoir of our cook stove, when there was a good fire in it—the stove, we mean, not the reservoir." John Tofte of West Fargo had a fourteen by eighteen foot house and a small sod barn. During one of the blizzards of 1880 the barn was completely covered by snow, but luckily there was a high pole in front of the barn door which stuck up through the snow and thus indicated where he had to start shoveling to get in. In the storms of 1888 his house was often completely buried and he had to shovel snow into his cellar to enable him to open his door and tunnel out of his house.

In the winter of 1882-83 Charles Hobart was caught short of coal in two blizzards. "The first time I had got out of coal I went to Buxton with a load of hay. They were out of coal but had a carload coming on that day's freight. It did not get in until so late that it was dark before I got anywhere near home." On his trip home he went off the trail in the blizzard and lost all concept of where he was until he found himself in a neighbor's bundle field (shocked grain) and from that point on he was able to guide his horses home. Hobart explained that in both cases he ran out of coal because the storms lasted so long and seemed to come one right after another.

Milford Stangeland and Peter Anderson, farmers near Fillmore, went twelve miles south to Esmond to get coal. But there was no coal at Esmond so they were forced to drive all the way back and then go on to Pleasant Lake, thirteen miles north of Fillmore. As they passed through Fillmore others joined them in the search. They were able to get coal at Pleasant Lake but on the way home they were caught in a blizzard and became lost. Since the horses seemed to know where to go, the drivers let the reins drop and the horses found the way home.

According to Mrs. Michael McMahon, the Larimore area had a mild winter that year that lasted until early March when the area experienced a three-day blizzard, the first of several during the month. On the third day the men became worried about "Grandma" who lived all alone in a shanty a short distance down the road. They found the shanty but it was "drifted clear over. Johnnie called but [received] no answer. They dug the snow away and Murphy opened the door. Johnnie stayed outside crying and cussing the country. Grandma was O.K. She and the dog had kept warm." [3]

Both Hobart and Probstfield agreed that the winter of 1886-87 was a cold one and a low of forty-six degrees below zero was recorded in the Valley. The temperatures were so low and stayed there for such a long period that Hobart was forced to get a better stove. He explained his predicament as follows:

I took my wood burning stove and changed it for one that burned either wood or coal. Then I bought a supply of hard coal. We found we needed it to keep from freezing. The house was not built very warm, and we had a cold winter. I kept a record, and the weather averaged 19° below zero for six weeks in January and February. . . . We hung a carpet around the stove, shutting off three-fourths of the room; and then [sitting between the carpet and stove] we could hardly keep warm. But we were glad to get where the water was good, and into a house fairly good.

The Hobarts had learned their lesson and they made more serious preparations for the following winters:

As the house was neither plastered or clapboarded, it became a question of what we were going to do to get through the winter. . . . We arranged for your Aunt Lizzie [Mrs. Hobart] to go down to Fargo, and stay with the family there through the winter, while my father and I stuck it out on the farm. I boarded up the back door, built a small lean-to over the front door, for my coal, and banked the house all around the north side up to and over the eaves, and banked the rest of it, except the windows, up to the chamber window. I used horse manure, old straw, and anything that would do. In the spring it took fifty loads to haul it away. We were quite comfortable.

Probstfield, sixty miles farther south in the Valley, had similar heating problems. On New Year's Day, 1887, he recorded a low of forty-one degrees below zero at 8 a.m. and a high of thirty-two degrees below zero at 11:30 p.m. On the previous twenty-two days the warmest temperature had been two degrees below zero and the coldest was forty-six degrees below zero. Unlike Hobart, the Probstfields relied on wood for fuel, but even with two stoves going, they were forced to close off all the other rooms except the two where the stoves were located. Mrs. Probstfield "nearly froze while cooking the meals," even though Probstfield, like the Hobarts, had used manure and straw for banking the house.

Still farther south, along the Wild Rice River in Richland County, at the Crawford's the severe storms started on December 20, 1886, and lasted continuously until January 27, 1887. "The storm hit like an explosion. . . . The snow was so thick that it bothered my breathing. This was the winter . . . that Father put me out of a window twice to go around and shovel away from the door. In this blizzard . . . many people were caught." Those who died in the storm were later examined by physicians and were said to have died of suffocation, "smothered by the density of the snow in the air and the force of the wind." In one stretch from January 12 to January 22, there were persistent high winds and heavy snowfall. The family was snowed in for six weeks and during that period did not see a single outsider. To keep warm in their one-room house with its two windows, they boarded up one window completely and hung a horse blanket over the other. There was little they could do about the doorway for they had to be able to get in and out. Finally they were forced to break a road to get some wood because they were running low. When they eventually got to town there was over a "half bushel of mail" waiting for them mostly from relatives in Vermont who were anxious to hear how they had come through the storm.

The Crawfords watered their cattle at the Wild Rice River about a mile from their farm. The winter was so cold and the water in the river was so low that it started to freeze solid forcing them to look for places where the river was spring fed. They chopped a hole in the ice at the spring and waited for it to fill with water, but the cattle could drink faster than the spring could provide water so it was a slow process. As the river froze the water became polluted from dying fish and the cattle did not want to drink it. The Crawfords were able to get water for household use from a small well of their neighbors' but that was not adequate to supply their cattle so they were forced to continue to water them from the Wild Rice River.

Mrs. Woodward, an immigrant who came from Wisconsin, complained about the "horizontal snow storms" of 1886-87, and concluded, "There is no use trying to live here unless the blizzard is combatted with trees, and that will take a long time." By January 19 the drifts were a foot higher than the eaves on the machine shed and she predicted that if there was one more storm they would have to dig tunnels to all the buildings. It was so cold that when her son, Walter, walked to Fargo to get the mail, he wore a buffalo coat, an astrakhan coat, an under coat, three pair of trousers, woolen underwear, and woolen shoes, forerunner to present-day Arctic boots. During one blizzard a horse named Pete walked on snow banks covering the tool shed roof. When he broke through the snow and his feet hit the roof of the shed, he refused to move.[4]

The winter of 1887-88 started out to be quite mild, but on February 9, 1888, Probstfield noted the "temperature [was] −50° too cold to warm up the school house—could not have school." On February 15 Edmund Probstfield started for Sheldon, located along the Northern Pacific. A blizzard arose with strong southeast winds and the temperature dropped rapidly to thirty-five degrees below zero. The train got stuck and five engines were needed to pull it back to Fargo. Edmund never got to Sheldon. Storms came regularly after that until the middle of March when R. M. Probstfield recorded that the snow drifts were the highest he had seen in his nineteen years on the Oakport farm. In March, 1888, Mrs. Woodward ended the worst of her six winters in the area. On March 28, after four months of blizzards, snow was piled "mountain high and still coming." These blizzards of the spring of 1888 are the most severe ever recorded by the weather bureau for this area.

The winter of 1888-89 was a pleasant relief for the residents of the Dakotas. Kate Glaspell of Jamestown wrote on December 1, 1888, that it was so warm that the city council decided to celebrate the good weather with a parade. The men put on linen "dusters," and straw hats, and carried palm leaf fans and sun parasols. After the parade lunch was served in Elliot's Grove and then baseball and other summer games were played. Mayor Albert A. Allen made a speech "commiserating the suffering of the shivering people of the East," and said they should come to North Dakota. After the speech a photograph was taken of the crowd.

However, no one in Jamestown did much boasting about the warm winter in the following year, and the Glaspells, too, discovered that it could become quite uncomfortable in their "pleasant five room, one story cottage. We had never heard of a storm window, a double sash, so only one thin pane of glass protected us" from the sub-zero temperatures. The frost became so thick that in order to see out a hot iron was held near the window to melt the frost. On one occasion when the Glaspells were invited to a neighborhood dance, the temperature was fifty-two degrees below zero, "too cold to leave the horses out," so the guests walked to the dance through two feet of snow. "Trifles like that did not interfere with our pleasure in those early days." The pioneer on the prairie might not have agreed in all respects with Mrs. Glaspell who, after all, lived in Jamestown. The farmer's wife, for example, who did not get to town or see anyone beside the family from November until April, might not have called those storms "trifles."

Emil Ankerfeldt recalled that during the first big storm of the winter of 1890-91, his mother had gone to visit their nearest neighbors on the far corner of the same section, roughly a distance of a mile and one-third. A blizzard came up while she was visiting with them and Mrs. Ankerfeldt could not get home for seven days. No one ventured out of the house except to take care of the livestock in the barn.

The Divets were hauling wheat to Wahpeton with five wagons at a time in the early part of that winter. One afternoon a blizzard suddenly rolled out of the northwest and in the whirling snow Guy Divet lost track of the four wagons ahead of him. When he observed that his horses had also lost their sense of direction, he remembered what he had been told many times—not to wander around in a storm. Divet knew that he could withstand a night out in the storm because in addition to his warm clothing, he had two heavy horse blankets, twenty-six grain sacks, and some hay in the bottom of his sleigh. So he turned the horses loose and tipped the wagon box upside down for shelter, using the sacks, blankets, and hay for insulation. He awoke the next morning to find the weather perfectly calm and the sun shining brightly. His horses were munching on a nearby haystack and his home could be seen only one-half mile away. Another of the Divet men who had lost his way spent the night in an abandoned settler's shack and returned unharmed.

Charles Hobart was fortunate in this same storm because when it struck he was safely at home. But the next morning he said there "was not a door or window downstairs that [I] could get out of. I went upstairs [his house was a story and one-half] and jumped out of the west window into the drift." Snow continued to pile up so that by the end of February, Hobart "could and did start from a few rods south of the house and walked up on the drift and looked down the chimney with my hands in my pocket." Some of his neighbors were snowed in worse than he. "John Anderson had hard work to get out of his house and a man living just south of Burnetts . . . had to be dug out" and then abandoned his house until the following spring.[5]

The Winter of 1896-97

The weather bureau office was established in Moorhead in the late 1870's. From its records, newspaper accounts, and by word of mouth it is easy to determine that the winter of 1896-97 is generally recognized locally as being the most severe suffered in this area. According to Edgar Olsen:

The fall of 1896 and the spring of 1897 will be long remembered as a period of heavy snows, blizzards, and heavier than average spring rains. Hay stacks were covered with snow and it was nearly impossible to get hay home over the drifted roads. There was so much snow that we just took the top off the stacks, then, when the rains came, they soaked right into the stacks spoiling the hay. There was water everywhere. There was great damage to property and loss of livestock in the spring flood of 1897, but no lives were lost in our area.

Probstfield gives a running account of what that winter was like: November 26, 1896, "snowing and drifting all day—worst storm for years." A few days later his daughter, Dorothea, walked to Fargo to take the train to Sheldon where she taught school but "she was unable to leave Fargo because the railroad was blocked." January 3, 1897, "Perfect gale—snowing and blizzard all day—worse than on Thanksgiving Day. Everybody hugging the stove." The next day, "blowing furiously, snowing and blizzarding all day—general weather worse than yesterday. Animals all shut in—unable to feed them. Everything drifted up. Snowdrifts 9 and 10 feet high." From January 17 through January 22 his notations were identical: "blowing and storming all day." January 30, "blowing hard, snowing and blizzarding all day." On February 9 there was excitement at the Probstfields. "Train got stuck—conductor Baker and Brakeman came over and got horse and cutter to go to town." Several days throughout February, "blowing, snowing, and storming hard all day, another immense amount of snow on hand." Another train was stuck in the snow nearby on February 24 and it took a large crew to shovel it out. In early March there was a week of "blowing hard and blizzarding all day" and then the accounts taper off as spring drew closer.

For Mrs. Mahon the terrible winter of 1896-97 "started with a terrific blizzard on election day, early in November, with such piles of snow that never went off until April. Water flooded the whole Red River Valley that spring and some flooded areas were nearly fifty miles wide."

For Iver Madsen, Jr., who was six years old at the time, the winter was one of great excitement. After every storm, the Great Northern had to send the rotary plow out to clear the tracks because the regular plows could not get through the snow. After each storm neighbors went around checking every house to make sure the inhabitants could get out. At the neighbor's house just west of the Madsens, the rescue party had to dig a long tunnel to get to the door because snow was piled over the eaves. The Madsen barn had an eighteen-foot high wall on one side and before the men shoveled the snow off the roof the children could start near the top of the barn and slide to the road 250 feet away. Iver remembered his father telling about a storm in which snow completely covered their original small barn. By the time they dug down to one of the doors, the cattle were showing the effects of lack of air.

C. H. Frey, who was seven years old then, recalled that there were several times that winter when no one went out of the house for a period of from one to three days. After the worst storm, several of the small homestead shanties were completely covered by snow. He has no memory of any loss of life because of the weather "for the early storms had made them cautious and they kept adequate supplies of coal and flour on hand." [6]

Ada Lockhart Gunkelman was eleven years old when the big blizzards of 1896 and 1897 enveloped the Kelso community. She liked to play out of doors and had a particularly good time that winter for snow was over the door of the hay loft and right up to the peak of their high barn. Before any farm chores could be done after a big storm "Father and one man had to shovel out of the house." After they got out they shoveled snow away from the windows because "Father was worried about not enough air getting into the house" which was two stories high. After the house was sufficiently uncovered, the men shoveled their way into the hay barn door and to the chicken house that was completely covered. The pump house and the water tank shed were also buried so that they had to carry snow in pails to melt it for the livestock, the chickens, and the household use for more than a week.

That winter was the worst the Andrew Overbys had experienced since leaving Wisconsin in 1880. Late in the fall of 1896 Overby was cutting wood by the Red River about seven miles from his farm near Wolverton. It seemed to be "such a nice day, but suddenly a blizzard was there." Crossing the unmarked prairie on his way home visibility was zero "and the oxen began acting strangly" because their eyes and nostrils were crusted with ice. Overby was forced to walk in front of them and keep their eyes and nostrils free so he could make it back to the farm. It was fortunate that his sleigh was well loaded with wood when the blizzard hit because he needed it all before the winter was over and he used all that he had stockpiled. Neighbors who ran out of wood had to use twisted hay for fuel or they sawed up their hayracks and burned them before there was a break in the cold weather.

The winter's worst single storm lasted about three weeks and is compared in intensity by the weather bureau to the three-day storm of March, 1966. When his house and barn were completely covered with snow, Overby gave up shoveling a path and instead cut a trap door in the roof of the house so that he could get in and out. He also had to brace the roof with poles to prevent a cave-in from the weight of the snow. The only part of the house that remained visible above the snow was the chimney; he added extensions to this as a precaution.

During one of the first storms he stretched twine from the house to the barn to serve as a guide. Later he had to cut a hole in the barn roof and brace it up just as he had done to the house. Because there was no loft, all the hay was stacked outside the barn and had to be forked into it through the hole in the roof. Like the Lockharts, the Oscar Overbys, the Jens Hagens, and others, Andrew Overby carried snow to the cattle in the barn where it was melted for water, because he could not get water to them and they could not get out of the barn. Overby had carefully stacked his cord wood alongside the house and each time he went out to do chores he carried a four-foot log back to the house where he sawed it into lengths that would fit into the stove.

Hans Krabbenhoft's father also sawed wood in the house much of that winter. He had to tunnel from the pump to the barn where drifts reached the bottom of the hay barn door. Krabbenhoft repeated an exaggerated story about that winter, one that was still in circulation seventy years later. According to the story, a settler had been keeping a seventy-five pound pig in a small three-cornered pen when the storm started. The storm became so fierce that the farmer had only enough time to put a door over the pen to protect the pig. The next morning the snow was so deep that he had to use a two-foot length of stove pipe to put down feed to the pig, and each day thereafter he had to add another two-foot length of stove pipe to his feed line until the storm subsided on the seventeenth day. When the snow finally melted that spring, a 400-pound hog appeared! [7]

The heavy snows of the winter of 1890-91 caused many anxious moments, but those same snows brought relief from the serious dry spells of the previous years. The resulting bumper crop was a turning point for many farmers who had decided that if the crop of 1891 did not prove to be profitable, they were going to give up farming in the area. The years after that until 1921 were encouraging enough so that there was even a serious overexpansion of farms and small service communities.

Floods and Drainage

The Valley was often exposed to excessive flooding in seasons following heavy snowfall. Because the Red River flows into territory to the north that is still frozen and because the river is almost completely lacking steep banks, flooding is an annual threat. O. A. Olson describes this uncertainty:

> You unpredictable Red of the North,
> You swelling cantankerous stream—

In the record flood in the spring of 1897 the water level was so high that in Dakota the Sheyenne, Wild Rice, and Red Rivers all overflowed their banks and joined to become one body of water. At the same time the South Branch of the Buffalo River and Whiskey and Stoney Creeks in Minnesota became one. The high water mark of the 1897 flood was imprinted on a tree at McCauleyville as a reminder of this.

The flatness of the Valley caused the early settlers to be apprehensive of potential flooding. Therefore, they carefully avoided settling in the low areas. One of the best examples of this trend is found in the history of the Felton region in northeastern Clay County. It was initially opened in 1880, but was not well settled until the state drainage canal was completed in 1895. The only crop that could be successfully harvested there in the early years was native prairie hay, but even haying was not extensive until after the canal had been built. In 1899 four hundred carloads of prairie hay were shipped out, most of it to the timber country.

Even the highest spots in the Valley, which had been selected by the cautious first settlers, were subject to occasional flooding. For example, in April, 1876, Probstfield spent the day making a roost for his forty-nine hens and three roosters in the shanty joining the house because it was "the only dry place I can find." This was the second time in his first six years at Oakport that his farmstead was threatened by flood waters. Probstfield had selected his Oakport farm site in March 1859 when the Red was at a very high level. In August, 1874, heavy rains caused some flooding. But the Probstfield farmstead itself has never been flooded, not even in the spring of 1897. On July 4, 1877, his crops were severely damaged by a flood so intensive that on that same day, eighty miles down the Valley at Fisher's Landing on the Red Lake

River, small buildings had to be tied down to keep them from floating away, and the river boat "discharged passengers into the upper story of the Russell Hotel." During the summer flood of 1901 the Sands Brothers of Alvarado lost 600 acres of grain to flooding and farmers in the area lost many horses from swamp fever spread by flies and mosquitoes.

It is estimated that from forty to sixty percent of the Red River plain was subject to periodic swamping, but the earliest settlers ignored drainage, which could have reduced this problem, or they simply chose higher ground. Bonanza farmers and other large-scale farmers avoided any section with low spots because they could not afford the additional cost of working around them. By the mid-1880's settlers were more numerous and so they were forced to occupy some of the lower areas. Proper drainage then became essential for a more intensive agriculture.

The drainage problem was most severe in the Manitoba portion of the Valley and by 1879 the provincial assembly had advanced funds for drainage there. Each year the project was expanded and in 1920 more than 1,342 miles of ditches had been dug, draining 1,103,760 acres and enabling 350,000 acres to be tilled for the first time. When James J. Hill constructed his railroad into the Valley in 1879, he became a champion for drainage and he constructed the first of many ditches financed by his railroad. His prodding and a gift of $25,000 were instrumental in getting the Minnesota legislature to appropriate funds for drainage. Progress was slow at first but by 1908 fifty machines were at work digging ditches.

In the North Dakota portion of the Valley, the drainage program advanced much more slowly. Only after intensive efforts by Hill did the agricultural agencies initiate drainage projects in Cass, Traill, Grand Forks, and Walsh counties. Because of extensive drainage, many counties in the Valley have seventy percent or more of their area in crop production, and some townships are nearly 100 percent tillable. Few regions in the world can match this record.[8]

Prairie Fires

The virgin prairie, even though it was the ultimate source of wealth, also offered one of the greatest threats to pioneer living. The native grass, which grew from two to eight feet in height, proved to be ideal for the rapid spread of prairie fires, the most dreaded phenomenon on the prairie. With few obstacles, such as graded roads, railroads, or plowed fields to stop them, prairie fires could spread so fast that no one could outrun them. A dugout, a water body, or a large plowed area provided the best shelter from a running fire, but because they were not always readily available, pioneers carried matches with them as the last desperate precaution. The reason for the matches is explained by Eva K. Anglesburg:

> But she could not reach that safe refuge;
> The shanty would soon be their pyre . . .
> Then into her mind flashed that proverb
> of the plains—Fight a fire with a fire!

Prairie fires sometimes covered large areas. One of the largest of such fires started north of Bismarck and spread east nearly to Jamestown. Alfred Sands said that in some areas around Alvarado the grass was so tall that plowing was almost impossible; consequently, many farmers, without giving a second thought to the eventual dangers, set the grass on fire. Such fires frequently ended in disaster. Prairie fires could occur at any season of the year but they were most common in the middle of a dry summer or after a frost in the fall.

In summer, the virgin prairie with its dry, matted grass and weeds of many years, "provided a perfect setting for the deadly fires which could be realistic nightmares for every family." There was little protection from these fires in the summer because fire breaks were not always present or were not kept cultivated. Fall, however, was by far the most dangerous season because of the great amount of dry stubble fields and the roughage stored around the farms. Many farmers were lax and sometimes they were so slow that the ground froze before they got around to working on their fire breaks. People on the bonanza farms did not suffer as much from prairie fires because in those areas there was more plowed land which greately reduced the fire hazard.

Railroads were both a curse and a blessing when it came to prairie fires. The Madsens faithfully plowed fire breaks around their buildings and their hay and grain stacks every year. They were threatened by a prairie fire once but, fortunately, they were saved by the Great Northern tracks less than a mile from their farm that served as a fire break. The Purdys of Wyndmere had a similar experience when a prairie fire, after burning several of their hay stacks, threatened their farm place. The fire was out of hand and the only obstacle in its way was the Northern Pacific Railroad track that ran just north of their buildings. But the track was enough to stop the fire and save the Purdys.

However, in many cases, it was the railroad that was responsible for the prairie fires. Mrs. Woodward recalled one fire in September, 1886, that was started by a spark from a Northern Pacific train and burned about 700 tons of hay. Most of the hay stacks were protected by plowed fire breaks, but this fire was so great that it jumped them. It moved so fast that additional emergency breaks could not be plowed fast enough to head it off. It eventually burned itself out. She stated that later the railroad company paid for all losses but "it is hay and not money that we need and want. We do not have enough hay left to last through plowing." Prairie fires continued in their neighborhood for another month that fall. Farms and schools were burned and some villages were seriously threatened. One fire in Central Cass County swept a path of more than ten miles in one day.

The Ankerfeldts also experienced fires which had been started by trains. Ankerfeldt reported that sometimes lightning also started prairie fires; other times farmers "just wanted to burn the blooming grass off [but after] the Soo Line came through sparks from the smokestack started lots of them. They had a big cover and screen on the smokestack but it didn't catch all of them." Plowed fire breaks and backfires helped stop fires, but "this was grazing country and the prairie was wide open," which added greatly to the danger.

Emil Ankerfeldt recalled an incident of the 1890's: "We were living at our second farm, Dad wasn't home, Mother and Uncle Ole were. We were just starting to build a new barn. We were playing by four hay stacks on the yard. Then there was the fire, I don't know where it came from but it came clean up to the haystack, then it went clean out, some gift of God." Ankerfeldt said there was no way to stop it because his mother and Uncle Ole could not fight it alone. A few days later another fire lit up the night sky for "miles and miles." They felt safe that time because "it was on the other side of the Soo Line."

September 27, 1886, a Great Northern locomotive set fire to the prairie near the Probstfield farm. Many acres of prairie as well as numerous hay stacks in the area were burned including nine tons of hay at Probstfields. "We all fought fire. Edmund plowed around [Peter] Lamb's stacks and saved them." The Lambs lived about a mile and one-half from Probstfield. If it had not been for a great deal of plowed land in that area, Moorhead could have been threatened because the fire was west of the railroad tracks so that they could not act as a fire break. On November 24, 1886, Probstfield "received check from S.P.P. & M.R.R. Co. $35 for fighting fire and loss of nine tons of hay."

Even though Probstfield's location along the river gave them an avenue of escape, they were aware of the threat of prairie fires. February 4, 1878, he noted, "prairie fires all around us." Five days later, "prairie fires still burning around us in all directions." On September 27 of that same year, "prairie fires all around, am worried about it spreading to grain stacks." The next day they plowed a fire guard all around the grain stacks that proved to be none too soon for in early October prairie fires came "right up to our plowing."

The Overbys at Wolverton lived in fear of prairie fires because some fire breaks in their neighborhood were not properly maintained and others were too narrow to be effective. Lack of roads and a limited amount of plowed ground added to the danger. When the Hovde farmstead was threatened by fire Mari dragged "their big Norwegian chest out on a plowed field and put their most valuable possessions into it." The Hovdes carried matches to enable them to set a "back-fire" if they were ever caught by a prairie fire.

The Hobarts' first close call with prairie fires came one spring in the early 1880's. The fire was noticed about 9 a.m. and they quickly set backfires around three farm places that were in the fire's immediate path. Several families fought the fire as it raged across the prairie until 5 p.m. when it "burnt itself out." In the fall of 1889 another fire threatened Hobart's neighborhood. "We ran the fire around Nicholis and Nelson's settings of grain. The boys took two horses and a foot-plow and I took three horses and the sulky plow. [Others] went to the house and helped the old folks protect the buildings. I helped Nelson plow around his remaining stacks." In September, 1882, a Hillsboro area farmer lost eight stacks of wheat from a prairie fire because he had not bothered to plow any fire break around his crop.

Prairie fires were especially bad in the fall of 1885 because of the dry season. While working with a threshing crew, some distance from his farm, Torkel Fuglestad had his first experience with prairie fire in October of that year. For three days he had smelled smoke and noticed a haze in the distance. When he noted that the smoke seemed to be coming from the general direction of his neighborhood, Fuglestad became worried about his family and went home. On arrival at the farm he determined that his house, his stable, and the hay stacks were in no danger, but that his wheat stacks were threatened. He had had a good crop that year and was happy to have one small and three large stacks of wheat to harvest from fourteen acres. The three large stacks burned in spite of his efforts, and only the small one was saved.

The loss of this crop forced him to go back to the threshing crew to make enough money for winter groceries for his family. Unknown to him, his neighbors threshed out the remaining stack of wheat for him free, and the stack yielded fifty bushels. Fuglestad realized how fortunate he was for other farmers had lost not only their total crop to the flames but also most of their livestock. That particular fire was not stopped until it reached the Sheyenne River, about twelve miles away. In spite of his narrow escape, Fuglestad made a blunder that fall that caused him to worry. He loaned his oxen to a neighbor after the fire for he did not need them while he was away threshing; consequently, he forgot to plow his fire break as protection for the coming year. Farther south along the Sheyenne River, fires threatened the Woodwards for more than two months in 1885. Newspapers reported fires everywhere in the area. One nearly burned the Woodward buildings but, fortunately, when they first noticed the fire the horses were all harnessed to the plows and so a fire break was plowed in the time that it took the fire to travel the three miles toward them. During that fall the trains were forced to stop running for a time because of the uncertainty of some of the bridges in the burned over areas. For two weeks in October the Woodward house was filled with smoke. "At times [it was] perfectly suffocating." Mrs. Woodward, who originally came from northeastern Wisconsin, said it reminded her of home when smoke from the Chicago fire filled the air.

R. D. Crawford portrays most vividly his experience with a prairie fire:

We had our baptism of fire in November, 1883. We made a firebreak around a bin of oats in the field over a mile from the house, which saved that. A half mile east of the house an uncle . . . had put up seven stacks of hay, about five tons each stack. Two evenings to a late hour had been spent in fire protection. We still had the buildings to be firebreaked on the north and seven stacks of hay [to be protected]. . . . In the afternoon of the second of November, we saw a boy get out of a wagon . . . and light the grass a half mile from the house. The wind took it northwest. Then the wind switched. . . . The stack of hay would be in danger . . . Father took me and brother Walter and went to the hay stack and started to set backfires.

Whipping out the line of fire adjacent to the stack and letting the other line burn in the opposite direction. We were busy and were not aware that the wind had changed [again] to the northwest, sending the fire straight at us. Father suddenly gave a shout, dropped the gunny sack he was beating the fire with, and grabbed us by the hand to run for the plowing perhaps 15 or 20 rods away. By the time we came near the plowing the smoke was thick and it was getting hot. We all went sprawling when we came to the plowing. As I rolled over to pick myself up the flames went by. By the time I was on my feet Father had started to run to the house, nearly a half mile. I helped Walter to get to the road (only a prairie track) and left him to come alone. He was nine and I was twelve. Father started a backfire as soon as he could, and carried it far enough west to intercept the oncoming fire, but had led out too fast so that the line adjacent to the house was about to get away. He motioned to me to whip that line out and threw his gunny sack to me and threw himself flat on the ground, exhausted. The backfire met the oncoming fire just as I got my line whipped out at the northwest corner of the yard. The main line of fire went by and spent itself in the pasture where the grass was short.

It was a close call. It was probably midnight when we felt safe to relax. Father had me lie down on the couch while he went out to look around. He got out a team and went southwest to the bin of oats, which he found to be safe. We finally got to our beds at 2 a.m. . . . At the time of this fracas my sister was only one day old.

After that experience the Crawfords took more pains with their fire breaks. They and others realized that fires could sometimes spread across sod clearings if the grass was not completely turned under. In some cases the fire got under the sod and burned through the break. For several years following that narrow escape from catastrophe, the Crawfords plowed two fire breaks around their yard and then burned the grass between the plowed rings.

Sod houses, if properly built with no lumber in the walls, apparently could withstand a certain amount of fire. One settler is known to have "escaped being roasted one night when a roaring prairie fire swept right over the roof of his house. He stayed indoors and let the elements roar." The *Hillsboro Banner* advised all settlers to build earth cellars a rod or two from their house as a place of refuge during prairie fires, blizzards, or cyclones. "It is the only form of sure protection for the settlers against wind, fire, lightning, and freezing." The practice of plowing and maintaining fire breaks continued in the area of bonanza farms until the late 1880's and in other areas until the late 1890's when sufficient land was under cultivation and roads were being built to make fire breaks unnecessary.[9]

Grasshoppers and Other Pests

There were also other natural disasters at the time. Farming and success in farming was often retarded by grasshopper invasions—actual or rumored. According to Ida Hall Crofford, "Grasshoppers darkened the sky in 1871 and ate the sides out of tents" that her father, Andrew Hall, had put up in Fargo. These four tents served as a family operated hotel that catered to Northern Pacific construction workers. While her father was out mowing the lawn around the tents, the grasshoppers "ate the linen coat from [his] back." Reputedly the grasshoppers got into the beds and "one big one landed on a dinner table and shed his outer covering right before the boarders." The hoppers hesitated at the Red River and piled up so fast at Fargo that they were piled "5 or 6 deep on everything." The *Moorhead Independent* reported that grasshoppers on the east side of the Red destroyed all the crops and the only thing that prevented the settlers from abandoning the area was the fact that they were able to obtain employment on Northern Pacific construction.

There was little grasshopper activity during 1872, but in the following year they attacked a wide area of the midwest. Much of Minnesota was systematically ruined from 1873 to 1877 before the plague subsided. Probstfield's concise reports unfold the entire story of the 1873 invasion:

> July 23, 1873 grasshoppers flying in
> July 26, 1873 grasshoppers landed in numbers
> July 27, 1873 grasshoppers eating oats
> July 29, 1873 grasshoppers destroyed oats, have
>   not bothered garden yet

An account of the 1873 plague in *The Record* stressed the invasion in the northern part of the Valley where grasshoppers were reputed to be so thick that they were piled up against fences and buildings eighteen inches deep. The railroad tracks were so slippery that the rails had to be sanded before the trains could start. One account from south-central Minnesota describes the intensity of the invasion in this manner:

Out of the clear blue sky came a calamity. The sun was darkened by flying millions of grasshoppers. Our doom was upon us. How serious it was we could not realize at the time. By nightfall the ground was literally covered. . . . The whole earth's surface for miles around was a seething mass of grasshoppers. Only those who were there and saw the terrible scourge can really comprehend the sight and what it meant to this settlement. These grasshoppers stayed and made a clean job of it. They laid millions of eggs in the ground. . . . I have seen hoppers so thick in a wagon road that the juice from crushed hoppers would run in a stream down the wagon tires. I must say that a boy, with bare legs and bare feet, was up against an awful problem to undertake to travel through a path in the grass or even an open road. The hoppers would soon have a boy's bare feet and legs raw and bleeding from the legions hopping against his bare limbs, and the continued squirming of those on the ground was awful.

The plague continued throughout much of the midwest in 1874 and, on July 17, Probstfield noted, "Grasshoppers heavy, oats badly damaged. Wheat not harmed yet. Buckwheat, beans, turnips, all cleaned out, corn, barley, potatoes, and garden only slightly damaged. Grasshoppers thick in Moorhead. [Andrew] Holes smoking them out of garden. We are smoking and chasing grasshoppers to keep them out of garden." His final comment was made July 25: "Grasshoppers left," and apparently for good reason—there was little more to ruin. At that time smudge fires were used extensively around gardens with apparent success, but whether it was economically feasible is debatable. Some farmers actually built smudge fires on wagons which they pulled back and forth across the fields. The big trouble with that process was that the grasshoppers flew out of range of the smoke and as soon as it had drifted by, re-entered the field.

At least two other methods were used to eradicate or to control grasshoppers. A sheet of iron about two and one-half feet wide and eight feet long was placed on runners and coal tar was put on the sheet. As the sheet was pulled horizontally through the field, grasshoppers flew up on it and stuck to the tar. Whenever this "hopperdozer" was filled, it was unloaded at the end of the field. Others used a flat, shallow tank, "sort of like a stone boat with sides," filled with about six inches of water and kerosene mix. The hoppers jumped into the solution and died. "We piled the hoppers up at the end of the field. They would really stink." Others used sacks which were held open with barrel hoops. Two men walked through the field holding the sack opening in a vertical position. "There would be a continual stream of hoppers going into the sack." Soon the sack was too heavy for two men to carry.

The grasshoppers reappeared in 1875, but Probstfield made no comment about them until August: "Grasshoppers bad again, did considerable damage. One 3½-acre piece of barley produced 31 shocks. I predict there will be no hoppers in 1876." Of his garden, which was always a mainstay of income, he wrote: "Prospects very poor for garden, have not sold a thing from the garden of over 3 acres yet. Garden pretty well eaten by hoppers."

Mr. Probstfield's prediction of no hoppers in 1876 was wrong, for they were back again and as bad as ever. James B. Power knew that the presence of grasshoppers as far east as Becker County was hurting prospects of the Northern Pacific land sales there. The Ericksons, farming just east of Hawley, had twelve acres in wheat, five in oats, and some potatoes as their first crop. Both the grasshoppers and a prairie fire ruined a portion of it. That year some homesteaders living east of Detroit Lakes started their move to the Valley. When they came face to face with grasshoppers near Audubon, they decided to return to their home. Probstfield confined his comments on grasshoppers in 1876 to July 15, 16, and 19: "Grasshoppers thick. Grasshoppers by the millions, tried to smoke them out of the garden. It was useless. Vegetables damaged." His final comment, for there was not another significant mention made on the subject up to 1900, was: "A good many [grasshoppers] deposited their eggs to brighten our prospects for next season. Farm covered with eggs."

In 1877, after five years of the plague, Minnesota's governor Pillsbury declared a day of prayer for "deliverance from this scourge. No one scoffed at this day of prayer. Even the atheists remained silent." How effective the prayers were cannot be determined but soon the grasshoppers started dying because they had become infected by parasites. On close examination they appeared to have "tiny red mites" under their wings which apparently were killing the grasshoppers.

The Overbys and the Hovdes each reported damage from grasshoppers during the 1880's. The Hovde's first crop of five acres of oats "looked so fine. Then one day at noon the sun was darkened suddenly and a cloud of grasshoppers settled on the little green patch. In an incredibly short time the field was completely bare. The hungry creatures roughened up the handles of forks and ate at the fence posts before leaving." Grasshoppers did not bother to any great degree after that until the 1930's.

Other pests also added to the misery of the homesteader. In 1873 Probstfield complained that gnats made it impossible for man or beast to work in the fields. Many farmers reported difficulty getting their oxen to work because they were fiercely bothered by gnats. The Madsens recorded that on some summer nights the mosquitoes were so bad that smudges had to be built to give protection to the cows and horses. Even with the smudges "the cows fairly bellow in their torment." People were bothered too because most houses lacked screens.

Not all of the pests were above ground either, for the Probstfield's gardening operation was also bothered by cut worms. Nothing was safe from grasshoppers, cut worms or whatever else bothered the farmers' crops. O. A. Olson faced every threat to crops in the area and he summed it up in these words:

> The cut worms chew; the wire worms eat
> All kinds of plants, including wheat.

Probstfield first reported cut worms in 1877 when his garden was nearly entirely destroyed by them. About the only defense available against such insects was actual picking by hand. In one day in 1883 the entire family hunted cut worms and "killed 1,600." [10]

Hail

Hail, always a threat to the man of the soil, made its impact on the area farmer and nearly every pioneer suffered from it. The ironic thing about the insects, the pests, and the hail is that the more they bothered the farmer, the more determined he became to fight back. The farmer's plight caused him to fight back either out of stubbornness, stupidity, or desperation. The hopelessness of the situation is once again described by Mr. Olson:

> Then hail destroys what hoppers can't
> And yet they plant.

Probstfield must have been an exception, for his extensive diary does not mention loss of crop due to hail, but, in spite of his good fortune, he was a co-founder and secretary of the Red River Valley Hail Insurance Company. Ada Lockhart Gunkelman, however, gave one account that could be repeated thousands of times with little variation. She remembered that whenever a particular crop looked good, her father would always remark, "It looks like I will have to give up a white hat this year," implying that Mrs. Lockhart could go shopping for new clothes. On one occasion while he was taking Ada into Kelso for her music lessons and to secure provisions, he repeated that favorite statement. She recalled how pleased he was with the looks of the crop. On the return trip they passed the same fields and saw that they had completely changed from a bumper crop into black ground because the hail had hit so hard while they were in town. The hundred pounds of sugar, the sacks of flour, the case of dried peaches, another of dried prunes, and a third of dried apples that he had purchased to provide for the threshing crew would not be needed that year, and Mrs. Lockhart would not get her "white hat." [11]

Drought

Wheat monoculture not only hastened the spread of weeds but it also must be partially blamed for some of the large-scale dust storms that, unfortunately, became part of life in the Valley. Many farmers who experienced the "dirty thirties" must have thought that the dust storms and drought of that time were the ultimate of natural disasters for many abandoned the area. When the Oscar Overbys were visiting Norway in the 1930's, they met a Norwegian native who had farmed in Dakota and returned to live in the woods of Norway for he "was sick and tired of the sand storms and bleak Dakota prairies."

Severe as the 1930's were, records indicate that the actual suffering from drought alone was more intense in the 1880's than it was in the 1930's. O. A. Olson, whose parents had lost a farm in the 1880's because of drought, and who lost a farm of his own in the 1930's for the same reason, knew well the farmer's determination against the nearly hopeless odds:

> With soil so dry that plants won't grow—
> They blindly sow.

Depressed wheat prices, weeds, and drought at this time gave the bonanza farms their first severe test and caused many of them to fail. The small farmer was plagued by the same conditions but was better prepared to face such disaster because generally he had a more diversified operation.

Localized droughts in Dakota in 1886 reduced grain yields by a third. The Woodward diary of April 10 reported, "The ground has never been as dry in seed time." Four days later the worst dust storm in their experience took place. "The wind blows without cessation and the dust flies in great clouds." The Fargo weather bureau estimated that the precipitation at this time was reduced by fifty percent in specific areas. The drought of 1887 was even more severe and widespread and very little harvesting was attempted in many counties. The drought of 1888 was spotty and localized and the crop in the entire area was below average. In 1889 the drought was described as "terrible." It was widespread throughout the central United States and "struck Dakota with great severity, producing much suffering and destitution."

J. B. Power, one of the great advocates of the region, admitted that low prices in addition to the drought had made farming a very costly enterprise for him from 1888 through 1890. Unable to pay his old and ever increasing bill at his grocery supply house in St. Paul, he explained:

The past two seasons have brought me heavy losses instead of profit on the farm, outside resources upon which I depended principally from land contracts, have failed me and it has taken my entire crop of this year to pay labor bills. Money cannot be collected here from farmers and banks are slow in putting it out.

C. H. Frey, who was born in November, 1889, at Harlem, North Dakota (now a ghost town), said that after the three dry years of 1887, 1888, and 1889, his parents were forced to give up their homestead and start over again in 1890 near Leonard. Probstfield's diary again gives a first hand, year by year, account of what happened specifically to him during that prolonged dry spell of the 1880's. Apparently he was not affected by the dry weather of 1886 for it is not until May 2, 1887, that his records indicate that things were "not right" as far as the moisture supply was concerned. "Took a survey of destruction done by the storm east of house and made the annex diagrams showing damage. All the dotted part is as good as scooped, in many places the ground is blown off as deep as the plow went last fall and the wheat still remaining on top of ground. Out of 55 acres . . . there are 30 acres destroyed."

The field Probstfield was describing is a quarter of a mile long and has railroad tracks and embankment on its east side. The north and west are protected by a sizeable grove of trees. That this field, a relatively small area and quite well sheltered, should be so thoroughly blown out, gives an indication of how dry and windy it was. On May 7, "winds. E. all day—clear hot blowing gale and carrying clouds of dust off wheat field into woods and river. Dust fifteen inches high is blown in piles about [the yard]. Nearly choked in house with dust. [The house was set partially in the woods.] Could not do anything today. Wheat seems to be totally ruined." July 24 he examined his crops and concluded, "Looked over barley in evening, dead ripe, but not worth cutting. Looked over wheat and find it poorest we ever had. About seven acres [of wheat] to cut yet for hay."

The season started the same way in 1888. On April 25 there was "strong gale, wheat blowing out as fast as sown. Boys are discouraged to sow more wheat." Conditions improved for about ten days later he had seeded 201 acres and moved his equipment to Douglas siding (about a mile and one-half south of Georgetown) to sow another 140 acres. After the grain was seeded the weather became very cold and windy. "We all took a good rest reading and guarding the heating stove." He celebrated the Fourth of July by walking "over the wheat fields and [have] seen enough of disgust—15 or 16 bus. per acre average is all I can possibly expect—the stand is not there to make more with the most favorable weather. Chances are good for less. Buckwheat is starting to climb over the wheat and pull it down." Those were his last remarks about the weather for the disastrous season of 1888. Little did he realize that the coming season would be the worst of all before the dry cycle would end.

Starting on May 4, 1889, Probstfields endured four days of "terrible storm [that] completely blew out 75 acres of grain." Because of poor weather in the next two weeks, Probstfield "discharged Wm Karges— as I see no prospects for being able to pay him. I don't see where the money can come from." On June 11: "No rain—grain drying out. This is the worst growing season we have had since 1864. Potatoes planted April 29 are not up yet." His comments about the growing season were finalized August 29: "Vegetables all drying up, river drying up so we can't hardly get or keep pump pipe in." They relied on the Red for their drinking supply as well as for their livestock.

Probstfield had gone through much in his nearly six decades and was prepared for the worst in 1890. At the beginning it looked like a repetition of the three previous seasons. "It was not fit to be out of the house at this place for clouds of dust flying. Nobody able to work it was a terror." On June 13 the worst was over and the drought was broken. "A terrific rain, after 7:45 p.m. The best we have had for three years . . . Jack MacDonald stopped in to put feed and flour in our granary to keep it from getting wet—went on home with team."

Probstfield's comments about the terrific rain correlate with the weather bureau records for June, 1890, was the wettest month since July, 1887. The weather bureau station was located at Center Avenue and Sixth Street on the second floor of Merchants Bank in Moorhead until July 1, 1889, when it was moved to Fargo. All weather reports west of the Red River were kept by volunteer observers, generally farmers or elevator men. Weather data were compiled by the War Department, using facilities of the Signal Service of the United States Army.

The long time average for precipitation for those months for the East Central Dakota Weather District is 13.30 inches, which is actually about 5.25 inches less than what was assumed average in those days. The details of the dry spell are given in a table in footnote 12 for Chapter VIII. The higher average probably was affected by the short period for which records had been kept and the relatively high average for the late 1870's and early 1880's. The average annual precipitation for the entire Valley is approximately eighteen inches, varying from fifteen inches near the American-Canadian border to twenty-one inches in the Wahpeton-Breckenridge region.

R. D. Crawford bitterly remembered those dry years and associated events:

The first dust storms began to appear three or four years after most of the sod was broken. It may be thought strange that such occurrence did not get wide publicity. It must be understood that *Dakota Territory* was being *promoted* and that anything at all derogatory must not appear in the local papers. Weather, wind, mosquitoes were only mentioned jokingly. The editor did not have to live on it, and besides the real estate men were watching.

Frost

Lack of moisture was not the only blow to the farmers locally during the late 1880's. Late and early frosts and a fluctuating wheat market at Chicago ranging from $2.00 to $.71 a bushel were also a decisive blow to both the homesteaders and the bonanza farmers. Because of steadily dropping wheat prices since their high point in 1882, many of the farmers were in no condition to take the additional burden caused by drought and frost. The spring of 1888 came early to the Cooperstown area and crops were well ahead of schedule, but by

June 1 they had almost withered away. Then heavy rains and intense heat came and the grain "bounced back."

On August 12 word came from the weather bureau in St. Paul that Dakota should be prepared for a hard frost on the sixteenth. Everyone made preparations—most of them futile. Fuglestad and many of his neighbors piled straw and other expendable material on the northwest corner of their grain fields and between 2 and 3 a.m. on the seventeenth of August they lit fires. Once he had lit his stacks, Fuglestad realized they would do little good because "it was like a drop in the ocean." After everyone in the neighborhood had finished with their fires, they "went to Froilands to have coffee, food, and smoke our pipes. It was so cold Froiland had to light a fire." By the time they were through visiting it was 4 a.m. and everyone was pleased to note that Froiland's thermometer registered 34°F. No one bothered to take into account that it was fixed to the chimney and a fire was burning. On the morning of August 17 the wheat fields were "frozen white—a new experience in this strange land." Fuglestad, not one to lament, said, "It was a hard blow—we were all in debt. Some harvested their wheat for chicken feed, some burned their crop and plowed, some rolled the wheat flat and plowed. I left the stand until spring, then burned, dragged, and seeded."

Fuglestad realized that any time spent on the farm that fall was futile because without grain he had neither feed nor cash income. "Then came the good opportunity. Barnes, a brother-in-law of [bonanza farmer] R. C. Cooper had gone bankrupt because of the poor crop." In an attempt to raise all the money he could, Barnes offered to sell timber from his land along the Sheyenne River at $.75 a load for all that one team could haul. Fuglestad accepted the offer and boasted that his team of strong, 1,200-pound oxen could pull "a good supply of elm logs." He stockpiled the logs on his farm hoping for a better year when he would have enough money to build a log house.

The following year, 1889, was dry in the Hannaford-Cooperstown area, just as it was in most of the region. Fuglestad's average yield from fall plowing was only five bushels. Most of his neighbors averaged that or even less. Fuglestad was lucky for he had plowed only twelve acres in the fall. The field that he had not touched in 1888 after the frost yielded eighteen bushels per acre. The fall of 1888 had been dry, but a heavy snowfall during the winter settled on the standing straw and soaked in during the spring, giving him additional moisture to withstand the low precipitation of the 1889 season. One neighbor, who was quite irked about the entire outcome, commented to

Fuglestad: "Yes, yes, the lazy ones get it. I who toiled and plowed get nothing. He who wandered to the woods and spent his time picking berries—he gets a crop." The price of wheat was up slightly that year because of the widespread Dakota frost. Fuglestad's extra thirteen bushels per acre helped him considerably.

Interestingly enough, the official weather records affirm that 1888 was most unusual. The temperature at the Moorhead station dropped to 20°F on May 13 and 14 and 28°F on June 1. Normally, the last date for the temperature to drop to 24°F at that location is April 22. The mean frost date at the latitude of Hannaford is September 20. On August 17, 1888, the official low for the weather station at St. Vincent on the Canadian border was 30.4°F.[12]

Short Memories

The newspapers in general reported the weather, both good and bad, but were much more likely to talk about the "Nile of America" or "America's only genuine banana belt" than about the adverse side of farming in Red River Land. The early newspaper sometimes blindly promoted the area. After weather conditions improved in 1890, and more specifically in 1891, the trying years of the late 1880's were often overlooked by the newspapers and the promoters. The newspapers of the area were quick to react to the bumper crop of 1891. The *Fargo Republican* printed a story that was repeated in several of the area newspapers. After knowing some of the hardships that the settlers had just lived through, the story seems too exaggerated to be acceptable. A special supplement to the *Warren Sheaf* of October 19, 1891, and many other area newspaper carried a long boastful story about the weather of the region and the bumper crop.

The promoters and newspaper editors were in an optimistic mood throughout 1891, but, as Crawford remarked, it was possible for the editors to speak in glowing terms about the wealth of agriculture for they did not have to make a living from it. In May, 1891, when a large number of Scandinavian immigrants arrived at Warren, the *Sheaf* commented, "They looked strong and healthy and by their labor they will help make our vast prairies blossom like a rose." [13]

The dry spell of the late 1880's changed the pattern of agriculture for the region. Many of the old timers expressed the fact that they, or their parents, had made up their minds to leave the Valley if 1891 was not a good year. In fact, many bonanza farms did sell out and settlers did leave. But those settlers who stayed reaped a golden harvest that helped them become well established. They enlarged their farms and profited from three decades of improved conditions which terminated with the collapse of farm prices in 1921. The bonanza farmers who remained diversified their operations or leased out much of their land on a share-crop basis.

FOOTNOTES

[1] Murray, p. 119; Probstfield.

[2] *Fargo Argus*, Nov. 19, 1881, Oct. 20, 1882.

[3] *The Record*, I (Dec., 1895), 15; Arnold, *Ransom County*, p. 67; *Fargo Argus*, Sept. 2, 1882; Fuglestad, pp. 13-14; Hobart, "Pioneering," VII, 211, 221; Madsen interview; Briggs, "The Great Dakota Boom, 1879-1886," p. 81; *Warren Sheaf*, Jan. 26, 1881; McMahon, NDIRS, File 195. A cord of wood measures 4 x 4 x 8 feet. In the 1870's and 1880's a cord sold for from $3.25 to $5.00 in the Moorhead area. Type of wood made a difference, but there was price fluctuation responding to supply and demand. Ten to fifteen cords was standard requirement for a normal winter's use, according to Norman B. Nelson of Western Minnesota Steam Threshers Association. Some authorities contend that there was little natural tree growth in the Valley and maintain that trees were planted by the settlers. This was not true for areas around streams because early travelers such as Hargraves and Ross comment on tree growth. The accounts of the size of trees and groves given by Thortvedt, A. Overby, Fuglestad, and Probstfield substantiate the availability of timber along the streams.

[4] Hobart, "Pioneering," VIII, 205-211; Probstfield; Crawford, NDIRS, File 290; Woodward, pp. 159-162.

[5] Probstfield; Glaspell, pp. 188-190; Woodward, pp. 219-221; Divet, NDIRS, File 69; Hobart, "Pioneering," VIII, 122-123; Emil C. Ankerfeldt, interview.

[6] Olsen interview; *Warren Sheaf*, Feb., 1897; *The Record*, II (June, 1897), 2; Probstfield; McMahon, NDIRS, File 195; Madsen interview; Frey letter.

[7] Gunkelman interview; O. Overby, *Retrospect*; A. Overby, "Sod House Days"; Hans Krabbenhoft, interview by the author Sept. 28, 1967; Stafne, p. 16.

[8] A. Overby, "Sod House Days"; *Moorhead Independent*, Jan. 5, 1900, p. 47; Torrison, p. 32; Alfred Sands, interview by Donald Berg, July 18, 1966; *N. D. Ag. Stat.*, No. 408, p. 6; Hans Krabbenhoft interview; Murray, pp. 134-135, 152-158.

[9] Fuglestad, pp. 9-12; Robert P. and Wynona H. Wilkins, *God Giveth the Increase: The History of the Episcopal Church in North Dakota* (Fargo, 1959), p. 34; Sands interview; Madsen interview; Pruett interview; Ankerfeldt interview; Probstfield; A. Overby, "Sod House Days"; Hovde, pp. 11-12; O. Overby, *Retrospect*, pp. 10-11 Hobart, "Pioneering," VII, p. 221, VIII, pp. 119-120; *Hillsboro Banner*, July 14, 1882, Sept. 29, 1882; Woodward, pp. 95, 97, 142, 143, 257; Crawford, NDIRS, File 290.

[10] Crofford, pp. 130-131; *Moorhead Independent*, Jan. 5, 1900, p. 19; Probstfield; *The Record*, I (Aug., 1895), 6; I. G. Haycraft, "1873-1877, The Grasshopper Plague," *With Various Voices, Recordings of North Star Life*, eds. Theodore C. Blegen and Philip D. Jordan (St. Paul, 1949), pp. 310-313; Madsen interview; Power letter to Billings, July 15, 1876, NDIRS, File 309; A. Overby, "Sod House Days"; Hovde, p. 11; Woodward, p. 230.

[11] Gunkelman, NDIRS, File 569; Gunkelman interview.

[12] O. Overby, *Retrospect*, p. 3; Briggs, p. 99; Power letter to Allen, Moon and Company, St. Paul, Minn., Jan. 13, 1891, NDIRS, File 309; Frey letter; Probstfield; U. S. Weather Bureau Official Records for dates used; *N. D. Ag. Stat.*, No. 408, pp. 88-89; *Minn. Ag. Statistics*, p. 42; Woodward, p. 125; Fuglestad, pp. 15-16; Crawford, NDIRS, File 569; Weather Bureau State Climatologist Chart prepared Aug. 21, 1967; The University of Minnesota Agricultural Experiment Station Technical Bulletin No. 243 (St. Paul, 1963).

PRECIPITATION IN INCHES FOR THE FARGO-MOORHEAD AREA FOR THE GROWING
SEASON 1887-1890, SHOWING THE DEPARTURES FROM NORMAL FOR EACH MONTH

	1887	Dep.	1888	Dep.	1889	Dep.	1890	Dep.
March	.26	−.57	1.04	+.24	.24	−.59	.59	−.27
April	2.45	+.06	1.43	−.96	1.48	−.70	.19	−2.08
May	2.57	−.40	2.20	−.77	1.71	−1.17	1.42	−1.46
June	3.77	−.60	2.98	−1.39	.96	−3.24	6.60	+2.40
July	6.40	+1.55	3.48	−1.37	1.95	−2.90	3.59	−1.36
August	1.45	−1.69	.92	−2.22	1.40	−1.74	3.69	+.55
Total	16.90	−1.65	12.05	−6.47	7.74	−9.93	16.08	−2.32

[13] *Warren Sheaf*, May 14, 1891, Oct. 15, 1891. The following is a good example of one of the many boastful stories found in newspapers of that day to help promote the region. The story originated in the *Fargo Republican* and was repeated in a special supplement to the *Warren Sheaf*, Oct. 19, 1891:

From every section of the great state of North Dakota comes the glad tidings of an enormous yield of the famous and renowned wheat.

The monotonous song of thousands of harvesters was ceased and has been superceded by the hum of Countless Threshing Machines as they Pour Out to A Waiting and Expectant World the Most Prolific Yield of Valuable Cereals Ever Garnered by the Fortunate Tillers of North Dakota's Productive Lands.

A Glorious Crop that will Chase the Gaunt Skeleton of Want, Destitution, Hunger, and Despair from the doors of the People of Famine Stricken Europe. Twenty, Twenty-five, Thirty, Thirty-five, and Even Greater Number of Bushels of Hard Wheat Grown from a Single Acre of Dakota Ground.

A Solid Phalanx of Figures With the Names of the Fortunate Men and the Location of the Farms upon Which the Following Yields are Reported. Extracts From the Reliable and Representative Newspapers of the State That will Prove Interesting Reading to the People of the Overcrowded Eastern States. Not a "boom article" in any sense of the Word, but a Plain Statement of Facts Vouched For by Well known Residents of the Great Commonwealth.

A Cereal Story of Entrancing Interest Related by Threshers as They Force a Golden Stream of Heavy Wheat upon the Billowy Tide of the World's Commerce. Among the Youngest in the Sisterhood of States, North Dakota Proudly raises Her Peerless Head and Murmurs, "Peace, Prosperity and Plenty on Every Side in My Imperial Domain."

Cereals Among the Clouds

Europe Admits that it has but little grain, and we must supply the Impoverished country from our groaning granaries. Must is the word. Let it be repeated—it must have good American grain, and we are willing to let it go. Have no fear that we will sell too much and run on the rocks of starvation at Home Sweet Home. Our Northwest has Millions of bushels and will divide with its Transatlantic neighbors on a strictly cash basis.

Golden grain is worth golden dollars, and we have no conscientious scruples against making an exchange of commodities. Grain goes soaring on the Chicago Board, and its movement skyward is unchecked by reports of great crops. And, all in all, Farmers will be happy, and gold will flow into their coffers in a big round stream.

Minnesota Never Fails, in her agricultural lexicon there is no such word as fail—drop the seed in the ground and nature will do the rest.

This season the Red River Valley has more fertile fields, bursting granaries, and fat pocketbooks than ever. No limit to the opportunities yet remaining in that rich valley for the industrious and intelligent. The Lake Park Region continues to demonstrate its value as a grain growing section—a condition not a theory confronts us.

Every prospect pleases—the farm lands are golden with grain, the Harvest is plenty, though laborers are few. What the farmers have done this year may easily be done again and again and again. Here are some specimen facts—comment is unnecessary and conclusions will present themselves.

Overby sod home in northern Wilkin Co. Had a wooden frame with sod exterior. Home was whitewashed with baked limestone and sometimes papered with the *Youth's Companion.*

Photo credit: Arthur Overby.

Interior of sod house showing the kitchen with magazine paper as wall paper. Homemade chair on right. Flour can, coffee grinder, and lamp on wall.

Photo Credit: State Historical Society of North Dakota.

Pioneer's sod house, sod barn, "stone boat" has sod on it. Note breaking plow, one window in house, none in barn. Either in Walsh or Cavalier County about 1895.

Photo credit: Fred Hultstrand Collection, NDIRS.

Second home of E. Stafne, 1878.
Their first home was of sod.

*Photo Credit: State Historical Society
of North Dakota.*

Tarpaper shack, grindstone, well, wash tubs, in Rock Lake area.

Photo credit: State Historical Society of North Dakota.

Mr. and Mrs. Andrew Tabbut on left, Maurice Tabbut on right. The Tabbuts came to Scambler Township, Otter Tail County, from Maine in 1891 and lived in this house until 1912. Note board to channel rain into barrel.

Photo credit: P. T. Tabbut.

Hand carved washbowl and washboard with a bar of home-made lye soap.

Photo credit: David Peet Museum.

Kitchen cabinet, cook stove, and dry sink with utensils.

Photo credit: David Peet Museum.

Homemade pitchfork, homemade wooden shovel, cradle scythe. *Photo credit: David Peet Museum.*

Pazandaks delivering grain to elevator at Fullerton, N.D. about 1909.

Photo credit: Ferd Pazandak.

Jack Anderson cook car, taken 1910, at Pazandak farm. Louise Anderson with pony. l. to r. Emmon Gronbeck, engine driver; Charles Olson, engineer; Miss Rawhauser, Nina Anderson, Mr. Barsten, Jack Anderson. Cooking for sod breaking crew. Pony used by girls for bringing supplies.

Photo credit: Ferd Pazandak.

Potato sorting shed which slid along the ground above a trench filled with potatoes. Grant farm, about 1910.

Photo credit: Donald Grant.

Loading grain Pillsbury, N.D. 1911, prior to elevator erection just after Great Northern built Surrey cut-off. Horse power sweep with tumbler rod is clearly shown.   *Photo credit: Roy H. Smith.*

Hay making, 1916. Esther Gustafson Olsgaard in rack, O. G. Gustafson, Hildur Lian (sister-in-law), G. O. Gustafson on mower, another relative on ground, Mrs. O. G. Gustafson on far right. Farm located between St. Hilaire and Hazel, Minn., Pennington County.

Photo credit: Mrs. Cedric Onan.

Surveying in area east of Devils Lake in 1890's.

Photo credit: State Historical Society of North Dakota.

Buffalo bone pile, Fort Totten, 1883, just before the arrival of the railroad. Capt. Edward Edson Heerman, Devils Lake hauled 700 tons of bones across to the railroad on the *Minnie H 2nd* in 1882.
Photo credit: State Historical Society of North Dakota.

Red River carts with loads of buffalo bones, somewhere in the area between Devils Lake and Pembina.
Photo credit: State Historical Society of North Dakota.

Threshing on Magnus Nelson's Wild Rice Stock Farm near DeLamere, Sargent County, 1882. Note straw elevator, traction-less steam engine, sacking of grain.
Photo credit: C. B. Heifort.

Hans Langseth of Wahpeton with beard 19 ft. 2 in. Mr. Langseth started growing his beard at age 28 and it was not shaved off until his death at age 79. The beard is at the Smithsonian Institution and reported to be the longest known.

Photo credit: David Peet.

Chippewa Indians who walked into Flaten Studio in Moorhead about 1885.

Photo credit: C. B. Heifort.

Ole Overby family, rural Cooperstown, 1896. l. to r. Edward, Oscar, on knee, born 1892, Ole, Peter 1882, Mrs. Overby, Elma born 1895, Casper, Alph, 1889. All the clothes worn by the children were made by Mrs. Overby.

Photo credit: Casper Overby.

Fisher, Minn. 1876, near the height of its boom as a railroad terminus. Russell House, Manitoba House, General Store.

Photo credit: Polk County Historical Society.

J. L. Grandin aground near Halstad after the flood of 1897 where it ended its days. Henry Reitan (b. 1891) used some lumber from super-structure to build a tree house. By 1910 it was completely dismantled.

Photo credit: Mrs. Esther Waite.

Barge from J. L. Grandin used as a floating bridge across Red River between Halstad and Grandin farms. Barge was used from 1897 to 1902 when the first bridge was built.

Photo credit: Mrs. Esther Waite

Building road to Cargill, Polk Co. (Corser Farm Horses) in 1900. One machine like this could move 125 cubic yards of dirt per hour. This is as much as fifty men with teams could do with fresno scrapers.

Photo credit: Richard Samuelson.

Road construction with fresno scrapers, east of Hawley on Hawley and Eglon Township line, 1905.

Photo credit: Mrs. John Elton.

First elevator in North Dakota at Fargo taking bulk grain from barges for transfer to railroad cars.

Photo credit: State Historical Society of North Dakota.

Main entrance to Northwest School of Agriculture, Crookston, 1921. Model T. Ford.

Photo credit: N. W. Experiment Station.

Madson Studio picture of Halstad-to-Mayville tour 1912 with twelve cars. Pilot car went ahead and marked the road with confetti at intervals. Pathfinder car led the other eleven. The two lead cars were furnished by Halstad auto liveries as a sales promotion. There were several flat tires while traveling across the roadless prairie. Everyone stopped to help get them fixed. Reos, Buicks, Metz's and Fords were used.

Photo credit: Mrs. Esther Waite.

The Shaver family moved to Saline, N.D. about 1900. They lived in the Comstock area for a few years in the 1890's. Note road.

Photo credit: David Peet.

Street in Fargo during flood of April, 1897. Showing dislocated cedar blocks used for the pavement of the street. Large building on right is Fargo Packing Company.

Flaten photo, Moorhead Fire Department, 1905.

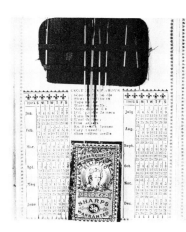

Portion of a larger brochure from Halland-Askegaard Store at Comstock, 1904. Note variety of goods.

TO EXAMINE OUR LINE OF

Dry Goods, Clothing,
Notions, Groceries,
Boots and Shoes, Hats and Caps,
Hardware, Paints and Oils
Furniture, Farm Implements
Lumber and Building Materials,
Farm Land Bought and Sold

HALLAND & ASKEGAARD,

COMSTOCK, MINN.

Bruns and Finkle Elevator A, Moorhead, 1879. Note use of oxen; sacks are two-bushel size made of canvas material.

Photo credit: Mrs. Edgar Olsen.

Larimore, 1893. O. H. Phillips office, bicycle and machinery dealer.

Photo credit: State Historical Society of North Dakota.

Bagley Store, Albert Lukkson, owner, 1910.

Photo credit: Clara Engen.

Griggs House, Grand Forks, 1882. Blackburn photo. Mr. and Mrs. C. B. Ingalls, proprietors, on middle Porch. Frank W. Wooley on hotel hack.

Photo credit: State Historical Society of North Dakota.

Rustad's Saloon, Moorhead, 1905. The building extended over the Red River.

Photo credit: NDIRS.

The Rathskeller, 1st Street and 2nd Avenue North, Moorhead, 1905. Owned by Thomas Erdel. This building contained a tunnel to help customers escape.

Photo credit: Ernest Schroeder.

Two jugs from Moorhead saloons dating to the period between 1889 and 1915.

Traveling road troupe advertising "Uncle Tom's Cabin" at Halstad, 1899.

Halinglad (dance) at Brooten, 1910. Olaf Thon, fiddler.

Christmas, 1896, Halstad. Candles used for lights, strings of popcorn, gifts were placed under the tree.

Photo credit: Mrs. Esther Waite.

Deerhorn Presbyterian Church, Wilkin County, 1899, shortly after construction.

Photo credit: Howard Peet.

The same Deerhorn Presbyterian Church, Wilkin County. Last services held in June, 1968.

Photo credit: Daellenbach.

Typical drinking and washing facilities in school house built in 1880 in Richland County. Note dinner pails.

Photo Credit: David Peet Museum

One room country school built in Richland County, 1880. W. J. Peet taught here in 1885.

Photo credit: David Peet Museum.

Sod shanty, 1884, Dakota Territory, Karl Rudd land on Maple River five miles from Sheldon. Anna Dirshimen taught school here in 1884.

Photo credit: Mrs. M. B. McGuigan.

Tarpaper shack in Rock Lake area.

Photo credit: State Historical Society of North Dakota.

Farm residence of James Holes, built in October, 1879. In 1970 the home of Mr. and Mrs. Charles Finkle (daughter of James Holes) at 1230 North Fifth Street, Fargo, North Dakota.

Photo credit: State Historical Society of North Dakota.

R. M. Probstfield home north of Moorhead, built in 1868, enlarged, sided, and painted in following years. This picture was taken in 1884. The house measured 28 x 34 feet and had 7 rooms for a family of 11 children and 2 hired men. House will become a state historical site in the future.

Photo credit: Ray Gesell.

After the blizzard. Taken March 20, 1893 in Richland County, North Dakota

Photo credit: State Historical Society of North Dakota.

Digging out after a three day snow storm, Milton, North Dakota about 1913. l. to r. Nellie Ward, Mrs. James Ward, James Ward, Jr., Hugh Ward on roof top.

Photo credit: Fred Hultstrand Collection, NDIRS.

W. J. Peet homes, 1890 and 1903, Wolverton, Minnesota   *Photo credit: David Peet.*

German-Russian farmstead between Ellendale and Wishek. 11 a.m. April 4, 1904.

Photo credit: John Redlin.

The Erickson homestead 6½ miles north of Fairdale, North Dakota in 1900. There were ten children in the Erickson family at this time. Martin Erickson at far right, age 20, John Erickson, 16, in doorway. The addition was built on to accommodate visiting relatives.

Photo credit: State Historical Society of North Dakota.

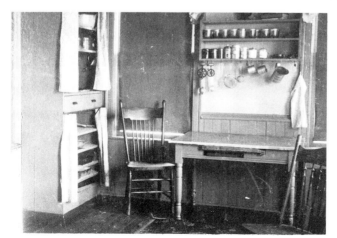

Model kitchen, Crookston School of Agriculture, 1919, Home Economics Rooms.

Photo credit: N.W. Experiment Station.

Home Economics model kitchen, Crookston Experimental Station, 1919. Note stove on left, waterpail, and dipper.

Photo credit: N.W. Experiment Station.

Baking stove in model kitchen, Crookston School of Agriculture, 1919. Note wood box, high oven.

Photo credit: N.W. Experiment Station.

Interior of a log cabin, 12' x 16', occupied until 1966. Most of the furniture actually used until that date by Martin and Oscar Nodsle, Erhard Minn.

Photo credit: David Peet Museum.

Christafor Nelson's rig in operation at Rollag, 1884. Canton Monitor machine. Note tongue on engine, wood cart, and rail fence.

Photo credit: Western Minn. Steam Threshers.

Self propelled thresher invented by Rev. Henry Sageng, 1908, 35 to 40 h.p., cost $3,500. Wing feeders on each side of the machine in rear. Only 21 of these threshers were made. This one used around Wolverton. The last farmer planned to make a tractor out of it but it lacked good traction.

Photo credit: Wilkin County Historical Society.

Horse power sweep stump puller used in eastern Clay County in the 1870's.

Photo credit: Western Minnesota Steam Threshers.

Horse power well drilling rig used in 1870's.

Photo credit: Draft Horse Journal.

Ten horse power sweep which operated the thresher by a shaft from the gear box, near Pelican Rapids, Minn. Note rail fence.

Photo credit: Mrs. M. B. McGuigan.

Blacksmith shop, Leonard, N.D. 1910. l. to. r. grindstone, trip hammer, anvil, water barrel, forge (hand operated) next to fire pot.

Photo credit: C. H. Frey.

Butchering at Benedict Farm Sabin, Minn. 1910. William Wussow hired man, Ferdinand Kelting, butcher, Ewald Benedict, with knife, John Huson, with rifle, hired man.

Photo credit: Mrs. Emma Mallinger.

Butchering during threshing time in Wilkin County, Nielsen Township, 1919. The boy is Ole Raftevold, man unknown.

Photo credit: Earl Tolbert.

l. to r. Olava Mickelson with pan for catching blood and a pail of hot water; grandson Orrin Knutson, Tommy Mickelson husband of Olava in back, Thore Myron. Myron and Mickelson came from Norway in 1882. Note hog on tree. Parke Twp, Clay County, 1912.

Photo credit: Mrs. Fred Melby.

Cleaning intestines for sausage after butchering at August Pankow, Hankinson, N.D. 1920's.

Photo credit: August Pankow.

Butchering at Abner L. Gray farm 1931 near Mapleton, N.D. l. to r. Emil Matthys, Abner L. Gray, hired man unknown, Dean Anderson.

Photo credit: Mrs. Marie G. Piersall, daughter of A. L. Gray.

Butchering 300 lb. hog. Note winch and tripod and little boy with big knife. Mr. and Mrs. Clem Kamrowski, Barnesville, Minn., on right.

Photo credit: Clem Kamrowski.

Probstfield family picture, 1890. Back row l. to r. Justus, 1866, Susan, 1870, Dorothea, 1872, Edmund, 1868, Cornelia, 1868, Emily, 1874, front row Walter, 1877, Mary, 1862, Mr. Probstfield, 1832, Josephine, 1882, Mrs. (Catherine) Probstfield, 1838, Arthur, 1879, Alexander, 1865.

Photo credit: Ray Gesell.

Red River cart train, near Canadian border. Eight carts operated by two Metis'.
Photo credit: State Historical Society of North Dakota.

Rose Frey and son John, farmers on the Sheyenne River south of Leonard, in town for "Crazy Days" 1906 version.
Photo credit: C. H. Frey.

Caledonia, N.D. 1875. Stage coach to Winnipeg.
Photo credit: State Historical Society of North Dakota.

Dry Goods department of Iver Lien store, Halstad, 1890's. Henry Reitan purchased a complete confirmation suit at this store in 1904 for $8.

Photo credit: *Mrs. Esther Waite.*

Iver Lien store showing leather department, and hardware department through archway. 1890's.

Photo credit: *Mrs. Esther Waite.*

Front view Iver Lien Department Store, Halstad 1890's. Note built up board sidewalk.

Photo credit: *Mrs. Esther Waite.*

Headquarters Hotel, Fargo, from the east. Northern Pacific tracks, crossing Broadway, in foreground. The building at one time served as hotel, depot, and county offices.

Photo credit: State Historical Society of North Dakota.

Interior of Rock Lake general store about 1895.

Photo credit: State Historical Society of North Dakota.

Front Street in Moorhead, 1874, showing ox and horse drawn Red River carts.

Photo credit: Mrs. Edgar Olsen.

Main street of Wolverton about 1913, now U.S. 75. Building #1 Town Hall, second floor used for dances. St. Anthony and Dakota Elevator with outside scale. #4 blacksmith shop; #5 Kirkhoven grocery; #6 Melbostad Livery Stable. Note straw and manure pile. #9 school.

Photo credit: Wilkin County Historical Society.

Millinery and dressmaking shop in Halstad about 1910. All dresses and hats made to order. Miss Johanna Opgrande had her high school graduation dress made here in 1907. She did not remember seeing a factory-made dress sold at the store.

Photo credit: Carl Opgrand.

Northern Pacific bridge taken from Center Avenue, Moorhead, April 7, 1897, by Flaten Studio. Building at lower right is old steamboat house. Steam threshing engines were placed on old south bridge to hold it down. At height of flood five railroad engines were placed on N. P. bridge.

Photo credit: Jim Fay collection, NDIRS.

Romness Band, 1908. l. to r. back row Hogan Skramstad, Jul Kastet, Peter A. Overby, Martin Leiberg, Andrew Kastet; middle row Casper Overby, Elmer Johnson, G. P. Overby, Albert Johnson; front row Oscar Overby, Anton Skramstad, Richard Kramstad, Alph Overby, John Stromme.

Photo credit: Casper Overby.

Mayville Opera House, 1890's. Note lamps at stage edge.

Photo credit: George Hilstad.

Emory Johnson Sporting Goods Store, Fargo, 1890's.

Photo credit: C. B. Heifort.

Bellmond baseball club, Bellmond, N.D. about 1900. Front row l. to r. Alfred Haugen, Andrew Halverson, Hildus Erickson, Simon Estenson, Olaus Vettern back row Eddie Olson, Olaus Myrland, Gust Torgerson, Peter Thompson. *Photo credit: Pioneer.*

Moorhead folks camping near Detroit Lakes. Believed to be a Flaten photo, 1893. *Photo credit: C. B. Heifort.*

Circus in Breckenridge-Wahpeton after 1900.

Photo credit: Lynn Skjonsby.

Steamer *Minnie H* on Devils Lake, late 1890's.

Club Day at Annie Stein's, Georgetown, June, 1903. Mrs. E. F. Krabbenhoft (Rosalie Schroeder) second from left.

Halstad church, 1896. Note planks on chairs, space heater, and kerosene lamps.

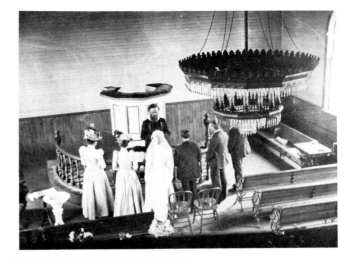

Wedding in Augustana Lutheran Church 4½ miles N.E. of Halstad, June 7, 1899. Andrew Nygaard and Minnie Josephine Davidson. Rev. O. A. Th. Solem officiating.

Photo credit: Mrs. Esther Waite.

Nygaard-Davidson wedding at Halstad. All day lunch and refreshments served at the farm home and an all night dance held in the bowery in the background. Music furnished by the Halstad band.

Photo credit: Mrs. Esther Waite.

Immanuel Church, Norman, Barnes County, about 1890. Note grindstone by wagon, cement box by water barrel, and helmets on steeplejacks.

Photo credit: NDIRS.

First school house in Enger Township and Steele County. Built in 1877 on Per Nyhus land. Picture taken about 1885. John Rorvig, teacher, far right, 3 Enger children in group. *Photo credit: Mrs. Del Nystedt.*

Emma Erickson Elton, age 22, teacher. Building erected 1884, picture taken 1897. Dist. #7 eastern Clay County. *Photo credit: Mrs. John Elton (Emma Erickson).*

Scrubbing day at Halstad schoolhouse, 1902. Johanna Opgrande in extreme upper left was in 7th grade, Henry Reitan in 5th grade at the time. Three lady teachers in back row. Mr. Henke, with glasses, was principal. *Photo credit: Mrs. Esther Waite.*

Clay County Teachers' Association, 1905, at Hawley. Young teacher rear right defied tradition and wore no hat. Students in group were county spelling winners.
Photo credit: Mrs. John Elton.

Early Minnesota consolidated school district school bus, Glyndon District, 1912.
Photo credit: Donald Grant.

New winterized school buses, Comstock, Minn. about 1909.
Photo credit: Rolf Askegaard.

School bus owned by Amenia and Sharon Land Co., Amenia, N.D. 1920.

Photo credit: Mrs. Max Dahl.

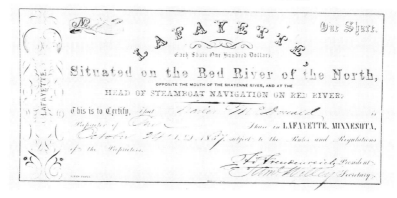

One share in the town of Lafayette, Minn., dated 1857 (north of Moorhead), acquired by R. M. Probstfield.

Photo credit: Raymond Gesell.

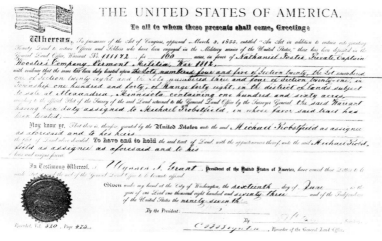

Bounty grant on quarter section in Oakport Township, Clay County, dated 1873, received by Randolph Michael Probstfield by assignment. This became the Probstfield farm and was not a homestead grant. Probstfield obviously purchased the bounty.

Photo credit: Raymond Gesell.

This Honorary Life Membership in the Minnesota State Horticultural Society was given to R. M. Probstfield. He had been an active member in the Society since 1880. *Photo credit: Raymond Gesell.*

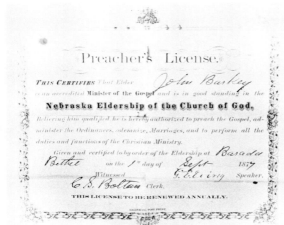

Preacher's license for a circuit rider, 1877, in Nebraska. John Barkey came to northern Minnesota in the early 1900's and rode a mule on his circuit composing five congregations.

Photo credit: Gordon Weiss.

Homestead claim of John Swenson for 80 acre homestead. This claim bearing President U. S. Grant's signature, is made of parchment which, according to authorities at Minnesota Historical Society, makes it very unusual. The farm is currently owned by Ringo Farm, Inc.

Certificate obtained through courtesy of the grandson, John W. Swenson.

CHAPTER IX

Till To Reap

Weeds

I<small>N THE</small> early years of agriculture in the Red River Valley, weeds were less of a problem than in later periods. The nearly complete lack of weeds on the Jens Hagen farm in its first year of operation (1873) was a great boon to the family. Corn, pumpkin, and squash were planted by merely poking holes in the ground with a stick. Because the garden was so free of weeds, "the vegetables were not touched until fall when they were gathered." The weed infestation increased only after the sod had been broken and weed seeds were imported with grain seeds. Then they multiplied rapidly. The thick, unbroken sod had not permitted most weeds to take root. The settlers, however, because they lacked time and good tillage tools, inadvertently permitted weeds to increase freely. As time passed and the weeds became better established, area farmers became disturbed by the almost impossible task of controlling them.

It would be wrong to leave the impression that there were no weeds at all in the area before farming was established. The settlers at the junction of the Red and Assiniboine Rivers (Winnipeg), for example, failed to get a potato crop in 1813 because of "late planting, a dry June, bad seeds, grubs, weeds. . . ." The large-scale wheat monoculture as practiced in later periods, particularly by the bonanza farmer, made the spread of weeds much easier because continuous wheat growing limited the effective control of weeds in contrast to more intensive methods for weed control used in the cultivation of row crops. Weeds definitely spread quicker in the area of the larger farm operations because of the presence of a greater proportion of black soil which was exposed to the elements. In addition, the lack of trees, hills, or other obstacles to obstruct the wind encouraged a more rapid spread of weeds.

By 1882 wild mustard was prevalent in the Valley, and shortly afterward, "wild buckwheat, lambs quarter, cockle, wild oats, Canadian thistle, French weed, and wild sunflowers also appeared." O. A. Olson was prompted to write about the changing conditions of the 1890's:

> In place of grain, now thistles grow,
> And yet they sow.

When agricultural leaders became disturbed enough by the weed problem, they promoted institutes to alert farmers to the seriousness of the situation. These institutes initiated the practices of summer fallowing, hand pulling, and weed cutting. There were always large areas, however, where weeds were not controlled or attended to because they were part of the public domain or because the individual farmer did not bother about them. Any partial eradication obviously was of little value.

Russian thistles were imported into the region in 1873 by Russian immigrants with some flax seed, but frequently weed seeds were also carried in the clothing, shoes, and miscellaneous packages of the new settlers. The thistle was confined to a single community for many years. When it finally spread, it nearly always seeded itself in plowed ground or in gopher mounds. As Crawford testified:

The prairies of the west were indeed virgin country. In 1881 there were none of the troublesome weeds, no dandelions, no purslane, no wild mustard, no plaintain. By the late '90's there were bull thistles, Canada thistles, cocklebur, wild mustard, wild buckwheat, pigeon grass. Since that time other weed pests have come in, quack grass, field bindweed, leafy spurge, Russian knapweed. Such are some of the vices of civilization. Our [Crawfords] first garden had lots of tough clods of unsubdued sod, but not a weed.

Conditions changed, and by 1893 the Russian thistle had taken such a foothold that it had spread over one-third of Dickey, Sargent, and LaMoure counties in North Dakota and was otherwise generally distributed in McIntosh, Ransom, Logan, and parts of Richland and Emmons counties. Many farmers completely gave up farming because of it and left the area, selling their quarter sections for prices from $200 to $500. By then the thistles were so thick that horses' legs had to be wrapped with burlap or other material to protect the horses when forcing them through the thorny patches of Russian thistles in an effort to cut them. (F. A. Bagg also wrapped his horses' legs with burlap to protect them from rust during the heavy infestation in his wheat in 1901.)

Continuous cropping of wheat, whether encouraged by the desire for quick profits, indifference, or honest ignorance, depleted the land

and hastened the weed problem. Stubble burning and shallow plowing also reduced crop production. The appearance of rust, smut, scab, and other blights was also hastened by continuous wheat monoculture. Not until the late 1890's did agricultural experiment stations produce any scientific controls to meet those problems and even then farmers were reluctant to follow their advice. Ironically, some writers of the nineteenth century reported that the only new crop introduced by the American farmers during that century was weeds. That was not entirely true, but as more land became cultivated, weeds were more numerous and troublesome. The farmers were not totally to blame for this, however, for science had done little to aid them in suppressing weeds in that century until after 1875. Scientific agriculture, as we know it today, reached new heights only after World War II.[1]

For many days all thirteen members of the Probstfield family and the hired man were occupied with pulling weeds. In June, 1886, several members of the family spent three straight weeks doing nothing but "pulling mustard and stink weed out of the wheat." Often the fields were wet with dew but entire crews went out each morning anyway to pull mustard. There were few jobs that were more hated by the farmers than pulling weeds. When laws were passed to enforce control of weeds, however, farmers stoutly opposed their enforcement.

In an attempt to prevent weeds from going to seed and also to prepare a better seed bed for the grain, farmers "dragged" their fields several times. The common "drag" was made from a forked tree with pegs of wood twenty inches long inserted into holes drilled into the prongs of the fork to serve as teeth. This "forked tree drag" was so high and narrow that it upset easily but this mattered little "for it did just about as good work that way." One acre a day was considered good progress with such an implement, which was so ineffective that several draggings were required to get the sod in shape before seeding, and several more were needed to cover the seed and help control the weeds. Some farmers in the Buffalo River settlement of six farms, who did not want to wait for the only drag available among them, used tree branches.

By the late 1870's drags were greatly improved by the use of steel teeth in a standard wooden frame, but three draggings prior to seeding and three after seeding were still common practice. Probstfield also used his seeder to cultivate summer fallow. The eight foot, two-horse seeder could be operated by any of his six oldest children. He wrote that "Dorothea [age 15] and Emilie [age 13] both out on seeders working summer fallow" while Mary (age 25) and Susan (age 17) hoed weeds in the corn field. Later, three of the girls were cultivating summer fallow with seeders.

Probstfield continued using the shovel type seeders as field cultivators until 1889 when he purchased a spring tooth harrow. This machine left the ground more ridged than he liked; consequently, he followed it with a "tooth harrow" to smooth down the ridges. Homemade cultivators to control weeds in corn did not scour well and were soon called "corn aggravators." These drawbacks explain why Probstfield and others did so much hand hoeing. The repeated corn cultivations which were necessary to eliminate weeds were hard on the corn and when Probstfield "finished plowing corn for the 6th time" in July, he probably most accurately described what he was doing because deep cultivating (i.e., "plowing") no doubt damaged the corn as much as it did the weeds.[2]

Grain Seeding

In spite of the many discouraging situations, the farmer is an eternal optimist. No matter how serious conditions are when spring draws near he anxiously awaits the opportunity to till the soil and plant the seed and renew his continued struggle with nature. Eva K. Anglesburg phrases this struggle so well:

> Each spring the age-old conflict is begun,
> But like the knights of old he does not quail.
> Not gold but freedom, that is the reward
> Of those who toil, co-laborers with the Lord.

Although mechanical seeding machines had been patented as early as 1799, and horse-drawn seeders had been in use since 1857, the pioneer Red River Land farmers, such as the Thortvedts, the Probstfields, and the Overbys, seeded their first crops by hand. Usually one of the children followed immediately behind the sower with a horse drawn tree drag to cover the seeds before the birds got more than their share and to improve chances of germination. Birds were a particular problem for the Thortvedts and the Probstfields whose fields were adjacent to wooded areas.

Hand broadcasting took one and one-third hours per acre, but, dragging, which had to follow the broadcasting immediately, was so much slower, that not much more than two acres could be seeded in one day. There was, however, one advantage in using hand broadcasting or the hand seeder—as soon as the fields were dry enough for a man to walk on, seeding could start. Probstfield, not one to wait for perfect weather, in 1872 started seeding on April 10 with the temperature at thirty degrees and "swales and coulies [*sic*] still so wet so I had to pick around to find dry land." In 1873 when the fields were still wet on May 27, he hand-broadcast oats on the previous year's stubble because he had not had time to plow the land.

With the advent of horse-drawn seeders, fields had to be drier before seeding could be commenced, but farmers even in those days were not always willing to wait until conditions were ideal, as described by Mrs. Woodward:

The farmers are elated over the early spring [April 7]. The country looks God-forsaken now. Everything is mud, and such mud, black and heavy and sticky like glue. I pity the men trudging through it all day on foot. Nobody can imagine what Dakota mud is like until he gets into it and tries to lift his feet. It sticks to the wheels until they are immense; yet the boys made eighteen miles [each] in it today.

Because of the open prairie, horse-drawn seeders were quickly adopted, enabling one man with an eight-foot, two-horse seeder to plant an average of sixteen acres per day.

The slowness of the dragging operation, however, still held them back. In an effort to reduce man hours, Hobart tied three mules pulling a three-section, fifteen-foot drag behind his eight-foot seeder, thus enabling him to seed and to double drag the land in one trip over the field. He continued this practice until he purchased a Dowagiac shoe-drill in 1889, "the first in our township . . . which worked so well that I sold four of them to my neighbors for Horton and Elkins [of Mayville] and they gave me a commission of five dollars each." The drill needed only a bushel of seed per acre in contrast to a bushel and one-half for the seeder. By the late 1880's, drills replaced seeders —J. B. Power purchased a press drill in 1888, Probstfield a Van Brunt Davis drill in 1890, and Ole Olson of Wolverton bought a twenty-shoe Superior Press drill in 1894.[3]

Corn Planting

Corn planters were even more primitive than grain seeders. The amount of corn planted in this area was never great, but most livestock farmers, even as far north as Gilby and Warren, raised a few acres of corn. Some of the earliest corn farmers in the area planted the seed by hand, using their shoes as a hoe to cover it. Later the hand hilldrop corn planter came into use. To mark the hills where the corn was to be planted, a board with wooden markers nailed on it forty inches apart was pulled first lengthwise and then crosswise over the field. Wherever the marks crossed, two or three kernels of corn were planted.

In 1896, thirteen-year-old Frank Liebenow planted sixteen acres in this manner at Chaffee. That fall the Liebenows shocked the corn in the field and bound the shocks with willow sticks instead of twine in order to save money. If a farmer wanted his corn shelled, he could do it by hand or put the hardened corn on frozen ground and let the horses trample on it. Or he could go "modern" and for $5 he could buy a hand operated Monitor Corn Sheller which could shell from five to ten bushels an hour.[4]

Harvesting and Threshing

Because area farmers soon realized that they could not take maximum advantage of the flat prairie without good harvesting equipment, they were eager to adopt the new reaper. In August, 1875, Probstfield went to the Chapin farm to see the Massilan and Marsh reapers being demonstrated and he observed, "It looks like Marsh is best." However, he waited until 1878 to buy a self-tie wire binder which "works pretty fair." In the 1876 the Hovdes purchased a three-horse, two-man "binder"; it was operated by one man who stood on a platform and bound the sheaves with stalks of grain while the other man drove the horses and was responsible for the sickle bar operation. They used this machine for many years before they purchased a "self binding binder."

The Ericksons of Hawley had a self rake reaper which they also used for cutting hay. In 1880 while Mrs. Erickson drove the reaper, her husband bound the sheaves and could almost keep up with her. When the grain had been bound into bundles, Mr. Erickson could shock in a few hours by moonlight what it had taken him all day to bind. Although the combination reaper-mower outsold the straight reaper by a large margin nationwide up to 1879, it was never popular with the Valley farmers. Mrs. Overby of Wolverton drove oxen on a six-foot Plano wire tie binder while her husband shocked "as fast as the oxen worked so he was always near the binder."

Unfortunately, wire did not prove to be a satisfactory binding material because it got into the grain and caused a significant increase in livestock deaths, it damaged milling machinery, and it was feared that in the long run it would even discourage flour consumption. Although wire tie binders were soon replaced by the more practical twine binders, farmers who had bought the wire tie binders were forced to continue using them because they were a sizeable investment which almost overnight lost their trade-in value. The Divets shipped two McCormick wire tie binders from their Minnesota farm to Richland County in 1880. The larger Pembina Farm used four wire tie and six twine tie binders in 1881. The McCormick dealer at Warren advertised self rake harvesters (for grain or hay), wire binders, or twine binders for 1881.

Bonanza farmer Oliver Dalyrymple was involved with the experimental use of twine as early as 1875, but its cost of $2.00 per acre discouraged its use on a large scale. By 1879, though, because of mass production and the great demand for twine in the Valley, its cost was less than that of wire. The Grandin bonanza alone used over a carload of twine in their first year. In 1885 the Woodwards averaged only twenty-seven cents per acre for twine for 600 acres of wheat and 500 acres of oats, yielding twenty and sixty bushels respectively. In that year the price was thirteen cents a pound, but by 1894, when North Dakota alone used over six million pounds of twine, it was down to seven and a fourth cents per pound. The following year, when one Fargo firm had sold 400 carloads of twine, Oliver Dalrymple had 155 self-tie twine binders in operation. Mass production had not only forced down the price of twine but it had forced the cost of the binder to less than $100.

The use of the binders did not reduce the length of the harvest day, however, because farmers significantly increased their individual grain acreage at that time. In 1886 Charles Hobart cut 320 acres of grain with one six-foot McCormick harvester by operating with two shifts of horses and men "nearly day and night." The first shift of horses started at 7 a.m. and were changed at 11 a.m., again at 3 p.m., and the final change came at 7 p.m. The last change of horses worked until the end of the day, which sometimes was as late as 1 a.m. On an average day these early binders could cut from eleven to seventeen acres. By the time the Overbys of Cooperstown were operating their entire 1,760 acres, they needed four binders and Mr. Overby spent "much of his time in the blacksmith shop keeping the machinery running." Generally, five shockers were required to keep up with the four binders.[5]

In 1866 David McCauley probably had the first threshing machine shipped into the Valley. The Probstfield diary of September 13, 1873, clearly states, "thresh machine came." It would have been the second machine in the area, although most historians credit the Hudson's Bay Company machine shipped to Georgetown in 1874 by Walter J. S. Traill as being the second one. Could this have been the same machine? Walter Traill had persuaded Probstfield and several other farmers to plant wheat, and Hudson's Bay offered to provide the threshing machine. For many years the Overby's at Wolverton relied on a custom thresher from Pelican Rapids who "threshed whenever he came and the weather was fit." Most homesteaders never owned their own rigs, although some farmers formed threshing "runs" which cooperatively owned the machines.[6]

Since the small farmers never knew when a threshing machine would be available and because there was intense competition with the bonanzas for labor, they had to continue stack threshing which frequently delayed threshing until the winter months. On the bonanza farms the custom of stack threshing was first broken because it would have been prohibitive in cost as well as in volume to continue the practice. The smaller farmers, however, continued to stack thresh for many years. The Divets stack threshed, "but the Adams, Dwights—the bonanzas shock threshed. Stacking was a woeful waste of energy, a source of added expense and delayed fall plowing; but both Father and [Uncle] Jim were expert stackers. . . . They both took great pride in this, and the practice with them therefore, died hard." Although Probstfield owned his own machine, he could not begin his threshing until December 12, 1881, because the bonanza farmers had had such a bumper crop that they were out-bidding the small farmer for labor.

Ten years later, with another record breaking crop, the homesteader was still at the mercy of the bonanza farmer. After Fuglestad and his neighbors had their crops all shocked, they found out that the custom thresher would not come to their smaller farms because of all the work he had already promised to do elsewhere. Threshing in general took longer than usual that year because wheat was running forty to fifty bushels an acre in the Hannaford area. Most small farmers were so impoverished by the previous dry years that now they were desperate to sell their crop at the prevailing good price of seventy-five cents. Fuglestad and his neighbors decided that they had no choice but to stack all of the crop rather than take the risk of leaving it in shocks. Only Ashland did not bother to stack his grain because no matter how big a crop he got, "the collectors would get the entire crop anyway so he didn't care."

At the end of October, Fuglestad and Ashland purchased a threshing machine and a steam engine for $600, promising to do the three remaining jobs the custom operator had previously contracted. Although those jobs took an entire week, they grossed $600, enough to pay for the machine. However, it was now the second week in November and just as the partners were ready to thresh their own grain, it snowed. It took two yoke of oxen instead of the usual team of horses to move the heavy machine and engine through the snow. By now it was so cold that they were unable to get water out of the frozen Sheyenne River and had to haul it from Cooperstown. Ice formed in the water tank and also in the flues of the engine constantly and a fire had to be kept in the boiler all night to prevent freezing. Snow and ice also bothered the operation of the threshing machine. The straw elevator would not work and two extra men were needed to pull straw away from the machine.

Even though it was November, they worked until 8 p.m. burning piles of straw so that they could see. "Most of the transient laborers became disgusted and went home. [But] the neighbors all helped the best they could." Cigars and liquor were offered to "liven the spirits. We paid three dollars a day for those short days, but we were glad to do it." Next, the rig moved to Aarestad's but after a big storm it was covered with snow and left standing between two half stacks. "Aarestad gave up," but a break came in the weather and Emil Korgagard offered to shovel out the machine and move it so he might get some threshing done. Fuglestad and Ashland threshed 1,200 bushels for him before the December weather became so cold that they had to quit. It was spring before those who had left their grain in shocks could thresh it, but by then it had deteriorated so much that it was graded as feed wheat and brought only twenty-five cents a bushel.

Although machine threshing was much more efficient than the old hand methods, it was far from an inexpensive operation. A penny post-card, circulated by J. I. Case in the area, advertised a six-horsepower tractionless engine for $500 and an eighteen by thirty-six inch steel separator with hand feed attachments and folding stacker for $380. Even such a small rig represented more money than many early area farmers had had to pay for an entire section of land. To avoid purchasing a machine and hiring men in 1884, their first year, the Woodwards hired their entire threshing done by the McKay custom threshers who had two complete outfits with six tents, two cook cars with four female cooks, and forty men. They did the complete job from shock to the granary for fifteen cents a bushel, at a time when local wheat prices were around sixty cents a bushel and the Chicago price averaged eighty-three cents.

In 1887, when "wheat [was] too low to hire threshing," Daniel Woodward purchased an Ames self-traction engine and an Advance thresher for $1,980, which included a ten percent reduction for cash. He also purchased a cook stove to feed the thirty-two man crew in the machine shed, and even an ice cream freezer. That year they threshed as much as 2,050 bushels per day. Such rigs required two band cutters to remove the twine, two feeders because they could not take more than a full bundle at once, two grain sackers, two or three men working in the stack, one separator man, one engine man, a water man, at least three men to handle grain at the granary, and ten to twelve bundle teams with six spike pitchers in the field. Oscar Overby joked that he had "the less strenuous assignment" of hauling water, but sometimes he had to get up before dawn to help clean and fire up the boiler before the bundle haulers arrived at 7 a.m. As machines improved, mechanical band cutters, self feeders, an automatic weigher, and a straw blower eliminated the need for six to eight of the men at the machine.

Probstfield was typical of the smaller farmers who established neighborhood rings to exchange help. In 1874, his second year in the threshing ring, he threshed 199 bushels of oats, 67 bushels of wheat and 46 bushels of barley at a machine cost of $16.70 or about five and a half cents a bushel. By 1876 he threshed 432 bushels in eleven hours at a machine cost of seven cents per bushel. Mrs. Probstfield had to furnish eleven breakfasts, twelve dinners, and twelve suppers for the crew. Later when Probstfield returned the labor given him by Bergquist, he, Alexander, 13, Justin, 10, and a hired man helped Bergquist with the threshing, while Mary, 14, helped Mrs. Bergquist cook.

One of the costs often overlooked in early threshing was that of sacks. Even for the relatively small acreage which Probstfield had in 1878, he needed 316 sacks in order to take the grain from the machine and haul it to the granary. These were two-bushel sacks and cost twenty cents each. To reduce the cost, they were exchanged between neighbors and many winter hours were spent patching them.[7]

Cost of Horses

Power to pull the farm machinery was expensive and it was not at all unusual for the pioneer farmer, regardless of the size of his operation, to have more money invested in animal power, either oxen or horses, than in land. Oxen were cheaper than horses, but even a good yoke of oxen could cost as much as a quarter section of land.

According to *The Record* the first legal transaction recorded in northern Dakota was on September 12, 1868, when four horses and one ox were sold for $553. In 1874 Probstfield purchased two horses, Fanny for $120 and Nelly for $140. In February, 1877, he paid $120 for a yoke of oxen and in April, 1878, he purchased two yoke for $275. In 1883 Hobart and some neighbors purchased a carload of horses which came from either Illinois or Missouri. A team of four-year-old, 1,200-pound grays, Gypsy and Norma, with harness, cost $400. He also selected a team of 1,400-pound four-year-old bays, Myra and Myrtle, for $400, including harness. The following spring Norma and Myrtle had colts, which were named Tony and Kit. Probstfield, who had been searching for horses for a few days in 1887, finally concluded, "Can't touch a good team for less than $400. Which no farmer can afford from his business." He eventually purchased a team of mares for $340 and a set of harness for $25.

It took only two dry years to bring the demand and the price of horses down about fifty percent from the peak prices which occurred about 1883 during the Great Dakota Boom. In 1889 the Woodwards valued their eighteen horses at $120 each reflecting market conditions. Hobart was able to purchase two teams—Bess and Buckskin for $250 and Dan and Nell for $200—but he concluded that horses at that price were too expensive and went into partnership with a neighbor to purchase a one-year-old Norman Percheron stallion for $250. He traded two two-year-old steers and three shares of $25 stock for his half of the animal. Later, they sold this horse and joined several farmers, including the owner of the Upson bonanza, in the purchase of a Percheron stallion for $2,500. Hobart said, "Mr. Upson was treasurer and manager and kept the horse; he made the cost of keeping about equal the income. I wanted to get out of it and I was lucky for the horse died a year or two later and all they had was a dead horse."

Poor crop years, an increase in the horse supply, and a decline in the rate of farm expansion dropped the price for horses each year during the late 1880's and into 1890 when horses averaged only about $100. On the other hand, lower prices encouraged some farmers to buy too many horses. Hobart's neighbor, Fred Turell, had thirteen of them on a half section of land which, according to Hobart, "was too many and . . . Turell was headed for trouble." Turell's creditors soon foreclosed because he owed too much on the horses. Horses were still considered choice collateral and, next to land, were most readily taken as security. Many times they were secured up to their full value. Ole Olson of Wolverton listed twenty horses as security with the First National Bank of Breckenridge in 1893 for $55 each, at a time when choice horses were selling for from $65 to $75 each.[8]

The pioneer farmer in Red River Land was able to secure treeless, stoneless, fertile prairie land at a very low cost. This land is what had attracted him to the area. His chief obstacle to progress, however, was the inability to farm properly the land he owned. Machinery was becoming available, but it was high priced as was animal power. This high cost made it difficult for these undercapitalized opportunists to take full advantage of an otherwise ideal situation. Some gambled with their opportunities more than others. If their timing was right, they prospered; if not, their burden became greater than ever. In that respect, little has changed in Valley agriculture. The 1880's with their dry years, low yields, low prices, and weed infestations provided the first severe test to the Red River Valley farmer.

FOOTNOTES

¹ Crawford, NDIRS, File 569; Murray, pp. 30, 159-160, 178-179; Brewer, p. 880; O. A. Stevens, *Russian Thistle: Life History and Growth*, North Dakota Agricultural Experiment Station Bulletin No. 326 (Fargo, 1943), p. 2; Dewey, pp. 12-15; H. L. Walster, "North Dakota's War on the Russian Thistle," *The North Dakota Quarterly*, XXIV (Summer, 1956), 95; Stafne, p. 14; Downing, NDIRS, File 166.

² Probstfield; Thortvedt, NDIRS, File 332; Jarchow, pp. 320-323; W. R. Gill and A. W. Cooper, "Tillage Tools," *Yearbook of Agriculture, 1962, After a Hundred Years*, ed. Alfred Stefferud (Washington, 1962), p. 421; Woodward, pp. 85, 131.

³ Danhof, "Farm Making Costs," p. 340; Jarchow, p. 326; Rogin, pp. 192-197, 200-203, 206, 209; *The Dakota Farmer*, March, 1885, p. 12, Jan., 1886, p. 12; Power to Magill and Company, Aug. 18, 1891, NDIRS, File 309; Hobart, "Pioneering," VII, pp. 202-224, VIII, pp. 118-123; Probstfield; A. Overby, Wolverton Township Records; Thortvedt, NDIRS, File 332; Woodward, p. 35; Crawford, NDIRS, File 290. Even though farmers of Red River Land adopted the horse drawn seeders and drills at an early date, the *Dakota Farmer* of March, 1885, still advertised the Hoosier Broadcast Seed Sower. Patented in 1857, this cyclone seeder sold for $5.00 and enabled a man to sow four to six acres an hour. In the 1860's an endgate seeder was perfected that enabled farmers to sow up to fifteen acres an hour. Before the disc drill became standardized, there were many versions of drills using shear blades on shoes to open the ground for the grain. Land rollers of either wood or steel were developed for the farmer who preferred to stay with the seeder rather than buying a drill.

⁴ Probstfield; Liebenow interview; Jarchow, p. 325; *The Dakota Farmer*, March, 1885, p. 12; Thornton, p. 3768.

⁵ Schmidt, p. 375; Rogin, p. 95; Probstfield; Hovde, p. 15; Elton, *Vaalhovd*, p. 34; A. Overby, "Sod House Days," p. 5; Divet, NDIRS, File 69; *Warren Sheaf*, June 15, 1881, Aug. 6, 1881; Murray, pp. 134-135; Benton, p. 411; Hobart, "Pioneering," VII, pp. 204, 215-218, 224. Hobart's hours seem long, but under ideal harvest conditions they are possible. In the 1968 harvest Norman Krabbenhoft of Clay County, who has an air conditioned cab on his combine, operated the machine continuously from 11 a.m. to 1 a.m. He harvested well in excess of 4,000 bushels of wheat in that period. Woodward, pp. 90-91; *The Record*, Aug., 1895, p. 14; Rasmussen, p. 23; O. Overby, *Retrospect*, p. 16; Crawford, NDIRS, File 290; Brewer, p. 881.

⁶ Rogin, pp. 154-176; Jarchow, p. 326; Rasmussen, p. 6; Holbrook, pp. 14-19, 34; Brewer, p. 883; Murray, p. 141; A. Overby, "Sod House Days," pp. 5, 17; *Hillsboro Banner*, June 28, 1956, Sec. V, p. 13; George N. Lamphere, "A History of Wheat Raising in the Red River Valley," *Minnesota Historical Society Collections*, X (Feb., 1905), 12-13. (Hereafter cited as MHS, *Collections*); Pruett interview.

⁷ Divet, NDIRS, File 69; Probstfield; Fuglestad, pp. 16-17; Jarchow, p. 324; Elton, *Vaalhovd*, p. 34; Hobart, "Pioneering," VII, pp. 205, 220, VIII, p. 129; *Hillsboro Banner*, June 28, 1956, p. 16; Hovde, p. 15; Frey letter; Woodward, pp. 47, 183-185; Rogin, pp. 172-176; Ernest F. Krabbenhoft interview. Mr. Krabbenhoft was born June 10, 1880, and has lived his entire life in the area. He was a prominent dairyman up to his retirement in 1942; Penny postcard ad of J. I. Case Company from the collection of Lynn Skjonsby; Power letter to Israel Lombard, July 18, 1878, NDIRS, File 209; *Warren Sheaf*, July 13, 1881; A. Overby, Wolverton Township Records; *Warren Register*, Aug. 31, 1887; Drache, *Bonanza*, p. 208; O. Overby, *Retrospect*, p. 35.

⁸ Probstfield; Hobart, "Pioneering," VII, pp. 203, VIII, pp. 118-129; Woodward, p. 136; A. Overby, Wolverton Town Records; *The Record*, I (Aug., 1895), (June, 1896); *The Dakota Farmer*, IV (Sept., 1885).

CHAPTER X

Of Those Who Toil

Even with a sizeable family, the pioneer farmer was not entirely independent of outside labor. Many settlers secured additional help during the peak work seasons by exchanging labor with their neighbors. Unfortunately, the peak labor requirements for most farmers came at the same time. Imported labor in the form of farm hands was just as essential to homesteaders and bonanza farmers as were the cowboys to the cattle country, or the miners and the lumberjacks on other frontiers. The drudgery and exploitation associated with farm work and the large numbers of farm laborers is no less significant to the development of this portion of America than the contribution of the more publicized individuals on the other frontiers.

Hired Help

This region of the bonanza farms with their large crews of men was one of the most dramatic of all farm frontiers, equalled only by the cattle frontier with its cowboys. "During the eighties, . . . the Red River Valley was the universal hobo magnet. Even bank clerks and counter jumpers were caught up in the excitement and induced by low railroad fares [half fare for any point between Fergus Falls and Binford] to see the American Valley of the Nile in its fullest bloom."

Because the railroads were aware of the need for field hands during harvest, they were very lenient toward them and allowed them and professional hobos to "ride the rods" into the area—sometimes as many as 100 on a single freight train. In one extreme case there were 400 men on a Great Northern train that went through Wahpeton. Some of these were professional tramps; others were poor, honest farm workers who were looking for jobs and were traveling as cheaply as possible. The towns along the railroad were particularly plagued by these transient workers and they drew nationwide attention with a drawing in *Harper's Weekly*, 1890, of idle farm hands lying on the loading platform at Casselton. To discourage them from loafing around Hillsboro in 1885, the hobos were rounded up by city officials and were forced to wear steel balls and chains. While wearing those "ornaments" they were made to work for the city. Most farms of any size near good travel routes experienced visits from transient laborers of all sorts.

Once when harvest was just starting, three tramps stopped at the Woodwards, who already had thirteen men working for them. They wanted to sleep in the barn. "They did not want to sleep with the hired men in the upstairs of the granary." They were not hired or allowed to stay. Two men stopped at the Probstfield farm one day at dusk and "wanted to do a little work *for supper*. I had no work and no supper for them—well supplied with whiskey." Others came and left in the same manner year in and year out. On one drizzly day during harvest, eight men looking for work stopped at the Woodwards and when they left, one of the farm hands, Pat Haines, a barber from Philadelphia, went with them. He had worked only long enough to make money to continue "his travels." A few days later another man, Nels Nelson, who "is quite tony wearing two gold rings, gold scarf pin and gold neck button [and] can read English a little," joined the crew. At that time the crew was getting up at 4 a.m. to feed and to harness the horses before breakfast.

Many of these transients were attracted to the area by extravagant promotional campaigns as illustrated by an article in the *Hillsboro Banner*:

Labor is always in demand at good prices. No matter how poor anyone is on coming here, by going to work he can earn in a week or two enough to enter a homestead or tree claim, or both cost $14 each. He is allowed six months to make improvements on his homestead . . . and a year on the tree claim. His wages during the first six months will amply able him to build a comfortable little cottage of boards and sod, and pay breaking and backsetting of, say 15 or 20 acres. He can work in the pineries the next winter. The following year he can work on a bonanza plus get 400 bushels off of his farm which will buy teams and machinery and make him an independent farmer at the end of two years.

According to the same issue of the *Hillsboro Banner*, opening and operating costs for a 160-acre homestead included $14 for land entry fee, $480 for sod breaking at $3 an acre, and $320 for backsetting for the same acreage at $2 an acre. Providing a house and a stable for horses added another $300 and other improvements on land cost $186. Seed and seeding expenses were supposed to be done for $300 while harvesting cost would amount to $850. The threshing bill would increase costs by $200, assuming a 4,000-bushel yield at five cents a bushel. Another $600 would be required for hired labor. The newspaper story carried an erroneous total of $2,750 instead of an actual total of $3,150. Either figure would have to be considered reasonable.

The paper assumed twenty-five bushels per acre at $1 a bushel or $4,000 gross, leaving a net profit of $850 in one year, including the fees and the breaking cost. A yield of fifteen bushels and a price of seventy cents a bushel would have been more realistic and would have ended with a loss in addition to the cost of living expenses. The article concluded, "The result is enough to tempt the Wall Street brokers to come to Dakota and become farmers, and many of them have done so." Certainly any individual who came to the area and had relied on the above figures would not have been a farmer for long. He would have become and remained a hired man for a farmer with better judgment.

Since some of the nation's leading economists of that day recommended that immigrants turn to the farm instead of the city as a place to find work, there was so much demand for laborers in Red River Land in the 1880's that the Northern Pacific required a $10 deposit of all who sought construction jobs at the end of the line. This deposit was required because so many men, intending to work for the railroad, were lured from the trains along the way by prospects of better jobs on the farms that the Northern Pacific officials never saw them when the train reached the construction sites.

While the bonanzas employed from 100 to 1,000 men each, nearly every homesteader who had more than a quarter section also employed one or two hired men the year around especially if they had livestock. Farmers with a section or more hired from twelve to thirty men for cropping season. Hobart, who farmed a half section, had two hired men in addition to his own large family for winter work. The Woodwards hired a permanent choreman even though there were two young men in the family who worked. The Woodwards, the Divets, and the Lockharts all had a dozen or more men during the entire farming season and when harvest time came the crews were increased to twenty-four or thirty.

The harvest crews, whether on the bonanza or the homesteads, represented a cross section of American society. Knut Hamsun, who later became a famous Norwegian author and Nobel Prize winner, worked on small farms and bonanzas in the 1880's and found that he had to work very hard under conditions more distasteful than those he had left in Europe. On one crew he worked with Germans, "two other Norwegians, a Swede, ten or twelve Irishmen and a few Americans." He preferred working with large crews because he wanted to study America and its people. Like so many other immigrants in the harvest fields, he "was afflicted with homesickness and often wept. My landlady laughed indulgently; she taught me the English word 'homesick.' " He frequently felt completely alone because he was just another foreigner and hired man, and could not afford to return to his homeland.

Many of the farmers never even knew the names or the backgrounds of their transient harvest hands. When two men were injured and two died after lightning struck the Woodward's barn in which they were sleeping, their names were not even recorded in the family diary. They were nameless cogs in the wheel that opened the frontier. Even Probstfield, who was particularly interested in people, never got to know more than the first names of some of his harvest workers and he often referred to them by their nationality: "Paid Swede that worked through harvest $20.95." Many men, however, were treated as one of the family and returned to the same farm for ten, fifteen, or even twenty years.

The W. J. Peets had a hired man who left each fall and returned on the same day in March for seventeen years. He never wrote ahead, but the whole family watched for him to come walking down the field road on that day. Because he had no relatives and no savings, he lived with the Peet family in his old age. At another time the Peets employed an ex-sailor, Pete Johnson, who had a crippled back and could only do handyman work. He worked for his room and board for several years. John Martin, who had been yard man on the Dodge farm for four years, decided that he wanted to spend his winters working in the woods rather than doing chores. When he left, the family diary noted, "We will miss him—he is like one of the family." About the middle of December he returned because "he said he got lonesome in the woods." [1]

Homesteaders to the east side of Red River Land, who had smaller farms, made a regular practice of stacking their grain and then going to the harvest fields of the bonanza farms. In some cases both husband and wife went to work on the bonanzas. Some came with teams and wagons from as far away as Illinois and Iowa and worked until corn harvest commenced back home. They were paid $4 to $5 a day for themselves, their team, and their wagon, and "when it was so d--- dark you couldn't find the shocks" it was quitting time.

A farm with a good reputation found it easy to maintain a labor force. A good reputation meant comfortable sleeping quarters for the farm hands and good food. Men expected to sleep in hay lofts, granaries, or machine sheds because only a few farms other than the bonanza farms had bunkhouses and the men realized that a one-room log cabin with seven or eight people in it did not have much more to offer in the line of comfort during the summer season than the out-of-doors. Some employers provided beds and bedding and others did not. There was certainly a variance in food and in cooks, but generally the food was abundant and wholesome and the labor force ate the same food as the family did. One supper menu at the Woodwards consisted of "boiled beef, vegetables, mince pie, doughnuts—such things and as hungry men like."

A common complaint among the women who had to cook for these big crews was their enormous appetites and their regularity at the table, even if they had not worked and had been up town during the day. As much as 500 pounds of flour was used on several of the large homesteads during a single threshing period. Butchering was a constant chore. In spite of Mrs. Woodward's efficiency and a daughter and a hired girl to help her, she was unable to keep up with the work. Consequently, they hired a man who had been a cook in Germany, on steamers, in lumber camps, and at summer resorts and hotels. "He is fat and lazy." With twenty beds to make as well as the feeding and threshing duties, the womenfolk still had all they could manage.

Some times farmers employed traveling custom thresher crews. These crews provided their own cook car. The custom thresher could fire his cooks if they were not good, but the homesteader was generally married to his so he could not fire her. Many of the cooks hired for the threshing crews cooked in lumber camps during the winter. Standard fare for cook-house meals included bread, butter, meat (beef, ham, salt pork), sometimes eggs, vegetables (beans, corn, or peas, all from large tins), sometimes fresh vegetables, and always potatoes. To top off the meal there was either raisin, lemon, sour cream, or dried apple pie, or dried fruit sauce (either prunes or apricots), cake (either pan or cup cakes) generally without frosting, coffee, and the ever-present molasses. Barrels of beans, sugar, dried fruit, and whole coffee beans, plus cases of other goods were all stored in preparation for the threshing season.

With so many men gathered on the farms for the harvest, trouble among them was bound to occur, especially during rainy spells or machinery breakdowns. On many farms men were forbidden to gamble because "it always led to fighting" within a single labor crew or between crews. Competition between various custom threshing crews was intense and tricks such as placing a horse shoe or a partial ball of twine in the midst of a bundle of grain could touch off a real war. Everyone wanted to put in all the time he could and when a "loaded

bundle" entered the threshing machine the resulting breakdown trig-
gered the action.

Sometimes minor irritations were enough to start a fight such as the
one that occurred between two Irish boys when "Tom said Felix
called him 'onproper names.' Each is minus a flannel shirt but have
scratches on their faces. They expected to be fired but if they settle
down David will keep them." Two other men, who had often disa-
greed before, had a fight in the barn while harnessing horses. Later,
one of them returned to the yard with his plow and announced that
he was quitting because he had concluded that the other fellow,
"Dutch Henry," would not give up the feud. The farmer agreed although he did not like to lose the man. "We hired the first man who
came along, we cannot afford to have a plow idle."

Not all transients who quit had such good reasons. Two Swedes
told Probstfield. "Want to quit, we have to *stand up* too early for $15
per month." On occasion, workers just quit. "Both wood choppers left
without saying a word." One man hired by the Woodwards to do farm
work was assigned to dig a cellar. He did not like that job and he was
next seen walking a mile down the road toward Mapleton. "He did
not even ask for his wages for one day. Good enough!"

Some of the men hired were very reliable and others were just the
opposite.

"Pat spread out wet hay from windrows and opened all hay cocks
being wet. Finished about 5 p.m. and *sat down*. Alfred worked all day
[butchering] then came home from the market at 10 p.m. Put horses
in stable without giving water or hay. Got up out of bed and watered
and fed them—good man! . . . Sunday hired Mennonite—Tues discharged same—paid him 40¢ for half days labor—worthless. . . .
[Later] hired man to shock—discharged him after 2½ days—no good."

Probstfield would not tolerate any insults either and "discharged
Beaton for making a remark this morning—'I wish I was done in this
hole.'" As stern as this may seem, a short time later when the men
were stacking wheat and making other preparations for threshing,
Probstfield purchased a gallon of whiskey for $4 to keep their spirits
up.

Whenever there were such large numbers of men around, personal
property had to be watched closely. "The men lie around the yard,
playing ball, resting, and washing their clothes. It is very trying to
have threshers on the place. Everything is upset. Pails, lanterns, and
all things moveable are missing. . . . The crew left, only stole five
blankets, some tools and other things, 'the rascals.'" However, they

got along well together, for there were no fights, "not a cross word nor quarrel all through" the season.

Not all men were problems for James Lockhart, who had a year round crew of four men and thirty at harvest time, fired only one man in all his years of farming. Even though the men were transients, most of them were trying to get a start in hopes of making a better living.[2]

Family Labor

The members of the homesteader's own family worked just as hard as the hired laborer. Sixteen-year-old Mary Probstfield did back-setting with a double yoke of oxen. What more was expected of a hired man? When her brother Walter was twelve and her sister Emilie was thirteen, one of their regular jobs was plowing with a sulky plow. While the children were plowing, Mr. and Mrs. Probstfield hand raked the harvested wheat field and carried the gleanings to the hog pen, and the hired man split logs in the woods for fuel for the steam engine. In her early teens, when they were short of men during threshing, Ada Lockhart Gunkelman drove the straw bucker which bucked the straw from the straw elevator back to the engine where it was used for fuel. When not doing that, she helped her mother and the hired girl cook and make beds for thirty men. She also helped with chicken and hog chores as well as pumped water for the livestock and for forty head of horses.

It was no different at the Divets, the Overbys, the Fuglestads, the Crawfords, or any of the other homesteads. Everybody had a job. However, at the Lessings, who had a half section as well as an extensive livestock operation, Elsie, 15, plowed for her father, and the other daughters had to work out-of-doors also. The eight children and the mother did most of the work. Teenage Elsie and Lena Lessing hauled wood with a four-horse team from the Sheyenne River to their home south of Mapleton. It is difficult to "understand how any female can do as much work as they do, yet it is plain that they are females."

At age eleven R. D. Crawford started out breaking three sections of land with a walking plow. From April, 1882, when he started plowing until he left home in November, 1894, he estimated that he had walked 90,000 miles; the original plowing and backsetting alone, using a twelve-inch walking plow, involved over 30,000 miles of walking. No doubt there were others who also plowed two miles per hour, for Crawford would not have had enough time to do that much walking in the years included. He bluntly stated that a farmer could not have existed without extensive use of his non-paid family labor.[3]

Hired Girls

Looking at the immense amount of work performed by the farm women of yesterday, a woman of today can come to only one conclusion—the farmer's wife must have had hired help. This was not always the case. The 1920 agricultural census indicated that only twelve percent of the farms had hired girls. A much greater portion of them had help occasionally, but only during times of childbirth, injury, or sickness. The average pioneer farmer could not afford domestic help and relied on his large family. The boys as well as the girls were expected to do their share of housework, barnyard chores, and field work.

Information about the duties of a hired girl was just as difficult to obtain as were comments about routine household duties. Apparently everyone assumed that such routine matters were not worth recording. Most family biographies had no more than one reference to the activities of the hired girl. Only five of the nearly fifty families interviewed or otherwise studied indicated that they had a hired girl for any length of time. These were the Hovdes, the Lockharts, the Ole Overbys, the Woodwards, and the Hobarts. All had special reasons for having hired girls. Mrs. Hovde became an invalid early in life; Mrs. Hobart had heart trouble; the Lockharts and Overbys operated larger than average farms; and the Woodwards received payment for hired help from an absentee landlord. The Overbys were also in the habit of helping new immigrants to America and having them "work out" their expenses.

Working out for the neighbors or working in town were accepted practices for a large number of the young women of that day. This work provided them with the opportunity to raise extra income for the family and to subsidize the farming operation. Even the Probstfield children were expected to help support the family with money which they earned. They were fortunate, however, because most of them received more than a grade school education and later they were able to earn much above average wages.

Hired girls generally received room and board and $2.50 to $4 per week and some received an extreme top of $5. These wages seem low by today's standards, but they did not appear that way to the pioneer farmer. When Mrs. Hobart had her first heart attack, "Mary Knutson was hired for $2.50 a week, plus room and board. This employment was for seven days a week with no vacations except an occasional free Sunday afternoon to visit her parents. She was with the Hobarts for a year and a half. After she left, a Fargo girl, Mattie Mitchell, worked for the Hobarts for several months. In 1888 they

Of Those Who Toil

hired Agnes Gilmore. In April, 1889, Julie Germstad was hired. Next came a brother-sister combination, Lewis and Nellie Olstad, who stayed into the threshing season of the second year when they both left because "threshing wages [on the bonanzas] were too much of a temptation." Nellie worked on the kitchen crew there. Both men and women were so fascinated by the drama of working on a bonanza farm with its large crew of men and parades of machines and horses that they preferred them to work on a small farm. Next, Hobart hired a man and his wife, Hans and Maria Thomson, who received the standard wage of $50 per month plus room and board.

Having a hired girl around was not always an asset, as the testimony of Mrs. Bernard Holes and Mrs. Woodward reveals. Mrs. Holes had two hired girls to help during the threshing season when she had her first baby. Those two girls fought with each other constantly. Late one forenoon, the fifth day after the baby was born and when preparations for dinner should have been in progress, Mrs. Holes noticed that there were no sounds coming from the kitchen. She got out of bed and walked out to the kitchen where she found both girls sitting, doing nothing. When asked what was the matter, one of the girls replied, "There's no wood in the house." The wood, kept in the woodshed next to the house, was normally carried in by the choreman, but because he was busy with threshing chores, he had not done the job. When the girls refused to carry in the wood, Mrs. Holes had to do it so that they could get dinner started.

In Mrs. Woodward's account of her experiences from 1884 to 1889 is another good example of some of the problems involved with hired girls. She wrote:

Fred brought a Swedish girl named Mary who cannot speak one word of English. I hate to bother with her but we must have someone. . . . Hired a married couple by name of Pascal, he is French, she is Yankee. . . . Walter brought a girl [Elsie] from Fargo who is seven months from Norway. If she had as good judgment as Roxy [the dog] I should be glad, but she says "yes" to everything so I cannot tell whether she understands or not. . . . The hired girl's sister is here with her and they stay in the kitchen and jabber Norwegian. They have been singing beautifully together there this evening. Elsie made some good fried cakes which is encouraging. If she could only understand English I could teach her housework. . . . I was nearly beside myself getting dinner for thirteen men besides carpenters and tinners with Katie [her daughter] sick in bed and Elsie washing. I baked seventeen loaves of bread today, making seventy-four loaves since last Sunday, not to mention twenty-one pies, and puddings, cakes and doughnuts. . . . The hired girl is a regular "hired" and I have to follow her around to cover up jars, tubs, and barrels. She seems to want the bottom piece in the pork barrel. But she is big and strong and knows how to work. She weights 170 pounds; Katie 102; I 116.

Later, in July, 1887, when ten men were hired to help during harvest, she wrote:

I might have secured the services of a Norwegian girl, just landed, but I thought if my soul must go, my body might just as well go with it. Ella Sampson [a neighbor girl] came to help us. Her mother is anxious to have her learn, and said I was to tell her to "stand up" in the morning.

Another time Mrs. Sampson came over and "helped all day on two dozen sheets and pillow cases. She has rubbed all day and Katie has sudsed and rinsed and hung them out."

Another couple was employed and everyone seemed pleased:

Mrs. Doyle a good, homespun-looking woman, nineteen years old. She and her husband have a farm in the timber of Minnesota. They are very poor so that four dollars a week was some inducement. . . . We have a good girl this time . . . did sheets and pillow cases from twelve beds. A big washing. The bedding from the men's beds was pounded in a barrel so that they need no rubbing.

The Doyles had to go back to their own farm after the threshing season was over, so when another season rolled around, Mary, an Irish girl from Fargo was hired:

Mary can pare potatoes, but if she is not watched she will have them on the stove any time. The other day they were about half cooked when I told her they would be done too soon. She said, "Well, I will pull the fire out." She can wash, but she doesn't know what to do with the clothes when she has rubbed them. If I were strong enough I should rather do the work myself. I did not know what a boon it was when I was too poor to have a hired girl.

Mary did not stay long. The next hired girl was Mary Magdalene, a fifty-year old French woman, who obviously knew how to do house work. "She, poor thing, is poverty stricken and has left a farm to come here and earn four dollars a week." Later in the summer Mary refused to blacken the stove when told to do so because she said that it was a man's job, so Mrs. Woodward did it. Before the summer was over the second Mary had left and the mother and daughter were alone again to do the work. "Katie baked a half bushel of cookies yesterday. . . . We have no help with the cooking. I might as well have my feet ache as my soul tried by the help we get, and they must all have four dollars a week for trying us." It was nearly impossible to hire girls during that August. A short time later they hired a Swedish girl who had just arrived in Moorhead and could not speak a word of English.

In their last year of farming in bonanzaland, the Woodwards had one of their better hired girls, Tilda Olson, a new arrival from Norway. Mrs. Woodward noted that she could not speak much English "but she looks right" and is "strong and clean." Mrs. Woodward wrote, "She can 'feestan' me," and praised her for being a good worker. Besides the baking of eight loaves of bread each day, she did the laundry for the crew. The latter chore carried some risk. "Tilda is washing the men's bedding and she has a lively lot of clothes. If we can manage to keep the house free from these insects we are thankful." No wonder the Woodwards did not want to have their hired men sleeping in the house.

Most hired girls did not have a pleasant life, for their work was hard and their hours were long. Crews had big appetites and there were few appliances to reduce the work requirements. Hired girls were not always treated as first class citizens although some families accepted them as a "big sister." Girls who worked in cook cars had an especially trying life. Sometimes the cooks were wives of crew members, but usually two single girls cooked for thirty or forty men. The girls in the cook car for a threshing crew in eastern Steele County received more attention than they cared from a "sticky lady lover." One evening after supper the "lover" was sitting on the steps of the cook car waiting for them to finish with the dishes. The girls were disgusted with his attentions so that when they were ready to dump the greasy dish water they managed to pour a tub-sized basin of it over his head. He was less attentive after that.

A girl did not remain a hired girl long if she was the least bit alert to the opportunities for young women. One newspaper article described the situation: "This territory is the place for young women. Not the worthless substitute which comes ready made . . . but the earnest, industrious young women who are willing to work and make themselves useful. There is a scarcity of such young women here, and of those that have come nearly all have married since their arrival." The article continued by citing the case of Miss Belle Clinton of Iowa who, after saving $100 from her teacher's salary, homesteaded 160 acres near Hillsboro and established a timber claim on another 120 acres. The following spring she took up another quarter section. The article anticipated that in ten years she would be worth $25,000, but did not follow up to report whether or not she had reached her objective by 1892. Miss Clinton did not come to Dakota to be a hired girl. She was a speculator, but she was, no doubt, comforted by the great opportunity open to women.

In spite of temporary hardships, young, single women, like all other early settlers in this area, were optimistic. A few, such as Miss Phelps, a friend of Mrs. Woodward, did very well. She and her sister had come to Fargo in 1881 with no financial resources. After working for a short time, they started trading in city lots and taking up claims. By 1885 they were "worth a great deal of money. They think that any energetic self-reliant young lady could find no place where she could do as well as in this territory." Mrs. Woodward was quite impressed with the good fortune of the Phelps sisters.[4]

Negro Laborers

Because there are only a few Negroes in Red River Land in contemporary times, many people have the idea that there were never any black people in the area in earlier days. Contrary to popular opinion, however, Negro laborers and some Negro homesteaders did come to the Red River Valley during the Great Dakota Boom. Ada Lockhart Gunkelman reported that when she was a girl of twelve one of her regular jobs was to cross the Red River at Hendrum and pick up farm laborers who had jumped off the train there. One day the only laborer available was a Negro, the first she had ever seen. When the buggy returned to the farm, everyone was surprised to see a large, black passenger in it.

About twenty miles south of Fargo there is an elevator and a large farmstead. These buildings are all that remain of a small community called Lithia. This settlement was formerly called Montgomery after William T. Montgomery who eventually owned 1,020 acres there in the 1880's and 1890's. Montgomery had been a slave and is believed to have been owned by a brother to Confederate President Jefferson Davis. He purchased section 11 in Eagle Township, Richland County, from the Northern Pacific Railroad. The farm is now owned by Ernest J. Israelson.

During his first winters in the area Montgomery lived at the European Hotel in Fargo. When that building was razed and replaced by the Forte Hotel, he purchased the lumber to build a large house for himself on his farm. Some of his closest friends were the Joseph Hollands family who had given up farming in Wisconsin because of the serious wild oat infestation there and had decided to come to Dakota in 1884. The Hollands, who were employed by Mr. Montgomery, were still living with him in November, 1885, when their son, George, was born. For several years after the Hollands left the employ of Montgomery in order to farm for themselves, he hired local women as housekeepers, but in the early 1890's he went south and brought back a Negro lady who worked for him for about five years.

As his farm expanded, Montgomery built an elevator on his land along the railroad and this became a local train stop. Whenever the Hollands got off the train at his station, he was sure to hitch up his team and take them to their farm. His early successes were somewhat diminished when he went into partnership with a not too successful Captain Hunt. He also lost money speculating on the grain futures market, but it was his own kindheartedness that hurt him most. He never was strict enough with his manager or his other employees and they were extremely careless with his equipment. This carelessness proved to be costly. He lost a fair sum of money in the fall of 1888 when he paid full market price for frozen wheat. Later when he learned that it could not be resold for milling purposes, he was forced to take a large discount on it. In the 1890's he sold his farm and joined some Fargoans in a land investment scheme in Canada. It proved to be a complete failure. Montgomery then returned to Mississippi where he worked as a bookkeeper. He was nearly blind when he visited Fargo after World War I but he could still recognize the Hollands and other friends by their voices. He was educated and had been well liked in the community.

Another Negro, Isham Evans, worked on a large farm near Page and later homesteaded there. One of his stepchildren farmed for many years in the Page area and a stepdaughter, Ella Nora Bryant, who had come to Page in 1884, spent her entire life there working for others. She was acclaimed by one Sunday School class to be the best example of a Christian person in Page. By contrast, the only other known Negro in that area was Henry Hubbard, who was arrested as a "rum runner" by United States Marshals.

One of several Negro farm workers who came each year for the cropping season was George Washington, who worked for two generations for the Holland family. He last appeared in 1925. The Hollands never knew anything about Washington's background, but they said he was an extremely good worker, a very polite man, and especially "good around the house." He always traveled alone. Another Negro who worked for them was known only as Ed. Ed told the Hollands that he liked working for them because they were English and he could understand them much better than he could understand the broken language of the Norwegians, the Swedes, and the Germans.

One Negro, who worked around Christine and Abercrombie, could speak Norwegian and was known everywhere in the area as the "Norwegian Negro." Other Negroes were employed on bonanza farms. George Hollands knew of two Negro barbers in Fargo, Mr. Gordon

and his helper, Ed, both of whom did very well in their trade up to
about 1895 when they went north to take up homesteads.

David McCauley had a black employee in the early 1870's. Augus-
tus Lewis, who was known in the Wilkin County Community as "Nig-
ger Gus," was born in New Orleans in 1859, the son of slave parents.
After the Civil War he stowed away on a river boat destined for Fort
Snelling where he was taken in charge by one of the officers bound for
Fort Ransom. He was well treated there but, becoming bored with
duties as an orderly, he escaped to Fort Abercrombie where he met
David McCauley and asked for employment. He remained in McCauley's employ as a groomsman until McCauley's death. Lewis worked
elsewhere in the Valley and became a well respected citizen. He died
at Mahnomen on May 28, 1936.

One Negro harvest hand was lynched from a Red River bridge at
Grand Forks in 1882. Even though some of the community's most respectable citizens figured in this case, there appears to have been no
noticeable prejudice toward any minority group in early Red River
Land for many white laborers also met with a similar fate from time
to time.[5]

Wages for Farm Labor 1873-1905

The cost of labor has always played an important part in the economics of farming. The initial cost of labor on the frontier was relatively high, but when the supply increased faster than the demand,
wage rates dropped drastically. In years of bumper crops, labor costs
rose sharply, reflecting the farmer's eagerness to collect his profitable
harvest.

Initially, most homesteaders had little reason for hiring labor and
could rely on family help and exchange labor with their neighbors.
However, after they had all of their land in crops, they were forced
to hire labor for seeding as well as harvest. During most of the 1870's,
Probstfield was able to hire winter labor for chopping wood at $1.25
per cord. The figure amounted to $1 per day.

All day labor, regardless of season, was hired on a no work-no pay
basis, and generally received $1 per day, except during the peak har-
vest season when it reached a maximum of $2. Day laborers were paid
only part of their wages each month to guarantee their staying
through the crop season. Men hired on an annual basis received an
average monthly wage of $20. Room, board, and washing were com-
monly provided for all the laborers.

Charles Hobart paid his hired man, August Rahm, who could speak
only Norwegian and who was "the hardest worker" he ever had, a

bonus of twenty five cents an acre for "anything over ten acres that he shocked each day." Rahm earned a $20 bonus one season for shocking 320 acres at an average of thirteen acres a day. Probstfield paid one of his grown sons $100 a year to keep him at home. This price was less than he had to pay labor of equal caliber, but probably more than most farmers' sons received for working at home.

The normal work day of the 1880's during seeding, haying, and harvest was long on the Divet farm. A chore man got up at 3 a.m. (sometimes 2 a.m. depending on how many teams he had to get ready) and filled the mangers with hay. After he gave the horses their oats, he called the field men to curry and to harness them. The men then went in for breakfast, which took about half an hour, and were ready for field work at full daylight. A full hour was necessary at noon to rest and to feed the horses. When it was hot, the horses were either changed at noon or an extra half hour's rest was taken. They were always in the barn by dusk. After supper, the men dried and brushed the horses. For this standard work day on most farms the men received $1 plus room, board, and washing.

In the mid-1880's, after the "flush" of the Great Dakota Boom had subsided, labor costs were reduced and the "best men" could be hired for $16 to $19 a month during the crop season and during the winter for $6 to $10 a month. Probstfield, who had willingly paid $2 a day for harvest and threshing labor in 1885, refused to pay $1.50 in the harvest of 1887. That winter he reduced the wages paid for making cord wood to eighty-five cents for elm and seventy-five cents for all other wood, which was down from $1.25 in earlier years. He employed a man to cut 500 cords at those rates.

During the dry spell of 1886-90, many men were forced to work for just room and board during the winter. The best fall work came to those who harvested potatoes, a rapidly expanding crop in the area. Pickers received two cents a bushel and a good picker could gather fifty to sixty bushels a day.

However, even the rapid rise of the potato industry could not stem the tide of the weak farm economy in the late 1890's. Many laborers were so desperate that they were willing to work for seventy-five cents a day. Local boys, who usually had first chance at available jobs, were satisfied to get $8 to $10 a month for the seven-month crop season. Frank Liebenow attended school whenever he could not find work and by the time he was twenty-seven he had saved enough to start farming for himself on a rented half section. He thought that both homesteaders and bonanza farmers were hard on hired men and he had seen fellow workers fired "on the spot because there always seemed to be many more available."

In addition to the bonanza farms, the major competitors for labor were the railroads. In 1883 the Northern Pacific Railway in North Dakota had over a thousand employees who received an average daily wage of $2.21. Five years later the railroad company employed nearly 1,400 men in the state at an average daily wage of $2.27. Although these wages were higher than those of farm laborers, they did not include the living costs of room, board, and washing. By 1901 the Northern Pacific had 2,535 employees in North Dakota and was the largest private employer in the state, but the average daily wage had dropped to $1.85. J. E. McCarthy of Wheatland started working for the Northern Pacific in 1903 and received fifty cents a day as a water boy and helper. In 1906 he was given full time status and received fifteen cents an hour for ten hours a day, six days a week. The following year he was promoted to section foreman at Magnolia (no longer in existence), half-way between Buffalo and Wheatland, and was advanced to $55 a month, which he said was excellent pay.

Torkel Fuglestad was fortunate to find a good haying job at a time when he needed to supplement his meager farm income. In the fall of 1883 he was paid fifteen cents per cubic yard to move dirt with a spade and a wheelbarrow to build the approach to a bridge being built over the Sheyenne River east of Cooperstown. This bridge was the first public one in Griggs County. After paying room and board, he was able to save $3 a day. He moved about twenty-six cubic yards of dirt a day, a very substantial achievement, and in one month he earned enough to buy groceries for the winter.

Often young people, who failed to see a future in farming because of its drudgery and risks, took jobs in town. In 1890 twenty-two year old Edmund Probstfield started working for the J. I. Case Company in Fargo for $55 a month and his eighteen-year-old sister, Dorothea, started teaching school at Sheldon for $35 a month. Alexander Probstfield, 27, took a job as bookkeeper at the East Grand Forks Brewery. R. D. Crawford, who had become very bitter about farming, went East to work in an electrical machinery factory in 1895 for seven cents an hour, ten hours a day for five days and nine hours on Saturday. He thought the job was better than farming because he had some time for himself with this "shorter work week."

Guy Divet started teaching school when he was seventeen years old, but since he did not like it, he bought a half interest in a livery stable at Hankinson which paid for itself and produced $1,500 in profits in the first year. Divet's partner lost most of the profits gambling one night at Lidgerwood; consequently, Divet became sole owner of the business. He soon earned enough money to pay for an education in law and went on to become a very successful lawyer.

Low as farm wages appeared to be, agricultural economy with its low margins and its many fluctuations, was not able to pay more. Walter Woodward, who was hired to manage the 1,520-acre Dodge Farm for $1,000 a year plus living expenses, was out of a job in 1889 after five years because the owner, Daniel Dodge, maintained that the farm was not profitable. Because he was unable to find a buyer, Dodge was forced to share rent the farm for many years. This example is proof that the smaller farmers were not immune to the same conditions that were bankrupting the bonanza farms at that time.

Because some of the early farmers in the Red River Valley lacked capital, they hired out to others with their teams and machinery in order to supplement their income. The price for this type of labor reacted sharply to the supply and demand and followed the same pattern as wages. Probstfield and his three yoke of oxen worked for the Hudson's Bay Company in January, 1873, for $2.50 a day. At the same time his hired man and five horses received $3.15 a day. In 1874 Probstfield paid $3 a day for a man and team with a mower for haying or a plow for breaking sod. On the per acre basis it was $2 an acre to break new sod and $1.50 for previously plowed land. By 1890 he had to pay as much as $3.50 an acre for breaking sod.

Seeding could be hired for $2.75 a day for a man, a team, and seeder unit, while cutting grain with a man, a team, and a binder unit cost $1.50 an acre, or when hired by the day, about $7.50 to $10 a day. Throughout the 1880's and early 1890's, except occasionally during the peak of harvest in bumper years when a man and team could demand $5 a day for a few days, the common daily rate was $2.25 to $3 for nearly all kinds of work.[6]

The farm laborer, male or female, played an indispensable part in developing the farmers' frontier. In the Red River Valley he was even more significant than in many other areas of the country because the farms, in general, tended to be larger here than on most of the other frontiers. He was important to the homesteader, but even more essential to the bonanza farmer. Fortunately for the individual laborers, many of them became farm owners or wives of farmers and in this manner achieved a goal that was not as attainable for the factory laborer of that day.

FOOTNOTES

[1] Rogin, pp. 131-132; Holbrook. p. 79; Theodore C. Blegen, *Norwegian Migration to America: The American Transition* (Northfield, Minn., 1940), p. 566; Blegen's book is a

fascinating account of Norwegian immigrants and their experiences in America; Arlo W. Anderson, "Knut Hamsun's America," *Norwegian American Studies*, XXIII, ed. Carlton C. Qualey (Northfield, Minn., 1967), p. 201; Knut Hamsun, *On Over Grown Paths* (New York, 1967), pp. 157-165; Hanna Astrup Larsen, *Knut Hamsun* (New York, 1922), p. 22; *Dakota Farmer*, V (Jan., 1886), 1; Woodward, pp. 92, 100, 151; *Hillsboro Banner*, July 14, 1882.

² Olsen interview; Holes interview; Pratt interview; Probstfield; Gunkelman interview; O. Overby, *Retrospect*, p. 16; Crawford, NDIRS, File 290; Knut Hamsun, "The Prairie," *The Living Age*, CCCX (Aug. 27, 1921), 549; *Hillsboro Banner*, July 14, 1882.

³ Probstfield; Hobart, "Pioneering,," VII, 226; Gunkelman interview; Woodward, pp. 157, 228; *Fargo Argus*, March 25, Oct. 19, 1882; Holes interview; Ankerfeldt interview; Emma Erickson Elton, *Eglon Memories: A History of Eglon Township, Clay County, Minnesota* (Hawley, Minn., 1967), p. 77; *Warren Sheaf*, July 15, 1891; *Our Page*, pp. 92, 93, 99, 169; Wilkins, p. 23; David Peet interview; Pratt interview; Woodward, pp. 43, 133-138, 173, 179, 192, 244-247. David Peet has an excellent privately operated museum of agriculture and domestic life in the Red River Valley.

⁴ *World's Work*, XL (Sept., 1920), 435; Hobart, "Pioneering," VII, 218-226, VIII, 118-125; Thortvedt, NDIRS, File 332; Probstfield; Rendahl, p. 14, Woodward, pp. 41, 44, 54, 84, 88, 90, 122, 179, 192, 222-239, 246; O. Overby, *Retrospect*, p. 35; *Hillsboro Banner*, Feb. 24, 1882.

⁵ George Holland, Hickson, N.D., interview by the author, May 12, 1967. The Hollands still live on the farm homesteaded by his father in 1886; *Valley Alert*, "Wilkin County Centennial 1868-1968," July 18, 1968, pp. 87-88; Wilkins, p. 23; *Our Page*, pp. 92-93, 99, 169.

⁶ Probstfield; Fuglestad, p. 7; Hobart, "Pioneering," VII, pp. 197, 213, 224, VIII, p. 127; Divet, NDIRS, File 69; Woodward, p. 9; Dakota Railroad Commissioner, *Annual Report*, 1886-1888; North Dakota Railroad Commissioner, *Annual Report*, 1890, 1896, 1901; Liebenow interview; *The Record*, II (Sept., 1896); Crawford, NDIRS, File 290; Sands interview; John E. McCarthy, interview by the author, May 18, 1968; Power Letterbook, XIV, 678, NDIRS, File 309; United States Statistical Abstract 1967, *Agricultural Statistics*, p. 663; *Alvarado Golden Jubilee 1905-1955*, p. 9. Large road equipment cost about $.15 a cubic yard to move dirt, but as much as 35 yards can be moved in one load. Fuglestad received the same amount per yard using a spade and a wheelbarrow. One man with modern equipment can easily do more dirt moving than 100 could with Fuglestad's equipment.

CHAPTER XI

Fun and Frolic

CHARLES CAVILEER, speaking about his experiences as customs inspector at Pembina in 1851 and later, said, "Only Pembina could boast of its log houses, Indian tepees, or wigwams, it had its hunters, its fishers, its traders, its Catholic Mission and Missionaries and the sound of its church bell could on the Sabbath Day be heard calling the faithful to worship, and with all that I found as much happiness in those days as with a more pretentious and civilized people."

Social activities for the pioneer farmer in Red River Land were limited by distance, by heavy work requirements, and by a lack of money. His social life consisted chiefly in visiting the neighbors and it was very non-commercialized in nature. As late as 1920 the average farmer in America lived a mile and one-half from his school, three miles from his church, and five miles from his trade center. In the Valley, the average distances in most cases were even greater because the farms were generally larger than in other parts of the nation. With such distances at a time when travel was restricted to a top practical speed of four miles an hour by horse, is it any wonder that social life was limited? It was not until after World War I and the appearance of the automobile roads that Community Clubs, sewing clubs, and other organized community entertainment became commonplace in rural America.

Some pioneers, who lived in the 1870's and later, have recorded their feelings about the social side of those times and have expressed no regret for having lived in that era. At least one felt that even though life may not have been "very thrilling," the changes "were not so apparent then" as in the twentieth century, and "all life was simple" but pleasant enough. Another, who saw the virgin prairie around Hope being turned under by ox drawn plows, said, "I'm glad that I saw those pioneer days and have witnessed the change that has taken place in every way." Others felt that they "were happier then than we are today—more grateful for the little things." From another part of the Valley came the comment, "They were great times. People were more satisfied in those days. You couldn't get anywhere so you were satisfied to stay home." You knew who your neighbors were and "you don't know them today [1966]." The children were easy to satisfy. Children liked to go to the Hillsboro bank because "Mr. Hanson, the banker . . . kept peanuts in his pocket" for them. A visitor at the Hovde home brought a bag of "store candy which was kept in the old chest [from Norway] and doled out on special occasions." That bag of candy lasted a long time.

Trips to town for strictly social or pleasure purposes were seldom made. Even the Woodwards, who were better educated and more culturally inclined than most pioneers, reported less than a dozen purely pleasure trips to Fargo in a five-year period, although it was only eight miles away. On one such occasion the younger set went to see a play entitled, "Called Back," presented by the Grismer-Davis Dramatic Company, a traveling entertainment troupe.

Fred Bill, Red River steamboat captain, said, "There was not much time for anything but digging hard to make a living, but occasionally the people turned loose, especially to give the children some pleasure. On July 24, 1877, Captain H. W. Holmes with the steamer *Selkirk* gave the Sunday School an excursion." The *Selkirk*, loaded with passengers, left Moorhead at 5 p.m. and went to Oakport, a distance of about seven and one-half miles by river and three miles by land. The boat returned to Moorhead with its joyous crowd at 9 p.m. The fare was twenty-five cents for adults and nothing for children.

Every little event made news in those days and even the daily papers of the larger towns had plenty of room for local social news. The *Fargo Argus* of the early 1880's had surveyed the eating habits of the guests at public places in Fargo and revealed that seventy-four percent of the men and fifty-nine percent of the women "did their feeding with a knife." This trait was considered evidence of the high ratio of immigrants in town. Unfortunately, a Grand Forks writer later used that information as proof that his city was more cultured than Fargo. Another local paper reported, "The month has been one continual round of excitment at Fargo" for it was the site of a Teacher's Institute, a Catholic convention, a Shriner's meeting, and statewide meetings of the dentists, the doctors, the sportsmen, and the Masons. To top it all off, the United States District Court had been in session all month. It is evident that there were things to do in those days, but since there were fewer people, not as many organizations were necessary to keep things moving as now.[1]

Organizations

Even in its most primitive state, the frontier country was not totally devoid of festive events and of organizations for the promotion of social life and community service. Probstfield was very community conscious and from the beginning he was active in several organizations. He was one of the founders of the Farmers Alliance, which carried on some of its most effective activity in this region. He was a leader of the Agricultural Society, whose major purpose was to enhance agriculture and agricultural expositions. Dues were $1 per year. Membership in the International Order of Odd Fellows was more costly for by the 1880's he was paying $6 a year, plus other associated costs.

On at least one occasion Probstfield was so short of cash that he attended the meeting but did not participate in the meal at the lodge hall but waited instead until he returned home at 10:30 p.m. for his meal. His remarks closing that day's diary were, "*Times are just splendid.*" In December, 1888, following one of the most disastrous years in northwest agriculture, he had spent the day renewing notes for another year at eight and ten percent interest, including one for household expenses. In spite of this predicament, the following year he made a $12.50 donation to the I.O.O.F. which would have to be considered a sizeable gift when one remembers that land prices were about $10 an acre and a man got $1.25 for a day's work.

The Odd Fellows Lodge appeared in area towns at a very early date. Dr. W. P. Cleveland helped organize the first I.O.O.F. Lodge in North Dakota shortly after he arrived in Caledonia in 1879. The Odd Fellows sponsored musicals, socials, and various other types of parties for members and their families. These activities played an important part in the social life of the community. On January 27, 1885, an insert in the diary, obviously written by one of the Probstfield children, read, ' Papa, Mama, Mary, Draper [a schoolteacher staying at Probstfields], Justus, and Alex went to Odd Fellows dance—cash expenses at dance $3.25." Several members of the family also attended dances sponsored by the Alliance and the Masons. Probstfield never indicated that he belonged to the Masons, so apparently these were public dances sponsored by them.

Probstfield was also a member of the German Society, with annual dues of $1, and others in the family belonged to the Agassiz Literary Club, which was active in Fargo-Moorhead at that time. Similar literary clubs functioned in many of the communities in the area. Students at the Moorhead Normal (now Moorhead State College) debated with members of many of these literary groups.

The Masonic order was also active in Red River Land at an early date. There was a "Lodge" in nearly every community of more than a few hundred people. Pembina has the honor of having Lodge No. 1 in the state. On January 5, 1882, the *Warren Sheaf* noted that a Masonic Lodge was being organized in Warren. A few months later Hillsboro organized Territorial Lodge No. 19 A.F. and A.M. which was renumbered State Lodge No. 10 when North Dakota became a state. The Masons secured quarters on the second floor of Morgan's store in Hillsboro. The I.O.O.F. had organized their Lodge No. 33 at an earlier date and, not to be outdone by the Masons, constructed their own hall, which they dedicated with a grand ball on July 30, 1882. The James Lockharts were active in the Forester Lodge at Grandin and they considered it an important part of their social life.

Dancing

Dances, private or organized, rated high on the list of social pastimes of that day and were commonly attended by entire families. As in lumber camps and in bunk houses on the range, men in the bonanza farm bunk houses often wore ribbons pinned to their garments to designate them as "follow partners" in the evening's dancing because women were so scarce. Walter Spokesfield, in an early history of Wells County, wrote that arrangements were made to have a barn dance at the Sykes farm in 1882. This dance was believed to be the first semi-public one in that county. However, it was only with great difficulty that sixteen women were obtained for the dance. He used a question mark after the word "women" and what he meant is left for his readers to surmise.

Everett Dick's *Vanguards of the Frontier* contains thirty-six references to dancing as a frontier pastime—far more than any other form of recreation. It was as difficult to keep hired girls in small communities as on the farms. In an effort to keep them entertained, Fargo, at least, had a special series of dances for hired girls. The first such dance was held on Friday, January 12, 1881, at the Continental Hotel. No doubt it was well attended by the girls and since men outnumbered women on the labor force of the bonanza farms at a ratio of twenty-five to one, there were probably plenty of partners on hand. The Warren House organized "social hops" for the girls of that town. Violin and organ music was provided by the hotel to complement these "pleasant parties."

The Madsens at Wheatland had a "neighborhood ring" of eight

families who held dances at a different home every Friday night. Most of the time they relied on two violins for music, but in later years some of the homes had pianos. Iver Madsen proudly noted that Bill Langer, later governor and a senator, was a member of their dance ring. Because entire families took part in these affairs, the crowds must have been sizeable since the Madsens alone had ten children. There was absolutely no drinking, but coffee and a big lunch were served about midnight. Mrs. Pratt agreed that "lunches were not just desserts like now, but big meals." She noted that if all members of their dance ring planned to be present they had to go to the Grandin Hotel which had a sizeable hall, but most parties were held in the homes. Music was provided by the "local orchestra." The Lockharts and the Pratts were in the same dance ring. Mrs. Pratt was well in her teens before she realized that commercial entertainment was available in the city. Her first experience with such events came when she was taken on the train to a circus in Fargo.

Christine Hagen made her first twenty-mile trip to Fargo when she was fifteen so that she could buy shoes and dress material for confirmation. Most of the Glaspell's social engagements "ended at ten o'clock [but] we had a dancing club that exceeded this a little and it was very enjoyable. It was called the 2 a.m. (quit at Midnight) Club. We found three hours of dancing sufficient," with lunch and chatter after that. In the summer time this Jamestown group did a great deal of front porch singing and horseback riding.

Not everyone who attended the dancing parties danced and many played cards or went outdoors. Cards cost only ten cents a pack. Pedro, a card game on the order of whist, was a favorite in the Grandin area. Sometimes the younger set took sleigh rides using heated bricks and hot water jugs placed in the hay to keep their feet warm. Heavy buffalo and horse robes also helped them keep warm. Then the traditional big lunch was served at midnight.

When the Overbys of Cooperstown had a house warming in 1902 for their third new house, planks were put on nail kegs for seats. Sawdust covered the new floor, and the new organ was used to supply music. "Conversation, fun and humor, singing and devotions, all seemed to serve a central need, to break barriers that had developed in the strenuous every-man-for-himself struggle to get settled and provide for eventualities."

The Overby's new house was large enough for their party, but the Mike McMahons were not so fortunate. At a farewell party "everyone came, ten of them I didn't even know. They took down the kitchen stove, put it in a corner and Tom Houston with his fiddle sat on top of it. Such a crowd and such dancing! They fixed a hanger outside for the coffee pot so they could build a fire under the boiler." Mrs. Mc-Mahon baked six pies and two cakes as her share of the lunch.

Sabin, in Clay County, had a musical organization called the Sabin Brass Band that was directed in its later days by Pete Becker. The band played "everywhere between Baker and Watt's Siding" for barn dances, house dances, and at the Sabin Hall. Baker and Watt's Siding are about fifteen miles apart with Sabin situated in the middle. The band members were paid by a collection taken during the evening and at extra large functions the members received $2 each for their efforts.[2]

Fairs

Fairs, or county agricultural expositions, early became a significant part of the social and the educational life of the pioneers. The social part, even though it was the lesser of the two purposes, was, nevertheless, important. Getting the farmers to produce and to exhibit samples of their crops as well as to view the success of other farmers' efforts was the chief educational purpose of the county agricultural societies.

Because of their educational and economic value, fairs were instigated soon after the counties were organized. The location of the fair frequently became a plum of the county political organization. Fairs were first created in Canada in the northern Valley. The one held at Portage la Prairie in 1872 probably has the distinction of being the earliest. In 1875 an annual provincial exhibition was established and by 1882 there were seventeen fairs being held in the province of Manitoba.

An early fair in Clay County was held in 1875 at Hawley, twenty-five miles east of the Red River. This area was the heart of the greatest concentration of Clay County farmers, reflecting the Scandinavian's urge to locate in the hilly and wooded lake country rather than on the prairie. R. M. Probstfield was an aggressive leader in Clay County agricultural and fair circles, and he was a lifetime member of the State Agricultural Society. When he attended the Clay County Fair at Hawley on September 22 and 23, 1875, he took the 7:00 a.m. train to Hawley and returned at 8:30 p.m. on the second day. His two days at the fair cost him $1.10 for train fare, $1.00 for meals, twenty-five cents for lodging, and $4.10 for "sundries." At the same time he attended a county political convention held in conjunction with the fair. Very likely most of the money spent on "sundries" was relative to the convention.

The next year, when the fair was held on October 12, he commented that there was "no farm exhibition of any consequence but the merchants were well represented by a creditable show." He again participated at a Republican meeting on the same trip. Probstfield had frequent exhibits both at county and at state fairs that eventually culminated in his winning third prize for his wheat exhibit at the Columbian Exposition in Chicago in 1893. In 1886 he reported attending the Minnesota State Fair for several days with total expenses, including rail fare, of $30.05.

The *Warren Sheaf* reported that the first agricultural fair in Marshall County was held in Stephen, November 12, 1891. Not more than a few hundred people could have attended these early expositions considering the small size of the communities that held them and the poor roads and limited population of the surrounding areas. Mrs. L. A. Schultz, a lifetime resident of Chaffee, about forty miles southwest of Fargo, said that no one in her family ever got to the Cass County Fair because it was too far to travel with horses. The rail connections were very poor because Chaffee was located at the end of a branch line. Furthermore, she added that they did not have the money to spend, even if they had lived closer.[3]

July 4

The Fourth of July was easily the year's big social event in most communities from Lisbon to Warren. There would be picnics with sack races, horse races, bicycle races, foot races, bands, speeches, baseball games, games for the younger set, callithumpians (a charivari), and balloon ascensions. The day usually ended with a big dance and a display of fireworks. It was always the largest crowd of the year in Lisbon. The *Warren Sheaf* boasted that over 500 people attended the celebration in Warren each year. In Kelso "even the Grandins and Dalrymples came." This event was one of the few occasions when these bonanza families mixed with the rest of the community. Horse racing was popular with the girls and as many as seven girls with their horses participated in a single race.

Ada Lockhart Gunkelman remembered how happy she was when her father got her a fancy riding horse and told her, "Now you can give that Dalrymple girl a race." Clark Dalrymple's daughter, Dorothy, who later married John Pollock, was a great horsewoman and the envy of the other girls. The bonanza families had more time and money for riding horses, bicycles, and "things like that" and had them long before anyone else in the community. Their influence caused many of the small communities to establish tracks for riding and harness races. Horesback riding and buggy rides were favorite Sunday afternoon pastimes of a great share of the farm children even though they commonly had to use work horses because their families could never afford any type of road or riding horses. Only a few had ponies for road travel.

In the 1890's the Fourth of July celebration was going as strong as ever and was still the biggest annual event. By then the Mission Society of Warren had begun sponsoring a celebration which was open to the public. The day started at 10 a.m. with prayer, instrumental music, and singing, followed by two orations. Dinner was served with background music after which the races were held with $200 in prize money. Horse racing had a $15 first prize, foot races $7 and bicycle racing $3. The lucky winner in the potato race received $5. The winning side in the tug of war got $10 as did the one who caught the greased pig. A "bowery dance" was in continuous session all afternoon and evening. The big day ended with fireworks.

In some communities, like Wyndmere and others where the Norwegian population was heavy, May 17 (Norwegian Independence Day) probably took precedence over the Fourth of July in importance. Until well after World War I, Norwegians came from as far as Iowa to help their Dakota friends in Richland County celebrate. The only social event of other national minority groups that in any way resembled the May 17 celebration by the Norwegians was the attempt of the Scottish-Canadian immigrants to honor Robert Burns. Because his birthday anniversary is January 25, the weather generally prevented the Scots from having an elaborate outdoor event. Kilts were a little drafty for January in Red River Land.[4]

Sports

A large number of people of the area took an active part in sports in the early days. Nearly every little community had its baseball team. Many churches also had their own teams in addition to the informal teams of neighborhood youth. Oscar Overby, who belonged to a church team, reminisced, "I can still see it [Romness] boldly sewed across the chest of our homemade baseball uniforms." He recalled how anxious he and his brothers were to get the uniforms out of moth balls each spring and to have their mother patch them up for the new season. Their team name was later adopted as the name of Romness Township in which they lived. Many families, like the Probstfields, the Madsens, and the Overbys, had enough children for a good game of "workup" when others in the neighborhood were not around to form two teams. Large farm yards, which were well grazed by the horses, and nearby pastures had their share of evening and Sunday baseball.

Larger communities had a more formal organization of their teams than did the cow-pasture players, but the rewards were the same. Ice cream was the common winner's spoils in the young group, and for the older "boys" who played organized town ball, the treat was more likely to be a "pony" of beer. Hillsboro organized its first official team on April 22, 1886. J. E. McCarthy of Wheatland remembered that Buffalo, Casselton, Page, and Cooperstown (and many more) all had horse race tracks with baseball diamonds in the center. Local celebrations had baseball in the forenoon and horse racing in the afternoon, and occasionally a second baseball game was held after the horse races. Initially only local talent was used, but in later years a few traveling teams made a living by playing baseball.

Sometimes circuses came to town. On one occasion 300 Indians, who came to Casselton with a road show, butchered and barbecued a steer "right on the grounds" as part of their show and for the Indians to eat. Mrs. Henry Woell, sister of the late Senator Bill Langer, related that even though her family lived only a few miles south of Casselton, she seldom got to town, "only when I had a toothache or to see a doctor." She felt that she was very lucky, when, at the age of twelve, she and the entire family went to a circus at Casselton. As a girl she played ball with her brothers, but she was twenty years old before seeing a "real ball game at Casselton" in 1904. Probstfield reported attending a traveling baseball circus in 1896, but most people seemed to prefer the home town type of entertainment, whether it was baseball or plays.

The Overbys had another Sunday afternoon diversion for they lived along the Sheyenne River and had a homemade rowboat that was used more for entertainment than for fishing. Oscar Overby said, "It was fine for lovers." The bridge over the Sheyenne River was a favorite recreation spot for the Overby family; they fished from it and swam under it.

Most of the sports activities engaged in by the pioneer families were relatively inexpensive. Baseballs cost only twenty-five cents in the 1880's and bats were often homemade. Probstfield mentioned a lawn croquet set which he purchased for $2 but not many lawns were kept up well enough for games. Incidentally, on the same date he had a shave and a haircut in Moorhead for thirty-five cents.

Surprisingly, many of the smallest settlements had roller skating rinks. Wheatland, which never had more than 150 citizens, had a roller skating rink in the late 1880's. Jamestown had a very active roller skating club that used a commercial skating rink located in a downtown building. Unfortunately, it was destroyed by fire at a very early date. The Probstfield children frequently went to Moorhead to attend roller skating parties at the commercial rink. Ice skating was also popular with them, but with the Red River less than 100 feet from their house, there was no need for them to go to any commercial rink. Bowling was also established in some communities at an early date. A bowling alley was reported in Hillsboro in the 1880's, but nothing more was mentioned about it. Hillsboro also had a sizeable opera house which was erected in 1882 and later converted into a roller rink.[5]

Hunting

Hunting has always been considered a part of frontier life. In pioneer Red River Land hunting varied from an extravagant sport for the rich to an economic necessity for the farm family. C. H. Frey said that in his neighborhood both hunting and trapping were definitely a necessity and were not done for sport. The Divets ate rabbits and used the skins for mittens. The Hagens wore caps, mittens, and moccasins made at home from skunk, badger, mink, muskrat, and beaver. All of these animals were numerous along the Sheyenne and Wild Rice Rivers near their home.

The Ankerfeldts reported that everybody hunted and ate rabbit until some information was put out by the government that rabbits had a disease that could be acquired by humans. Some people "were scared by this" and did not hunt rabbits from then on. The Pruetts, living near the Sand Hills, and the Probstfields, who lived near wooded areas along rivers, all hunted and trapped extensively. Probstfield noted in his diary that one Sunday in November, 1886, "a wagon load of boys came over—we all went hunting in the woods." Obviously they combined sport and utility in their hunting and trapping.

The Valley and surrounding area also served as a great sports attraction for many well-to-do people from the Twin Cities or other cities further East. One army general and his friends came in from the East in a special railroad car which sat on a side track at Wyndmere for a week at a time. Each day they went into the Sand Hills to hunt whatever they could find. They shot "so many grouse and prairie chickens" that some of the natives wondered if there would be any left. Pheasants were also plentiful. They even had a "fellow by the name of Alexander who came up ahead of time to train dogs for hunting." Another group, "big shots from St. Paul," sent men ahead to get the dogs ready and set up camp before they came. They came for geese and ducks and shot more than they could take home with them. There were no limits then, but they did not want to be bothered with the fowl—it was "just sport, you know."

Mrs. Pratt remembered there were many well-to-do people who owned farms in the Grandin area but did not really care too much about the farming operations. They wanted the farm only for a place to live in the summer as well as for hunting, and they invited friends from Fargo to come out on weekends. "I think they did this instead of going to the lakes." Mrs. Pratt knew one such family—the Knights of Fargo. The greatest number of hunters came in the fall when the ducks and geese were migrating. James J. Hill was probably the best known of the "big shots" who came to hunt in the area. Each fall he came in his private railroad car to hunt prairie chickens and ducks. He always had a small company of friends with him.[6]

Music

Music, so much a part of personal and commercial entertainment, was also found among the early settlers of Red River Land. Tales of wagon trains and nights on the prairie all mention the sound of the harmonica and the violin, for few other instruments were available. Many of the early churches functioned for years before they were able to secure either a piano or an organ for their services. Until the advent of the railroad, the shipment of such a sizeable, heavy item to the frontier was nearly prohibitive for the person of average means. Many of the earliest organs and pianos from the East were shipped by water to Hudson Bay, then to Fort Garry, and finally up the Red River to their destination.

Those who owned pianos or organs were marked as the well-to-do of the community because the instruments represented a sizeable investment, comparable to the cost of building a house or the purchase of a piece of equipment, such as a binder. Nearly every bonanza household had a piano or organ which, of course, was commented on by other residents. "The Walkers had a Grand Piano on their farm. Even though they did not stay on the farm in the winter but resided in Boston." However, the Probstfields, although never well-to-do, also had a piano or an organ as early as any of the farm families in the area, and the first notation on music in the family diary was on June 24, 1876, when "Mary got elementary music book for piano." The following day's entry read, "Commenced teaching music to Mary, that is not knowing much myself, assisted her a little to understand musical terms." (Probstfield's German heritage showed itself in his spelling of the word "music" for frequently he spelled it "musik.") On October 4, 1876, he sent an order to Child Brothers of Indianapolis for an organ. Its initial cost was $107.50, boxing $3, organ stool $3.50, and book of music $2 for a total of $116. When the organ arrived on November 16, 1876, the freight was $14, which boosted the total cost of the organ to $130.

At that date land in the area could be purchased for $1.25 an acre and much was sold under the Northern Pacific bond exchange program for less than fifty cents per acre; so the organ easily represented the price of a quarter section of land. Probstfield did not have cash to pay for the organ so he borrowed $100 from Stocke and Wamback of Moorhead at ten percent. When hard times developed because of the dry weather, he was forced to sell the organ to a country church in Cass County. Several of the Probstfield children took music lessons on either the piano or the organ, often making the three-mile trip to Moorhead on foot. Music lessons cost fifty cents each.

The Probstfields were not alone in an effort to improve the cultural level of their family. When the Overbys on the Sheyenne River purchased their organ, Mrs. Overby commented, "I hope at least one of you boys can find something else to do than to follow the tail of a horse." Living ten miles from town presented a problem when it came to taking lessons, but an instruction book accompanied the organ so that "each had to learn to master the organ by himself." The Overbys were very musical and during the long winter evenings members of the family "stood in line to take their turn at the organ." They had a reed organ many years before they owned a piano. After several years, it appeared that Oscar Overby was the most gifted musician of the family and his parents were so pleased that they encouraged him to practice on the organ. His practicing caused him to "miss many turns at chores" which annoyed his brothers and sisters who had to do his work.

Just after the turn of the century, Carl Wade, a piano salesman from Fargo who had heard about Oscar's ability, persuaded the Overbys to buy a Bush and Gerts piano. He offered free room and board and the use of his personal piano whenever Oscar came to Fargo, ninety miles away, for lessons. Initially, Oscar took piano lessons in Cooperstown, often making the ten-mile trip on foot. It took nearly three hours each way. In winter his father arranged to haul his wheat to town on lesson days. The trip, over snow-covered fields with heavy loads of wheat, took three hours or more. Sometimes, when the weather was cold and he could not keep warm under the heavy cowhide and horsehide robes, Oscar walked along beside the sled.

This country boy, who later earned his Ph.D. in music, felt embarrassed about coming to music lessons bundled in layers of "old fashioned" clothes when all the other pupils were "high class city girls from Cooperstown." Sometimes his hands were so cold that he had to let someone else take his turn so that he could keep his hands on the radiator an extra half hour to thaw them out. In all, taking lessons meant a great deal of effort, for the trip averaged about seven hours, often under trying conditions. In 1909, after several years of lessons at Cooperstown, Overby switched to Mrs. Langlie in Fargo where he spent a full fall term taking lessons. In light of the fact that none of the Overby children had ever been in Fargo, this was a great privilege for Oscar. His efforts were not in vain, for before he was graduated from Concordia College, he became a teaching assistant in music there. Later he became a professor of music at St. Olaf College.

Mrs. Pratt's experience as a music student in her youth at Grandin was somewhat different. Her music teacher Bessie Hyde took the train from Fargo and spent the day in Grandin giving lessons. She had competition from another teacher in Hillsboro who also came by train and spent one day each week there. The hotel had the first piano in Grandin and the teachers rented it for the purpose of giving lessons. Sometimes they went to the homes of the pupils. Pianos or organs were necessary to the hotels of that day because so many of the community parties were held in them.[7]

Lyceums and Chautauquas

Probably the earliest predecessors to the lyceum in Red River Land were magician shows held at Pembina and other lower Red River settlements during the early 1800's. The usual admission to these shows was one buffalo sinew, one of the most prized articles of barter in early Red River trade. These sinews, which were about two feet long and two inches wide, came from the flat of a buffalo's back and were the finest material available at that time for use as sewing thread. A sinew could be split as wide or as narrow as desired and a thread could be ripped the full length of the sinew.

The lyceum, which in later years followed these early shows, was one of the most popular forms of entertainment in small communities. From the early 1880's through the 1890's frequent lyceums were held at the schoolhouse, about a city block from the Probstfield home. For several years the lyceum was a weekly affair and was duly recorded in the family diary. Unfortunately, Probstfield frequently did not record what was featured. Quite likely learned people from Fargo and Moorhead were invited out there to speak, or to debate. Discussions were also held by residents of the district. The local lyceum season started in October and ended in March, but sometimes meetings were held in the summer too. Probably most farm families did not attend them as religiously as the Probstfields who were close to the school and more alert to the needs of the times and the community.

Other lyceums were held in the Odd Fellows Hall, the Opera Hall, and the City Hall in Moorhead, with topics varying from matters of local interest, such as county agricultural or historical societies, to a lecture on tariffs and agriculture by the Reverend T. B. Nash in 1888. A large meeting at Fargo in March, 1895, featured Eugene V. Debs as speaker. Another time "Cranberry Jones came down . . . and gave a rattling good speech at the Lyceum" on the farm problem. Probstfield paid Jones $10 on behalf of the Farmers Alliance for his efforts.

The biggest single educational and social event between the 1880's and World War I that was not local in origin was the Chautauqua. In some respects the Chautauquas served in the developing period before well organized community groups were completely able to fill local needs. These meetings, which were generally held in large tents supplied by traveling group, were well publicized and drew people from many miles around. A major portion of their program was devoted to scientific and literary topics, but much attention was also given to religious subjects, sometimes causing them to compete with the church. The Chautauquas probably had the best programs available to rural America in those days for both their personnel and their objectives were of a much higher caliber than those of most other traveling cultural organizations. They easily overshadowed the small traveling minstrel shows which were another major outside entertainment available at that time.

For about twenty years Chautauquas were quite active in Grandin, Hillsboro, Wyndmere, Arthur, Hope, Fargo, Devils Lake, and many other communities in Red River Land. Mrs. Pruett felt that they were very "elevating experiences"; however, she remembered one time when a young girl, who was supposed to be a distinguished violinist, dropped her instrument and the music continued, revealing that the child violinist had been pantomiming all the time. A less humorous event occurred when a storm blew the big tent down at Hope and the program had to be moved to the Opera House, "the center of most activity."

The best publicized, and largest of area Chautauquas, took place at Devils Lake in 1895 from June 28 to July 21 with an average daily attendance of 800. The railroad gave special rates and people came from fifty miles around. The three-story Oakwood Hotel had been built to accommodate those in attendance, but the crowds were so great that most of them had to be quartered in tents. At the 1879

Devils Lake Chautauqua, which lasted for sixteen days, Judge Norris of Nebraska was the featured speaker and there were others of national repute. Two women speakers led sessions on "Western Womanhood." In addition to the three sermons a day and the Bible study, were musical presentations, bicycle races, baseball games, and excursions on the lake. With such a full program, is it any wonder that the Chautauquas were popular?

Opera houses and hotels were the centers of most community activity. These buildings were majestic for that day. Hope House in Hope was 50 by 110 feet and three stories high with forty rooms. The Grand Pacific Hotel, which opened in Moorhead in 1881, boasted of being the finest hotel between Chicago and the Pacific Coast. This three story structure "had 101 carpeted bedrooms, each with bath, hot and cold water, and gas light furnished by the Hotel's own gas plant." Built at a cost of $150,000 by pioneer Moorhead miller, Henry Bruns, it was purchased in 1896 by James J. Hill, who had it torn down. The first major building in Fargo was the Headquarters Hotel constructed by the Northern Pacific to house guests, government offices, and to serve as the railroad station. The original hotel burned on September 22, 1874, and was immediately rebuilt.

The Warren House, which had a steady stream of activity, served the Warren community well with dances, socials, lectures, and concerts. A typical "musical" was given by the Warren Band and Glee Club on the evening of January 27, 1882. Admission to the concert was only twenty-five cents but combined tickets to the "supper, Grand Ball, and Concert were $2." The numbers listed on the program were:

"The Bonney Blue Flag"
"Greeting Glee"
"Galapode Quadrille"
"The Vagabond"
"Sweet Bye and Bye"
"English March"
"The Girl I Left Behind Me"
"Stars of the Summer Night"
"The Mocking Bird"
"Moonlight on the Lake"

"Come Where the Lillies Bloom"
"The Girl that Keeps the
   Peanut Stand"
"The Irish Washerwoman"
"Matrimonial Sweets"
"Sulton Polka"
"Fairy Moonlight"
"Co Ca Che Lune"
"Yankee Doodle"

The stockholders of the Hillsboro opera house boasted, when they finished their building in 1882, that it would seat 500 people. This building was certainly more than adequate for any crowd that might have gathered in Hillsboro at that time. In 1891, when the Crookston community dedicated its new opera house, many people from Warren attended the grand opening. The *Warren Sheaf* editor wrote, "Crookston is to be congratulated on having such a magnificent temple where the dramatic art may be cultivated."

As might be expected, not all entertainment was on such a high cultural level. Probstfield made one notation that indicates there were occasional activities that might not necessarily be classified as "cultured." "Stayed in town to attend I.O.O.F. Lodge meeting, no meeting—not even hall opened, all went, it seems, to Fargo to see a *leg show* at a dollar a person for each attendant. Good!!" [8]

Home Parties

Most of the social life in the early days in Red River Land was home centered. The amount of outside entertainment, of course, varied with the location of the farm. The Ankerfeldts of Ransom County, for example, had little social life during the winter months. One of them said, "They had some dances and that was about all. There wasn't much going on and no place to go, unless you walked." They did not have any horses and their oxen were fine for farm work, but much too slow to use for purely social purposes. The Crawfords in Richland County realized that their lack of social life was caused by their:

Unfortunate location. We were in sort of a no-man's land between two arteries of travel. There was no regular travel past our place. It was a two-mile break-out to the north to the prairie road that branched southwest from the Wild Rice River bridge to Skunk Lake, and went past the Judd farm, which later became the Fairview farm. Once plowing was over and freeze up came, things were reduced to a low tempo.

They considered themselves "socially holed up" about five months each winter and "some never went out—they just chafed in monotony." The Divets had a similar experience, but even though the large number in each family helped break the monotony, they all felt the pressure of the long isolation. Those who were located nearer villages or in more thickly settled farming regions did not complain so bitterly.

The Probstfield diary again and again provides a good picture of what happened in the social sphere. The Probstfields did not suffer from isolation like the Crawfords, the Divets, and the Pruetts, for they were near the railroad tracks and the main road running north out of Moorhead. Mr. Probstfield took part in several civic organizations which gave the family broad social contact. Regular callers at the Probstfield home were many of the prominent early families of the area including the Hutchinsons—one of the very early families of Georgetown—and the James and Andrew Holes families.

Andrew Holes, reputed to be the third settler in Moorhead and a member of the first board of county commissioners in Clay County, secured the land which the Northern Pacific needed for its Red River crossing. James Holes was known for his forty-bushel wheat crop in 1875 that became the basis for much of the promotion that enticed bonanza farmers to come into the area. The Probstfields were friends of the Sargents of Goose River country, also prominent in early railroad land speculation. They were even able to list the Bollmans of Georgetown, well known bonanza farmers, as one of their social acquaintances, though it was not common for the ordinary farmer to associate that closely with bonanza farmers.

Other local families who were among the regular social callers at the Probstfield home were the Benedicts, the Kiefers, the Heatons, the Wilsons (first Clay County Auditor), the Videens, the Harrises, the Lambs, the Wambacks, the Bergquists (a brick manufacturer and Moorhead's second settler), the Stockers, the Schroeders, and the Cannings from Hendrum (a "political buddy" of Probstfield). The Probstfields were an active family, not lacking in friends or amusement. To celebrate July 4, 1876, Probstfield and his children, Mary and Alexander, drove to Moorhead where they "celebrated in good style, stayed at the ball in the evening at Schoolhouse . . . until 1 a.m. Then stopped at the George Whitemarsh hotel." Total expenses for the day were $2.50. Later that summer the family drove to Anton Jansens at Moland on the Buffalo River where they had a "surprise dancing party—never slept until the next night."

On July 1, 1883, Probstfield went to Lorings to help plan the Fourth of July celebration. On the afternoon of the Fourth, the Wilson and the Probstfield families celebrated by having a picnic at the Gilbertsons. That evening everyone went to the dance at Lorings which lasted until 4 a.m. Expenses for the day were $3. On New Year's Eve, 1883, the Probstfields went to a dance at Hannahers. It was a cold day—the high temperature was eighteen degrees below zero—but this apparently was no deterrent, for a few days later another dance was held at the schoolhouse. The high that day was twelve degrees below zero and when the dance was over at 4 a.m. it was twenty-six below.

As the Probstfield children became older and held more parties on their own, their father's comments became somewhat amusing. July 8, 1883, "several young folks came from town, had a picnic by the river." June 24, 1888, "another picnic, nine other families over." February 7, 1889, "Surprise party, too many here to mention. Cleared dining room at 8 p.m. for dance—kept racket up until 4 a.m." November 22, 1889, "had big party, full house from 9 p.m. to 3 a.m." January 17, 1890, "14 guests all from Dakota side, racket all night." January 31, 1890, "6 of the family were at Kennedys for surprise party I suppose, came home 5 a.m."

During the dry years of 1887 and 1888, Probstfield was in one of his most serious personal depressions. On Christmas Day, 1887, he wrote, "Children took a ride to Fargo to see the results of the fire" which had occurred December 23 in the opera house block. His closing comments for that day were, "A very tame Christmas indeed." On December 24 and 25, 1888, he described the economic impact of the drought on their Christmas festivities:

Today is Christmas Eve! What shall I say? Not since I have a family did I see such a blight as now. We always had something for the children—but this year absolutely nothing—no money to buy. I have yet 45 cts. in house—which I must save for oil which we must have. No coffee but (chickoree [sic] essense) pseudo coffee. Tea—like prairie hay. Butter for show only when strangers are here. Still we have enough to eat—potatoes, flour, and cabbage, but lard and meat sometimes scarce. We are ragged and not sufficient rags if cold weather comes. Nearly everyone in the house needs new shoes but no prospect of getting them. I am wearing a pair of boots (with the assistance of a pair of rubbers left by somebody in the house a visitor C. G. for whom they were not good enough) [C. G. was Charles Gesell who later married a Probstfield.] 3 years old last June.

Edmunds pants is out *behind and before*. But what is the use to go into detail. Buried with debts without any prospects to ever crawl out. The boys and girls growing up virtually slaves to stomack [sic] and interest and taxes. I write this down, so that if we ever get out of the slough of despondency as a retrospect. If I was twenty years younger I would probably take a more hopeful view of the situation. I suppose I am soured by too many experiences similar, in my younger days, when I had more energy left.

Justus came home about 8 p.m. and brought home apples, pencils, and nuts to keep up poor Santa Claus. Of course all on tick! [meaning it was all charged] Christmas dinner good without the usual extras though. R. J. Bell and Chas. Gesell called 2 p.m. with a load of presents for the whole family. Mrs. P. and self broom brush with hanging case [still in possession of the family]. A box of cheroots for the smokers. Dressing case for Nelly. Writing case and gold pen, envelopes, paper, etc. for Susy; shopping case for Dora. Workbag for Milly. Set dominos for Walter. Book for Arthur. Book and fine speaking and crying doll with reversible head for Josephine.

Probstfield knew that times could not continue to remain that difficult for any great period. By the mid-1890's Probstfield was in his sixties, but times had improved and he was able to play Santa Claus again, which was more characteristic of his nature.[9]

Newspapers and Magazines

It is generally accepted that present-day Red River Land farmers do a reasonable amount of reading. Even in the early days, the long winters and the isolation made reading popular. The cash grain operations with a minimum of winter chores were partly responsible. The local weekly and the paper from back home were the two most thoroughly read items. Mrs. Woodward gave the impression that life would have been even more trying if it had not been for newspapers, magazines, and books. Trips to the post office were as frequent as possible under the conditions. "Without material to read we could not live here . . ." expressed the thoughts of many who sat through the long winters. More than one old timer interviewed expressed amazement that their eyes held out under the great amount of reading they did with such poor light. Reading material was treasured. "The Mc-Auliffe's, our closest neighbors, are a very intelligent family, and we exchange much reading with them. We furnish reading to our German neighbors, the Lessings, who never had any before."

Newspapers became popular immediately so they overexpanded as much as any other enterprise in Minnesota and North Dakota. Newspapers were published locally as soon as it was feasible, and sometimes earlier than that, for everyone hoped that his community would become a great center and this could happen only if there were a local paper to do the "booming." In fact, pioneers sensed that early area papers were reluctant to print too much about events that might slacken immigration into the area. After one severe winter storm thousands of head of livestock and 200 people were reported dead, but one settler said, "Local papers do not talk of the blizzard only the Chicago papers."

"In 1890 North Dakota had about 125 newspapers and only 50 incorporated towns and villages," making the papers nearly as numerous as the "blind pigs" that dotted "dry" North Dakota. By 1915 there were 347 weeklies and nearly a dozen dailies. After the area was completely settled by the World War I influx, the number of weekly papers dropped to just over 100, while the number and the influence of the dailies increased. The same experience basically held true for the Valley counties of Minnesota. The decline in newspapers for the Red River Valley was not as drastic as it was in the central and western areas of Dakota or the northeastern area of Minnesota. The *War-*

ren Sheaf of March 30, 1881, described its relative success with the following pun: "Why are a true lover's visits like a successful newspaper? Because they commence weekly, then become semi-weekly, then tri-weekly, and then daily with the Sunday supplement thrown in."

Apparently the first newspaper in Red River Land was the *Red River Gazette* published at Glyndon in the spring of 1872 by E. B. Chambers. Probstfield paid $1 for a six-month subscription to it in 1873. In 1873 this paper was moved to Fargo and was renamed the *Fargo Times*. Probstfield subscribed to it in August for $1 a year. Moorhead had its first newspaper, the *Red River Star*, in publication in July, 1873, under the leadership of W. B. Nickles (or Nichols). Major Edwards had the *Argus*, Fargo's second paper (later the *Forum*), in circulation by 1879.

George B. Winship, one of the first men on the scene at Grand Forks, transferred his equipment used in publishing the *Caledonia* (Minnesota) *Courier* to Dakota in 1879. He built a new 12 by 22 foot building at a cost of $150 and published the first issue of the *Grand Forks Herald* on June 26, 1879. In July, 1881, the *Herald* became a semi-weekly and had four pages of eight columns in width and measuring twenty-three inches in length. By November it had become a daily. The *Herald* was not the first paper in Grand Forks for George H. Walsh, who had shipped his printing equipment from St. Paul to Moorhead and then down the Red River in 1875, put out the first issue of *The Plaindealer* on July 2, 1875. It served as the official paper of Traill County until a newspaper was founded there in 1879. *The Plaindealer* quickly became a daily but, unfortunately, its office plant burned down in 1881 and took six years of valuable local history with it in its files.

Although only twenty buildings were erected in Inkster in 1884, in its first year, A. H. Smith started the *Inkster Review* in a "handsome" new 24 by 18 foot office. The first issue was dated July 16, 1886, but in spite of the *Review's* success, Smith decided that the new boom town of Park River had a greater future and the paper closed after fifty-five weeks. Inkster was then without a paper until Tom Tallant started the *Inkster Times* on July 28, 1888, with the apparent backing of liquor interests. In October, 1888, the *Inkster Tribune* was started with the purpose of combating Tallant who was active politically, but the town of less than 400 people could not support two newspapers, and after fifteen issues the *Inkster Times* closed. The *Tribune* succeeded and Inkster was assured of a newspaper for many years.

The *Hope Pioneer* was printed in Minneapolis for three months before facilities were moved to Hope in 1880. The purpose in establishing a paper there so early was to boom the community with an intensive newspaper campaign to attract the attention of outsiders. The plan was a success and promoters J. A. Steele, S. S. Small, and E. W. Steele, who called themselves the Red River Land Company, Inc. and who owned 50,000 acres, which they had purchased from the Northern Pacific, moved into Hope.

Too many people started too many newspapers in small towns that could not support them. Hillsboro, with eight weekly newspapers at one time in the 1880's, is an example of such overexpansion. Only the *Hillsboro Banner*, established in 1879, has been able to survive. Its three English language competitors were the *Traill County Blade*, the *Traill County Free Press*, and the *Traill County Times*. The four weekly Norwegian language newspapers were the *Alpholds-Basunen*, the *Statstidende*, the *Avia Guten*, and the *Fremtidende*. With seven failures out of eight attempts, very obviously Hillsboro newspaper business has had proportionately far more failures than farming in that wealthy agricultural county.

With such small communities so close to each other, the newspapers competed in all respects except for the most intimate local gossip. For example, the L. J. Marjacks, who lived south of Hillsboro near Grandin, could have been well serviced by the Hillsboro paper, but Grandin had its own *Chronicle*, so they took that smaller, but more local, paper. The same could be repeated for many other families, except that the local paper would be the *Hunter Times*, the *Casselton Reporter*, the *Richland County Globe*, the *Hannaford Enterprise*, the *Griggs County Sentinel*, the *Wyndmere Missile*, or the *Kittson County Enterprise*.

If you were Norwegian, the odds were that you received either the *Normanden* from Fargo, the *Decorah Posten* from Decorah, Iowa (for Trondjheim Norwegians), the *Viser Gutten* from Story City, Iowa (for Stavanger Norwegians), the *Ugeblad* from Fergus Falls, the *Nordisk Folkeblad*, or the *Borne Bladet* from Minneapolis. One of the homes received four Norwegian language newspapers. Because they were natives of Scotland, the Marjacks subscribed to a Scottish language newspaper. The Swedes, the Germans, and even the Danes had their own language newspapers. Some of them were published in Chicago and others in smaller communities with a strong foreign element, such as Decorah, Iowa, where a Norwegian magazine, the *Ved Arnen* was also published. This magazine was a supplement to the *Decorah Posten*. *Ved Arnen*, loosely translated, means "by the fireplace." "Ole and Per" was the favorite comic strip in many homes. Johanna Opgrande said her parents always made the children wait to read the comics because the parents were so excited to see what "Ole and Per" were doing.

Farm magazines, especially the *Farm Stock and Home*, the *Northwestern Farmer* (now the *Farmer* published in St. Paul)), and the *Dakota Farmer*, were the most popular among farm families. *Woman's World* was the most frequently mentioned woman's magazine, but the *Ladies Home Journal* was subscribed to also. The *Youth's Companion* was the most commonly mentioned magazine for general family reading. Some families also received *Boy's Life*. The Probstfield and the Woodward families subscribed to many more publications than the average pioneers. Probstfield was a regular subscriber to the *American Agriculturalist* ($1.75 per year), the *Farm Journal* ($2.00), the *Iowa Homesteader* ($2.00), and the *Northwestern Farmer*, the *St. Paul Pioneer Press* ($1.25), the Barnesville-*Chronicle* ($1), the New York *Sun* ($1.10), the *Red River Star* ($1), and the Moorhead *Independent*. The Probstfields were outdone by only the Woodwards in total number of magazines and papers purchased regularly. The Woodwards were avid readers and whenever one of the men went to town he purchased a book or a magazine to which he did not regularly subscribe. On one weekly mail call they received thirteen papers and magazines. They subscribed to the *Chicago Times*, the *Milwaukee News*, a New York paper, the Fargo *Argus*, and "three Republican papers," plus *Harpers Monthly and Weekly*, the *Graphic, Frank Leslie's Illustrated, Scribner's*, the *American Agriculturalist*, and "*Puck* which is so plainly illustrated it can reach the dullest brain." Both the Probstfields and Woodwards had complete sets of encyclopedias, the *Brittanica* and *Chambers* respectively. One of the Woodwards had every book in the *Cobweb Series*.

However, the average homesteading family probably could afford only a newspaper or two, a farm magazine, and one book—the Bible —which was "much read" in many of those homes. Jig saw puzzles became popular for winter entertainment. During a "puzzle craze" in the area in the late 1880's, "they [were] on every counter in Fargo." Playing cards at ten cents to twenty-five cents per pack also provided inexpensive entertainment for those who did not condemn card playing for religious reasons.

The long and intense storms of the winter of 1888 caused newspaper editors to show some ingenuity. When the railroads were unable to deliver newsprint, the local papers were printed on brown, blue, red, or any other colored paper they had on hand, just to get the paper out.

The great efforts put forth by the pioneers to get their mail is proof of their craving for contact with the outside world, even if it was "just" the daily paper.[10]

FOOTNOTES

[1] *World's Work*, XL (Sept., 1920), 436; Glaspell, p. 189; *Hope of the Prairie*, p. 50; Gunkelman interview; Edwin Ankerfeldt interview; Hovde, p. 14; Woodward, p. 195; *Fargo Argus*, Jan. 27, 1883; *The Record*, I (June, 1895), 29; Fred A. Bill, "Early Steamboating on the Red River," *NDHQ*, IX (Jan., 1942), 82.

[2] Probstfield; *Warren Sheaf*, Dec. 3, 1881, Jan. 12, 1881, Jan. 5, 1882; *Hillsboro Banner*, June 28, 1956, Sec. III, p. 10, Aug. 25, 1882, July 14, 1882; Gunkelman interview; Walter E. Spokesfield, *The History of Wells County, North Dakota, and Its Pioneers* (Jamestown, N. D., 1928), pp. 45-47; Everett Dick, *Vanguards of the Frontier* (Lincoln, 1941); Ernest F. Krabbenhoft interview. Mr. Krabbenhoft was a member of the Sabin Brass Band.

[3] Murray, p. 160; Probstfield; *Warren Sheaf*, Nov. 12, 1891; Letter from L. A. Schultz, July 20, 1966.

[4] Pruett interview; Pratt interview; Gunkelman interview; Frey letter; *Warren Sheaf*, June 15, 1881, July 1, 1891; Probstfield.

[5] O. Overby, *Retrospect*, pp. 10-24; Probstfield; McCarthy interview; Mrs. Henry Woell interview; A. Overby, "Sod House Days," p. 3; *Hillsboro Banner*, June 28, 1956, pp. 6, 11. Hillsboro's first athletic star was Duncan Cameron who became state champion bicycle rider and skater. Glaspell, p. 189.

[6] Frey letter; Emil Ankerfeldt interview; Divet, NDIRS, File 69; Pruett interview; Probstfield; Pratt interview; McMahon, NDIRS, File 195; Stafne, p. 14.

[7] Robert Heckman, interview by the author, May 24, 1968 (Heckman owns an organ which was shipped via the Hudson's Bay route); Gunkelman interview; Probstfield; O. Overby, *Retrospect*, pp. 18-26; Pratt interview. Unfortunately for the Probstfield family, the church that purchased the organ did not keep track of what happened to it. The family has attempted to locate the organ in an effort to restore all of the early furniture of the home.

[8] Probstfield; Pratt interview; Pruett interview; Bettschen interview; *The Record*, June, 1895, p. 13, May, 1897, p. 8; Healy, p. 12; *Hope of the Prairie*, p. 2 (Hope was named in honor of Hope Steele, wife of E. H. Steele, an early large land owner. Steele County was named in his honor. For another version of how Hope got its name, see *Hope of the Prairie*, p. 5 and *Bonanza*, p. 71.); Euren; *Warren Sheaf*, April 19, 1891.

[9] Emil Ankerfeldt interview; Crawford, NDIRS, File 290; Madsen interview; Pratt interview; Glaspell, p. 189; A. Overby, "Sod House Days," p. 15; O. Overby, *Retrospect*, p. 22; McMahon, NDIRS, File 195; Probstfield; Gunkelman interview; Glenn E. Johnson, "Here, There, Everywhere," p. 12; Stafne, p. 21.

[10] *Warren Sheaf*, March 30, 1881; Robinson, pp. 164, 525-527; Woodward, pp. 23, 28, 26, 43-44, 103, 116, 197, 214; Ernest Schroeder interview; H. F. Arnold, *History of Grand Forks County with Special Reference to the First Ten Years of Grand Forks City* (Larimore, 1900), pp. 130-131, 140-141, 117-118; H. V. Arnold, *Inkster*, pp. 76, 88-91, 127; *Hillsboro Banner*, June 28, 1956, Sec. I, p. 13, Sec. II, p. 1; Pratt interview; Holes interview; Olsen interview; Gunderson, p. 88; Edwin Ankerfeldt interview; Frey letter; Thortvedt, NDIRS, File 332; *Hope of the Prairie*, p. 15; Pruett interview; Probstfield; A. Overby, "Sod House Days," p. 4; Bill, p. 203; *Moorhead Independent*, Jan. 5, 1900, p. 41; Glenn E. Johnson interview; Stafne, pp. 49-50.

CHAPTER XII

The Silent Prairie

E. V. SMALLEY, a well known agricultural writer, had much to say in the 1890's about the lonesome lives of the pioneers who settled on individual farmsteads. He pointed out that European farmers usually lived in villages and enjoyed a full social life in the village compound. The women had a chance to talk to each other in the village and to visit each other's homes frequently. Children had playmates close at hand; the school and the church were convenient places to get together. The old men sat outside in front of their houses and spoke with all those who went by. The mailman and the peddler made their daily rounds. The homes of these European farmers might have been small and meagerly furnished, but they were well built and for centuries they had offered good protection against the weather. Such a pleasant social setting helped to offset the many hardships and the monotony of a peasant's life.

Isolation By Design

This picture of the old country was a decided contrast to the life of the American farmer on the western frontier. Here he lived in isolation, often in order to satisfy the requirement of the Homestead Act. The long, cold winters of Red River Land were ideal for "the natural gregarious instinct of mankind to assert itself," and to gather around each other's hearth fires. But the American farmers' houses, set in the middle of the farms, were too far apart for much visiting. Besides, the pioneer could not afford a solid, weatherproof house like his European counterpart, so he often existed miserably in "a flimsy wooden frame house and if it were not for tar paper and sod he would find himself covered with snow or dirt after each storm." They had left "pleasant little homes in neat farm villages of Europe [or

New England] to settle in sod or tar paper houses on the bleak prairie of America." Because of his poverty, the pioneer's home was frequently a "cramped one room house with one window" and from that window all he could see was the wide open prairie, his own straw stack, and occasionally smoke arising from his neighbor's house, anywhere from one-half to five miles away. O. A. Olson explained his father's first impression of the Dakota prairie:

> Go West, young man, said Greeley:
> Go West, where land is free.
> I went, I saw, I settled
> On a prairie without a tree.

From the first storm in November to the last in April, there was little social life for the early settlers except a bi-monthly trip to the general store in the nearest village. This trip was made by all the members of the family if the weather was good and the village was not too far away. At the store the men liked to sit around the stove and talk to find out what had happened in the world since they had last been to town. If the trip was too long or the weather too severe, the men of the family went to town alone to get the provisions. Many times conditions permitted travel only by foot. Social calls on the neighbors "were not what they should be because everyone lived too far apart and the weather and roads too contrary."

The frontier lacked homogeneity not only because of the distance between the homes, but also because the settlers had come from so many diverse areas that they lacked even a common language and a common background. This great disadvantage kept them apart even though they strongly felt the need for social intercourse "which next to food, clothing, and shelter, is an essential to life." One contemporary writer asked, "Is it any wonder that there is a great amount of insanity among the settlers?"

Being isolated on the frontier presented another problem to the early settler. Often he was forced into idleness and economic unproductivity during the long winter months. In Europe, most farmers relied on some craft which kept them occupied during the winter and gave them additional income. On the American frontier only those who lived relatively near to towns had any chance for extra employment. The only other supplementary income which the settler had was his wife's efforts and ability to make butter, cheese, or sausages to sell or to exchange them for groceries. When American farmers were asked why they did not build in communities, their usual reply was that "the chickens and cattle would always get mixed up if they lived that way." There was "a crusty individuality about the average American farmer [which he has inherited from his environment] that does not take kindly to the familiarities of close association." [1]

Isolation By Nationality Groups

The Red River frontier was unique in that it contained two distinct classes of settlers—homesteaders and bonanza farmers. Within the ranks of the homesteaders, some were cooperative and others were as individualistic and as independent as they could be. Some were very sociable and mixed freely, while others were loners and completely ignored those around them.

One of the most divisive handicaps to community spirit was lack of communication that arose because of differences in language, in nationality, and in customs. The high percentage of foreign born in the area and the presence of the bonanza farmer tended to delay making the area a real melting pot. Generally, the immigrant had the smallest farm; the transplanted American had the next largest operation; and the well educated and well financed American operated the bonanzas. There were exceptions, but it was not until uniformly hard times hit local agriculture, or when the second generation grew up, that nationality and class lines broke down.

There was no established pattern as to where farmers settled, except that they were inclined, if possible, to settle in areas with people of a similar background from Europe or eastern America, or adjacent to established homesteaders. Many, however, emigrated individually, and if they did not have relatives or friends on the frontier, settled at the first location that pleased them or where they secured their first jobs. Clay County, one of the earliest settled counties in this area, illustrates the irregular settlement pattern. In 1875 it had 1,451 people living in six townships, including 475 people in the village of Moorhead. Glyndon Township, including the rapidly growing village of Glyndon, had 244 people. The Buffalo River settlement in Moland Township founded by the Thortvedts totalled 135. Three townships —Hawley with 162, Lund (now Tansem) 135, and Parke, 190—were on the edge of the Red River Valley, indicating the strong attraction the Scandinavian newcomers had for these rolling, forested, and wetlands areas.

National origins for the county in 1875 listed the Norwegians with 355, English 115, Canadians 57, Germans 53, Swedes 47, Irish 46, Scots, 21, as well as five other European countries and thirteen American states. The tendency to settle in nationality groups continued, and by the 1890's this pattern was multiplied in other counties on both sides of the Red River. In the Cooperstown-Hannaford area seventy to eighty percent of the rural settlers were Scandinavian; Canadians, mostly of Scotch descent, were the next largest group.

Some communities were closely knit with everyone participating in the activities; others existed purely for economic reasons and were divided into many factions. The community of Hope, for example, felt sure that it was the most hospitable of all towns in Red River Land and the *Hope Pioneer* asserted: "Nearly all the early settlers of Hope were rather young people coming from large cities, exceptionally well educated, cultured, and hospitable. As a result Hope was a delightful community to live in."

The census figures might not have born out the contention of the editor, for the bulk of the settlers were farmers who came from overseas or from other farming areas, and they were not well educated. The Hope community was represented by many nationalities—Canadians, Danes, Norwegians, Swedes, Germans, Scots, and the American born "who were well educated and from the city." This democratic spirit even persisted in religious circles for when one of the first churches organized, it elected Danes, Swedes, and Norwegians as trustees to represent the most numerous groups in the congregation.

An old timer from southern Cass County, when asked what nationality most of the people in the Norman community were, answered, "Yah, I reckon mostly Norwegians. Nearby there was that church outfit at St. Benedict. They all lived in that town along the one main street. Not out in the country like other farmers. They were French-Canadian. There was one Scotch-Canadian who lived on the Scott farm way down by Lisbon." [2]

How one looked upon the friendship and cooperation within his community depended a great deal on whether one was from the minority or the dominant nationality group. Emma Erickson Elton, living in the predominantly Norwegian community east of Hawley, felt that "there were hardships and much physical work in those days, but I believe, less mental strain. Neighborliness and hospitality were unlimited." The Olsens of Hannaford shared those sentiments: "Life was full of hard work—cooperation with neighbors was essential." In the Norwegian community around Hillsboro, Anders Johnson's neighbors shared some of their crop with him when his failed. Ole Olson Hovde implied they would have done the same for any of the other settlers.

Such expressions of friendliness were not universal in all communities. Mary Woodward, who had grown up in Vermont, had spent most of her married life in Wisconsin, and had come to Cass County when she was in her late fifties. She was not overly impressed with the friendliness of her neighbors. On the other hand, traveling people and individuals who were lost were reluctantly permitted to spend the night at the Dodge Farm because, as Mrs. Woodward implied, "it was the only human thing to do." She personally had not visited a neighbor or gone to town for a period of three years and expressed the feeling that she was not sure she would even know how to act if she finally did get to town. However, prominent people did come out to the farm to have tea with her, including Mrs. Harry O'Neil, the first white woman to settle in Fargo.

Mrs. Woodward's diary of New Year's Day, 1886, noted, "There are three families near us, kind Irish people. . . . They seem to hold themselves rather aloof." About two years later when the Woodwards stopped to "borrow" some water from a neighbor who lived one and one-half miles from their farm, they discovered that the man there had died during the previous winter. "Nobody keeps track of neighbors out here. People come and go; families move in and out, and nobody asks whence they come or whither they go. . . . I have lived here for six years and I do not know who occupies half of the surrounding farms although they are in full view." She became acquainted with only two families in the neighborhood—Harry Green, who courted Katie Woodward, and the Lessings. Only the Lessing girls came over to visit, however, because the parents were Germans and "too busy" to visit.

While living in Minnesota, the Divets had participated in an active social life of dances and lyceums (consisting of speeches, debates, essays, plays, spelling matches, handwriting contests), or just plain visiting. By contrast, in their first four or five years in the Valley, they had "absolutely nothing in the way of social activities." A nearby settlement of Germans held dances and other neighborhood parties, but the Divets did not know these people well enough to be invited to any get-together. Their communication with the Germans was:

. . . very restricted, for we could not understand each other. . . . [It was not] that there was anything unfriendly in our relationships, it was just a matter of lack of mutual interests and probably aloofness on the part of all concerned . . . however, there was no real social intercourse. We exchanged ordinary neighborly courtesies, borrowed things back and forth, stopped and talked when we met on the road, or when our teams happened to meet at the line between farms, but there was nothing in the way of parties or other gatherings.

The Germans of Richland County had regular get-togethers at least every Sunday which they referred to as "it,"—"It is meeting today at Ziegelman's." As the Divet children grew into their teens in the mid-1880's, they desired more social contact. After they had lived in the area about six years, Guy and his sister "broke the social ice":

We knew that some five miles to the north was a family of Stebbins [S. E. Stebbins near the headquarters of the Downing bonanza], Americans, but we had never met them. So one day Eunice and I caught our riding horses and started north to get acquainted with the Stebbinses. . . . We met a delightful family, Walter and Minnie Stebbins several years older than we were, Agnes and Rolland and Ralph all about our age. We were invited to stay to dinner, which we had fully expected . . . We were informed that half a mile north and a mile west was another family of Americans. Andrus was the family name. [An "American" was anyone who could speak English and was acquainted with the customs.]

When church services were held the next Sunday at the Root home, the Divets saw to it that the Stebbins and the Andrus families were given special invitations to come. "There we all met again, [this time] with the older people who also got acquainted, and our social life in Dakota began." The following summer, when the Divets met the Borgens and the John Hektners of near Mooreton, their social circle had grown to five families and they began having dances in each others' homes. With the children all growing older and the communities becoming more settled,

it was only a short time until the public dances at Mooreton and sometimes at Dwight, and later at Hankinson, became a part of our regular planned entertainment . . . Later we added people to the north and west of Mooreton especially from Antelope Township, a Scotch settlement. Gradually, too, we got acquainted with the people in the German settlement and began to be invited to their dances and parties.

The Crawfords, who lived north of the same German settlement, had similar social experiences:

Our situation was in great contrast to the conditions in the settlement of Germans to the south of us. They lived to themselves. We could have scarcely anything in common with them. In winter they spent much of their time visiting and making the rounds. Around Dwight there were enough American families with a strong nucleus in that village that pretty much offset the isolation that many families went through. Throughout the [Dakota] Territory there were probably not many communities like it.

Charles Hobart felt very alone during that first year when he worked at opening his farm near Cummings. He became well acquainted with only two couples from April through November. For weeks he did not see another individual. During their second year the Hobarts became acquainted with two more families—the Barnums and the Pasholts. "Mr. Barnum called one day, and said he had heard an American family was living there; after that we saw him quite often. As he [Barnum] had no team I helped him with mine and he helped me build my house." Later they exchanged trips to Buxton to get the mail.

R. M. Probstfield, who had come to Minnesota in 1856, was certainly considered an "American" by 1870 when other settlers began to arrive and his diary has only vague references to nationality. In 1894, when walking back to his farm from Moorhead, he was given a ride by a "Norwegian farmer living on the Buffalo near Kragnes." Probstfield, who at that time was very active in politics, enjoyed the ride because the Norwegian and his wife were "arguing woman suffrage." Although Probstfield was well educated and associated easily with influential people, at the same time he shared neighborly feelings for the settlers in general, and they usually felt very much at home with him. The Probstfields enjoyed a great variety of social activity because of their many acquaintances.

In addition to the difference of nationalities, the presence of the bonanza farmers had a rather subduing effect upon the social life of the early settlers. These well financed bonanza farmers who came from eastern states seemed to be so wealthy that they were not looked upon with favor by the average homesteader who generally referred to them as the "big farmer" or the "aristocrat." It happened occasionally that even some homesteaders, who developed sizeable farming operations, were mistakenly associated with bonanza farming and thus were out of favor with the early settlers. Some of these, like the Divets and the Woodwards, understood the psychology involved and realized that they were operating on a scale too large to be acceptable to the homesteader, and yet not large enough to be more than "noticed" by the true bonanza farmer.

Whenever possible, the bonanza farmer avoided conflict with the homesteaders for he knew that they were envious of him. His social contacts with them were limited. The children of the bonanza farmer attended school in Fargo, Minneapolis, or institutions in the East, and many became college graduates in contrast to the meager schooling of the homesteader's children. The apparent great wealth of the bonanza farmer overawed the homesteader and no doubt made him feel quite uncomfortable when in the presence of the bonanza farmer.

As time passed inevitable conflicts arose when bonanza farmers enlarged their holdings. In such cases of conflict the bonanza farmer generally won out because of his greater financial strength. Frequently he bought out the homesteader which only increased the friction between those two groups. Even the tolerant Charles Hobart expressed resentment toward the bonanza farmer when he referred to him as "the big farmer" in a way that did not imply warm friendship. Without a doubt, the homesteader looked upon the bonanza farmer as a serious threat to his way of life.

Besides the bonanza farmers who were the "aristocrats" of the rural areas, there were also the "social elite" in the villages and towns who made the homesteader feel out of place, even though it was the business the homesteader brought into town which made these merchant families prosperous. Their huge and elaborate homes in the towns and villages are testimony that these families prospered considerably more than the average homesteader did. These homes, frequently called "castles" by the "outs" and even occasionally by the "ins," still remind those living in the Valley area nearly a century later of the "glorious" past.

It is an established fact that many of the homesteaders earned some of their first dollars as employees of the merchants in town and of the bonanza farmers. Ole Olson Hovde encouraged members of his family to come over from Norway. His two half sisters, Mary and Lena Larson, worked "in the homes of the aristocrats. For early in the history of Hillsboro the scions of educated and well-to-do families from the East such as the Sarles, Wilsons, Kelleys, and Kingmans came to the town and community." The Hillsboro community could even claim the sons of two "cotton kings," the McCains and the Suttons, as residents. Many communities thus developed a smug, comfortable social class at a very early date. However, it must not be forgotten that among those merchants, financiers, and professional people, many paid the price of pioneering because their fortunes were closely linked to the success or failure of the homesteaders. When large numbers of homesteaders failed in periods of adverse weather or prices, many from the other classes failed too.

Even the Chinese found their way to the Valley. According to the *Warren Sheaf*, "A 'John Chinaman' hailing from Red Lake Falls arrived on this morning's train. He is looking up a location for a laundry." Three weeks later the paper carried the following ad: "Chinese laundry. Hop Sam, prop. First Class Wash Done. Rooms back of Slee's Store, Warren, Minn." How Hop Sam came to settle in Warren is a mystery, but there was no denying that his services were sorely needed there as well as in many other communities too. However, social life for that enterprising Chinaman was no doubt as restricted as it was for a lone German family who settled in the midst of a community of Norwegians.[3]

Those Lonesome Days

In general pioneer family life was particularly harsh for the women. O. E. Rolvaag's novel, *Giants in the Earth*, does great justice to the hardships of pioneer life, especially those suffered by the women. Monotony, in many respects, was the greatest enemy of the pioneer woman's life. As already mentioned, she was barred from visiting with her neighbors either by distance or by difference in language. Mrs. McMahon said, "Those were lonesome days. No papers, no mail—we had to go seventeen miles to Larimore for the mail—and no church. Just the vast prairie. I could see so far and there wasn't even a tree anywhere. I used to look and look as far as I could see if I could see anyone coming . . . I always used to hang a lantern out when anyone from our place was away. It brought many a lost wayfarer to us!"

In November after "freeze-up came and no more farm work could be done except taking care of the horses and cattle . . . the hired man had packed his trunk . . . and Father took him to Wahpeton, eleven miles. As the wagon rolled out of the yard, [R. D. Crawford's] mother said, 'Now we are alone again'." During the winter of 1886-87, "none of the family except my father saw a soul from the outside. We were holed up. The blizzards and high winds were almost continuous. In one stretch of six weeks Father did not dare to venture out [but] finally he had to get wood."

This enforced isolation soon had a telling effect on the pioneer woman's character for she became increasingly timid. "A big price was paid for the development of the plains states. No one can ever know how much of that cheap wheat was produced by child labor [and overworked mothers] . . . It was in 1894 [that] I tossed a 480 acre farm over my shoulder. My mother spent four years [October, 1890, to March, 1894] in the hospital at Jamestown with a mental breakdown because of the hardships, anxiety, and isolation of the pioneer period. The children paid too. . . ." Those were the feelings of one who left Dakota as a young man after his mother returned from the mental hospital. He never quite got over being bitter about the price his family paid for being pioneers. O. A. Olson explained why his father stuck it out through the dry period of the 1880's before he finally lost his farm:

Most of my neighbors have vanished
For they could not live on dust.
They inscribed this line on their wagons:
"Back to the fleshpots or bust."

Soon after the Hovdes arrived in Traill County in 1871, Mari Hovde complained that the loneliness of the life was frightening and depressing. "Not even the birds or insects to disturb the quiet." Others in their neighborhood "agreed that there was neither bird nor insect life on the prairie, with the exception of mosquitoes, the first year that they came." The terrible strain and rigors of pioneer life, and the bearing and the caring for children with the lurking fears and the constant dread of prairie fire and Indians, all had taken their toll, and by 1883 Mari Hovde, in her thirties, paid the price of pioneering—she became an invalid and remained so until her death in 1929.

Ada Lockhart Gunkelman related that her mother endured a similar experience. When Ada was away at college she was called home to Kelso to take over the housework because her mother, in her mid-thirties, had "become very crippled from overwork." [4]

Guy Divet came to Dakota as a nine-year-old boy and grew up in a prosperous family. He tells a story that reveals the fate of two women:

My mother died [at about age 55] holding my hand. A contributing factor to her passing was the crushing burdens of the prairie frontier. She was one of many women who helped to subdue those wild lands and turn them into the fertile homelands they are today. Constituting a monument to their unconquerable spirits.

That new prairie settling was hard on women. There was always pressing work to be done, and lots of it; little time for rest or relaxation for mind or body; nothing but hope for the future.

Before that time came many of the wives and mothers were worn out, their strength absorbed, their early graves yawning; and so it was with my mother. Some women survived, but those not young when this prairie life began were victims of the hardships the loneliness and the monotony of the daily grind, and the prairies devoured them.

Mrs. Divet "had been a school teacher, a woman of considerable culture and pride." Guy remembered that while they were still living in southeastern Minnesota, she always dreamed and talked much of the day when she might visit her girlhood home in Wisconsin. "Several times such a trip was just on the verge of realization when some unforeseen farm event would prohibit it." Her hopes were blasted again and again. "Then came the talk of Dakota and [once more] the dreamed-of-trip was postponed. . . . Father was sympathetic, but without much sentiment. His ambition was to become a great land-owner, and here was the opportunity ready made, and he pressed it hard."

The Divet brothers were a team and they both worked hard. Work was the order of the day. The Divets continued to operate their 386-acre farm in Olmsted County, Minnesota, while they were developing their 1,920 acres in Richland County. Mrs. Divet had to work double time to keep up. Shortly after the Divets moved to Dakota, another son, Walter, was born. Guy Divet wrote, "Mother was overworked and rundown, and she never fully rallied. . . . There were crews of hungry men to be fed and housed; there were the younger children to be cared for and guided; and even when bedridden and in extreme physical distress, she rose and set things right in any emergency."

After a good year, very likely 1891, Daniel Divet informed his wife that she could make her long dreamed of trip to Wisconsin. He told her that on her way she could stop in Minneapolis to buy new clothes.

"Wisconsin," she said, and bitterness dripped like acid from her tongue. "Yes, I suppose we could stop in Minneapolis and buy clothes. But you can't buy me a new body to put them on, or feet which will wear shoes, or a hat that will cover my straggling hair, or anything at all to cover this hideous bag [a goiter] that hangs at my throat. You can't make me look like anything anyone would recognize. My brother, Del, wouldn't believe it was I." "No," she finally declared, "it's too late now. I don't want to go," and she fled the room followed by father. What happened between them then I do not know, but the trip to Wisconsin was never mentioned again in the family circle. Yes, my mother was, in very truth, a part of the grist of the frontier's mill, taken for toll in the interests of the generations to come. I wondered, when I held her hand that day she died, if somehow her poor disfigured and tired out body might not somehow be returned to look like the photograph of her that now lies in the Richland County Historical Society's files . . .

At that time I felt a terrible resentment toward father . . . But years have softened my feeling, and I realize now that, concealed in that apparent callousness, was a great compliment to my mother and proof of father's love and affection for her. For her changed appearance had never once been apparent to him, she was the bride he brought from her Wisconsin home so long ago—her form, her face, her hair, her feet —had not changed. She was the graceful, young woman he had first loved, and I think he still saw her with the pompadour she wore then, a slender figure instead of the shapeless one that wore its ugly "Mother Hubbard" . . . I think Father had never seen her imperfections, nor noticed the disfigurement of the goiter. He saw her as his girl bride, until that day of her terrible outburst.

Grist for the Mill

The Divets, as a family, made their mark as prosperous farmers in the new frontier society with Mrs. Divet, more than anyone else, paying the price of success. Within the Divet neighborhood there were many who also paid a price, but who failed as farmers. A neighbor of the Divets, who lived about three or four miles distance, was Ned. The Divet children never learned his last name. Ned came to Richland County about 1881 and lived in a sod-walled shanty with a board roof. He spent his first year building his shanty and breaking some of the prairie. When fall came he returned to Oshkosh, Wisconsin, to marry Margie. In the winter of 1881-82 Ned and Margie left Wisconsin for their new home on the frontier. Ned was very proud of his wife and stopped in at the Divets "to show her off to the only other 'American' family in the neighborhood. They accepted our invitation to spend the night, and somewhere a place was found for them to sleep," although the two-room house was already crowded with five children and four adults. Guy Divet remembered that Margie was about twenty, very attractive, and "we all liked her at once."

During the winter months that followed no visits were exchanged between the Divets and their new neighbors. Then, one day in March, "Ned drove through to us with the news that his wife was not well, and acting queerly—and would mother come over to their shanty and see her as soon as the weather relented a little." Fortunately, mild weather soon came and Mrs. Divet had her son, Guy, drive her over to Ned's place. After visiting several hours, the two returned home. Guy observed:

Mother was very grave and silent during the homeward journey. That night, after I was in bed, I overheard her tell my father that Margie was expecting a baby early in September and she was sick and out of her mind with loneliness and fear . . . she wanted to go back to Wisconsin. Ned was nearly crazy with worry and grief. Mother suggested that Margie be brought to our house, where she could give the girl some care and companionship. Father resisted but mother won out. She insisted Ned and Margie must have help . . . and some relief from the loneliness and monotony of her days.

Ned and Margie came over and a bed was set up in the "big room" of the shanty for Margie. This was the room that served for the so-called "living room" of today, where everyone gathered, and which was used for everything except sleeping room for the family. To give Margie some privacy, a curtain was hung around her bed in the corner, but she was able to hear our voices and keep in contact with other's lives and interests and this, together with good food and mother's loving care proved a wonderfully recuperative treatment.

While Margie's health improved, Ned worked for the Divets and helped them with his team. The Divets finished their field work earlier with that extra help so they took their entire crew over to Ned's place and did all of his spring field work for him in one day. In about a month "Margie had recovered sufficiently, both physically and mentally, to help mother with cooking and other house work." In another month both Ned and Margie, with new hope and courage, were able to return to their shanty. Ned struggled with two horses and a walking plow to add another thirty acres for the next year's crop land. To do this he had to spend most of his time in the field, leaving Margie alone.

We did not see much of Ned and Margie all summer because we, too, were driven with work and it was not easy to visit neighbors who lived three or four miles distant. When we did see Ned he was always worried. Mother got to see Margie once and was distressed because she did not know who was going to care for the baby. Men must work and women must weep and on the prairie women did both.

Ned came over to the Divets one day and informed them that it appeared as if Margie's baby would be coming sooner than expected. He inquired if Mrs. Divet could come over when Margie's time came, if he would come over to get her. "That was the way things were done in those days; to get a woman of kindness and experience like my mother, to attend in such an emergency, was a luxury then."

About a week later Ned came dashing over in the pre-dawn darkness. "My mother piled out of bed and was off and away, on what she declared later was the wildest ride she had ever taken. Across the prairie humps and gopher mounds that rocked and bounced the wagon and its occupants." On the way over to the shanty Ned said that he had had to tie Margie to the bed to keep her from following him. Mrs. Divet commented that they arrived none too soon. For two days she sat with the "screaming, agonized wife, who babbled about her child, which she visualized as already born and perishing in the winter snows. This was varied with screams for her mother and pleas to take her little Lucy, as she called her coming baby, home to Wisconsin."

After a few days Daniel Divet, accompanied by his nine-year-old daughter, Rena, went to visit Ned and Margie and to get his wife, for by now it was necessary that Mrs. Divet return home because they were busy with harvest. Rena was left with Margie to act as nurse and housekeeper, and do whatever possible to make Margie comfortable. Mrs. Divet promised to come over every few days to see how things progressed. Guy commented that "Rena never married. She was so affected by what she experienced in those few weeks at Ned's cottage with the half crazed mother and depressed father that she became a lifelong cynic about marriage." Margie regained her senses and had partially recovered in about a month. She "turned out to be a very capable young woman, vigorous and eager in her care of home and child." After Rena left Ned's place to return home, the Divets saw little of the family until after harvest.

No doubt Ned thought much about the future during those months, concluding that Margie and the baby would not be able to pull through the coming winter. He decided to sell his crop, give up his homestead claim, and return to Wisconsin. After harvest he used the Divet's shop to convert his grain wagon into a modified covered wagon for the trip back. Mrs. Divet visited with Margie several times after harvest. There was concern in the little neighborhood about the young couple, but, according to Guy, "Prairie families were pretty good at minding their own business and not interfering with that of their neighbors and while there was some discussion in our family as to the wisdom of such a move, it was pretty well agreed that Ned was right in his determination to take the young mother and her child back home."

On November 1 the covered grain wagon with binder canvas cover, camping equipment, dishes, tools, a little sheet iron stove, provisions, and sacks of oats for the horses came slowly across the prairie. Margie and the baby lay on a mattress cushioned with straw while Ned had his bedroll for sleeping under the wagon.

Several of the neighbors came over to the Divets where a little surprise farewell was quickly organized:

Margie talked with us, full of hope and renewed confidence, though she was far too ill to raise up from her bed. [When they were about ready to leave, one of the Divet hired men] grasped Ned's hand and asked, "How much money you got, Ned?" Awkwardly Ned responded, "Oh, I'll get by all right," hanging his head a little in embarrassment. "How much you got?" Old Bob insisted. " 'Bout twenty dollars," replied Ned. "Seven hundred miles from home, a sick wife and baby, cold weather coming on, and you got twenty dollars," said Old Bob. Then he added, "An' I think you're lying at that!" Old Bob reached into his pocket took out some silver and a couple of bills, dropped the money into his hat, and said, "That's all I got."

Without another word the hat was passed around and into it went something from everyone, we children scurrying into the shanty to delve into our hiding places and came back with a few nickels, dimes, and pennies. Mother found a couple of bills to add to the accumulation. Then Old Bob solemnly counted the money and wrapped it in his old red handkerchief. "Thirty-six dollars and eighty cents," he said, and tossed the bundle into the wagon bed where Margie and the baby lay, "and God knows that's little enough." With tears streaming down his face Ned mounted his wagon seat, and ashamed of his tears, slapped the lines on the horse's backs and drove away.

The farewell party broke up after that with most of the people shaking their heads in pity and disbelief.

Four weeks later the Divets received a letter from Ned, postmarked Winona, Minnesota, informing them that the baby had died. Some church society had taken care of the burial. Ned wrote that he and Margie were both prostrate with grief but still determined to get to Oshkosh. Ned had made good time on his trip to Winona, averaging twenty-five miles a day, but he slowed down after that. Just before Christmas a second letter arrived from Ned. Margie had died two hundred miles away from her longed-for Oshkosh. Ned wrote that he had sold his wagon and team for $150 to pay for Margie's burial expenses and he would walk the last two hundred miles. "That was all. It was the last [anyone in Dakota] ever heard from Ned. Thus, not alone the women but babies, too, often strong men and able ones were grist to the prairie mill."

When Ned left Dakota he gave Daniel Divet the key to his shanty and asked him to look at the place from time to time. Ned said that if he never came back, Divet could take all that was left behind. Eventually Ned's claim was "jumped," so Daniel and Son, Guy, drove over to check on the shanty. They found little in the home. "On the stove was an old iron teakettle and an iron pot, some of the dishes they had used for their last breakfast, still unwashed, a few old garments and on the little shelf an old clock." Guy described the clock which contained a weather barometer that had the figure of an old man who forecast foul weather and when the figure of an old woman appeared it forecast fair weather. "There was also a little homemade crib with a small soiled tick filled with hay, a little quilted blanket of brightly colored calico pieces, and a little china cup with 'Lucy' in pretty blue letters on the side."

Daniel and Guy talked it over after they had examined all of Ned's belongings and decided that there was nothing worth saving. On the other hand, they decided that it was not proper to let them fall into the hands of strangers either and concluded that they should burn the house. They gathered some hay from the little sod barn and piled it into the crib. Then they broke the chairs and the table into kindling wood and put it under the crib. Once the fire started, they "went outside to watch with reverence" as they thought of Ned and Margie.

The little shanty burned quickly. After examining the sod barn they decided to leave it untouched. As they were about to leave, Guy remembered that "Father looked back when the last ember was dying and said more to himself than me, 'The end of a homesteader's dream.'"

When writing about the event much later, Guy Divet noted:

As I look backward down through the vista of 60-odd years, since the day I saw Ned's little home go up in smoke, I see many things . . . but nothing comes back to me more vividly as the burning prairie home we watched that day. We never heard from Ned again. This was part of the growing pains of that great prairie empire . . and these people of whom I write had their tragic and greater share.

Ned and Margie were not the only ones who paid the supreme price to conquer Red River Land. At a later date, when the Divet children and some friends were out hunting not far from the Divet farm, they came across a burned-out spot on the prairie where the outlines of a shanty foundation were still visible. Nearby were five acres of ground that had been plowed some years before. A flat piece of sandstone marked a grave with the inscription: *MARY AND BABY GOOD BI* [sic]. Beside it were a cold chisel and a hammer. Even though this was in the Divet neighborhood, no one was ever able to determine who "Mary and Baby" were or learn the father's name.

There were many graves on the frontier without even markers. Knut Hamsun, the famous Norwegian author who spent a few years in the 1880's working on farms in this area, recalled such a burial. His first job when working for a pioneer farmer was to dig a little grave near the woods. As soon as Hamsun finished digging the farmer came from the house with a little coffin and placed it in the grave. Because neither could understand the other, he motioned to Hamsun to cover the grave and then turned away. "But dear God, didn't he come back again? No. He worked at something in the outhouses and pretended to be busy. I could not make it out, shuddered and felt bad. The body of a child had been buried, that was all. No ceremony, not even a hymn. They were young people . . ."

When the Thortvedt's "Uncle Andres Gjeitsta" died in March, 1871, "the neighbors got together and buried him on the river bank of his land." A couple of hymns were sung at the graveside. Because there was no finished lumber available for making a coffin, a wagon box was taken apart for the purpose. In November, 1875, Mrs. R. M. Probstfield gave premature birth "to a boy born dead." A neighbor, Mrs. Jacob Wamback, came over to help. Mr. Probstfield "made [the] coffin and buried him." Five days later he concluded the sad event with a simple: "Mrs. P. up in the afternoon—feels better."

No Wallflowers

Helena Huntington Smith, author of *Pioneers in Petticoats*, disagrees with the common belief that the frontier was "hell on women [as many] ladies claim they had the time of their lives." She admits that there are a great many contradictions among the women themselves, but sums up her opinion as follows: "Successful pioneering was a matter of temperament and constitution, combined with width of pelvis, which was luck, a factor not to be overlooked." Not all pioneer women agreed with Hamlin Garland's epitaph on a pioneer woman's grave which read, "Just born an' scrubbed an' suffered and died."

One young woman, who had traveled to the plains by ox wagon with a small baby, reported sixty years later that "she had worked hard all her life and had no time for worry and it's worry and not work that kills." This woman, who reared nine children, always had a big crew of men to cook for. At the Saturday night dance she was always a terrific dancer—outlasting her husband by many years in that respect. Frequently one of her sons had to substitute at the "romping, stomping parties for her partner." Another woman, who spent a great deal of time out of doors working with her husband, said, "What woman, youthful and full of spirits and the love of living, needs sympathy because of availing herself of the opportunity of being with her husband while at his chosen work in the great out-of-door world?"

Mrs. Woodward frequently noted in her diary that she was lonesome, but what she seemed to notice most was the complete lack of trees in contrast to her former home in Wisconsin. She spent a great deal of time in what she called her "observatory," which was the east upstairs window. Here she daily peered through a spyglass toward the green woods along the Sheyenne or to see if anyone was walking across the prairie. On the evening of her second anniversary in the area, this fifty-eight year old woman noted, "They have been short years for me for I have had plenty to do. I have enjoyed my life here very much and have never wished to leave." True, for many pioneers, life was more difficult than for the Woodwards, but few had such a broad view of the overall problems and opportunities that the frontier presented.

Christine Stafne, who lived through the period from the 1870's to World War II, was impressed by the rapid improvement in pioneer life and observed that the 1880's "did not compare to the hardships in the 1870's." To her the pain of the farm depression of the 1920's, when so much of what they had worked for was lost, exceeded all the adversities of the first two decades of pioneering.

Helena H. Smith has suggested the phrase that the frontier was "hell on horses and women" must have been uttered by a man because she was unable to find a "single woman who agreed that life was hell, or a grandmother old enough to admit that it had ever been so in her day." There were no "wallflowers" on the frontier; every school teacher and every hired girl got married. The conclusion reached by researchers on pioneer women is that some women, and also some men, were just not suited for frontier life. Some hated dirt floors; some hated the thought of cooking with buffalo chips; some hated not having frequent social contact; and some just hated the loneliness.[5]

FOOTNOTES

[1] Smalley, p. 380; Harry F. McLean, "Presentation of the Statue of a Pioneer Family to the State of North Dakota," *NDH*, XIV (Oct., 1947) 282-284.

[2] *Hope of the Prairie*; Gunderson, pp. 19-26, 40-42, 60, 70-75; Murray, pp. 68-70; Olsen interview; Pratt interview; Emil Ankerfeldt interview.

[3] Elton, *Vaalhovd*, p. 36; Olsen interview; Hovde, pp. 16-20; Woodward, pp. 113, 144, 242; Divet, NDIRS, File 69; Crawford, NDIRS, File 290; Hobart, "Pioneering," VII, 206; Probstfield; *Warren Sheaf*, March 5 and March 26, 1891; Mrs. Leif Christianson, interview by the author, June, 1968. Mrs. Christianson is the descendent of a family of southern planters.

[4] Cavileer, p. 213; "State Geographic Board Report on North Dakota," *NDH*, II (Oct., 1927), 54; *Fargo Forum*, Feb. 28, 1961, p. 25; Crawford, NDIRS, File 290; Hovde, pp. 18-19; Gunkelman interview; McMahon, NDIRS, File 195.

[5] Divet, NDIRS, File 69; Hamsun, *On Over Grown Paths*, p. 160; Thortvedt, NDIRS, File 332; Probstfield; Elton, *Vaalhovd*, p. 30; Pruett interview; Helena Huntington Smith, "Pioneers in Petticoats," *American Heritage*, X (1959), 37-38, 101-102; Woodward, pp. 52, 82, 145; Stafne, pp. 34, 69.

CHAPTER XIII

God on the Prairie

Roman Catholic missionaries traveled in central North America with French fur traders as early as the sixteenth century and were well known for their work among the Indians. Catholic leaders realized that missionaries and priests in the new country had to be practical men with a good knowledge of how to erect buildings and how to farm. They had to be men of sound judgment and of great ability, as well as men of religious zeal and piety. The new frontier was no place for weak men. On September 18, 1818, Father Joseph Severe Norbert Dumoulin established a church, a shop, and a school for his parish at Pembina.

The St. Francis Xavier Mission (now the Assumption Catholic Church) is the oldest functioning congregation in the American sector of the Valley and its early years were encouraging. By September 13, 1822, there had been 49 burials, 60 marriages, and 394 baptisms. The congregation has occupied five church buildings (three made of logs, one of sawed lumber, and the present one of brick and stone). Up to 1969 this congregation has been served by sixty-eight priests.

Religious Development

Although the Hudson's Bay Company had been functioning in the area since the 1670's, it had encouraged very little religious work other than reading from the Prayer Book to the men at the posts. But in 1820 the Company decided to send a chaplain into the area and provided the Reverend John West with £150 a year to do mission work among the Indians and among the settlers in the Red River area. The Reverend West held his first Anglican service in Pembina on March 15, 1821, and later described it in this manner:

I preached to a considerable number of persons assembled at the Fort. They heard me with great attention; but I was often depressed in mind, on the general view of character, and at the spectacle of human depravity and barbarism I was called to witness.

West worked hard among the early Red River settlers trying to raise their moral and cultural level. Father Dumoulin once referred to him as "that fanatic" because West had married many Swiss Protestant girls to Roman Catholic soldiers.

Many frontier historians assert that religion was one of the major factors enabling pioneer men and women to endure the loneliness and the hardships. Religion was a part of life for the pioneers. To them, it was a vital, moving thing. Pioneers had to be very resourceful and they sensed that only some "higher power" could help them endure. With few of the comforts and aids of civilization available, pioneers longed for the reassurance given them by men of God. This statement does not mean to imply, however, that there was no religious indifference on the frontier. The booming liquor traffic and the fact that men were sometimes fired if "they would not work on Sunday" give testimony of the antireligious feelings of many settlers. In the earliest years of settlement there was little outward evidence of Christianity except within the home until a man of God, usually in the form of a traveling preacher, appeared and religious services were started.

The first "Episcopal form of worship" held in what is now North Dakota was a marriage service conducted in July or August, 1871, by N. P. Langford, a layman, at the second crossing of the Sheyenne River (Valley City). In June, 1872, Dr. A. D. Forbes, M.D., held services in the construction camp of the Northern Pacific Railroad in what is now the city of Fargo. To the east of the Red River, the friend of the Indians, Bishop Henry B. Whipple, commissioned the Reverend Joseph A. Gilfillan to follow the Northern Pacific's progress west. Reverend Gilfillan traveled along the road and held services at principal towns about every two weeks starting in 1872. Following the construction of the line, he hoped to establish congregations at Detroit Lakes, Glyndon, Moorhead, and Fargo. When he arrived in Moorhead, he was surprised to find a Presbyterian, the Reverend O. H. Elmer, there ahead of him.

The Reverend Elmer had been conducting services in Moorhead since October 22, 1871, using the Chapin House as a church. The Reverend Elmer helped Gilfillan hold services in a railroad coach during the summer of 1872. Later in the year Reverend Gilfillan was invited to use the old converted school house that the Presbyterians had acquired under Elmer's leadership. The Reverend Elmer prepared the fires and got the building ready for services for his fellow worker. In

August, 1872, Gilfillan held the second recorded church services in Fargo when a Northern Pacific engineer, General Thomas R.. Rosser and his wife Betsy, invited him to read prayer and conduct communion in one of the tents which then made up the Fargo townsite. Five communicants attended the service.

The traveling preacher of all denominations held services wherever he could get listeners. The first sermon preached at Bismarck, Dakota Territory, in 1873, was delivered under unusual circumstances. One Sunday morning all the railroad construction men gathered around the tables in a gambling house to play poker. Suddenly a stranger entered the room, mounted an unused table, and began reading aloud from a Bible. The first impluse of the poker players was to stop this disconcerting activity with a bullet, but then they decided to let him go on unless he should try to stop their game. But the stranger attended strictly to his own business and won the respect of the gamblers. At the close of his impromptu sermon the men passed the hat and collected $40 in poker chips. The proprietor presented the purse to the preacher and informed him that the chips represented money. He could "play them in" or he could "cash them in." He also offered a pistol to the preacher to make sure things were "square" if he wished to gamble. The minister declined the invitation to gamble and cashed in the chips.

In some communities the first church meetings were held in a tent on the Sabbath and a congregation of eight or ten people was considered large. There were no organs, no pews, and often no chairs. Many times the traveling preachers and evangelists held prayer meetings in the larger homes, and as the crowds increased, they moved to the school house or, as in one case, to the local store where the minister used a whiskey barrel for a pulpit. In Hillsboro, services were held "in the hall over Pete Morris's livery barn" or in homes. As the community grew, the traveling preacher recognized the need to organize a congregation as the Reverend H. Harstad did in Hillsboro in 1874.

The preachers had a difficult life, traveling under all conditions of weather and encountering many antagonists. Some preachers were even permitted to carry guns. But they also found homes where they were welcomed because of the news they brought, the companionship they offered, as well as the Word they delivered. The Overby family on the Sheyenne was a good example of such a home and the traveling ministers made it their regular stopping place. The house was crowded, but there was always room for another. He made himself useful and chopped wood, helped in the garden, or even did chores so that the work could be finished earlier in order to have an evening of church service.

Until a church was built in the 1890's, the Overbys at Wolverton always had the traveling preacher stay at their home when he preached in their community. The Hovdes at Hillsboro were hosts both to itinerant missionaries and to preachers who usually stayed a couple of days at a time. The preaching and the singing often attracted other people to the homes.

The traveling missionary was not universally welcomed; nevertheless, he was generally treated with respect. The arrival in Cass County of Mr. Fenn, a student of theology from New York in June, 1888, showed a typical reaction of pioneer communities to such visitors:

[He is] trying to organize a Sabbath school among us heathen. I do not think he will succeed as nearly all the families with children in the neighborhood are Catholics, and it is difficult for Catholics and Protestants to have any unison . . . He had consent of the school board to use the school house. No man seems willing to take it in hand and Katie [the local teacher] doesn't like to.

But apparently young Mr. Fenn's persistence paid off for he sold Bibles and books of Bible stories. He appeared at the Woodward home several times because he sensed that they were leaders in the community and within two months several of the Woodwards were going to Sabbath School and on one Sunday all of the hired men went too.

[They said] they were going for the purpose of quelling any disturbance which might arise. Last Sabbath a young man who worked in the neighborhood cracked parlor matches under his heels, laughed aloud, and talked so that he disturbed the school. None of the men said anything to him, so Katie asked him to leave, which he did. He came again this Sabbath to have more fun, but when he saw the crowd was against him, he left without going inside. The hired men said they had boxing gloves in the wagon as they didn't want to kill him.

The urge for Christian fellowship among many of the earliest settlers in the Red River Valley was so strong that occasionally they put aside denominational differences and held union services in private homes or in other suitable buildings whenever a pastor was available. Most of the early traveling preachers were Presbyterians, Baptists, or Methodists. They usually came on the Northern Pacific Railroad and stopped at the towns along the way to minister to all, much like the military chaplains.

In the newly settled community of Lisbon, for example, a Union Society was formed which held services in a tent during the spring and summer of 1881 and then moved into a roughly built log structure for the winter. By the summer of 1882 the Methodists, the Presbyterians, and the Catholics were numerous enough there to establish individual congregations. The arrangement of union services proved satisfactory until language barriers became more pronounced when so many foreign settlers came in during the Great Dakota Boom.

Denominationalism received more emphasis and soon each national group had its own church, with the Norwegians going to the extreme by establishing four synods within the Lutheran church. In the Sheyenne Valley John Hogenson, who preached in Norwegian, had "marked talents for leadership in religious and public activities," and served as a lay preacher and later played "a leading role in separating a group of neighboring farmers from our Lutheran congregation to form a new 'left wing' congregation of Methodists. . . . He could read and converse in English so the Norwegians, who had no opportunity to become proficient in a foreign language" went to him for much advice. In this way he influenced them.[1]

"Moonlighting" Ministers

As early as colonial times in America most preachers were expected to provide for their family's livelihood by practicing a second vocation. The same was expected of them in Red River Land. The traveling preachers, who were also the first resident ministers in the area, were overworked and underpaid. Their salaries ranged from $28 to $495 annually for one large conference. In the 1870's resident pastors of the Dakota District of the Methodist Church had an average annual salary of $300 including house allowance. Many were paid even less and received corn, wheat, flour, hay, vegetables, or meat instead. Consequently, many of the early ministers in the Red River area were forced to combine preaching with farming.

On July 4, 1871, the Reverend Jonas Ostlund, who was probably the first permanent resident minister in Traill County, "squatted" on land belonging to the Northern Pacific. The railroad objected to this action but after much negotiation he won clear title to the land and eventually was able to accumulate 320 acres. His farming operation succeeded, even though he spent much time away from it while serving the religious needs of several communities in Traill and Steele counties.

Another "squatter" was the Reverend C. Y. Snell, a Baptist minister from New Brunswick, Canada, who moved his family to Strabone Township near Inkster in 1881. Like Ostlund, Snell's preaching activities did not seem to affect his success in farming, for by 1893 he had acquired a full section of land. However, the Snells received much publicity for one of the most gruesome events in the annals of crime in the Red River area occurred at their farm. While Reverend Snell was away on a two-week preaching tour at Mayville, his hired man, George Miller, murdered Mrs. Snell and their eleven-year-old son, Herbert.

The murder was not discovered until a week later when some neighbors stopped at the farm to investigate because the place seemed so quiet. Noticing that the animals appeared starved, they entered the house and found the two bloody bodies frozen to the beds. Fortunately, the three eldest children were attending school in Grand Forks at this time and, therefore, escaped death. Law enforcement officials soon captured Miller in Minnesota.

The Reverend Daniel C. Pehrsson also combined farming with his preaching duties. A veteran of the Civil War, he had preached in large eastern cities for fourteen years and in order to avoid losing his investment of wartime savings in Northern Pacific bonds, converted them to one and one-half sections of land near Wheatland. Although this was a large amount of land, Reverend Pehrsson managed to continue his preaching. However, he was forced to hire additional help to operate the land.[2]

Upper Valley Congregations

One of the earliest "men of God" in the Upper Red River Valley was Father Baptiste Genin who spent three days at McCauleyville in 1865 with two other priests ministering to local settlers, half breeds, and soldiers at Fort Abercrombie. The results of their three days of mission work eventually led to the founding of the St. Thomas Parish at Kent. Farther upstream, Father Ignatius Tomazin served the Bohemian settlers from 1868 to 1879, celebrating his first mass in a dugout just west of the Red River north of Wahpeton. The congregation held services in many locations in Breckenridge and Wahpeton until they erected a frame church in 1877.

One of the first Protestant congregations formed in the Upper Valley was Hamar, on the trail between Fergus Falls and Moorhead, near present-day Rothsay. The first services were held at the Sletvild home on November 2, 1870, and ten children were baptized at that time. When the congregation was formally organized in 1874, Reverend T. Rosholdt was called as pastor and was paid $70 for holding seven services a year (two of which were to be on Sunday) besides ministering to the needs of the congregation. The entire congregation worked to erect a log church and subscribed the $146 to pay for it. Logs cost twenty-five cents each. The benches had no back rests and the church was intolerably cold in the winter time. When the members could not keep warm with their overcoats on, services were moved to the school house.

In 1880 when the Richland Lutheran Congregation of Abercrombie decided to build a $2,500 church, each member was assessed one-half cent per bushel of wheat grown to cover the cost of the building and to pay itinerant pastor T. Vetelson's salary of $93.

In 1872, six Norwegian families organized the South Wild Rice congregation, holding services in the Martin Johnson cabin until 1874 because it was the largest in the community. After that they met in the new 18 by 22 foot school house. Each family was assessed fifty cents annually to cover rental of the building. The "Ladies Aid" organized in 1883 conducted bake and sewing sales, served church dinners as well as lunches at various farm auctions in an effort to raise money to support missions, orphans, the parochial school, and to purchase items for the church and to loan money to farmers in need. In 1887 the "Ladies Aid" purchased a large chandelier for $71.65 which lighted the entire church; in 1890 they purchased an altar set for $23.12; and six years later paid $117.20 for a new altar and pulpit, in addition to the materials and labor when the church was painted. The church treasury was annually replenished through a congregational auction sale to which goods of all kinds were donated, including livestock, machinery, and produce.

Several Norwegian families who settled on both sides of the Red River south of Fargo and Moorhead probably held the first Norwegian language services in that area in the fall of 1871. Because of their nearness to the railroad, they received visits from itinerant pastors until October, 1872, when the Reverend Niels T. Ylvisaker helped organize the congregation at the home of Peter P. Nokken, south of Moorhead. Five families, eight single men, and one woman were listed as charter members. The congregation erected a church in Moorhead, but in 1878 was forced to sell it because of financial difficulties.

In 1890 the congregation decided to build another church south of Fargo (along present U. S. Highway 81) and members provided all the labor to build the church, the altar, the pulpit, and the communion rail. All were still in use in 1969. Salem, probably the second oldest Lutheran congregation still functioning in the state of North Dakota, is surpassed in age only by the Aal congregation in Traill County. It was organized two months earlier than Salem.

Typical of many of the small congregations formed as a result of the language barrier was the Immanuel Lutheran Church of the Missouri Synod organized at Davenport in 1886 by only nine people. This German language congregation held services every fourth Sunday and shared its pastor with three other churches, each of which paid $7 to $10 a month toward his support. But like so many others, this congregation was unable to maintain itself during the post World War I agricultural depression and most of its members joined the nearby Norwegian Lutheran Church.

Social Function of the Church

In addition to satisfying the spiritual needs of the settlers, the church also played an important part in their social lives. This function was important in days when social life was quite limited. Visits from the itinerant preacher provided a time for friendly visits as well as for spiritual stimulation. In the absence of a minister, neighbors often got together for Sunday devotions and filled out the day with conversation and hymn signing. Christenings and weddings were festive affairs, and even funerals were an opportunity for meeting friends and relatives.

When Ole Hovde's daughter, Mattie, married Even A. Nelson, a Norwegian clerk in the Hans Johnson Mercantile Company in Hillsboro, there was a big celebration. Both the Reverends Hillerud and Jacobson officiated at the 6 p.m. service, after which over 100 guests attended the wedding dinner held at the farm home. The neighborhood ladies had spent several days making the preparations and a large tent, decorated with Japanese lanterns, had been erected. A sudden rain storm forced many to spend the night in the tent, but that only added to the fun.

Quite a contrast to this gala affair was the wedding held at the Charles Hobart farm home, when Lewis Wright, a hired man, and Agnes Gilmore, a hired girl, were married. Only the Hobarts as witnesses and Mr. Phillips, the minister at Cummings, were present. This wedding was the only one Mr. Hobart had ever attended "except one other and of course my own."

In some communities the church was also the center of most Chrismas activities, though in others the celebration of Christmas was more home oriented. But in no instance did Christmas have the commercial atmosphere of today. The "Christmas tree" was used almost exclusively in the church. One congregation had a "big church tree which was an oak wrapped with strips of green cloth and had apples hung on it, with chains of popcorn and cranberry for decorations." Many congregations decorated the tree with candles and had gifts for the children beneath it.

Most families did some sort of home decorating for Christmas, but the customary evergreen was not always available. In one instance a wild plum tree was decorated with apples, popcorn, and paper cutouts. One prairie family used a tumbleweed which the children had rescued from a nearby fence line.[3]

Pioneer ministers, just like pioneer farmers, were optimistic about the future. Everyone wanted to build churches and before long there were more than could be properly used. After the dry years of the late 1880's and the resulting exodus of settlers, churches were found to be in surplus. This same situation had already repeated itself at earlier times in rural America and has remained a problem to the present. The problem is well illustrated in the following:

It is evident to anyone who travels the country roads in America these days that the country church, as we have known it in the past, is falling into decay. And it does not take the reports of extensive religious surveys to convince one that perhaps two-thirds of the country and village churches in the United States are either losing ground or are standing still in membership and in influence in their communities. When the surrounding population has been falling off rapidly as it has been in most country districts, it is inevitable that many of the existing churches should be given up. They merely go the way of all things which are built upon insufficient foundation. They fail because they are not big enough to live. For the present era is one of the big things and it is not surprising that the country church has responded to the challenge.

The above quotation, which could be applied to the Red River region in the mid-twentieth century, was written about the eastern corn belt by Mary Atkeson in 1920. Those who do not learn from history must relive it. Even though rural areas in the eastern part of America were already on the decline when the Valley was being opened, real estate promoters and others were so optimistic that even the church overexpanded. Prominent individuals donated lots to a church because it would enhance the value of land they owned around the church. Lumber companies advanced credit too liberally to newly formed congregations. This credit caused small congregations to become heavily indebted before they could really economically justify themselves. Local promoters tried hard to get at least three or four denominations represented in their community to assure more rapid growth of their town.

Hillsboro established a pattern that was typical of many communities. Before church building came to an end in that community, there were eight churches—the Presbyterian, the Congregational, the Baptist, the Catholic, the Methodist (American), the Methodist

(Scandinavian), the Synod Lutheran, and the Free Lutheran—all in a community that never had more than 1,400 people. However, Ellendale to the southwest, a village of 1,800 population, still had fourteen churches in 1966. Other communities had done nearly as badly, but probably Ellendale holds some kind of unofficial record for over-expansion.

The Deerhorn Presbyterian Church in Wilkin County is an example of one of the rural churches in the Red River Valley in which the membership leveled off shortly after its organization and, after a long, gradual decline in membership, was eventually forced to close. This church was organized March 14, 1891, by sixteen people—four cou-' ples, six single men, and two single women. The congregation applied to the Red River Presbytery for half-time services of an available pastor and promised to pay $115 annually toward his salary. On May 31, four additional members brought the total to twenty.

No regular services were held until June, 1895, but then more new members enlarged the congregation so that services had to be held in the school house. In April, 1898, the congregation decided that the time had come to erect a church building. A structure 24 by 36 feet with fifteen pews seating ninety people was erected. The Reverend Asterwood served as foreman and construction started on June 6, 1898, on an acre of land donated by John Hult. The total cost of $1,080.78 was raised by means of a $300 loan from the Board of Erection, $182.67 by the King's Daughters (ladies of the church), $106 in donated labor, and $492.11 from subscriptions.

In the early years the congregation raised money as it was needed. In 1900, after two hanging lamps were purchased, there was a balance in the treasury of seventy cents. The next year $162 was raised by subscription and after the pastor was paid $159, the balance was $3.70. In 1903 the members voted to raise an additional $12.50 for the purpose of taking care of the church building. By 1912 the pastor's salary was $194. The organist received $18 for her services. The following year, however, she was paid only $5 because there were $15 in well expenses at the manse. By 1927 it was voted to have services every Sunday during the summer and into the fall as long as the weather was favorable, and to pay the minister $10 per Sunday.

Membership reached its peak in the 1920's with just over ninety on the rolls when the nearby Olivet Presbyterian congregation voted to join Deerhorn. With exodus of farmers in the 1930's and consolidation of farms in the community, membership dwindled down to thirteen and it was decided to close the doors in 1968.[4]

Father A. A. A. Schmirler, in his history of Page, wrote about religious developments in the Page area:

The first settlers were a resourceful people, and brought the twin patterns of organized Christian living with them into the promised land . . . education and public worship. However, spiritual actions, like the soul of man himself, need a material base. Thus, indirectly, religion can suffer for lack of the physical media it needs.

In Page the overexpansion of the churches caused nearly every congregation to go through a long period of indebtedness and hardship. One pastor who had suffered many years with his struggling congregation commented, "When I die I want to go to hell for a little while so I can watch the people of Page who will be there frying."

Oscar Overby, who became professor of church music at St. Olaf College, recalled his early Christian farm home and his parents' faith:

I could never figure out how she [Mother] managed all her jobs and could come to the end of each day with a playful temper and generous smile . . . and how she loved to have us join her in singing favorite hymns by the new organ before we went to sleep. During the hymn-sing father was always sitting ready with his *Postil* to lead us in devotions and prayer as a final *Amen* to the day. I would consider this the most priceless part of anyone's bringing up.

Regular church services were held in the homes in the Overby's neighborhood starting in 1882, but it was not until 1897 that there were enough settlers to justify building the Ringsaker Lutheran Church. Overby commented about that event:

Folks who were already getting adjusted to democratic living, had deep affects on our family members in many respects. . . . We at once began to feel a new sense of community and closely knit social life. The church came into clearer view, and was soon to occupy a central place in our interests.

By 1890 many people had already left the Red River area and the overexpanded churches felt the drain, forcing them to retrench.[5] Ministers were forced to serve in three to seven point parishes because one small congregation could not support their own minister. The problem of building too many churches remained with the Red River area as well as other regions of rural America for many decades. Changing times caused rapid depopulation in farming regions after World War II and forced reorganization within the greater church, resulting in the consolidation of many rural congregations. This process is still going on.

FOOTNOTES

[1] Atheson, *The Women on the Farm*, pp. 204-210; Wilkins, pp. 5-6, 10-12; Arnold, *History of Grand Forks*, pp. 123-124, 128-131, 139-143; Euren; Edward Everett Dale, *Fron-*

tier *Ways* (Austin, 1959), pp. 213-214; Probstfield; Everett Dick, *The Sod House Frontier 1854-1890* (New York, 1937), p. 334; Father Gerald Weber, Mrs. Arnold J. Christopher, Martin H. Lutter, "St. Francis Xavier Mission at Pembina: Advent of Christianity in the Upper Midwest," *Red River Valley Historian*, II (Autumn, 1968), 3, 1, 31-33; McLean, p. 282; O. Overby, *Retrospect*, pp. 11, 20-23; A. Overby, "Sod House Days," p. 12; Hovde, pp. 11-15; Probstfield; Woodward, pp. 231-235.

² O. Overby, *Retrospect*, pp. 10, 25; Hovde, pp. 11, 16; *Hillsboro Banner*, June 28, 1956, Sec. V, p. 2; Pehrsson letter; Arnold, *Inkster*, pp. 55-61; Olsen interview; Fuglestad, p. 7; Hobart, "Pioneering," VIII, 122; *Warren Sheaf*, Feb. 23, 1881, Dec. 3, 1881, Dec. 17, 1881, April 20, 1887; Pratt interview.

³ Dale, pp. 214-227; Arnold, *Ransom County*, pp. 66-67; *Hillsboro Banner*, June 28, 1956, Sec. II, p. 4, Sec. III, p. 10, Sec. IV, p. 5; Hovde, p. 16; *Our Page*, pp. 59-62, 126-132; Mrs. Elizabeth McCradie,, letter, Aug., 1967. Mrs. McCradie is the daughter-in-law of James McCradie, a settler in Quincy, which is now a ghost town in Elm River Township, in 1878; *Pioneers*, p. 87; Gilbert Haven, "Feathers Dropped from a Flying Wing," *Zion's Herald*, XLIX (Oct. 31, 1872), p. 518; *The Valley Alert, Wilkin County Centennial Edition 1868-1968*, July 18, 1968, "Salem Lutheran Church," Horace, N.D., a typed history. O. G. Nokken, "Peter P. Nokken Family," a typed history; pp. 21, 22, 23, 25, 26; Lorraine Moe, "Richland Lutheran Church," Christine, N. D., a manuscript submitted to the Red River Historical Society; Leone Flaa, "St. John's Lutheran Church," Abercrombie, N. D., a manuscript submitted to the Red River Valley Historical Society; Typed history of the Salem Lutheran Church; Lois Ward, "North Star Presbyterian Church," Humboldt, Minn., a manuscript submitted to the Red River Valley Historical Society; Mary Ann Bernath, "Christ Episcopal Church," St. Vincent, Minn., a manuscript submitted to the Red River Valley Historical Society; Barbara Colliton, "Immanual Lutheran Church," Davenport, N.D., a manuscript submitted to the Red River Valley Historical Society; *The Valley Alert*, Sept. 5, 1968; "The Minutes of Session of the Deerhorn Presbyterian Church," Wilkin County, Minn. from 1891 to 1968, provided by Mrs. David Peet; Fay Hubbard, letter to Reverend William Van Dycken, May 24, 1968.

⁴ Records of the Deerhorn Presbyterian Church.

⁵ Atheson, *The Women on the Farm*, pp. 204-210; *Our Page*, pp. 59-62; O. Overby, *Retrospect*.

CHAPTER XIV

Heal Thyself

CHILDBIRTH was one of the greatest causes of anxiety to women on the frontier. Emotional problems resulting from births appeared to be every bit as serious as the physical. Medical science was crude and doctors were lacking, so the women had to suffer. The first non-Indian child born in what is now North Dakota arrived on March 12, 1802, in the Alexander Henry trading post at Pembina. She was the daughter of Pierre Bonga and his wife, who were both Negroes. The first child of two white parents in the Red River Valley was born on December 29, 1807, at the mouth of the Pembina River, but the child was taken to Scotland the following summer.

The second child born of white parents arrived on January 6, 1808, on the open prairie a few miles from Pembina with only a wigwam for shelter. This girl, daughter of Pierre Lagimonière, a trapper and fur trader, grew up to become the mother of Louis Riel, who is famous for his rebellious activities along the Red River. Marie Anne Lagimonière had her second child under no less trying conditions. While traveling with her husband across the prairie on horseback in search of game, with their three-year-old daughter strapped in a moss bag on one side of her saddle and provisions in a packet on the other, Marie's trained pony spotted some buffalo and gave chase. During the chase Marie Anne was unable to control the horse and just before she was about to fall, her husband managed to overtake them and stop the horse. Marie Anne dismounted and shortly after gave birth to a son.

Childbirth

Because of the slowness of travel and the distances involved, many children were born while their parents were enroute to the frontier. This condition added to the hazards of childbirth in a day when few doctors were available. In 1872, Louise Carpenter, who was traveling west with her family in a covered wagon, died while giving birth to her seventh child just as they reached Fort Abercrombie. The saddened Carpenter family had no choice but to continue its journey, without a mother, to their destination somewhere in Walsh County.

Generally the pioneer woman made extensive preparations for the lying-in period by making bread, cookies, and any other food items that could be prepared in advance and stored. Frequently the women in the neighborhood (if there were neighbors) helped by making baby clothes and bringing over soup, "mush," and baked goods after the birth. Each community usually had a midwife. These were "generous women, untrained but willing and with experience, who could be called on at such times," even to go places outside of the neighborhood. Just as Mrs. Divet rushed out of bed when Ned came for help, others were aroused in the same manner. Mrs. Thortvedt was called very early the morning of December 15, 1870, to help deliver Theodore H. Skrei, the first child born in the Buffalo River settlement.

Mrs. Probstfield, who raised eleven children, was called on many times to act as midwife. In September, 1876, she spent an entire night and the following day helping her neighbor, Mrs. Harris. The baby was born dead and Mrs. Probstfield stayed until after the burial. When the Hovdes had their first child in 1872, Mrs. Anders (Goner) Johnson, who served that community for many years, acted as midwife. Ada Lockhart Gunkelman reported that her mother, Mrs. James Lockhart, had a "little kit and some tools" and acted as the "doctor" in the Kelso community. Delivering babies and preparing bodies for burial were her most frequent jobs.

Mrs. Bernhard Bernhardson served for years as midwife and "doctor" in the Comstock community. When Mrs. Bernhardson became older Mrs. Ole Nelson took over some of the duties. Mrs. Nelson worked particularly hard during the flu epidemic of 1918 even though she was quite elderly at that time. It is generally accepted that most of the natives of that area, who were born before 1910, were delivered either by Mrs. Bernhardson or Mrs. Nelson. Most midwives were not paid directly for their services but were usually remembered at Christmas or on their birthdays.

Christine Hagen Stafne, the eldest daughter of the Jens Hagens, recalled her experiences with childbirth. "It was on a hot summer night, July 16, 1877, at the age of fourteen, that I first officiated as midwife. How proud I was when I called the boys and Father from the granary where they slept in the summer, for I had prepared breakfast and had our new baby sister washed, dressed, and ready for display."

Christine married Erick Stafne, March 3, 1883, and on November 26 their first child, Albert, was born. Mrs. Galchutt, the community midwife, accompanied by a Finnish woman, was there. The Finnish woman came "only on very special cases," such as first babies or problem births. In the weeks prior to Albert's birth, Christine had been very busy putting the finishing touches on a new cellar. "The next few days after Albert's birth were days of leisure for me, in fact, it was only at such times that I was ever idle." She boasted that she even had Erick Hoel's daughter, Ingeborg, over as hired girl for a few days. Ingeborg's mother never missed bringing food and visiting whenever Christine had a baby. She always brought "sweet soup" (fruit soup) and "römme gröt" (cream mush). Mrs. Christine Baudette came to see Albert, too, and tears streamed down her face as she held him for it brought back memories of the six children she had lost in a diphtheria outbreak.

Of the ten children born to Christine, it was the birth of the sixth child, Edward, that forced her to seek quick help. On February 21, 1894, while the men were in the woods chopping trees and the three oldest children were in school, Christine was home with the two preschoolers baking lefse when she felt the first labor pains. She sent young John to get Kari Jacobson, who lived a mile down the road. Kari arrived just in time to bring "Edward into the world without much fuss or confusion. After Kari had washed and dressed the new baby, and we discussed his good health and appearance, she sat down by my bedside and we had our usual cup of afternoon coffee."

Pioneer women had great faith in the midwives of their communities and only in extreme cases were doctors called in. The service of doctors was difficult to obtain because they were located only in larger communities or on military bases, and often at least twenty-four hours away. A doctor could be a dentist, a medical doctor, a veterinarian, or a fake, but if he carried the title "doctor," he was welcomed. On at least one occasion a young doctor was called and, after sitting with the expectant mother through twenty-four hours of labor, he broke down and confessed that he had never delivered a baby and did not know what to do. He packed his bag and left and a neighbor lady was called in to take over.[1]

Epidemics

Even though the pioneer woman felt insecure when she was facing childbirth, the isolation and the inability to get help plagued her even more when epidemics struck. Typhoid, diphtheria, and pneumonia were almost certain to end in death, but scarlet fever, measles, and even simple infections could be just as deadly. Small pox, mumps, appendicitis, or the "terrifying whooping cough for which we drank the horrid tasting mare's milk," and many undiagnosed illnesses also took their toll. The limited knowledge about medical science is apparent from a few illustrative cases.

In 1877 Probstfields had a siege of sickness which lasted over a month. His diary for December 3 read, "Andy getting worse, Susy and Mary not any better. Dora very bad. Mrs. P. thinks that she cannot live until tomorrow. Mrs. Harris came over this evening to watch part of the night—to let Mrs. P. get some rest." On December 4 Mr. Harris went for Dr. Wilson at 6 a.m. and returned with him at 9:20 a.m. The next day Lizzie Nelson came in the morning and stayed "all day and all night." On December 7 Mr. Harris came over to sit with the family so that Probstfield could rest. Andrew Holes, prominent early settler, came over the following morning with apples and lemons and offered to have Mrs. Holes come over to help out. Dr. Wilson made his second visit on December 12 and stayed for four hours checking on all members of the family. He said that Dorothea had passed her danger point and would recover. Some entry about sickness was made daily until December 30 when Probstfield noted that every member of the family had been sick with what he termed "violent measles."

When the Probstfields recovered, their neighbors, the Harrises, fell ill. On January 1, 1878, Probstfield spent the day caring for little Homer Harris. When his twenty-four hours were up, Mrs. Probstfield took her turn. When she returned after her day of sitting she reported that the boy could not live until noon. Mr. Probstfield went over to continue the vigil and at 12:15 the boy died. "A very sad day [with] Mary, Alex, Justus, and Edmund all over to watch corpse of their friend Homer Harris."

In the spring of 1878 the Probstfields went through another prolonged period of illness which climaxed by the middle of April. After Mrs. Probstfield had become very ill and could not take care of the family, Mr. Probstfield was driven to a state of exhaustion when the children, Andy, Justus, Edmund, Dora, Nelly, and Walter, were all sick at one time for a period of several days. During that period Probstfield noted, "Mrs. P. thinks she is better. I think not so." Very depressed, he wrote. "I think I shall have to build a hospital." Later, when the other children, Alex, Susy, and Mary, were sick, he stated. "The house *is* a hospital. Where is this going to end?" On December 21, 1890, Edmund Probstfield was taken sick. "It is not like typhoid." Dr. Kurtz was called but he could not determine the nature of the sickness and "advised isolation and not to have visitors." Probstfield noted that the doctor was "apprehensive" because this was an unfamiliar disease. Two days later Drs. Kurtz and McLean visited Edmund but "[could] not settle on what was ailing Edmund but it was not smallpox as was known to them" and all they could advise was isolation. Probstfield himself was a lifelong sufferer from rheumatism and his wife suffered more than her share of illness throughout the years, although she lived to be sixty years of age and he seventy-nine.

Typhoid epidemics were common in the early days of settlement because many people, including Probstfields, took their drinking water from the rivers. It was believed that if one drank water after it ran between two stones "it was purified and alright [sic] to drink," even though cattle were watered from the same stream. Others, like Mrs. Woodward, doubted the purity of the water and when everyone on their farm was sick during the spring of 1885, she reasoned, "Perhaps the water is more unhealthful this spring. It does not seem to quench the thirst. The water we use for drinking should be boiled, but we have no time to take care of ourselves." The *Warren Sheaf* carried many articles about people who died from typhoid as late as November and December of 1891. It seemed that when one person in a community was stricken there was suddenly an epidemic. At such times people became terrified because they realized their helplessness in combatting the disease and the only thing they could do was to isolate themselves as a preventive measure.

In some areas, such as Eglon Township, Clay County, the Board of Supervisors acted as a board of health to prevent the spread of the disease and to provide relief. They acted under instructions of doctors from Lake Park, only ten miles away. The township records indicate that from 1877 to 1889 there were nine deaths blamed on diphtheria and seven on whooping cough. Tuberculosis was the next big killer causing seventeen deaths from 1877 to 1906. Appendicitis ranked third as a cause of death among the people of Eglon Township which had a population of less than 500 at that time.

The most distressing fact was that these diseases and sicknesses took such a large toll of the young people. Christine Stafne, like Emma Elton, was disturbed over the needless deaths of small children who died from colds, pneumonia, dysentery, and stomach problems caused by improper food. She lamented that every smallpox or diphtheria epidemic was sure to take one or two members from each family. Oscar Overby noted that most of the scattered graves in their area were those of young children.

Jens Hagen, skilled carpenter and coffin maker in the Wild Rice-

Abercrombie area, buried his youngest son, Theodore, with several other children in an isolated grave on the Gunness farm near Abercrombie after the diphtheria epidemic of 1887. When "the terrible scourge of diphtheria entered the [Cooperstown] settlement" and took its toll, several babies were added to the list of departed. After that diphtheria epidemic Carl Flisaram, neighbor to the Overbys, donated a site on a hill because a "burial ground became urgent . . . in the new cemetery crude handmade headstones began to rise. . . . These early headstones were of special interest to [children of the Overby family] because some of them were quarried out of the hills and inscribed in bold script by our father."

Emma Elton and Guy Divet both recorded details of the diphtheria epidemic of the winter of 1886 and 1887 that was the most severe in the Red River area and was known as the "diphtheria winter." The first known case in Richland County occurred at the Downing bonanza farm, but soon several cases were reported throughout the neighborhood. Communication between families ceased, but even the precautions of isolation seemed to be in vain, for suddenly the entire neighborhood was sick with diphtheria. When farmers went to town for provisions they drove to within forty or fifty rods of the homes of the afflicted families and called to them. If provisions were needed, those in the house answered. On return, the provisions were left at a pre-determined spot and someone from the distressed family walked out to pick them up.

To make the situation more difficult, a series of storms hit the area making it impossible for doctors to travel. Fred Divet, ten-year-old brother of Guy, was the first and most seriously afflicted in that family. When it was decided that Uncle Jim Divet should go to Wahpeton to get Dr. C. W. Arbuckle, he had to walk because of the heavy snow. He dressed warmly and took "several slices of meat with him in his coat pocket." The snow was so deep that it took him three hours to get to the buildings of the Fairview bonanza farmstead, only three miles away. Everyone in the house watched until he got to that point. Guy's father realized that by traveling at that rate the doctor would not arrive before evening of the second day. About an hour before sunset of the second day one of Divet children sighted Jim walking across the snow-laden prairie with Dr. Arbuckle's team following his footsteps. By then, all five of the Divet children were sick with diphtheria. On top of that, Jim had frozen one of his feet while walking to Wahpeton. Dr. Arbuckle stayed overnight at the Divets, but all he could recommend was that everyone be kept as warm as possible and be given hot, raw alcohol to drink.

After he was well rested and had done what he could, Dr. Arbuckle prepared to return to Wahpeton. This time, because of Jim's frozen foot, Guy's father had to lead the way. The twenty-six mile round trip took Divet two days. While in Wahpeton he purchased provisions as well as a pick axe and a spade. When he brought the spade and pick axe into the house, Mrs. Divet reproached him for being so thoughtless and frightening the children because they knew the purpose of those tools. Soon little ten-year-old Fred started gasping for breath because the hot, raw alcohol was no longer effective in keeping his throat clear. As he felt his breath being choked away he began to struggle, and for more than ten minutes his father forcefully held him down while the other four children and the mother "watched in terror."

Little Fred did not survive the attack. A few days later two neighbors braved the danger and, using Divet's newly purchased tools, dug a grave for Fred. They prepared the body for burial and remained with the family until Fred was buried on a corner of the Root farm southwest of Wahpeton. In the spring, Florence and Cyrus, two other Divet children who had died a few years earlier, were reburied beside Fred. Uncle Jim planted a single box elder twig at the head of the triple grave. It grew up into three trunks reminding the Divets down through the years of three who were no longer with them. That tree was still growing in the 1950's when Guy Divet wrote his account of pioneer life.[2]

Medical Aid

Many injuries and sicknesses occurred from the normal occupational hazards of making a living on the frontier. Even the simple task of digging a well, which was one of the first jobs to be done, involved potential danger. Cave-ins were frequent because diggers were not always careful about putting in curbing as they went deeper. Because pioneers were unacquainted with the potential danger from underground gases, many died from exposure to them. The *Hillsboro Banner* of July, 1882, reported that Peter Hanson and John Fosberg both died from being overcome by gas while digging a well.

John Bernhardson, son of Comstock's first settler, was shot in the arm while hunting game. A tourniquet was applied to stop the bleeding and the patient was given whiskey to relieve the pain. The doctor from Wolverton was summoned and determined that the arm had to be amputated. Several men held Bernhardson down while the doctor removed the arm. Other than the whiskey, no pain killer was available. In spite of his ordeal, Bernhardson lived to be an old man and was known to be one of the hardest workers in the Comstock community.

Horses sometimes saved men's lives, but on many occasions they were also responsible for injury or death. Smashed faces, kicks in the groin, broken pelvises, or smashed toes were frequent in the days of horse power agriculture. Gust, Charles Hobart's hired man for many years, suffered a common injury when he was kicked in the face by a colt as he entered the stall with feed. He was severely hurt—one eye was closed and his lip was badly cut—but it was threshing season and Gust "would not lay off and worked every day!"

In the early 1880's Jens Hagen purchased a team of horses that proved to be very mean. One morning fifteen-year-old Clement went out to harness them. When he failed to return to the house, his father went to the barn where he found Clement trampled under the horse's feet with a crushed head and a broken leg. He survived, however, and when the doctor arrived three days later he set the leg without benefit of any anesthetics. For several months Clement could not utter a sound, but, as his sister Christine philosophically wrote in her later days, "Nature proved to be a wonderful healer aided by prayers and determination." Farm hands realized all too well the hazards of sickness or injury while on the job. "To die as quickly as possible or to recover speedily were the only desired alternatives, for medical aid and hospitalization were unobtainable."

Torkel Fuglestad became seriously ill while working on a railroad construction crew and set out for his home, fifteen miles away, because there was no medical help at the camp. As he walked he became weaker and weaker and, realizing that he could not reach his home, he turned toward the nearest house. He was so delirious by the time he reached it that he did not recognize his neighbors, the Aarestads. Their sod house "now had windows and a wooden floor. . . . There I lay sick for a month with typhoid fever. It never occurred to us to summon a doctor. We did not have the means for that and we had lately come from Norway where it was not customary to run for the doctor when one felt a little under the weather." Frequently pioneers added to their own suffering by not calling a doctor because they were afraid of the expenses involved.[3]

Probably many of the medicines and the cures known and used in pioneer days were worse than the afflictions. The medical kit of Mrs. James Lockhart contained "Ward's liniment, epsom salts, and castor oil." Some midwives used chloroform, which was applied with a handkerchief. Sometimes it was applied by the expectant mother herself if no one else was available. The old practice of bloodletting was still used in the Comstock area where it was referred to as "kopping." Its purpose was to relieve aches and pains. For many years Nils Egge was recognized as the "official kopper" in the area.

The practice of dentistry was no more refined than medicine in general. Haken Pearson, the "dentist" for the Comstock community, used a very simple mail order catalog plier. He had no other equipment or tools and used no pain killers. Like the neighborhood barber and the midwife, he did not ask a fee, but assumed that there would be a donation. The Probstfields, because they lived close to Moorhead, had the benefit of a trained dentist who extracted at least three of Probstfield's teeth. With a family of eleven children, he probably pulled a good many of theirs himself. On December 14, 1887, he "paid Dr. Davenport $.50 for pulling tooth." In May, 1895, and in February, 1896, he had others pulled and the fee was still fifty cents. Ernest Schroeder recalled that Dr. Brendemuhl came by his father's farm one day and was stopped by a hired man who was working in the field and wanted a tooth pulled. "The doctor pulled it right out in the field."

Infections from cuts and bruises, so common in farming, frequently meant death to the pioneer because of his ignorance and his carelessness. Mike McMahon, who later homesteaded near Larimore, cut his leg while working for the Great Northern in 1879 near Evansville, Minnesota. The cut was deep and he bled profusely:

He lay there, with over a hundred men around him and no one knew what to do . . . [Mrs. McMahon] tried to get Grandpa McMahon as he was always good at knowing what to do when anyone was hurt . . . Someone had gone on horseback the twenty miles for the doctor. [The nearest doctor was probably at Fergus Falls.] He came the next day and tied up the foot. . . . On the fourth day his foot was starting to pain him. Just when we were wondering how to get him to a doctor a traveler came along in a wagon. He said he was selling books and couldn't be in Alexandria, thirty-five miles away, until late that night but Pa went along with him.

While Mike's foot was healing, his family stayed with a German family three miles outside of Fergus Falls. "Doctors were hard to get and there was no such place as a hospital in those days."

Mrs. McMahon had a second experience with an axe accident. After the McMahons had settled in the Larimore area, a bachelor neighbor, Herman Hankie "cut his foot really badly." He drove over to the McMahons with his ox team and asked for "a piece of cloth to tie up his foot. We brought him in and fixed him up and he had dinner with us. How he did enjoy the dinner." Hankie commented that he had been batching it on the farm for two months and this was his first good meal in that time. Nothing was said about the infection or how they kept the wound clean, but reference to "a piece of cloth" gives some idea about the lack of concern over bandages.

Ignorance and fear of the cost of treatment aroused Mrs. Woodward to comment on medical care after an accident that happened to one of their neighbors on May 28, 1888:

Mrs. Sampson came running over today saying that one of her boys had broken his leg yesterday. They splintered it with lath, but he cried so hard that they took the lath off. She wanted some liniment. . . . Her husband was going for the doctor "if the boy couldn't stand up by noon." Walter [Woodward] went over with her. He says the leg was so badly swollen that he could not tell whether it was broken or not. The Sampsons own a quarter section of land and sixteen head of cattle and could afford a doctor.

Three days later Katie Woodward and her boy friend, Harry Green, went over to the Sampsons. Green recognized the seriousness of the situation and said the boy needed a doctor and, if necessary, the township would pay the bill. Katie noted that the boy's bed was only a foot from the cook stove and she was quite disgusted with his care. So was her mother who commented, "if the Lord tempers the wind of the shorn lamb, that may be the cause of the freeze up last night, 28 degrees, June 1, 1888."

Drastic measures were sometimes necessary in order to get relief. According to Helena Huntington Smith, one pioneer woman noticed that the hired man's finger was swollen and it looked as if gangrene had set in. When she observed green streaks running up his arm she knew something had to be done at once. She convinced the hired man that the best way to detect blood poisoning was to have the afflicted person lay his finger on a block of wood and look up to the sun. The superstitious hired man was taken in by the story and agreed to put his finger on the piece of wood, which just happened to be the chopping block. As he looked straight up into the noon day sun, with one sharp blow of the axe the woman of the house chopped the finger off. Shortly after they were able to get a doctor who testified that the woman's "surgery" more than likely saved the man's life.

The urgency of the gangrene case demanded prompt attention. Most of the time it was the woman of the family who was the best immediate source of help. Eva K. Anglesburg, poet of the Dakota prairies, vividly describes what was without a doubt a common experience for the pioneer farmer:

Blood from his hands was streaming; The yellow lamplight shone
Upon a thumb half severed, A palm gashed to the bone.
Although his face was ashen, Quite casually he said,

"Get out your needle, Mother, and take your stoutest thread;
For here's a bit of stitching I'd like to have you do.
No need to call a doctor when I can come to you."

Oscar Overby used good common sense in regard to medicine of those days. "We had doctors in Cooperstown, but with roads practically impassable at times . . . we were left with our own home medicine and improvised cures." Having nothing better to turn to, the pioneers purchased patent medicines with vigor in hopes that one of them might be a cure. The newspapers and magazines all carried numerous patent medicine ads to take advantage of the pioneer's isolation and desperation. An illustration of the various forms of such ads was carried in the August 20, 1881, issue of the *Warren Sheaf* where on one page there were eleven ads—one for axle grease, another for horsepowered threshing machines, another on religion, and eight for patent medicines. Each medicine advertised was entirely different from the others, but all of them boasted that they were the "genuine wonder drug pain killer."

Each nationality group had its own special patent medicine for a cure-all. The Germans used Alpenkräuter essence which came in a tall, square bottle. They took it one, two, or three times a day, depending upon the seriousness of their ailment, imagined or real. The ironic thing about this and other patent medicines with their high alcoholic content is that they were standard fare in some of the homes where alcoholic beverages were considered taboo for religious reasons. Occasionally they also provided a relief to those whose conscience would not permit them to make home brew in legally "dry" Dakota.

In Scandinavian homes the old standby was called Kuriko. Oscar Overby reported that every Norwegian pioneer's home had Kuriko and the bottles were used for many purposes after the medicine was gone. The mother used them in her pantry and the children carried drinking water to school in them. In the Fuglestad home Kuriko was the only known medicine until after World War I. Kuriko came in a sixteen-ounce bottle and sold for $1.65 to $1.90. The label on the Kuriko bottle, printed both in Norwegian and English, read:

Dr. Peter's Kuriko Laxative Carminative/Stomachic and to help relieve indigestion or gas when associated with constipation. Prepared from Senna, Fennel, Peppermint, Spearmint, Mountain Mint, Horsemint, Sarsaparilla, Sassafras, Hyssop, Blessed Thistle, Dittany, Ground Ivy, Johnswort, Lemon Balm, Sage, Spikenard, Yarrow. Alcohol 14% by volume.

The time proven family medicine of Five generations compounded from foreign and domestic herbs and botanicals. Used by millions since 1869. Made available for two generations previously to the settlers of Pennsylvania, Maryland, and Virginia by old Dr. Peter Fahrney and his son, Dr. Joseph Fahrney.

This medicine is designed to help relieve constipation and the following troubles when only associated with constipation: upset stomach, indigestion, coated tongue, flatulence (gas), loss of appetite, headache, nervousness, restlessness, and loss of sleep. The carminative/stomachic action helps create a feeling of warmth and comfort in the stomach and helps expel gas from the stomach and intestines.

Probstfield mentioned a number of remedies in his diary which were no doubt considered seriously in those days. Recorded in his 1879 diary was a remedy for smallpox: "One ounce cream of tartar dissolved in one pint of water. Drink at intervals when cold. Is a never failing remedy for smallpox." Probstfield credited his long time friend and early settler in the Georgetown area, E. R. Hutchinson, with the following remedy for diphtheria: "Take 10 grains of sulfho [*sic*] carbonate of soda and dissolve in tumbler half full of cold water. Take from one-half to full teaspoonful every hour until better, then one, two or three hours according to circumstances."

On July 27, 1885, he copied a remedy from the *New York Sun* called cholera mixture, reputed to have been first published in 1832: "Take equal parts of tincture of cayenne, tincture of opium, tincture of rhubarb, essence of peppermint, and spirits of camphor. Mix well. Dose: fifteen to thirty drops in a wineglass of water, according to age and violence of attack. Repeat every fifteen or twenty minutes until relief is obtained."

Although Probstfield was a lifetime sufferer from rheumatism, there are only two references to this ailment in his diary. On February 24, 1888, "Very lame with rheumatism this morn and bad cold so I could hardly stir. Tried electric battery all week with so far, no beneficial results and so far no benefit from medicine." On a miscellaneous page of the 1890 diary, he recorded a "Recipe for Rheumatism: One ounce of iodide of potassium, three ounces of cuchena, one quart of brandy. Mix thoroughly. Dose—one teaspoonful before every meal, three times a day. No good for me—tried it."

When Christine Hagen's brother Olaf fell into a pan of scalding water and seriously burned himself, his mother applied grease that was either wild goose grease or hog lard and then put stove soot over it. The use of stove carbon, a standard ingredient in many home medical applications, was based primarily on superstition. The Hagens were well educated people. So were the Woodwards, and still they used a wide assortment of cures. In December, 1884, Mrs. Woodward was very sick and sent Walter to Fargo for medicine. He returned with "Cherry Pectoral [a cough medicine], Buche's German Liniment, two bottles of medicine from the doctor, peppermint brandy, besides oranges, candy, and gum. If all this does not cure me I ought to die." She lived.

About three years later this hardy lady, in her sixties, noted that she had been taking brandy and quinine for a lingering cough. Her last comment about illness was that she was having chills and fever and Katie "did my head in cold cloths, my feet in cabbage leaves, made me sage tea and crust coffee, gave me a Dover's powder, and is now giving me rhubarb and soda. She knows how to do everything correctly."

Hired men, who did not have access to proper care, had their own ideas on how to cure their ailments. Itch was a common ailment among these men and was generally caused either by dust or by lack of washing, or both. Although the standard doctor's prescription for itch was sulfur and lard, some men tried white liniment which was available because it was used in the barn as a rub-down for horses. The liniment burned so badly that it was more of an irritant than a cure. Henry Schroeder had one hired man who used a mixture of kerosene and liniment whenever he had a cold.

Ads in the *Dakota Farmer* in the 1880's demonstrate the widespread desire to take advantage of a populace who had little medical knowledge. North Star Lung and Throat Balsam was recommended as a "sure cure for coughs and colds." For immigrants and travelers, Ayer's Sarsaparilla was an "effectual cure for eruptions, boils, pimples, eczema, etc. that break out on the skin." These disorders were the result of life aboard ship and apparently many of the immigrants had acquired them. It was also advised as the "best medicine for everyone in the spring." Ayer's Ague Cure was reputed to be the only remedy known "certain to cure Fever and Ague permanently, by expelling the malarial poison" from the body. It was guaranteed to leave no ill effects upon the system. Then there was Dr. W. W. Clarke's Oil of Arnica which cured "catarrh, chilblains, rheumatic pains, and is the best general purpose or household liniment now in use." The ad continued that all were aware of the great curative properties of arnica.

People suffered, and sometimes died, from mental as well as physical ailments. The women were probably more subject to insanity because they generally were more lonely and overworked, but the lonely bachelor on his isolated farmstead, like the sheepherder on another frontier, was also a victim of mental anguish. The Burdicks, while still living at Owatonna, Minnesota, had to flee their home one night when their hired man went insane and chopped his way through their bedroom door. Some of the mentally disturbed were fortunate enough to have a kind and understanding family who took care of them. A few, like Mrs. Divet and Mrs. Crawford, received treatment at special institutions such as the Jamestown mental hospital. A large percentage of the mentally afflicted, however, received no attention.

In addition to church and township welfare groups, sometimes a benevolent community helped a needy person as was true in the case of Mrs. Creminiski of Wright, a small settlement near Warren. Mrs. Creminiski had gone blind and J. R. Smyth circulated a subscription for her benefit. Enough money was raised so that the unfortunate lady could be taken to an "expert oculist" for treatment.[4]

Doctors

Doctors on the frontier were few and far between. The earliest ones were generally at military posts such as Fort Abercrombie, or else they were employed by the United States government to work among the Indians. Like the itinerant preacher, there were also traveling doctors who had their shingles fastened to the side of their covered wagons. Dr. W. P. Cleveland of Caledonia had the distinction of holding license number 1 to practice medicine in North Dakota. Dr. Cleveland, a distant relative of President Cleveland, was graduated from medical school in 1879 and came to the Red River area soon after. He served at Caledonia from 1879 until 1901 when he moved his practice to Fargo.

The Probstfield diary has very few references to the absence of doctors because they lived so near Fargo and Moorhead, two of the earliest and largest communities in the area. On February 20, 1888, there was enough sickness in the Probstfield home to justify getting a doctor. "Justus went to town for the doctor at 10:30 p.m. was back with the doctor at 11:30 p.m. Took doctor back to town at 2:00 a.m. and returned home at 3:00 a.m." The doctor was no doubt pleased that his patients were so close to town.

In his later life Charles Hobart recalled that he was awakened one night by his neighbor, Chris Nelson. "It was as dark as a pocket," and the Nelsons wanted Hobart to take his driving horses and go to Buxton to get Dr. James Grassick. On his way Hobart got off the trail and could not see so he had to walk ahead of the horses until he hit a fence. He followed the fence line until he again found the trail. He had to awaken people in Buxton to find out where the doctor lived. Dr. Grassick tied a lantern to the dashboard, which helped them see their way to the Nelsons. Other trips that Dr. Grassick made were even more trying. On one of them his sleigh became buried in soft snow and he had to unhitch the horses and let them go while he went on on foot. When he finally came to a house he was so exhausted that he fell into a heap when the door was opened.

In 1890 the Probstfields received a telegram stating that their eldest daughter, Mary, who was teaching at Sheldon, had had spasms and requested that they bring a doctor on the first train. The doctor and Mrs. Probstfield were prepared to make the forty-mile trip by freight train if necessary, but there was none until 7 a.m. the following day. Mary apparently pulled through all right. Twelve days later, on May 10, the diary noted, "Mrs. P. returned from Sheldon." No comment was made about the doctor's fee.

Emma Erickson Elton noted that the closest doctors to her family home near Hawley were in Moorhead, a distance of twenty-seven miles. The Eltons called a doctor only twice between 1875 and 1906. Getting a doctor meant taking a buggy four miles to Hawley and then telegraphing to Moorhead. The doctor took the late train to Hawley after his day's work and was taken to the farm by a buggy, which had been standing at the depot since earlier in the day. The doctor stayed overnight both times and was taken back to Hawley the next morning to catch the early train to Moorhead. The Erickson family, though twenty-seven miles from a doctor, was fortunate because they were close to the most heavily traveled rail line in the area and could secure medical help with relative ease. Later, Hawley and Lake Park both acquired doctors. The Lockharts at Kelso, though thirty-six miles from the nearest doctor at Fargo, were also located on a well traveled rail line and, therefore, had an easy access to a doctor. However, only in extreme cases was a doctor called because most people relied on the experienced women of the area to treat them.

The Madsens appreciated what it meant to live close to the railroad towns of Buffalo and Wheatland for these two towns had doctors—Dr. Clark at Buffalo and Dr. Fish at Wheatland. When one of the Madsen boys caught pneumonia, Dr. Fish drove out every day for two weeks before the boy died. When Charles Hobart's wife suffered her first heart attack, the family went through much anxiety traveling by buggy and by train to make the forty-eight miles from their farm near Cummings to a doctor in Fargo.

Mrs. Mike McMahon, who had "doctored" more than her share of injuries, had her greatest scare when a bull attacked one of her sons. The lad was knocked down in a mud puddle and butted by the bull, but not trampled. Somehow they managed to get the bull away and carried the boy to safety. Mrs. McMahon reported, "Pa was in Larimore so I sent a [hired] man on horseback eight miles to McCanna to call the Larimore doctor. [Larimore was seventeen miles away] The doctor got to the farm at ten o'clock that night and found Mort badly crushed but no bones were broken."

The Andrew Overbys, who homesteaded in 1882, were without doctor's care until 1904. Dr. W. D. Wolverton came to Wolverton in 1890 to farm but did not practice medicine. About the same time a doctor settled across the river at Christine and later built a doctor's hospital, the remnants of which are still standing (1969). Some of the very first settlers in that area secured medical service from Fort Abercrombie until the Fort was abandoned in 1877, just when the first heavy movement of settlers began arriving. Before local medical help was available, the most serious cases were taken the twenty-five miles to Moorhead. For example the bill for August Anderson's care, paid November 13, 1896, covered: twenty-four visits by Dr. Daniel C. Darrow of Moorhead, charge $24.00; medicine for twenty-four days, $2.50; room, board, and care at the S. W. Bryant House in Moorhead, $1.49 a day for a total of $35.75; total bill $62.25. Because Anderson was unable to pay, the Wolverton Township treasurer paid the bill as part of the township relief system.

It is apparent that doctors spent a great deal of time traveling to their patients. This travel was obviously a great waste of their valuable time and no doubt it did much to discourage doctors from serving in frontier communities. A good example of the dilemma caused by travel and by overwork was the experience of Dr. Flatin Olsen Blekre of Hatton. He was a graduate of Norwegian medical schools who came to the Red River area in the 1870's. During a diphtheria outbreak in 1882 he was so exhausted that after one call his horse returned home with the unconscious doctor lying in the buggy.

Many doctors traveled from one community to another and had scheduled hours in each town. Dr. Beach carried an ad in the *Warren Sheaf* announcing that he would be available at the Medicine Lodge in Warren every Wednesday. For some of the more remote communities such weekly medical service was all that was available for years.

There was at least one female doctor practicing in this area at a very early date. The *Medical Women's Journal* of 1930 carried an article honoring Dr. Helen Knauf Wink as the pioneer woman doctor of the Northwest. She began her practice at Jamestown in 1883 and had many patients in the rural areas outside of Jamestown.

Two of the earliest dentists to come to Red River country were A. T. Bigelow and S. J. Hill. Dr. Bigelow, the first dentist in northern Dakota, arrived in November, 1876, and by December boasted that his receipts were $385. His office was in a barber shop where he rented a barber's chair for $1.50 a week which, he asserted, was more than the chair was worth. In spite of his rather lucrative practice, no other dentist entered the area until March, 1878, when S. J. Hill arrived. Dr. K. W. Woodward, an early dentist in Jamestown, had a regular circuit that included scheduled trips to New Rockford, Minnewaukan, Oberon, and other points in the James River Valley.[5]

The lack of good medical attention increased the burden of the pioneers of this area. Many sizeable communities did not have doctors until the 1890's, but even then roads were so poor and farms so isolated that trips to the doctor or the dentist were made only in extreme emergencies. The doctors who were here, however, were seriously overworked because there were so few of them and because of the hardships under which they were forced to work.

FOOTNOTES

[1] Weber, p. 33; O. Overby, *Retrospect*, p. 19; Smith, p. 102; *Warren Sheaf*, May 8, 1968; Healy, pp. 1-8; A. Overby, "Sod House Days," pp. 14-15; Thortvedt, NDIRS, File 332; *Moorhead Independent*, Jan. 5, 1900, p. 18; Gunkelman interview; Evert, Ch. III, p. 5; Stafne, pp. 26, 35, 44.

[2] Rendahl, p. 12; *Fargo Forum*, Feb. 29, 1961, p. 25; O. Overby, *Retrospect*, p. 19; Probstfield; Edgar Olsen interview; *Warren Sheaf*, Nov. and Dec., 1891; Elton, *Eglon Memories*, p. 5; Divet, NDIRS, File 69; Woodward, p. 75; Stafne, pp. 18, 26, 38.

[3] Burdick, p. 8; Dick, pp. 459, 502; *Warren Sheaf*, May 14, 1891; *Hillsboro Banner*, July 14, 1882; Evert, Ch. III, p. 6; Hobart, "Pioneering," VIII, 120; Fuglestad, p. 6; Woodward, p. 66; Stafne, p. 30.

[4] Smith, p. 102; Gunkelman interview; Evert, Ch. III, pp. 6, 7; Probstfield; McMahon, NDIRS, File 195; O. Overby, *Retrospect*, pp. 14, 19; *Warren Sheaf*, Aug. 20, 1881; Author's note: One of my grandfathers, who was quite opposed to alcoholic beverages, used his Alpenkräuter regularly. It came in a square bottle with German language on the bottle and on the box. He secured his "medicine" through an ad in a German language newspaper which he subscribed to until his death in 1946 at the age of 84. Dr. Carl Simison, M.D., stated that during the 1930's the alcoholic content of these patent medicines was increased to about 30 percent. He is aware of at least four patent medicines that had the same basic ingredients printed in different languages to appeal to national groups. Dr. Simison also commented that stove carbon was universally used by pioneers in their medicines; Label from a bottle of Kuriko; Woodward, pp. 228-229, 57-58, 166, 247; Schroeder interview; Stafne, p. 16; *The Dakota Farmer*, IV (May, 1885), pp. 3, 11, IV (Oct., 1885), pp. 3, 10.

[5] Dick, pp. 92, 115; Probstfield; Elton, *Vaalhovd*, p. 36; Gunkelman, NDIRS, File 569; A. Overby, "Sod House Days," p. 8; A. Overby, Records of Wolverton Township, Wilkin County, Hobart, "Pioneering," VIII, 118-126; McMahon, NDIRS, File 195; Madsen interview; *Fingal Enger Family History*, p. 11; *Warren Sheaf*, Jan. 19, 1882; *NDHQ*, IV (July, 1930), p. 277, a short article in a series on significant historical events of North Dakota; *The Record*, I (June, 1895), pp. 1-2; I (May, 1896), p. 11; *Pioneers*, pp. 46, 82; Stafne, p. 66. Mrs. Rendahl and Christine Stafne both were sure that the influenza epidemic of 1918 was the worst epidemic suffered in their lifetime. Both agreed that the shortage of doctors was felt more intensely at that time than in any prior epidemic. That, coupled with the intense fear that many people had which prevented them from aiding the afflicted, apparently compounded the problem.

CHAPTER XV

Sundries

A<small>LL</small> <small>THROUGH</small> history liquor has been big business. The Red River frontier was no exception for liquor played an all too important part in the lives of many of the area's pioneers. In pre-settlement days liquor was a major problem among the troops and the Indians and there is no reason to believe that drinking did not exist on the farmers' frontier. The only moderation in the use of alcohol might have resulted from the fact that farmers were more likely to be family men.

Liquor was one of the commodities hauled in great quantity by Red River carts and by steamboats. Liquor was so common in all periods that frequently it served as the barometer of the economy. Because Portland, Dakota Territory, imported four barrels of whiskey to every one barrel of flour in the early 1880's, it was judged by the *Argus* editor to be a "boom town." Considering the number of liquor establishments in many communities compared to other business firms, the liquor trade took in more than its share from the pioneers.

Liquor

Liquor arrived on the Red River frontier along with the first shipments of food. John Lindstrom, who had moved from Douglas County, Minnesota, to Grand Forks County in 1870, told of a "Frenchman called Jack" who had a place of business across the Red River from the Hudson's Bay post at Georgetown. Jack sold flour for $15 a barrel, salt pork for thirty cents a pound, "black strap" molasses and kerosene for $2 a gallon, and most other supplies at about "three times as much as at the general stores." He also maintained an "under the counter" trade in whiskey. This "business" was brought to an abrupt end by troops enroute to Fort Pembina. Two soldiers traded some candles for whiskey in order to discover where the supply was hidden. Early the next morning some of the troops entered the kitchen and got into an argument with Jack in order to attract his attention while the others were filling their canteens with whiskey. Because the keg was nearly full, there were not enough canteens so the troops carried off the ten-gallon keg and Jack's entire supply of whiskey. Three miles down stream they "had a glorious time" at Jack's expense. "This wound up Jack's saloon business, for he was afraid of having more customers of that kind."

Even though the liquor business was risky, it was highly profitable. A new saloon erected in Jamestown in the early 1870's did $1,800 worth of business in its first week. This amount equaled the gross cash income of about a half dozen quarter section homesteaders for a full year. Ole Thompson's house, which served as a stage depot at Comstock, contained a bar room. "Regular" guests were served beer, but important guests were served "pons," a hot strong drink made of whiskey, hot water, and sugar. Frequently a flame was lit on top of the drink as an added attraction.

Beer was used as a part of sales promotion at the Hudson's Bay Company store at Caledonia. A barrel of beer was placed in a convenient spot in the center of the store with a dipper available so that everyone could help himself. Perhaps the beer helped soothe the ruffled homesteaders, most of whom were in debt to the Company. Brainerd, Minnesota, an important Northern Pacific railroad town, had one general merchandise store that attracted customers by having a barrel of whiskey, with drinks on a "help yourself" basis. This policy shocked one of the early missionaries who worked among the railroad construction employees who, he felt, were "graduates of wickedness."

James J. Hill was concerned about the problem of alcoholism and on one occasion he "discharged three division superintendents [for drinking] and told the mayor of Breckenridge that if he didn't straighten up the town he would move the roundhouse" out of town. Hill had a way of making his word stick as many bonanza area communities came to realize. But, it was not only the merchants who dispensed free liquor to promote business. Charles Hobart recalled an auction at Cummings in the 1880's at which "there was some wild bidding; I laid it to the fact that there was a man circulating through the crowd with a pail of whiskey and a tin cup urging everyone to help himself." No doubt this was the doing of a clever auctioneer.

In the 1880's and 1890's there was a sufficient market for beer around Fargo-Moorhead to support local breweries. The *Fargo Argus* noted that "Brewer Kraenzlein has received his machinery and expects the brewery to be in ship-shape in two weeks." On that same day Kraenzlein advertised that he would pay "top cash prices" for barley delivered to his brewery. Apparently the area barley made good brew, for once the brewery got into operation the *Argus* reported that "Kraenzlein's new brewery has brewed five times this week and Mr. K. has been compelled to order a beer pump three times the size of the one first put in."

An inventory of saloons in several of the towns in the Valley indicates the scope of this business. In 1874, when Ida Hall Crawford went to Jamestown to teach school, the town consisted of four Northern Pacific buildings, two stores, a blacksmith shop, four houses, a school house, and two saloons, both were doing "big business." It reminded her of the desperate conditions when Fargo was "practically dead" and the people were "all too poor to get away" after the bankruptcy of the Northern Pacific in 1873. They just sat and "ate the fat off of their ribs." However, according to Mrs. Crawford, "bad off as the town was, Mr. Chapin fairly coined money in his saloon" which he started after he resigned as manager of the Headquarters Hotel. Within a year's time Chapin was investing money in land on the edge of Fargo.

Fargo had its share of excitement until statehood and prohibition both came to North Dakota in 1889 and life became more sedate. A Wisconsin editor, who had visited Fargo in 1882, jotted down his impressions: "All Fargo . . . may be styled the needy villain's general home and the common sewer for all wickedness from St. Paul and Minneapolis. Such are the penalties of greatness, however, for if Fargo were not such a miniature Paris, there would be no villainy concentrated in her limits, more than those of neighboring towns." Bismarck, by this time, was becoming a reformed city. In 1872, in its first year of existence with a population of only 200, it had witnessed seventeen killings on its one street, but by 1883, when it became Territorial capital, Bismarck was going through a transition. In the previous year "horse-racing was going on in the main street throughout Sunday, all the stores were open and gambling and drinking were . . . universally . . . publicly indulged in." Three years later the chief reminder of the once wild, carefree days was "in the number of saloons and of otherwise respectable people who patronize them. Eastern and southern men who settled there in considerable numbers had brought with them the concept of law and order."

Grand Forks, which was settled later than Moorhead, Fargo, or Bismarck, did not have its big boom until 1880. At that time it had a population of 300 living in not more than sixty buildings, and forty-five of those were saloons. George Walsh, pioneer citizen, was so disturbed that he gave $100 to get a minister into town. When the Reverend Woodward P. Law arrived, he was forced by the lack of housing to take quarters in a bachelor's cabin with three other men who kept their expenses down by a cooperative housekeeping venture. In 1882, shortly after Larimore had been created as a railroad junction, and had only forty houses, it had nine saloons, and nine hotels that sold liquor.

Hillsboro, formerly Hill City, with 600 residents in 1882, became the booming rail center of Traill County. Besides its six general stores, one dry goods store, two weekly newspapers, one physician, one livery stable, a flour mill, and two grain elevators, it had six saloons and five hotels that served liquor. The Headquarter's Saloon on Main Street boasted of "dining rooms where the hungry will be served with refreshments of every description from a Champaign [sic] Supper to Pig's Feet." Eating in restaurants was not as commonplace for the average householder then as it is now, but with such a menu, who could resist?

Apparently liquor overcame the judgment of one of Hillsboro's leading citizens and provided the basis for the following tirade in the *Hillsboro Banner* in 1882:

A little incident occurred at one of our hotels one day last week of no minor magnitude in the annals of indecency, unchastity, and obscenity in which one of Hillsboro's fine gentry was the principle [sic] actor. What do the law-abiding citizens of our beautiful and prosperous city think when we tell them that virtuous innocence is in jeopardy right here in our midst? Little did we think that there was anyone in Hillsboro possessing the form of a human being, who would so degrade themselves as to be guilty of an act so ungentlemanly and offensive to civilized society. We withhold the place, name, and nature of the occurrence as being unfit for public perusal.

In 1871 Moorhead was known as the "Wickedest City in the World" with streets that were the arena for "the toughest bunch of men that ever got together. Gambling houses flourished, open day and night, bars never closed. Women . . . thronged [the] saloon dance halls of these epic times." The Midway, the House of Lords, The Bucket of Blood, The Gold Mine, The Three Orphans Saloon, and The Rathskeller over the Rhine were six of the forty-two saloons that lined the streets of Moorhead by 1898. Shortly afterward the number of saloons reached a peak of forty-eight at a time when the city's population was 3,000.

Most of the saloons were located near the bridges leading to Fargo in order to accommodate the citizens of Dakota which had prohibition. The "higher class saloons" seemed to be closer to the north bridge while the "lower class real dives" were located around the south bridge. However, these structures were elegant compared to the first frontier tent saloons. Rustad's saloon had brass footsteps on its stairway to show the customers the way to the bar. Another had personally engraved "stone" mugs which cost from $3.50 to $4.00 each.

Murphy and Young owned The Three Orphans Saloon, one of the "fancy ones [with] an awful long bar. It was 150 feet long. They had three cash registers—one in the middle and one toward each end. Three bartenders worked at each cash register. They specialized in 'the Klondiker' which was a ten cent beer in a tall mug that was just a little over a pint. Most saloons sold nickel beers." This establishment was quite a contrast to Fred Amb's place which did not have a single chair or table in it. All it had was a bar and it was not much of a place to hang around, but it served nothing but the best liquor with a big carry-out trade.

While The Three Orphans was noted for its long bar, The Rathskeller over the Rhine had its tunnel which led to the basement of the Erdell house. The Rathskeller was a "fancy place" which catered to the elite, who sometimes found it prudent to make a hasty, but inconspicuous, exit. Since most of the churches were opposed to drinking, many of the "elite" felt that their prestige would be damaged if they were seen drinking. The tunnel gave them a chance to avoid such embarrassment. After the Erdells no longer operated it, the Rathskeller became a "dive." The Erdells later started a coffee roasting business, which was the predecessor to the Pioneer Coffee Company of Moorhead.

As unusual as the tunnel in the Rathskeller was, the trap door which was rumored to be in the porch of one of the saloons on the river front was probably the greatest oddity of the Moorhead saloons. The saloon cannot be identified by name, but it was near the south bridge and had a porch that hung out over the river. Apparently if a "drunk" became too "pesky he was led over the trap door and received a free bath in the Red River." The existence of this trap door cannot be positively verified, but so many old timers have repeated the story that one becomes convinced that the trap door was a reality, at least in the minds of every Moorhead citizen, if not in fact.

Maybe the drunks were not really dropped through a trap door, but certainly many of them were thrown out, after their bank rolls were taken. The Olson Saloon was known for its rough bartenders who, after beating their victims, tossed them out of a back door which was several feet above the ground and had no stairway. One time they went too far and "beat up" a drunk using a board with nails in it. This incident caused the arrest of Olson and the bartender. The

Olsons were prominent citizens on Third Street and no case was brought against them, but, according to Jim Fay, the bartender "skipped the country when he got out on bail."

The Gletne Saloon, which was operated by Thompson, had an added attraction for its customers. On the second floor above the saloon was the "Tidlie Theatre"—a burlesque house.

"The Glommer," (whose real name will remain anonymous) was an important figure among the forty-eight saloon operators in Moorhead. The term "Glommer," according to saloon slang, meant one who grabs anything loose. In the case of "the Glommer," his business was to round up cheap food for the "low class saloons." It was often spoiled meat, which had not been accepted by C.O.D. recipients at the depot, or meat that had become spoiled in the stores. He also got the livers from the Fargo Packing Company and a small meat packing firm in Moorhead. The livers were hauled out by wheelbarrow and on more than one occasion he was caught trying to sneak hams out with the livers. The meat that "the Glommer" secured was sold to the saloons and set out on the table or the bar to attract customers. It was free as long as you bought an occasional drink.

The offering of free food was a common practice of low class saloons in those days to help promote the sale of "John Barleycorn or White Mule." "The Glommer," who headquartered at the Rustad saloon, was suspected of having raided many chicken coops and hog pens in the rural Fargo-Moorhead area when his other sources of supply ran out. Unfortunately for him, when he was finally caught, "the Glommer" was tried by an all farmer jury, several of whom had been victims of his raids. According to Ewald Benedict, "the Glommer" was convicted after he stole chickens from the Grant farm south of Glyndon. The Grants had their chickens marked with notches between the toes and they were identified while in "the Glommer's" possession. He spent his last days at the Minnesota State Prison at Stillwater.

East Grand Forks shared with Moorhead the reputation of being the most "wide open" of all the cities in the area. The Northern Pacific realized this at an early date, however, and had already made Fargo its local headquarters. Liquor, brawls, women, and high priced lots discouraged potential Moorhead and East Grand Forks investors, causing many of them to locate in Fargo. In the years prior to 1889 when a prohibition law was enacted in North Dakota, the criminal element from Brainerd, Staples, and other railroad towns to the east seemed to concentrate in Moorhead and Bismarck as the Northern Pacific construction work moved west. Here the United States marshals had their greatest problems.

On one occasion the officials of Moorhead were warned that a gang of men had boarded a freight train at Staples and were heading west with Moorhead as their goal. A large citizens' posse, organized by the sheriff, was stationed east of Moorhead at the crossing of the Northern Pacific and the Great Northern to wait for them. All of the trains had to stop at this junction and it was the intent of the sheriff to keep the men from getting off. However, the gang had anticipated such action and had spread themselves along the entire train, making it impossible for the posse to stop them from jumping off. The leader jumped out and the gang quickly followed. They marched to the Moorhead City Hall and took over the park where the Moorhead fire station is now located. Washboilers full of coffee and food were provided by restaurants and citizens of Moorhead in an effort to avoid begging or looting for food. After sizing up the situation, the leader thanked Moorhead for its hospitality, and the gang marched out of town. After a few days they drifted back in singles or in pairs and the streets of Moorhead were jammed, just as they were after a rain or after harvest when the men were paid off, but no damage was done.

The combination of large numbers of single farm laborers and the over-abundance of liquor establishments provided an ideal setting for houses of prostitution. At the beginning, these flourished in the area around Eleventh Street and Cedar Avenue in Moorhead. In the early 1900's, when H. H. Aaker, president of Concordia College, became mayor, he banned them. Many of the prostitutes then went to Minneapolis or to the lumber camp area around Bemidji where the lumbering industry was at its greatest volume. Others moved just across the river where their establishments remained until they were displaced by "urban renewal."

Not all drinking was limited to the towns. Liquor in the bunkhouses on the farms was a constant problem and could not be tolerated with so many men in close quarters. Gambling and drinking were the greatest sources of trouble for both the bonanza farmer and the family farmer who hired help. The Woodwards, the Pratts, the Lockharts, and the Holes, all of whom hired about thirty men during the peak work loads, said that men were easy to handle when they were kept busy.

It was during the rainy spells, especially during harvest, that trouble came. It was fairly easy to keep the men from drinking at the beginning of the season because most of them were broke and it was customary not to pay them until the season was over. However, gambling was more difficult to stop because the men who won were willing to take winnings "on the cuff" until pay day. Gambling, like drinking, also caused the men to fight with each other. Fighting, of course, created another serious problem for the employer.

Mrs. Woodward's diary vividly portrays an all too common pattern of the tribulations with the harvest hands on the farms of the area:

Walter brought a man home from Fargo, he had saved $60 in the harvest season. He started drinking, took a bed at the Minnesota House and the next morning he had no money. Half of the money that is earned in Dakota goes in that manner. . . . Frank Beady came just after the Fourth, ragged and dirty, with not a cent in his pocket. Now [August] he has fifty dollars which burns him; so he must strike out for Mapleton where, I fear, he will deposit it in a saloon. [After threshing] town is full of men who have sweated and toiled, and many will leave their money and go out [leave Dakota] as they came in, with nothing . . .

The harvest of 1888 was not good because of dry weather and an early frost and the country was overcrowded with men who arrived in advance of the limited harvest. Out of sympathy, the Woodwards hired a new man from Fargo who was drunk when hired and had no money. "He looks as though work would come hard. The country is full of such men in summer and fall who work like slaves and then leave every cent in the saloons."

Although building bees were not as common in the Red River area as they had been on earlier eastern frontiers, parties, called "hoe downs," were frequently held to celebrate the erection of sizeable buildings. These were not unlike the barn dances so common in more recent times in rural America. Crawford noted that the major ingredients for such affairs were "a fiddle, beer, whiskey, and sometimes a gallon of alcohol in case the whiskey ran out." When the Lessings, German neighbors of the Woodwards, finished their new granary in 1887, they invited all the young men and women in the neighborhood to a "hoe down." Mrs. Woodward was pleased to see all the young couples galloping by on horseback on their way to the Lessings.

The next day the Cass County sheriff stopped at the Woodwards to arrest some of their hired men for breaking the peace. These "outsiders" had not been invited, but they had gone over to join the fun and had stolen a keg of beer that Mr. Lessing had laid out in the grass to keep cool. After they had emptied the contents, the men were sufficiently brave to invade the dance in the granary. They not only cut in for partners, but also started making speeches which interfered with the music and dancing. When a trial was held in Fargo, Mr. Lessing became very angry at being questioned and swore at the lawyers. He could not understand why he was being cross-examined. Judge Plummer dismissed the case at that point and all of the accused men were freed.

Probstfield continued the European practice of supplying harvest hands with beer and ale as a "morale booster" during the long, hot, hard days. Between May 12 and August 25, 1883, Probstfield purchased eight half-barrels of beer from the local brewery for $24. The first half-barrel was used up between May 12 and May 21. Two others were purchased during threshing time and one-half barrel was used between August 12 and 25 when the men were haying every day. Beer was used socially by the family and another one-eighth barrel was consumed one Sunday afternoon when the Lorings, C. Schriber, and the Rudolphs called on the Probstfields.

Probstfield did not hesitate to admit that he used his share of liquor. This trait may have been considered part of his heritage, but he was seriously plagued with rheumatism and liquor was as effective as a pain killer as any medicine available. However, he determined to "taboo" liquor and tobacco in his New Year's resolution for 1875 when his records indicated that his expenses for those items had been $62.90 out of a gross income of $1,243.25, which was $81.28 short of covering his total expenses for the year. Probstfield and his friend Hutchinson discussed liquor on other occasions. On December 31, 1873, "Hutch renewed pledge to abstain from liquor during the year 1874—ditto myself." He kept a strict accounting of all his expenditures and even on his trips to political conventions, fairs, and the like, he seldom purchased more than one seventy-five-cent pint of whiskey. Sometimes he did not record liquor as such, but referred to it as "sundries."

The Overbys on the Sheyenne River were sober, God-fearing people who quickly saw the impact that alcohol made on isolated rural people. Excessive drinking was one of the main reasons the traveling preacher tried to speed up plans for organizing a congregation and building a church in their area. However, the presence of a church did not put an end to drinking either, for Overby remembered one Sunday morning when "our neighbor Betsy brought her herd of kids to church on a hay-rake. They were perched all along the row of tines, bouncing and laughing in chorus with every bump of the road. Her husband, as usual, had spent the night trying to find his way home." Betsy's husband wasn't the only drinker in the Sheyenne Valley

"The other neighbor . . . who when the spring flood came, tried to cross the river in his lumber wagon. . . . The box floated away from the chassis and carried him merrily down the swift current, while the horses wandered home with the chassis and no driver. We have long wondered what his wife was thinking."

The Reverend V. E. Boe, the second pastor of the Ringsaker congregation, upset one of the established customs when he was invited to marry a young couple "who were not the most active in the church." After the ceremony the crowd began "waiting and waiting for the preacher to leave, so the fun, the dance could begin." When no one showed any leadership in getting festivities started, the preacher began a song fest and story telling to keep the party going. "The community had its first wedding carousal, with the local pastor, instead of the usual beer keg, taking over the life of the party!" [1]

Prohibition

Prohibition had strong support at an early date in the area. Many citizens were disturbed by coroners' testimony of numerous deaths on the open prairie by freezing while under the influence of alcohol. By 1880 temperance groups were being formed in most of the communities. In the election of March, 1881, at Glyndon, which had been founded as a temperance town, an all-temperance slate won when only two "wet" votes were cast. Warren had several well organized, sizeable temperance groups that held regular meetings and carried on a full schedule of activities. After Cass County went strong for prohibition in the election of 1887, citizens predicted that the saloons would be moving across the river to Moorhead.

When the first prohibition elections took place in the 1880's, some of the saloon keepers developed subtle ways of fighting the trend. To continue in business without further irritating the public, the saloon keepers of Caledonia renamed their establishments "Temperance Saloons." They openly sold groceries and candy and kept "wet goods" under the counter or in the back room. When the Prohibition Party swept the slate of Traill County offices, this undercover business was forced to come to an end.

In some respects the community of Page spearheaded the prohibitionist movement in the area. The open fight for prohibition in Page started during the summer of 1883 with an organization called the "Page Temperance and Literary Society" which had actually superimposed itself upon the Settlers Mutual Aid and Protective Society of Page. The Page historian, Father A. A. A. Schmirler, described the initial events:

The Reverend Gentleman [Rev. P. P. Purrington] warmed by the beginning zeal of being in a new place, may not have been aware of the actual status of organization. Now tee-total abstinence, historically, is not an essential part of Protestantism. But in our area, at this time, all three Protestant denominations were setting a torrid pace in that national, popular reform movement, Temperance—and incidentally, women's suffrage. Rev. F. H. Baldwin, Presbyterian, had set up one new congregation south of us, on a basis that only tee-total abstainers from alcoholic drinks be admitted to membership in the church, for that was his view. People who heard Rev. E. Preston, Methodist, preach at Tower City, and in the Minnie Lake and Ellsbury areas, recall that he held the same uncompromising way of thinking which we hold toward Free Masonry . . . If Reverend Purrington hoped to make this a Baptist town (as he naturally would) he must have felt constrained to keep the lead in the temperance effort.

Because of a wide divergence of views in the community by 1885, the Society lost some of its zeal for temperance. When a saloon opened at Page, the November 20, 1885, paper boasted, "Page now has all the advantages of civilization—markets that defy competition, religious services to guide the morals, a public school that is second to none, and all kinds of business well represented—in fact, everything from Page is the best; even Page whiskey will braid the legs of a philosopher as easily as the legs of a cowboy." At that time Elizabeth Preston (later Anderson) spent two years teaching school at Page and after observing an intoxicated youth, decided to go into temperance work.

Later, when she was invited to join a sewing society, she persuaded the ladies "to organize a W.C.T.U. instead." At that time she confronted L. B. Hanna, later state senator, governor, and congressman, with the Prohibitionist movement. She personally felt that, although he professed Prohibitionist ideals, "in reality [he] evaded the issue." His political enemies declared that politician Hanna did not make a positive tie with the movement until the prohibition law had been in effect for twenty-four years. According to A. A. A. Schmirler, Elizabeth Preston Anderson was a zealous crusader who "seemed to have lost the distinction between command and counsel," differing from L. B. Hanna who had much more wisdom about the way in which mankind functioned. For nearly forty years, as head of the North Dakota Women's Christian Temperance Union, she had such staunch supporters as Fargo attorney Charles Fremont Amidon, leaders from the Farmers Alliance, Grand Forks businessman R. B. Griffith, and George B. Winship of the *Grand Forks Herald*. Strongest voices in opposition to the movement were those of the *Fargo Argus* and the *Bismarck Tribune*. In 1889 while teaching at Amenia, Mrs. Anderson became acquainted with Robert M. and Charles M. Pollock, Fargo attorneys.

This trio was very instrumental in drafting a prohibition clause for the North Dakota constitution.

Both geographically and economically, the Red River Valley was divided into "wet" and "dry" areas by politics. The era of North Dakota prohibition had a particular impact on Minnesota border cities whose destiny it was to furnish liquor for the "dry" Dakotans from January 1, 1890, until national prohibition became law in 1920. Hallock, Warren, East Grand Forks, Crookston, Moorhead, and Breckenridge, in addition to all the small villages along the border especially felt the "beneficial" results of the Dakota prohibition. Warren, seventeen miles east of the Dakota border in Minnesota, had a booming liquor business. With a population of only 500 people in 1892, the city council decided to limit the number of saloons to five and to set the annual license fee at $750. Moorhead, with its forty-eight saloons and 3,000 people, set its license fee for each saloon at $1,000 annually. With so much revenue being paid into the city treasuries each year, is it any wonder that the liquor interests were influential there?

To attract business away from "dry" Fargo, the more prosperous Moorhead saloon keepers provided transportation for potential customers in the form of horse drawn vehicles called "jag wagons." Those that used the south bridge went down Front Street as far as Broadway, while the north bridge operator went down N. P. Avenue to Broadway. The wagons were not permitted beyond Broadway, although initially they operated through much of downtown Fargo. The drivers of these jag wagons were bartenders such as Lars Fenstad of the Emporium who wanted a change of routine. They provided free round trip transportation, but were more concerned about getting customers to Moorhead than they were about returning them home. Youngsters who were friendly to the wagon drivers saved street car fare by hitching rides, especially when they were westbound.

Sometimes the jag wagons went out to the bonanza farms to pick up entire loads of thirsty harvest hands. One is reputed to have gone as far as Rothsay, about forty miles from Moorhead. Some of the jag wagons delivered liquor to Fargo customers, but this practice was met by stiff resistance and such deliveries were stopped. The most unusual of all jag wagons was owned by John Haas, who operated the Midway, one of the elaborate saloons along the old street car bridge between First Avenue North in Moorhead and N. P. Avenue in Fargo. Haas had a battery powered conveyance used for special customers. It seated only three and was quite a novelty on the streets of Moorhead and Fargo. Haas later operated the House of Lords, a well known tavern.

Although officially banned from North Dakota on January 1, 1890:
[Liquor] was easily obtainable. You could order what you wanted
from representatives of . . . Minnesota liquor houses who had agents
traveling the countryside taking orders. As I remember some railway
or express agents would also serve as agents for liquor dealers. They
would keep some shipments on hand under the subterfuge that they
were C.O.D. shipments consigned to some John Doe. By paying
charges, walk-in customers would get the liquor.

Law or no law, the North Dakotans were determined to have their
liquor and devised many schemes to have it smuggled in. Liquor was
shipped to North Dakota railroad stations and people using fictitious
names, not always John Doe, came in to claim the merchandise.
These names were pre-arranged with the Moorhead liquor dealers. J.
E. McCarthy said that when he was a young boy and he first saw people he knew giving wrong names, he was disturbed, but soon he
learned what it was all about. Sometimes the cartons were opened and
people got only one bottle with the depot agent acting as the retailer.
Wheatland, where such activity took place in the depot, formerly had
nine saloons or hotels where liquor could be obtained in pre-prohibi-
tion days.

At Hunter the elevator manager served as the chief dispenser of
illegal booze and had regular express shipments consigned to him.
Customers came to the elevator to do their "business" and a few minutes later were seen departing from the basement of the manager's
house. According to the local store keeper, the elevator manager was
not the only liquor dealer in town. The Webb-Kenyon law prohibiting
the use of common carriers to transport liquor into a dry state made
liquor traffic more difficult. At Portland, the name of L. O. Orvin was
the standard alias used by many people to obtain their beer or whiskey shipments. When the depot agent at Portland was arrested for
what the citizens called "brine picking" (i.e., smuggling booze), he
was not convicted, but traffic slowed down after that forcing the
thirsty ones to go to Minnesota communities.

Liquor interests had ways of getting around the law. One of the
most popular ads in those days read, "Hamms Non-Toxo prepared especially for Dakota trade. Non-intoxicating malt beverage on the
market less than 2% alcohol." The breweries tried to give the impression that this was some kind of tonic—at least some people referred
to it as "tonic."

The Peterson Mercantile Company, originally owned by Martin
Hector of Fargo, was one of the big wholesale liquor firms of the area.
Each fall Company representatives came to the Moorhead post office

with old beer cases full of thousands of liquor price lists that were mailed to people in Dakota. Other firms did likewise, but not on such a large scale. Before every holiday the money order business at the Moorhead post office "was really terrific"—all the orders coming from the Dakotas to the Moorhead liquor firms. The Moorhead post office did not have an adding machine and its business at certain periods was so great that postal employees borrowed a machine from local business firms. After one Fourth of July business rush, the adding machine tape was sent to Washington to convince authorities that a machine was necessary for the Moorhead post office. One arrived shortly.

Each year, before the Fourth of July particularly, long strings of Northern Pacific express cars were loaded at the Sixth Street depot and put on the side track, most of them loaded with beer. About July 1, an entire train, called Northern Pacific No. 7, was made up to deliver these cars to their destinations in Dakota. Several of the large breweries from other areas had branch offices in Moorhead at that time.

Jim Fay said that in the early 1900's, "Clay County was very wet and Moorhead was full of saloons. We had blocks and blocks of them." It is difficult to separate fact from fiction about everything that happened to "drunks" in downtown Moorhead, but apparently enough people were becoming unhappy with the situation so that it was possible to get a "dry movement" started.

The first break came in 1910 when a special agent of the Indian Bureau posted notices in every liquor place in Moorhead stating that in September they would be out of business because they had been violating the law. The government's case was based on treaties with the Sioux and the Chippewa Indians dating to the 1850's that prohibited the use of intoxicating liquors by Indians in specific areas including Moorhead. Immediately, seventy-five members of the saloon keepers' association set out to defend themselves. Because they contributed $48,000 in license fees to the city treasury each year, they received broad support from Moorhead residents, even from some who did not imbibe. Three prominent lawyers, "including the mayor and city attorney, not directly connected with the liquor business, went to Washington" to study the records. They appealed to the authorities there that the Sioux Outbreak of 1862 had basically destroyed the value of the early treaty. They apparently convinced the authorities for the Moorhead liquor interests were allowed to operate freely for a few more years, but their days were numbered.

Because of the adverse publicity that Moorhead received from its forty-eight saloons with a population of 3,000, Moorhead saloon keepers decided that the number of their retail establishments must be reduced. Once again Indian agents were successful in stirring up the people, particularly after they succeeded in restricting the sale of liquor in the area north of the Buffalo River. Through mergers, the number of saloons was reduced to forty in one year, but the license fee was raised to $1,200 for each saloon so that the city revenue would not be reduced.

The next year the number was reduced to thirty saloons and the license fee raised to $1,600. To aid their cause, the saloon keepers employed speakers from as "far away as Chicago" to warn what would happen to Moorhead if all the saloons were closed. Meetings were held, and before the election, a big tent was pitched and a high powered campaign was centered around the liquor problem. One speaker from Chicago even warned that "if Moorhead went dry, you would be able to hear ants walking down Front Street." The "dry" campaign disturbed many people who, although not particularly favorable to liquor, were concerned over the loss of $48,000 to the city revenue if all thirty businesses should be closed.

However, opposing forces were too strong. Spearheaded by the Reverend Martin Anderson of Trinity Lutheran Church, the dry group was able to get a county option bill introduced into the state legislature. F. H. Peterson, prominent local lawyer and former Minnesota state senator, provided the legal support and the bill passed the legislature early in 1915. On May 17, 1915, an election was held and, although the city of Moorhead voted wet by a slim majority, the out-county vote was overwhelmingly dry. When liquor licenses expired on June 30, 1915, "they came in from all directions . . . to see the last big blowout in Moorhead." There were "a lot of empty buildings in Moorhead when the saloons went out. The city council cut salaries . . . and did a lot of trimming because they were losing $48,000 in revenue."

As soon as the legitimate liquor dealers were put out of business, illegitimate retailers, commonly known as "blind pigs" or "blind tigers," replaced them. They were already in operation in many locations in North Dakota, and now they opened up in Minnesota. In fact, some dealers in Dakota had been operating quite openly, actually transporting liquor to the workers in the harvest fields. The sophisticated little town of Grandin was able to maintain a "blind pig" throughout much of the prohibition era. It was located in the hotel and was patronized by "the best people." Even the "blind pig" operator was reputed to be "just as nice a man as he could be."

Bootleggers and stills did not become a part of the life of this area until national prohibition was established in 1920. Former Governor Norman Brunsdale said, "the last seven or eight years before national prohibition, I don't think there was a bootlegger in the whole of Traill County. But after [that event] you had so many bootleggers you couldn't keep track of them. They brought it in from Canada and elsewhere."

Mr. Brunsdale recalled that when he was building a house in 1925 he was in a hardware warehouse in Portland looking for a "certain type of ornamental gutter" when he came across some tubing and other materials obviously used to make stills. The materials had been purchased by the hardware firm in the 1890's when many of the early settlers had hit upon the idea that they might improve the quality of the "alkali" drinking water by distilling it. Apparently the results did not prove practical and the stills went into inventory for thirty years. Suddenly they were in demand in the 1920's and the Portland hardware dealer moved his complete stock of ancient still equipment without placing a single ad in the local paper.[2]

Tobacco

The tobacco habit was almost as irritating to the farmer who hired help as was the drinking habit. Much more tobacco was chewed than was smoked, but its habit forming qualities were as conspicuous then as now. As a pioneer tobacco farmer, Probstfield was well aware of the effect of tobacco, for he fed it to his horses to worm them. He also complained because "the habit" had cost him $6.80 in pipes and tobacco in 1874. He vowed to quit smoking, but never did. For him, tobacco raising was profitable because it provided him with horse wormer and tobacco for his own needs, and usually with a surplus which he sold for twenty-five cents a pound.

Probstfield had only himself and his family to worry about. Other farmers who employed large numbers of men had to see to it that tobacco was available. On Ada Lockhart Gunkelman's bi-weekly trips to town, she always had to get large quantities of tobacco for the men. "I remember how much tobacco was used in those days—mostly chewed." Miss Lockhart did not object, for she and her sister saved the snuff and cigar containers "and decorated them to make fancy little gift boxes."

The Crawfords apparently did not look upon the tobacco habit so kindly:

In the summer, no matter how urgent the farm work, a team frequently had to be pulled out of the field to go to town for tobacco. Those days tobacco users—chewers mostly—were sewed up by Lady

Nicotine and were just about incapacitated without it. . . . Father had a German farm hand for haying. In the midst of it his tobacco ran out. Ordinarily a trip to town for supplies was made every two weeks. That trip had just been made and there was no real need of going again. But [the man] was in a weak state—had no energy seemingly. To get the haying done, Father had to take a team out of the hay field and go to town for tobacco.

None of the Woodwards smoked or chewed and they not only disliked the habit, but they were also afraid of fires caused by smoking because the men slept in the granary. After the Woodwards had moved the sleeping quarters to the machine shed, they felt more secure. To discourage the men from smoking, Woodward painted a large "NO SMOKING" sign on his machine shed with a skull and cross bones to vent his own feelings. He detested having to bring back tobacco on his trips to Fargo or Mapleton.[3]

Much information about liquor consumption in the Red River Valley was recorded because the area was divided between the "wets" and the "drys." This division tended to magnify greatly the impact of liquor on the towns along the western border of Minnesota. Activity in these towns was at a high pitch by comparison to the more sedate life in the eastern border towns of North Dakota. The contrast was significant, and it was not until national prohibition took effect in 1920 that the difference was removed. The prohibition laws apparently did not prevent immigration into North Dakota, but they did cause the people there to expend much energy in an effort to secure what the law said they could not have.

FOOTNOTES

[1] Arnold, *Grand Forks*, p. 46; Probstfield; Evert. Ch. II, p. 18; *Fargo Argus*, Oct. 28, 1881, Jan. 14, 1882; *Hillsboro Banner*, Feb. 24, 1882, July 14, 1882, June 28, 1956, Sec. 5, p. 13; Crawford, NDIRS, File 290; Hobart, "Pioneering," VII, 204; Crofford, pp. 131-135; Euren, "Moorhead Highlights"; James Fay, interview by Donald Berg, Aug. 11 and 12, 1966; *Fargo-Moorhead Directory 1898-99*, V, pp. 257-258; Larimore, p. 39; Woodward, pp. 94, 138, 180, 187, 237; Pratt interview; Gunkelman interview; Holes interview; O. Overby, *Retrospect*, pp. 11, 23-26. Mrs. Bernard Holes is the daughter-in-law of James Holes, Sr. who had the now famous forty bushels per acre wheat crop in 1875. This set the stage for James B. Power and his bonanza scheme. Andrew Holes (brother of James, Sr.), early Moorhead realtor and surveyor, secured the land for the Northern Pacific when it crossed the Red River. McCauleyville, at its peak in 1870, had seven saloons out of fourteen places of business. In 1876 at the peak of the boom for Fisher's Landing, that village had twenty saloons out of a total of thirty businesses. Ewald Benedict, interview by the author, May 14, 1969.

[2] Pratt interview; O. Overby, *Retrospect*, p. 33; *Warren Sheaf*, March 30, April 6, 1881, March 31, 1892; *Pioneers*, p. 39; Robinson, pp. 258-259; *Our Page*, pp. 64-69; Fay interview; Olsen interview; McCarthy interview; Bettschen interview; *Fargo-Moorhead Directory*, p. 258; Norman Brunsdale, interview by Donald Berg, July 16, 1966. Mr. Brunsdale is a former governor of North Dakota and a large-scale farmer. He noted that

while he was governor a still was uncovered in the power plant of the state penitentiary. Some inmates working in the dairy barn were discovered to be very intoxicated and even though they did not talk, authorities realized that there was an internal supply. The still was attached to the smoke stack in such a manner that all odors were drawn off. A note in the *Warren Sheaf*, Dec. 20, 1894, sheds sidelight to local humor and the fact that Norwegian jokes were in existence in those days. The article read: "Have you heard about the Norwegian farmer who drank a glass of yeast, thinking it was buttermilk, before he retired. The next morning he arose three hours earlier." Weekly prayer sessions were held in the schoolhouse at Galchutt because people were concerned about liquor. Later, groups organized to fight openly the sale of liquor. A friend of the Stafne's died in their home from the overindulgence of patent medicine which he consumed for its alcoholic content. Stafne, p. 49.

³ Probstfield; Gunkelman interview; Crawford, NDIRS, File 290; Woodward, p. 210.

CHAPTER XVI

The Little Country School

HARRY F. McLEAN, a pioneer settler, in a memorial address, paid special attention to what the pioneer thought about education. Not all pioneers might have agreed with McLean, but apparently enough of them did so that schools were quickly started. McLean said:

Think not that the tar-papered shack or the sod house had no expression of culture . . . I have seen the rude school with no equipment, with no transportation except what each furnished for himself; where there were no special grades but a patient desire to learn.

There was little formal education available on the frontier for, as Oscar Overby said, "farming was a greater purpose in the calculations of the settlers than book learning." Many of the settlers, however, had received an education before they moved into the Red River area and most of them were quite determined that their children should be educated too. Many mothers and some fathers conducted "school" at home with a very limited supply of books until formal schools were organized.

Early Schools

Pembina has the distinction of being the first community in the American sector of the Red River Valley to have organized schools, one private and another public. In September, 1818, William Edge arrived at Pembina from Fort Garry to help construct a school as part of the St. Francis Xavier Mission. A log cabin was built adjacent to the first log church and served as the schoolhouse for many years. A public school was organized in Pembina in 1871 and its classes were held in any available building until a schoolhouse was erected in 1876.

The Reverend O. H. Elmer, who conducted the first religious services in Moorhead, was also responsible for holding the first school session there in the summer of 1872, using the church facilities as a schoolroom. Fargo also had its first school session in the summer of 1872 with Mercy Nelson acting as the teacher. Frank Pinkham and his sister, Alvina F. Pinkham, were the next two teachers in the Fargo school system. Both the Moorhead and the Fargo schools were financed by funds raised through subscription.

Of the counties adjacent to the Red River, Wilkin County probably had the first organized school system. On April 11, 1872, the Wilkin County Board of Commissioners created three school districts and built a one-room school in Breckenridge at a cost of $1,000. The first teacher was Miss Jessie Blanding who taught there for two years during the academic school years of 1873 and 1874.

The first order of business of the Clay County Board of Commissioners after their organization on January 31, 1873, was to authorize the creation of school districts. On February 13, 1873, because of the leadership of L. H. Tenney, the Glyndon school district became number 1 in Clay County, with Moorhead number 2, and Woodlawn (now Parke) number 3. By April of that year the Moorhead school district was functioning and one of its first duties was the floating of a bond issue and the levying of a tax of eight mills to cover the twelve percent interest on the bonds. School opened on June 1, 1873, and ran for five months with Mary Farmer as the first teacher and with five students enrolled.

Five additional school districts were organized in Clay County in 1873, but plans were also laid out for seventy-four districts to be created as needed. Many of these school districts were never in debt until the advent of rural school consolidation with the passage of the Holmberg Act in 1911. Members of the school districts signed individual notes to raise money to pay the teachers' salaries. Many business firms, including Barnes and Tenney of Glyndon, agreed to "charge" or to take notes from individuals in the district for the cost of the building materials and supplies needed for the schools.

Many settlers saw to it that their children attended school as soon as one was available. Ole T. Berg, who was six years old when he arrived in Otter Tail County from Norway in June, 1882, said he had to commence a five-month school session at once. There was no organized school district in his community where Clay, Becker, and Otter Tail counties met, but parents in the neighborhood agreed to pay for a teacher and they hired Josephine McLeod, daughter of the miller at Cormorant, who taught there for two years.

R. M. Probstfield was most anxious to get a school organized in his community north of Moorhead, but in the meantime he held "school" at home for several winters. By 1876 there were enough settlers living in the Probstfield neighborhood so that the "community organized" school could hold classes in the winter months. On December 9, 1876, his diary noted: "Commenced school today." The 1877 winter term did not begin until January 14, 1878, because the weather had been so severe in December. On December 2, 1878, the third winter term commenced with Probstfield as the teacher, and his children, Justus, Edmund, Nellie, and Susy, among those in attendance. Apparently Mary, 16, and Alexander, 13, had already "finished" their basic formal education. On January 6, 1880, Probstfield took the initiative in establishing a formally organized school district and township by making the rounds with a petition and collecting the necessary signatures.

Among the items carried in the *Warren Sheaf* regarding school activities, one of the first stated that the public schools there closed on Friday, March 21, 1881. A three-month summer term which ended on August 6 had an average attendance of thirty-four out of the forty pupils enrolled. The *Hillsboro Banner* reported that seven students took their final written examinations on August 23, 1882, when the Caledonia summer term ended. The average daily attendance had been twenty-seven out of thirty-five students enrolled. The Grandin school summer term of two months had ended on August 4. Out of thirty-two students enrolled, nine had perfect attendance. In the same issue of the *Banner*, District 23 of Traill County advertised for bids on a new schoolhouse that was to measure 18 by 24 feet with twelve-foot posts. In 1882 the Oakport School, which the Probstfield children attended, had a ten-week summer term extending from early May to about the middle of July. Anne Swindell taught several sessions in that district in the early 1880's.

Oscar Overby said that "school was limited to poorly conducted three month terms" because children were needed to help during the long work seasons on the farm. In his rural school Overby and a cousin were the only two students in his grade and they were "the first ever to complete the eighth grade [1906] in our district and receive county diplomas." C. H. Frey said that in the Leonard area the school term was quite irregular, depending upon the weather and the farm work. In some years the term was two months; in others it was five months. School started after freeze-up and lasted until the fields were ready to be worked in the spring, but winter storms kept school closed much of the time in between. The Sands children attended school near Alvarado which had a term of five months—half in the fall and half in the spring.

The Cass County school taught by Katie Woodward in the 1880's, had a summer session that ended in mid-July after which there was a vacation until the end of August when a three-month fall session started. This fall session, which ended in early November, was followed by a short session that was held during February and March. At Wyndmere, Fay Purdy contracted to teach six months a year— three months in the fall and three months in the late winter and early spring. Even though the standard school year in most of the rural districts throughout the area from the 1870's through the 1890's was only five to six months long, the important fact was that there were schools. By 1888 Dakota Territory (including both Dakotas) had 4,124 schools and employed 5,744 teachers signifying the progress that had been made in the 1880's.[1]

Early Teachers

Teaching school in pioneer days was a vocation that required great dedication, for teachers' salaries were only slightly higher than wages for farm hands. However, professional requirements were minimal. For example, Fay Purdy, who attended a two-week Teachers Institute at Rockwell, Iowa, and six weeks at Mayville Normal School after she was graduated from rural school, signed a contract to teach at the Krogness School north of Wyndmere. But, before Miss Purdy could teach she had to take and pass a teacher's examination given at the Red River Valley University (now the State School of Science) at Wahpeton. Her expenses for the two days in Wahpeton while taking the exams were $1 for room and meals but only fifty cents for keeping her horse at the livery stable because she furnished her own oats and hay. She received $28 a month for the three-month fall term and $31 a month for the late winter-early spring term. Her supervisor was Dr. Hager, the first County Superintendent of Schools in Richland County. Miss Purdy had nine pupils for both terms of her first year.

Katie Woodward was not so fortunate, for she had an average of twenty pupils in her Cass County school. There were seven pupils the first two years that Ole Berg attended school in Becker County, but after that the enrollment gradually increased until there were twenty students when he was "graduated" from country school in 1891. C. H. Frey attended school at Leonard and in one session the teacher had sixty students of all ages. She was probably the busiest school teacher in the entire area for, because of the sparse population, rural schools seldom had such large enrollments. Mrs. Pratt said that the Grandin school, which started out as a one-room school, eventually had seventy-five pupils in all eight grades and three teachers.

Ada Lockhart Gunkelman and Guy Divet both attended rural

schools and later taught locally. Ada Gunkelman said that her father had her bring books home from school so that he could study them also. Many other parents did the same, especially when some of the first high schools were opened. Ada said that when it was time for her to take the eighth grade examinations, she had to go to another teacher, who was also a farmer. The examinations were given six miles from the Lockhart farm so that Ada had to get up at 4 a.m. and ride her bicycle to the teacher's farm. She took her examinations sitting under a shade tree, finishing them at 5 p.m.

After attending school for a few years, Guy Divet took his eighth grade examinations at the farm home of William House near Lidgerwood. House was not only a farmer but also County Superintendent of Schools in Richland County. Divet obtained a third grade certificate and at the age of seventeen started teaching in a rural school two miles from Hankinson. While teaching at Hankinson, Divet earned extra money on evenings and Saturdays by unloading carloads of cord wood at fifty cents a car. Each flatcar held eight or nine cords which took him about two hours to unload.

After graduating from Moorhead High School in 1887, Cornelia Probstfield attended Moorhead Normal School for one term from December 6, 1887, to September 13, 1888. She was a member of the first graduating class at the Normal School and was nineteen years old at the time she took her examinations for a teaching certificate and signed her first contract for $35 a month (considered a high salary) to teach at Buttzville. All but the two oldest Probstfield children attended high school and Moorhead Normal. Whenever they used a horse to travel to school they had to pay a ten cents livery stable fee. In the winter time the Probstfield girls boarded at the Jay Cooke House for $15.00 a month while attending Moorhead Normal.

Standard charges paid by teachers for room and board varied from $2 to $3.50 per week, which represented a great cost for one who made from $28 to $35 a month. The teacher hired to conduct the first school in Polk County in 1874 at Fisher's Landing was paid only $10 a month which was raised by donation, but was given free room and board. Even though the expenses were high and the pay low and most teachers had to walk a long distance to the school, which usually stood alone on the prairie; teachers were not difficult to obtain. Probstfield, who did most of the corresponding for his school district, nearly always secured a teacher with the first letter he wrote to a teacher's training institution. Only once did he have to advertise for a teacher; he did so by placing a want ad in the *St. Paul Pioneer Press*.

There were probably more male teachers in the frontier schools than female. In many cases one of the more educated farmers in the district took the examination for a teaching certificate. Were they "moonlighting" farmers or "moonlighting" teachers? In some districts it was necessary to have men teachers because severe discipline problems were encountered. Oscar Overby observed that:

The lady teacher would find herself surrounded by a huge rough crowd of all ages, some perhaps even in their 30's and 40's, newcomers and native hermits all mixed together. Discipline could often vanish to allow a free-for-all fist fight, or mean tricks of many hues, such as when a boy would get a ladder, climb the roof with a lid and seat himself on the chimney and smoke out the whole crowd, including the delicate, "citified schoolma'm." . . . There was a time when the frontier was inclined to produce an army of naughty boys, who were always master minds at figuring out new tricks and ways to derail school routine.

Mabel Lamb said that one of the tricks her pupils most often played on her was to put a live mouse in her center desk drawer. After the first few such experiences, she was able to detect the trick by observing the behavior of the students and noticing that "something was up." She then waited until the pupils were watching her before she opened the desk drawer and was sufficiently "surprised" to cause great laughter.

Not all teachers were as good humored as Miss Lamb. Ole Berg said that even with a man teacher (until about World War I), the big whip always "hung on the wall by the blackboard," although he never used it much. Ole got into a "good fist fight" during one recess. The teacher made the boys come into the school and told them to continue the fight in front of him. Berg said "both of us were too ashamed and too scared to carry on the fight, but we were warned that next time the whip would be used." He added, "I never had another fist fight at school." Mabel Lamb said that in all of her years of teaching she only "rapped a child once" even though her career included teaching at a school east of Barnesville which was "known for having bullies."[2]

School Facilities

After looking through her spyglass, Mrs. Woodward noted, "I can see three larger schoolhouses than I ever saw in Wisconsin: one in Fargo, one in Mapleton, and one in Casselton; besides four country schoolhouses all painted white. The Dakotan of the next generation should be an educated person." This comment gives the impression that schoolhouses were quite prevalent, but actually Mrs. Woodward could view fifteen miles in every direction because there were no hills and few trees or farm places to obstruct her line of sight. She was talking about the schools in more than four townships. Schools were usually one and one-half to three miles from most farm homes. Guy Divet, who walked "several miles" to school as a student, had to walk two miles to his school after he started teaching. Mrs. Erwin Tweton said the school which she attended was two and one-half miles from her home and she never remembered getting a ride in her eight years of grade school. In the winter all the children in her family used homemade skis. The five Divet children were permitted to use a horse and to ride the "pung" (Divet's word for homemade bob sled) after the snow got too deep for them to walk.

Probstfield commented several times that the children "nearly froze" returning from school, even though they had less than a mile to walk. Emma Mallinger had a mile and a quarter to school but she said, "I was lucky for Father was generous and would come after me with the team in stormy weather." Little Mary Hovde had less than two miles to school but Mike Johnson, a big neighbor boy, walked past the Hovdes and in bad weather he carried Mary on his back. If the weather was "too bad" Mike stayed overnight at the Hovdes rather than go "all the way to his home."

The McMahons, who had six children in school in 1899, decided that rather than have them fight the elements all winter, it would be simpler for the family to move to Grand Forks. The McMahons were quite prosperous by that time and they could afford to hire a married couple to do the chores while the children attended school in the winter months.

Every farmer fought to have the school built as close to his farm as possible. After the school fire in Caledonia in 1909, the people of that district had a special problem because the district was divided by the Goose River and none of the parents wanted their children to have to cross the river to get to school. In the late 1880's a new school site had to be determined in one district in Cass County. Every farmer took his hired help along to the meeting in order to get votes to build the school closer to his farm. There were many heated arguments before the issue was settled. When the first Moorhead school was built in 1873, the school board was accused of building "way out in the country," and that argument has been used in regard to each new school building project ever since. The Overbys on the Sheyenne were lucky when the second schoolhouse was built in their district for it was only a quarter mile from the Overby farmstead and the children could run home at noon for hot meals. For the Overby children that ended carrying their dinner to school in one-gallon syrup pails and their drinking water in *Kuriko* bottles.

Cynthia Jones, who taught school in Clay County south of Moorhead in the late 1890's, tried to improve the noon lunches for her pupils. She boiled potatoes each evening and brought them to school the next day where the students took turns frying them on a small kerosene stove in the rear of the schoolroom—an early version of the hot lunch program. In the winter sometimes potatoes were placed on the heating stove to bake. Mabel Lamb held basket socials to raise money for canned soup, cocoa, and crackers to supplement the sandwiches brought from home. This enterprise was not always successful because some of her pupils would not eat food that came out of a can.

Ole Berg was not as fortunate as the Overby children because he had three miles to walk to school. Not once in all his years of walking to school did he get caught by a storm at school or get a chance to stay at a farm place closer to the school instead of going home. The Bergs lived in the hilly area west of Pelican Lake where storms were less severe than on the open prairie. Ada Lockhart felt that she was lucky for she got to spend several nights at school because of storms. In their district every family provided extra robes which were left at the school so that the children would have bedding in case of storms. There were always "enough big boys" at school to take care of the fire wood, to carry water, and to help the little ones get home after a storm. The district officials were quite strict about making the students stay at school if a blizzard came up. Mabel Lamb had to keep her children overnight at the school on several occasions and "all they had to eat was leftovers from their noon lunch."

If there were no school house in the community, any available building was used for classes. The first school for the Sands children at Alvarado in 1886 was held in an abandoned sod house from which the frame window and the door had been removed. Ole Berg's first school was in a granary on Jim Holiday's farm. The students who were reciting sat at a table, "like a picnic table," and the rest of the students sat on planks "along the wall." The table and the planks were of a "rough, unplaned lumber and nothing was painted." The next year these same seven students and their teacher, Miss Josephine McLeod, were fortunate to have a log house for their school because one of the families agreed to "have school in their home from June through October."

The students had to carry their drinking water because the farm well was so far from the log cabin. Nearly everyone who was interviewed commented on the fact that each student carried his own water to school or that "the big students" took turns carrying water from the nearest farm. Water was used sparingly, and in every case a galvanized steel pail and common dipper were used. Not until after 1900 did the crock jar with a spigot appear for "individualized" drinking. In his third year, Ole Berg attended school for nine months in a new schoolhouse that had seats which held two students each. He never had to "share a seat with a girl." When the ninety-four year old Ole Berg was asked if he had ever missed school, he replied, "I skipped a few days to do farm work but I was interested in school so I didn't skip much."

The first year that Edwin Ankerfeldt went to school it was conducted in an "abandoned farm house on Ollie Helgrude's place." After 1892 they used a discarded "railroad section house." The thing Mr. Ankerfeldt remembered most vividly about that year was watching "them build a new railroad grade." His final comment about school was that "we didn't have much time for school in them [sic] days." Guy Divet's first year of school was held upstairs in the William Root farm home. The parents of the students provided funds to employ a teacher and Root donated the space. It was the only house in the area with an upstairs.

In Divet's second year of school they had a "certified" teacher, Miss Edith Brooks. Mrs. E. D. Washburn taught seven students in the first rural school near Hope in 1889 in an abandoned 12 by 14 foot claim shanty. The first schoolhouse in Jamestown in 1874 was described by Ida Hall Crofford:

The school in which I taught for four months was a mere shed. . . . The roof did not leak, but the sides were not even battend, and there were wide cracks. . . . There was no chair for the teacher and the desks for the students were full length boards and so high [the] younger pupils used to rest their chins on them. . . . I gathered up the books and put them in a box at night covering them to keep them dry in case of rain. . . . They were all good children and very glad to have a school. We certainly had a good time.

Fixtures in the early schools were at minimum and frequently homemade. Ole Berg remembered that besides a desk and a stove in his school all they had was a blackboard and big globe. Later they got maps and book shelves and some books besides the regular texts. At the Hovde school everyone sat at one big table next to the stove. Probstfield made two of the first benches for their schoolhouse in December, 1875, and after that his diary had frequent notes about additional fixtures that he had made. Fay Purdy hung pictures on the wall between the 2 by 4 studs of her single boarded schoolroom to make it more pleasant.

When their district was formally organized, all the members donated labor and supplies to enable construction of a building. Each fall members of the school board hauled manure to the schoolhouse for "banking the building" in an effort to make it more comfortable. Mabel Lamb said that this banking was an absolute necessity because in one of the schools in which she taught her "feet froze all day." In January, 1888, Probstfield spent several nights in the schoolhouse in an effort to catch the thief who was stealing fire wood from the district's woodpile. Members of the district took turns hauling and making wood for the school's needs. This procedure was common in areas where timber was available. One day in December, 1881, Probstfield delivered five cords of wood to the school. He also hauled a load of new desks from Moorhead and, in addition, made a special trip to get the new school teacher. On November 3, 1883, members of the district cooperatively built a wood shed against the schoolhouse so the fuel supply would be safe from thieves and would remain dry. Six days later the entire neighborhood turned out to look for the school teacher who got lost on his way home from school. "He was found and safely brought home."

Several of those interviewed commented about the odors in the school room caused by a combination of the lack of regular bathing on the part of the students, the drying wet garments over the stoves, and by the heating equipment itself. Oscar Overby commented:

The round heater in the middle of the room had much attention when the teacher tried to wield the shovel and poker on cold morning. Some mornings when temperatures were low we kept our heavy wraps buckled or until mid-noon, perhaps grouped around the heater with our feet on the nickel rail. By mid-afternoon the whole room took on different odors. The daily shower baths were unknown in frontier homes. In some families they were confined to the category of special Christmas treats.

In an effort to keep the schoolhouse clean, regular "scrub days" were held about once a month. In many school districts the students did the scrubbing, but in some areas the mothers came to do the job. To keep the dust down and to make it easier to keep the wooden floors clean, the boards were thoroughly soaked with oil. Although the oiled floor presented somewhat of a fire hazard, this was felt to be offset by healthier conditions brought about by less dust.

The Budget

In contrast to today's huge school budgets, educational costs were very low in the early days. Costs per student in rural areas prior to 1900 were, in many cases, under $25 per year. With the exception of the year when the schoolhouse was built, salaries were the largest expense a district had and they seldom exceeded $200 per year. Mabel Lamb said that a teacher was supposed to get paid $3 a month extra for doing janitor chores but she personally collected only $9 during her entire teaching career.

Most rural school buildings, if they were built as schools, cost less than $500 each. Even the large 30 by 60 foot, two story brick building erected by the Moorhead School District in 1873 cost less than $5,000. However, by the 1880's some school buildings in the larger communities were costing as much as $15,000.

The first list of expenses in the Probstfield school district was dated December 23, 1875, and included two geography books for $.90, three slates for $1.05, ten slate pencils cost only $.10, a single United States history text for $1. The entire supply purchase for that year was $3.05.

Members present at the first school meeting on October 8, 1881, when those in Probstfield's neighborhood formally organized a school district and decided to erect a building, declared that a five mill levy should be established to finance the cost of building a schoolhouse. It was also decided to levy an additional two mill tax to pay for the teacher's salary, the fuel, and the school fixtures. School expenses, except the teachers salary, from April 23, 1884, to March 6, 1886, were $149.52. Items listed in those bills were: blackboards, chairs, fire wood, erasers, chalk, maps, a water pail, colors, and cleaning the school.

From March, 1886, to January, 1890, with an average annual enrollment of twelve students, total expenses, except the teacher's salary, were $129.07. Average annual cost per student including salaries was about $27. The largest single item in those last four years, other than salary, was for cord wood. In 1887 no tax was levied for school purposes because no additional money was needed. In September, 1890, Probstfield wrote: "Levied ½ mill tax for school district, still have balance of $300." It is probably quite safe to assume that most rural schools in the area were operated on similar budgets.[3]

The Three "R's"

In the larger systems, such as Moorhead, Fargo, and Grand Forks, and later in smaller communities, students were commonly divided into three or four groups for the purpose of teaching. The Moorhead School Board decided to build a schoolhouse in 1873. They agreed to operate on a graded basis and they built a four-room school to take care of the four groups. They did not have eight grades until after 1880. The Warren district is typical of districts that started with a one-room ungraded school in the late 1870's. By 1890, it had evolved to a four-room graded system. In 1890 the Warren school had forty-eight students enrolled in the primary group, thirty-eight in the intermediate, forty-four in the grammar school, and thirty-four in the high school.

The rural country schools functioned on an ungraded basis, usually in one room. All the students were assumed to be on the same basis at the beginning, but each worked at his own pace and progressed as rapidly as he could. Ole Berg, at the age of six, started with the first reader, as did everyone else when he began school. However, there were older students, who started with him, but who were able to go ahead with the material by themselves and who got ahead of the younger ones. The basic gauge to school progress was the student's ability to read. Students were placed in school according to where they were in the "readers." When Ole Berg quit school on his sixteenth birthday, he was "one-third through the fifth reader" which was good enough progress to permit him to pre-register at Concordia College. However, financial problems on the farm caused by three dry years prevented his attendance at Concordia.

The reader, although the basic learning device, did not correspond to any specific grade in school. In addition to reading, spelling, penmanship, geography, hygiene, arithmetic, English grammar, American history, civics, physiology, domestic science, elementary agriculture, and manual training were taught in the larger graded schools. Some of the courses, such as manual training, penmanship, and hygiene, were conducted for all of the students at one time. Others, such as spelling, arithmetic, geography, and reading, were taught to small groups according to the group's rate of progress. While one group was having class at the front of the room, the students in the other groups were preparing their assignments. This situation meant that the student in the one-room rural school had to learn to concentrate. It also meant that he could learn from those in classes ahead of him because he could listen to their recitations, as well as those of his own group.

Moorhead started its high school program in 1879 and smaller communities, such as Warren, were not far behind. Generally the schools in the smaller towns of the area established their high schools in the late 1890's or the early 1900's. High school attendance was encour-

aged by the consolidation movement and "Eighth Grade Graduation," though still the cherished goal of most scholars, was no longer
recognized as the end of one's formal education. Some of these high
schools were very small at first. Mrs. Carl Opgrand said that when
she attended the Caledonia school there were four teachers in the system—one for primary, another for intermediate, a third for grammar
school, and the principal, who also taught all of the high school
courses. In Mrs. Opgrand's last two years of school, the principal, Mr.
Tracy, had to teach as many as eight courses in each session and had
to alternate them so that the students could get all the prescribed
high school credits. In her junior year, Mrs. Opgrand was the only
student in the Latin III class.[4]

Doran, in Wilkin County, claims to have been the first consolidated
school system in Minnesota established under the Holmberg Act, and
Glyndon, in Clay County, was apparently the second. Many new
four- and eight-room brick schools were built during this time of consolidation and horse drawn school buses were adopted to bring the
children in from the country. Mrs. Carl Opgrand said that on her
route to school the bus had to travel ten miles and it was sometimes
necessary to board it as early as 6 a.m. In periods of cold weather, it
was necessary to use robes and heated bricks to keep warm. Girls
wore long underwear and heavy home-knit black woolen stockings.

On one occasion the horse drawn school bus on which Mrs. Opgrand
was riding tipped over three times while traveling three miles because
the snow was thawing and easily gave way. Mrs. Opgrand laughed
when she said, "No one was even hurt though for the sleighs were
built low to the ground and the snow was soft." She might have
added that a speed of two miles an hour is not very dangerous. She
was disappointed in one respect for in eleven years of riding on the
horse operated buses she was forced to stay at her "storm home" in
Caledonia only once.

"Public English" school was not the only education available to the
youngsters of the Red River area. In addition to ten sessions of regular school, Ole Berg attended five annual one-month sessions of Norwegian school. This was a private school where the students paid $20
for the month and studied the Norwegian language and culture. The
teacher was an elderly Norwegian immigrant who spent his retirement years in America doing this work. Mr. Berg said that because of
"this special school I could write Norwegian better than most of the
other immigrants and had to write many letters to parents and sweet-
hearts in Norway." He had one neighbor who regularly walked five

miles to the Berg farm in order to have Ole write letters to his girl friend in Norway.

By contrast, Oscar Overby remembered how his teachers tried to get everyone to speak the English language. Overby said that except for reciting in class or talking to the teacher, everyone spoke Norwegian. One teacher offered anyone in the school the "large sum of $.50" if he could go an entire week speaking only English. No one ever got that "great prize" for they always forgot themselves when out playing and spoke Norwegian. Language differences sometimes presented a problem. Mabel Lamb had one student who spoke only German. Neither she nor any of the other students could understand him.

Most of the school age youngsters in the area also participated in some form of religious education. For some, this education was conducted in the home by the parents until a congregation was established. In the Hovde neighborhood, parochial school was "rotated" every two weeks among the homes of those who had children attending. Because there were not enough people in the Overby neighborhood in the Sheyenne Valley, the Overbys hired a teacher to come in and conduct parochial school for their children. In Emma Mallinger's parochial school at Sabin, all teaching was conducted in German. In addition to the regular subjects necessary for confirmation, they frequently read German literature in the afternoons when all other assignments were finished.

The school was important to the early settlers of the Red River frontier and many expended much effort and expense to insure their children's chance to become educated. However, there was apathy, too. Frequently no one other than the school board members attended the annual school meetings. Nevertheless, schools were started, and, like too many other institutions in the area, there were soon more than could be adequately supported. The inevitable consolidation forced upon the people by changing economic and technological conditions brought about frustration, bitterness, and emotional upset because each neighborhood lost some of its identity in the process. Other than the church, nothing was closer to the hearts of the people than the little country school.[5]

FOOTNOTES

[1] McLean, pp. 282-284; Glenn E. Johnson, "Here, There, Everywhere"; *Valley Alert*, July 18, 1968, p. 39; Weber, Christopher, and Lutter, p. 1; Stan Cann, *Fargo Forum*, Feb. 28, 1961, p. 25; *The Moorhead Independent*, Jan. 5, 1900, p. 19; Ole T. Berg, interview by the author, July 31, 1969; Probstfield; *Warren Sheaf*, March 21, Aug. 6, 1881; *Hillsboro Banner*, Aug. 25, 1882; Pruett interview; O. Overby, *Retrospect*, pp. 13-22; Frey interview; Woodward, pp. 54, 235; Crofford, p. 132.

[2] Pruett interview; Woodward, pp. 66, 106; Gunkelman interview; Divet, NDIRS, File 69; Probstfield; Torrison, p. 33; O. Overby, *Retrospect*, p. 14; Ole Berg interview; Miss Mabel Lamb, interview by the author, Aug. 5, 1969. Miss Lamb taught rural school for many years in Clay County.

[3] Woodward, pp. 32, 168; Divet, NDIRS, File 69; Lamb interview; Tweton interview; Hovde, p. 14; McMahon, NDIRS, File 195; Mrs. Carl Opgrand, interview by the author, July 2, 1969; Glenn E. Johnson, "Here, There, Everywhere." When the first high school was built in Hunter, students from Arthur were actually able to take the train morning and night to get to and from school; Bettschen interview; O. Overby, *Retrospect*, p. 14; Sands interview; Ole Berg interview; Ankerfeldt interview; Gunkelman interview; Pruett interview; *Hope of the Prairie*, p. 13; Crofford, p. 136; Mrs. D. H. Sillers, interview by the author, Aug. 3, 1969; Probstfield; Pratt interview; W. Frank McClure, "The Countryman Has the Better of It," *World's Work*, II (Oct., 1901), p. 1307; Torrison, p. 33; Mrs. Emma Mallinger, interview by the author, Aug. 5, 1969.

[4] Glenn E. Johnson, "Here, There, Everywhere"; Ole Berg interview; *Warren Sheaf*, April 2, 1891; Mrs. Carl Opgrand interview; *The Valley Journal*, May 1, 1963; *Valley Alert*, July 18, 1968, p. 57; O. Overby, *Retrospect*, p. 2; Hovde, p. 14; Stafne, p. 21; Gunkelman interview; Lamb interview; Mallinger interview.

[5] Glenn E. Johnson, "Here, There, Everywhere"; Ole Berg interview; *Warren Sheaf*, April 2, 1891; Mrs. Carl Opgrand interview; *The Valley Journal*, May 1, 1963; *Valley Alert*, July 18, 1968, p. 57; O. Overby, *Retrospect*, p. 2; Hovde, p. 14; Stafne, p. 21; Gunkelman interview; Lamb interview; Mallinger interview.

CHAPTER XVII

The Garden of Eden?

THROUGHOUT history farmers have realized a great portion of their profits from appreciation of land values. Many settlers on the Red River frontier took extreme risks in securing sizeable blocks of land and were frequently wiped out. The dreams and resulting failure of the family of O. A. Olson were typical of what was an all too familiar happening on the Red River frontier:

> I thought when I filed on this homestead
> That I'd reached the goal of my quest.
> But I'm packing my "traps" in "a schooner"
> To abandon my claim like the rest.

Land Costs

Martin H. Johnson, who had been a lawyer and a school teacher in Iowa, came to Petersburg in 1883 with $100. He spent $14 for filing fees on his homestead claim and $4 on materials for a 7 by 9 foot claim shanty. A few years later he paid $12 filing fees on a 160-acre tree claim and shortly after paid $200 for a quarter section to a vacating homesteader. In less than a decade Johnson had acquired 480 acres for an initial cash outlay of $230. By 1895 he had purchased three more quarter sections on contracts for $650, $700, and $1,050, and was renting a school section for $27.50 a year, or just over four cents an acre.

H. D. Hurley speculated in a less risky manner. He had been a railroad conductor for fifteen years and decided to invest in some of the fertile prairie he had heard about. He purchased 160 acres in 1880 for $850 and paid an additional $800 to have it broken, making a total of $1,650 invested in 160 acres. He rented the farm on fifty-fifty shares and with the bumper crop of 1881, plus a good price, he netted $1,350

310

above all costs in his first year. He invested the profits in another quarter section in 1882 and the next year decided to quit his conductor's job and go farming. By 1895 he owned 1,400 acres and had become a director of the First National Bank of Fargo. He certainly had done much better as a farmer than he would have done as a railroad conductor.

Ferdinand Adams, a German immigrant, started buying land at Reynolds in 1882 for $125 per quarter section. In 1886 he paid $1,500 for a quarter section and $1,850 for another quarter in 1889. As he prospered he continued to buy additional quarter sections. In 1895 he agreed to pay 5,500 bushels of wheat to be delivered over a four-year period for a quarter section. This was at a time when wheat was selling at $.50 a bushel, making a purchase price of $2,750, or about $17 an acre.

At the same time that Adams was having a great success, only a few miles away Charles Hobart purchased 320 acres near Cummings for $6.50 an acre, a total of $2,080. He gave a note for the entire amount to James W. Jenkins of Peoria, Illinois, at twelve percent interest and a second note of $100 to Mr. Harwood for his realtor fee. Writing about this investment fifty-two years later, Hobart said, "This . . . started a debt to Mr. Jenkins that was to run until after his death, nearly thirty years later, and which amounted at one time to over $8,000. It ran at 12 per cent for several years, and then at 10 per cent, and later at 8 per cent."

While Adams was adding to his holdings and Hobart was struggling with his, in the 1880's, many others were selling out because they considered farming unprofitable or found pioneering too difficult. The Crawfords had paid $1.90 an acre for land in 1879. The first years were good, particularly 1882 when they sold wheat for ninety cents a bushel. When the price of wheat started a long decline in 1883, the Crawfords became discouraged and when the opportunity came to sell their farm for $17.50 an acre in 1890, they seized what they considered an excellent chance to get out of farming. In their reminiscences, the Crawfords were bitter over their farming experience, even though their land had appreciated in value over eighty percent per year during their eleven years of ownership, and they received a large sum of money when they sold the farm.[1]

Taxes

Although taxes are a major concern of farmers today, they presented a more serious problem to the pioneer. Even though the tax per acre (as shown in the table found in footnote 2 for this chapter) appears relatively low, in many cases a great portion of the total tax bill was on land not yet in production. Generally taxes, as well as interest, which had to be paid in cash beginning with the first year of ownership, were a major drain on the settler's limited cash resources.

Actual taxes in relation to land values are generally lower today than they were when the area was first developed. The table found in footnote 2 for this chapter illustrates the steady rise in average tax per acre nationwide and gives a specific illustration of a quarter section belonging to the Overby family in northern Wilkin County. Except for a brief period, this farm has remained in one family and has always had homestead exemption on it. The buildings are modest by today's standards; but no doubt when built they were quite adequate. Land values generally have increased about twice the rate that the taxes have. Unfortunately for the farmer, his earning power per acre has not kept pace with either the increased taxes or the price of land.[2]

Production Costs

Generally the farmer has little control over the price he receives for his product, therefore, his cost of production is an important factor to his success. The lower a farmer's production costs are the better a chance he has for success. The farmer of the early 1880's had between a three or four to one advantage over the farmer of the 1960's in purchasing power from his profit on an acre of wheat, based on local production costs and market prices for both periods. The pioneer's chief handicap was that he was limited in the number of acres he could farm. With the sharp drop in prices in the mid-1880's, there was little margin of profit so that much of the early advantage was lost.

R. D. Crawford, who had watched his father and other farmers in their Richland County neighborhood slowly lose the battle against natural elements and low prices, was able to state very simply the farmers' position: "The family [farmer] usually had children, so did not have to hire and he *did not* keep books and did not know his costs. He just knew that when wheat was around a dollar a bushel he had some money left at the end of the year."

Reliable production costs from specific farms varied from $5.58 to $7.56 per acre in the 1880's with $6.40 being a realistic average. This average was obtained by using a cost of $.42 for plowing, $1.50 for seed and seeding costs, $.38 was added for cutting and shocking expenses, threshing labor and delivery to the elevator. Those costs totalled $1.20 and were direct cash costs for the operations performed. Added to them was $.40 for depreciation on machinery and $.20 for depreciation on horses. Upkeep on horses amounted to another $.40, cook and food costs increased expenses by $.30, twine averaged $.30, additional threshing costs were $.80, and all other incidentals were another $.50, making total operating expenses $6.40 an acre. To this figure a land cost would have to be added.

Production costs were based on the following figures: oats $.30 a bushel and horse hay $4 a ton. The horse was to be fed sixteen pounds of hay and sixteen pounds of oats on work days and on idle days only twenty pounds of hay. Wages were figured at $20 a month and $1.75 a day for harvest hands with board charged at $.30 a day. It was assumed that a man with four horses could plow four acres a day and a man with three horses could seed six acres a day. A harvest crew of two men with a three-horse binder could cut and shock twelve acres a day. A sixteen-bushel yield at production costs of $6.40 per acre meant a cost of $.40 a bushel.[3]

To determine the settler's margin of profit, a table in footnote 4 of this chapter illustrates income received for wheat during much of the period of settlement in the Valley. Small farmers with limited volume could not possibly have lived from the profits of wheat. From 1874 to 1897 the price of Number 1 Hard wheat ranged from a low of $.35 a bushel in 1885 to a high of $1.75 in 1876. Home grown products which were used by the family and the appreciation of land were the salvation of the homesteader.[4]

Red River Land and the Great Plains received much adverse advance criticism by people in high places of America in those days. John Wesley Powell, director of the United States Geological Survey, was the one from whom the people heard the most locally, but he had been preceded by other powerful figures such as General Hazen who said of the area: "It [is] a barren waste, fit only for Indian and buffalo." Daniel Webtser at an earlier date was even stronger in his objections: "What do we want with this worthless area, this region of savages and wild beasts, of shifting sand and whirlwinds of dust, of cactus and prairie dogs? To what use could we put those great deserts . . . ?"

Yields

In spite of those pre-settlement pessimistic accounts, newspapers of the 1870's through the 1890's boasted of twenty- and twenty-five-bushel wheat yields in the Red River Valley. Actual production figures, however, do not support such optimistic claims. There were some good yields, however, on the virgin soil in the early years of production as indicated by James Holes' record yield of forty bushels per acre on forty acres which sold for $1.50 a bushel in 1875. The following year Probstfield raised thirty acres of wheat which averaged fifteen and one-half bushels per acre, a more common figure. The drought conditions, which started in 1886 and continued through 1890, affected yields decisively. In 1887 Probstfield averaged eight and one-half bushels from 124 acres and the following year he reached his all time low when 140 acres at Georgetown averaged four and fourtenths bushels. For a comparison over a ten-year period, the wheat yields on the Grandin bonanza averaged seventeen bushels per acre using the best management available. It is safe to assume that the homesteader, who was generally less progressive and not as well equipped, had smaller average yields. Fuglestad's yields ranged from a low of five bushels per acre in 1888 to a maximum of forty-five bushels in 1891. His average was eighteen bushels. Hobart's highest yield from 1882 through World War I was twenty-two bushels. In any case, the farmers were not reaping the abundant harvests that the newspapers and the promotion agencies led outsiders to believe.[5]

J. M. Gillette, a prominent area sociologist who had observed the changing fortunes of the farmers from the early 1900's through the 1940's, sensed what farmers had long realized—that to a great extent they were quite helpless. Late in his career he wrote: "Farming is just an incident in the midst of a great complex, in a national and international maelstrom, and . . . farmers alone cannot do much about it."

Prices

What happened in early Red River Land was proof of the farmer's helplessness, even though many times the farmer himself compounded the problem. The price of grain was relatively high in the early years of settlement. The rapid opening of the region, the development of the railroad, and the increase in mechanization, however, helped to glut the wheat market, and prices were brought down in the following decade. Local wheat prices rose sharply in 1876 because the full impact of the freight reduction from $.30 to $.15 a bushel was felt and Canada suffered a severe drought causing a local shortage. At the same time, the price of flour in Moorhead rose from $2.50 a hundred to $5.

When wheat prices declined in 1877, Probstfield shipped his wheat directly to Duluth. Although he received $.80 a bushel gross and $.64 net, which was $.04 more than the local market, he had not counted on a five percent loss in transit; consequently, he gained only $2.71 on the carload. His receipt on a carload of 400 bushels of wheat read: 379 bushels and 40 pounds of wheat at $.80 a bushel, $303.73. Freight charges at $.15 a bushel totalled $56.95, inspection fees, $.20 and commission $3.80, leaving a net of $242.71.

Early in 1879 the effect of the drop in wheat prices was being felt in the area. Probstfield "drove to Town P.M. to get money . . . bank had no money. Had to take a draft for $300 to send to Minneapolis to pay on land. The atmosphere about the Fargo banks—business feels as if they were going to prepare to shut up sharp."

But rising prices and good yields helped to contribute to the Great Dakota Boom which started in 1879 and collapsed with the bumper crop of 1884. R. D. Crawford said, "Abundant wheat crop had to be sold at prices about equal to, and in many instances, below the cost of production. Farmers complained that, with abundant crops, they could make nothing that year; that they had cropped their land for the benefit of elevator companies, grain commission men and millers."

Prices continued to drop and yields decreased in the following dry years, reaching a low point in 1887 when Probstfield received $367 for his wheat crop after holding back his seed for the next year. His harvest and threshing expenses were $269, leaving $98 income. "Live on *wind* old fellow with your family and take coats of tar and feathers for winter clothes if somebody will furnish some gratis!!! . . . What will the harvest be!! What will the farmers be? dogs!!!"

R. D. Crawford's version of their experiences in that year is very similar:

In November 1887 [Crawfords] took two loads of wheat to the elevator and got the magnificent price of 48¢ a bushel . . . it was just about this time that certain operators began to quit. The large farms [bonanzas], six of them from 12,800 acres to 27,000 acres in Richland County, began to make changes. Smaller operators who had less capital and no boys to take the place of hired hands were the first to sell or rent. Those who had to hire help were up against it.

The frost of August 17, 1888, and the extreme drought of 1889 prevented Probstfield from paying long past due accounts and the bill collectors descended upon him. "What next? I feel that I have a race with a lot of hungry wolves, that I am very nearly tired out—that the number of them is increasing and also their appetites and that I can last but a few—what?"

The decade of the 1890's started where the 1880's left off—low wheat prices and much of the wheat in such poor condition because of excess moisture that it could not be sold. When Hobart discovered that his wheat was heating, he opened the bins and spread the wettest wheat on the ground to dry out. After it had been stirred and aired out, it was mixed at the ratio of about one-third wet wheat with two-thirds dry wheat. In this manner he sold a few loads at every elevator in Cummings, Buxton, Hillsboro, and Mayville before the buyers caught on. However, by doing so he was able to get $.50 to $.60 a bushel for Number 2 grade wheat.

Many of the farmers who had not left the area in the 1880's vowed that 1890 would be their last year if conditions did not improve. Although 1890 was not prosperous, it held enough hope for improvement to cause most farmers to hang on for still another year. Prices held well in 1891 and in some areas there was a bumper crop which stemmed the liquidation of farms. Probstfield went on a "settling expedition" and paid off $340.83 on fourteen accounts.

The improvement was short lived and before all the crop of 1891 was sold, prices started to drop again. By 1894 new lows were reached when the price for Number 1 Hard wheat was $.45 on the local market and less in communities without rail and elevator competition. Intense pressure by newly organized farm groups was put on the elevators and the railroads to reduce their rates. These rates were not excessive except in isolated towns without competition. Hobart hauled his wheat an extra ten miles to Hillsboro to take advantage of three cents more per bushel, even though it took about twelve extra days to haul in his crop. Hovde frequently bypassed the Hillsboro elevator and hauled his grain to Fargo. He could make two trips a day to Hillsboro, but it took him three days to make the round trip to Fargo. The price differential was $.15 to $.20 on a sixty-bushel load that grossed him $9.00 to $12.00 for three days' work, less about $3.00 road expenses.[6]

Alternative Income

The agricultural economy remained extremely sluggish during most of the 1890's. In order to survive this agricultural depression, many farmers did whatever they could to bring in additional income—they hauled grain ten to thirty miles farther for a few cents a bushel more; they peddled vegetables, pigs, calves, sheep, and beef. All of the farmers' products, however, brought less than they had brought in most of the two previous decades. Railroad work and bonanza farm labor helped considerably. The Sands of Alvarado worked frequently on the Woodward bonanza (at Warren), and felt that "if it had not been for that farm and for work on the railroad, no one could have survived."

The more alert farmers were always looking for potential new crops. Probstfield raised tree seedlings for Fargo-Moorhead markets and in April, 1896, sold 100 shade trees to Concordia College for $10.

After the DeLaval separator was introduced, some communities tried to establish creameries. Many of these had relatively short lives and were closed by the late 1890's. It was believed that sugar beets could be successfully grown in the area and a first rate beet factory would cost only $200,000. Interested farmers were encouraged to send for packages of sugar beet seed, but there is no record that many of them did so. Sugar beets were not grown commercially in the area until after World War I.

Garden crops were commonly ignored by most farmers in this area because they required too much labor, even if the return per acre was great. By 1890, however, potatoes could no longer be overlooked as a commercial crop, for hundred-bushel potato yields, when compared with fifteen-bushel wheat or twenty-five-bushel oats yields, were very attractive from an income standpoint. Potatoes could stand intensive cultivation and provided an excellent rotation crop on land that had become excessively weedy from continuous small grain production. Potatoes were eventually responsible for keeping the Valley "on the map" after the initial success of the bonanza wheat operations had become a thing of the past. Wheat, generally the traditional frontier crop, is not a strong competitor when land values rise, for row crops and livestock tend to push it out of the rotation.

Clay County, under the leadership of Henry Schroeder of Sabin, took the lead in potato production. He had come to America from Germany in 1871, but he did not come to Clay County until 1878. He homesteaded a quarter section on the Buffalo River near Sabin and eventually increased his holdings to about 4,000 acres. By 1899 he had 260 acres of potatoes that produced 34,000 bushels. Schroeder was partially responsible for large-scale commercial potato production in the Valley.

Roy Johnson, prominent Red River Valley historian, gave George W. Bilsborrow of the Alden Farm, Wolverton Township, Wilkin County, credit for introducing certified seed potatoes into the area. Bilsborrow came from New York in 1894 and became a leading specialized potato grower. Much of his success was because of the lack of potato diseases in this virgin area and he produced an average of 100 bushels per acre for his first fifteen years with yields varying from 75 to 250 bushels.

C. W. Mundstock, who settled southwest of Barnesville, wrote about his success in the potato business for the benefit of the Wilkin County Publicity Club:

I am not an adept in telling my moderate success with a pen. I can handle a gang plow or a cultivator to much better advantage. In the spring of 1895 I purchased 80 acres of land where I now reside, at $10 per acre, going in debt for every cent of it, as I only had three horses and a wagon to start with. I used my credit again to purchase two cows and the necessary farm machinery. On Sept. 1st [sic] of that year I found myself $1700 in debt, but in three years I had all this paid, and purchased another 80 acres at $12 per acre and paid for all that with the next years crop. In 1902 I started to raise potatoes, together with my other farming operations, planting four acres. A fine crop with good prices netted me $135 per acre that fall. I have increased my acreage every year since. In 1905 I purchased 400 acres more of land adjoining at $30 per acre. . . .

Mundstock credited potatoes for his success, even though he did not possess the best land.[7]

Profit and Loss

O. A. Olson, after a lifetime of experience working with farmers, said:

Farmers are a hopeful set
The more they farm the less they net.

Inexpensive land, low taxes, and a large amount of family labor should have made farming a prosperous enterprise in the early Red River area. It was for some. Others also lived well through the years and were able to educate their children because they could borrow against their land which constantly increased in value. Some managed to stay in farming because of land appreciation, but they were not able to provide a satisfactory standard of living. There were many who sold out at the first good opportunity and left for another frontier, or more likely, for a job in the city. In this respect even the fertile Red River Valley was no different from some of the less endowed frontiers of America.

The Probstfields, for example, lived well, but, in times of agricultural distress as in the late 1880's, they understood what it was to tighten their belts. Probstfield's financial accounting for 1874 as illustrated in a table in footnote 8 of this chapter tells the story of one pioneer's struggle. Probstfield did not have wheat at that time because he realized that without proper machinery, wheat raising was unprofitable. Using every means available to the family for earning income, he was unable to balance the budget and ended 1874 with a deficit of $85.38.

A similar story can be told about the 1,400-acre Kingman farm just outside of Fargo, owned and operated by H. D. Hurley. A detailed study of the Hurley operating statement is found in footnote 8 of this chapter. Hurley's five-year summary points out that he was able to provide well for his family of five children out of farm income and still was able to come up with a net operating profit of $19,579.59. Hurley, who was recognized as one of the most successful farmers in Cass County, had an average net income of about $2.80 per acre per year, or fourteen percent on market value of his land in addition to family living expenses and appreciation of his investment. The significant point is that Hurley had a sizeable farm. Had it been one-half as large, he would have had only a three and a half percent return on the market value of his property because the family living expenses, in that case, would have represented forty percent of his farm operating expenses. Had he farmed only 600 acres, he would have been operating at a loss.

The major problem with the small farmer, therefore, was lack of volume. He had to produce enough to pay his expenses and provide for his family. This was not easily done, considering the very limited amount of machinery on the early area farms. After adequate machinery was available, his greatest single obstacle to success was low prices caused by the increased production. Weather and undercapitalization were the most apparent secondary factors that prevented adequate returns. But in spite of the hardships agriculture encountered in the Red River Valley, the number of farms increased until the 1940's when intensive mechanization forced farmers to increase the size of their operation, thereby reducing the number of farms.

By the 1870's, farm magazines became increasingly concerned with the decline of rural prosperity. L. H. Bailey, professor of agriculture at Cornell University in New York reported that the question most asked of people in agricultural colleges at the turn of the century was, "Can I make a farm pay?" His reply, in an extensive article, was, "Yes, if you like it." An elderly pioneer farmer who was asked a similar question expressed his sentiments quite differently: "What do I think of the joys uv farmin?" snorted the old farmer, "What do I think about a hen's hind legs? I think there ain't no sech thing!" [8]

Not all of the settlers of the Red River area would have agreed with the old timer, for many shared the feelings of Harry F. McLean, who expressed himself in the following words when the State of North Dakota paid homage to his pioneering parents:

I look back on almost sixty-five years of life. . . . I look back to the familiar sod shack and the log cabin; to the primitive road; to the time when the pioneer went out on the broad prairie and cut hay wherever he found—the hay free for his cutting; where he . . . followed the stream in search of fuel and got it for the taking. It cost him nothing but labor. . . . He thought little or nothing of it. It had to be done and it was done. He was too busy for crime; too much engrossed in the practical work of living to interfere with the right of his fellowman and he was under the stern necessity of protecting his own, he had no one to do things for him. He did them himself or he went without. . . . The old days were the time for strong and persistent men and women—truly the survival of the fittest. Many could not stand the pace and drifted on or drifted back. The weeding out process was severe; but it left a society that was sound at the core. . . . To them life was real and there was little veneer.[9]

Pioneering in Red River Country, as on any other frontier, was a test of man's endurance. To those who failed to meet the challenge, the area remained a naked prairie, but to those who succeeded, it became a Garden of Eden.

FOOTNOTES

[1] *World's Work*, XL, 17; Probstfield; *Fargo Argus*, Oct. 12, 1882; *Fargo Forum*, Dec. 10, 1955; *The Record*, I (June, 1893), No. 2, p. 31; (Sept., 1895), p. 10; (Dec., 1895), p. 14; (Jan., 1896), p. 16; (April, 1896), p. 19; Thortvedt, NDIRS, File 332, p. 42; Hovde, p. 11; Bohnsack, NDIRS, File 451; Crawford, NDIRS, File 290; *Hillsboro Banner*, July 14, 1882; Arnold, *Ransom County*, pp. 69-71; Hobart, "Pioneering," VII, 225, VIII, 124-127; *Moorhead Independent*, Jan. 5, 1900, p. 35; Liebenow interview.

[2] *Historical Abstract of the United States from Colonial Times to 1957*, pp. 289-290; A. Overby interview and real estate tax receipts; Probstfield; McMahon, NDIRS, File 195; *Hillsboro Banner*, Sept. 1 and 29, 1882; *The Record*, I (June, 1895), p. 14; (Jan., 1896), No. 8, p. 16; Conn Bjerke, Treasurer, Clay County, interview by the author, April, 1968; Thomas K. Ostenson, "Relationship of Real Estate Taxes to Land Values in North Dakota and Selected Counties," Department of Agricultural Economics, North Dakota Agricultural Experiment Station, North Dakota State University, Nov. 15, 1967. Taxes on real estate for 1968 and 1969 were not used in the table because of a sharp reduction in homestead taxation caused by the newly instituted sales tax in Minnesota;

AVERAGE TAX PER ACRE NATIONWIDE AND SPECIFIC TAX ON 160 ACRES
OF OVERBY HOMESTEAD IN WILKIN COUNTY

Year	National average per acre	Overby 160 acres Per acre	Gross
1883	....	$ .078	$ 12.55
1890	$ .13	.145	23.24
1897	..	.07	11.19
1900	.13	.187	29.92
1904	....	.142	22.76
1908	....	.195	31.28
1910	.19	.151	24.24
1920	.51	.331	53.08
1930	.57	.645	103.34
1940	.39	.599	95.98
1950	.69	.969	154.49
1960	1.22	1.41	226.28
1964	1.51	2.09	334.48
1967	....	2.73	437.12

[3] Arnold, *Inkster*, p. 39; *Dakota Farmer*, IV (Sept., 1885) 5; *The Record*, I (Sept., 1895), 31; Probstfield; Woodward, p. 136. During the period from 1874 to 1897 Probstfield's recorded sales on oats and barley ranged from a high for oats of $.70 in 1874 in contrast to an average of $.30 during the 1880's and 1890's. His high barley price was

Kingman Farm Operating Summary 1891-1895

	1891	1892	1893	1894	1895	5-Year total
Family expense	$ 976.58	......	......	......	$ 968.51	......
Household	1,806.65	......	......	......	2,195.65	......
Wages	3,352.12	......	......	......	2,106.40	......
Interest	801.01	......	......	......	481.03	......
Taxes	180.76	......	......	......	294.65	......
Operating capital	1,437.15	......	......	......	1,292.94	......
Improvements	6,507.72	......	......	......	5,098.79	......
Total expenses	14,961.99	12,603.58	12,463.49	7,347.87	12,882.97	60,259.90
Total income	19,910.73	9,721.82	6,570.69	10,170.93	17,760.74	64,134.91
Apparent annual profit or loss	$+4,948.74	$−2,981.76	$−5,892.90	$+2,823.08	$+4,877.77	$+9,774.93[sic]
Capital improvements charged as operating expenses						15,804.66
Net operating income for five years						$19,579.57

Probstfield Expenses and Income 1874

Expenses		Income	
Food	$258.26	Fish sold	$ 54.90
Shoes	18.80	Gov't. work, milk, hay, board, house rent	316.22
Books, papers	15.77	Vegetables sold	247.80
Clothing	43.90	Beef, hides, wool	624.26
Tobacco and saloon expenses	62.90		$1,243.25
All personal expenses	$ 399.63	Deficit for the year	$ 85.38
Seeds, chickens, oil, Grange dues	69.65		
Hardware, lumber, harness	59.02		
Machinery, etc. not paid for	290.50		
Paid for horse	60.00		
Taxes, labor, threshing, other farm expenses	449.63		
	$1,328.63		

$1.00 in 1875 with $.50 being the most frequently recorded price during the next two decades.

⁴ Probstfield; Hobart, "Pioneering," VIII, 125; Fuglestad; Drache, *Bonanza*, pp. 132-133;

ACTUAL PRICES RECEIVED BY SETTLERS IN RED RIVER LAND
FOR WHEAT FROM 1874 TO 1897

Year	Low	High	Year	Low	High
1874 .... $ ..		$1.50	1885 .... .35		$.72
1875		1.50	1886 .... .40		.63
1876		1.75	1887 .... .43		.62
1877		.85	1888		.73
1878 .... .64		.86	1889 .... .55		.78
1879		.83	1890 .... .74		.90
1880 .... .68		1.12	1891		.75
1881 .... .68		1.50	1894 .... .45		.65
1882 .... .71		1.50	1896 .... .49		—
1883 .... .70		1.06	1897		.76

⁵ Probstfield; Crawford, NDIRS, File 290.

⁶ Hobart, "Pioneering," VIII, 120-126; Probstfield; Hovde, p. 15; For additional details on wheat prices in that era see Drache, *Bonanza*, p. 208; Crawford, NDIRS, File 290.

⁷ Probstfield; Sands interview; *Moorhead Independent*, Jan. 5, 1900; *Alvarado Jubilee Booklet*, p. 32; *Truth About Wilkin County*, p. 31; A. Overby interview; *The Record*, II (April, 1897), p. 16; Murray, pp. 134-135.

⁸ Probstfield; *The Record*, II (April, 1897), p. 16; McCarthy interview; L. H. Bailey, "Can I Make A Farm Pay?" *World's Work*, I (March, 1901), p. 549; A. P. Hitchcock, "The Joys of Being a Farmer," *Country Life in America*, XX (July 1, 1911, p. 46. See tables on page 321.

⁹ McLean, pp. 282, 284.

Acknowledgments, Bibliography and Index

Acknowledgments

T HIS BOOK, like most others, is not the product of the author alone.
The North Dakota Institute for Regional Studies (indicated by NDIRS
in the notes and bibliography) deserves much credit for making available a great deal of information and its expert staff. The volumes of
material collected and organized by Dr. W. C. Hunter, Professor Leonard Sackett, and Professor Dean Stallings deserve praise for the broad
background material it provided. Dr. Seth Russell, past chairman of
the Institute, and Dr. Archer Jones, current chairman, are to be com-
mended for their faith in this project by providing means for specific
research. Mr. Donald Berg did an outstanding job of interviewing
scores of "old-timers" who were still living in 1966. Many have since
died, but history has recorded their deeds. Mr. Berg, under my personal
direction, proved to be a tireless researcher. He deserves much praise.
Thanks to Frank Vyzralek of the State Historical Society of North
Dakota, for hunting down those hard-to-find items. Mr. Oswald Daellenbach and Mr. John Hest, both professional agriculturalists, provided
expert photographic service for the illustrations. Their enthusiasm and
interest made picture-collecting and reproduction an exciting activity.

Thanks to Dr. Carl Bailey, Dean, and Dr. Walther Prausnitz,
Chairman of the Department of English of Concordia College, and
Mr. Howard Peet, Assistant Professor of English, North Dakota
State University, for their reading and expert advice in an effort to
make this a readable history. Mr. Peet served as grammarian as well
as reader, a task which required burning the candle into the morning
hours. Dr. Warren Kress, Associate Professor of Geography at North
Dakota State University, tutored me as well as gave expert help for
the better part of two weeks preparing the maps. Only good friends
would provide such dedicated assistance.

Dr. Leo Hertel, editor for the Institute, provided guidance for the entire project. His deep insight into the problems that an author faces can come only from being a "real pro" in the business.

Dr. Robert G. Dunbar, Professor of History, Montana State University; Dr. Stanley N. Murray, Associate Professor of History, University of North Dakota; and Dr. Bill Reid, Associate Professor of History, North Dakota State University, all specialists in western or agricultural history, gratefully served as professional readers. Their expert advice on technical problems as well as certain style corrections was a major contribution.

Thanks to Kay, David, and Paul, for doing housework and yard work to help keep things going smoothly while their parents were busy writing, editing, and typing.

And to the hundreds of friends in the Red River area who have supplied me with pictures, information, and leads to the past, thank you. It is a great joy to have such a large number of people give so much encouragement. There is still much material stored in the trunks, attics, and writing desks of the homes of this area. It is my hope that those of you who have access to this material will release it so that still more can be written about this fabulous land of the Red River.

Any author comes to feel a close relationship to the area about which he writes and to those who he has interviewed for the sake of recording the past. It is with deep regret that I list the names of the following pioneers who were willing to share their personal remembrances that helped make this book possible but who did not live to see it in print: Mr. Arthur D. Askegaard, d. 1970; Mr. Randall Curry, d. 1969; Mrs. Max (Eleanor Reed) Dahl, d. 1968; Mrs. John (Emma Erickson) Elton, d. 1968; Mr. James F. Fay, d. 1969; Mr. George Hilstad, d. 1969; Mr. Edgar I. Olsen, d. 1969; Mr. Daniel F. Pehrsson, d. 1970; Mrs. John (Dorothy Dalrymple) Pollock, d. 1969; Mrs. L. A. (Clara Martin) Schultz, d. 1969; Mr. D. E. Viker, d. 1968 and Mrs. August Hoppe, d. 1970.

HIRAM M. DRACHE

Bibliography

UNPUBLISHED MATERIAL

Ankerfeldt, Edwin. Interview by Donald Berg. Fargo, June 21, 1966.

Ankerfeldt, Emil. Interview by Donald Berg. Fargo, June 13, 1966.

Bailey, Carl L. Interview by the author. Moorhead, May 10, 1968. Dr. Bailey, a professor of physics at Concordia College gave information on binder wire.

Benedict, Ewald. Interview by the author. Moorhead, May 14, 1969.

Berg, Ole T. Interview by the author. Rural Route 2, Pelican Rapids, Minn., July 31, 1969. Mr. Berg was born in Norway on Sept. 1, 1875 and came to Minnesota in the spring of 1882.

Bernath, Mary Ann. "Christ Episcopal Church." St. Vincent, Minn., 1967. A typed manuscript in the files of the Red River Valley Historical Society.

Bettschen, Louis. Interview by Donald Berg. Arthur, N.D., Aug. 3, 1966.

Bjerke, Conn. Interview by the author. Moorhead, April, 1968. Mr. Bjerke, treasurer of Clay County, supplied information on tax rates on land in past and present.

Bohnsack, Charles. Interview by Leonard Sackett. Fargo, Nov. 18, 1954. File 451. When they came to Wisconsin from Germany in 1854, the John Bohnsacks lost two children during their forty-two days at sea. In 1878 Bohnsack filed a triple claim in what is now Section 14, Bohnsack Township, Traill County, North Dakota, and a single claim shanty was built. One quarter was in his name, another in his brother's, and a third in his nephew's. Bohnsack had an easier start than most homesteaders in bonanzaland, for he had sold his 70-acre farm near Sheboygan, Wisconsin, for $7,000, a large sum for pioneers in those days. With seven of his horses he was able to break and backset about 100 acres in his first year. Bohnsack's extra cash served him well in another respect for it enabled him to make many loans to neighbors, ranging from $35 for a cow to larger amounts for machinery and land. Interest rates were high in those days and few of the loans were defaulted so "he did alright" on them.

Brunsdale, Norman. Interview by Donald Berg. Mayville, N.D., July 16, 18, 1966. Mr. Brunsdale, a former governor of North Dakota, is a large-scale farmer who had other business interests that gave him extensive contacts.

Christianson, Mrs. Leif. Interview by the author. Moorhead, Minn., Jan. 20, 1968. Mrs. Christianson is a descendant of a plantation owner who left the South to relocate in Traill County.

Collins, Mrs. Tom. Interview by the author. Barnesville, Minn., Jan. 10, 1968. Mrs. Collins presented information on the comparative prices and values of clothing.

Colliton, Barbara. "Immanuel Lutheran Church." Davenport, N.D., 1968. A typed manuscript in the files of the Red River Valley Historical Society.

Crawford, R. D. "The First Pioneer Years in Dacotah Territory, 1881-1882." A typed

328 *The Challenge of the Prairie*

manuscript written in 1954, in the Archive of the North Dakota Institute for Regional Studies. (Hereafter cited as NDIRS.) File 290.

————. "Notes." A typed appendage, 1943, to *The Checkered Years*. NDIRS, File 290. Mr. Crawford, who was born at Rochester, Minn., in 1871, lived in the area described in *The Checkered Years* from 1881 to 1894.

Divet, A. G. (Guy). "The Divet Story." A copyrighted story from the *Fargo Forum* and *Richland County Farmer-Globe*, March 1, 1950. NDIRS, File 69. Among the Irish settlers who came to bonanzaland in the 1880's were Daniel and James Divet, sons of Irish immigrants, who headed west from Wisconsin in either 1866 or 1867. The Divet Brothers, as they preferred to be known, got as far as Byron, Minnesota (near Rochester), where they became successful farmers. "Dakota Fever" was just beginning to affect them in 1879 when a realtor approached them with an offer of six acres of Dakota land for each acre of their Byron farm. The Divets owned 386 acres in Minnesota and wanted ten to one. However, they eventually traded at five to one, receiving 1,920 acres (3 sections) in Dakota, plus the right to operate the Minnesota farm for three more years, and a sum of cash which gave them operating capital to open their new Dakota land. A. G. (Guy) Divet, son of Daniel Divet, who was born in 1871, was nine when his father took him on the train to Wahpeton to stake out their new farm. Guy was permitted to go because fare for the second passenger was almost nothing. Meals were $.15 and by sleeping with his father he saved the $.25 lodging fee. However, at the Green Tree Hotel in St. Paul his father had to pay a separate fee of $.45 for supper, lodging, and breakfast for Guy. Their passenger train "flew" west at twenty-five miles an hour. When they got to Richland County they sought out the 2" x 2" x 7' surveyor stakes which indicated proper identification of their sections.

"Downing Papers." NDIRS, File 166.

Euren, Helen R. "Moorhead Highlights During the 1800's." Moorhead, n.d. A mimeographed fact sheet in the files of the Moorhead Public Library.

Evert, Jon D. "History of Comstock, Minnesota." Dept. of History, Concordia College, Moorhead, Minn., 1968. A manuscript containing an excellent community history to be published at a future date.

Fay, James. Interview by Donald Berg. Moorhead, Minn., Aug. 11, 12, 1966. Mr. Fay, born in Moorhead on Dec. 14, 1883, wrote historical articles in local papers for several years. He knew Moorhead through his work as a postal employee from 1902 to 1945.

Flaa, Leone. "St. John's Lutheran Church." Abercrombie, N.D., 1967. A typed manuscript in the files of the Red River Valley Historical Society.

Frey, C. H. Letter to the author. Lisbon, N.D., July 10, 1966. Mr. Frey, the son of pioneers who lost their first homestead, was born near Harlem, N.D., in 1889.

Fuglestad, Ed. Interview by the author. Moorhead, Minn., Dec. 15, 1967. Professor Fuglestad is the son of Torkel Fuglestad, who homesteaded in 1882 near Hannaford, N.D.

Fuglestad, Torkel. "A Fuglestad History." Concordia College, Moorhead, Minn., 1937. A typed manuscript in the possession of Professor Ed Fuglestad.

Gesell, Mr. and Mrs. Raymond. Moorhead, Minnesota. The author spent several weeks in research and conversation at the home of this couple who are both grandchildren of Randolph M. Probstfield. The Probstfield diary is very likely the most extensive personal family record existing in the Red River area today. It has been a great honor to receive exclusive use of those valuable documents.

Goggins, Pat. Letter to the author. Feb. 3, 1969.

Gunderson, Dora J. "The Settlement of Clay County, Minnesota, 1870-1900." Unpublished Master's Thesis, University of Minnesota, Minneapolis, Minn., 1929.

Gunkelman, Mrs. R. F. Interview by Donald Berg. Fargo, Aug. 1, 1966. Additional material also found in File 569. Mrs. Gunkelman's father, James T. Lockhart, Woodstock, Ontario, son of a member of the Ontario assembly, had a great future ahead of him in Canada, but caught "Dakota Fever" after a trip west at the age of 15. In 1885 Lockhart and his future bride traveled to St. Thomas where they were married. Mrs.

Lockhart worked at the hotel in St. Thomas where she had to keep an eye on the Indians who were always around trying to "steal things," until 1886 when a daughter, Ada, was born. With his team and a scraper, Lockhart worked for two years on railroad construction and by 1887 he had accumulated enough money to buy a farm for $.25 an acre, including filing fees and a claim shack. He opened this land in his spare time in his third year with the railroad and by 1888 he had enough land opened to quit his railroad job in favor of farming. The year was a complete failure because of a severe frost the night of August 16. They abandoned the farm at St. Thomas and in the spring of 1889 moved to Kelso Township, Traill County. Lockhart traded an "old nag" for the rights to a quarter section and his wife filed a homestead claim on another quarter. The couple had $200 cash which they recognized was more than "any farmer around them had except the bonanza people." Lockhart quickly recovered from the crop failure of 1888 and bought quarter sections at every opportunity and by age 50 he owned 3,000 acres. His brother Joe, who came to the Valley at the same time, had accumulated an equal amount. He also provided financial backing for his son-in-law, R. F. Gunkelman, to get started in the grain business. Most of the Lockhart's early neighbors, first in St. Thomas and later in Kelso, were Scotch and English who had come from Canada and, like the Lockharts, were better educated than the Scandinavians who came later. The Canadians had little trouble with the Scandinavians except "for a rif over establishing schools."

Hartl, Albert V. Letter to the author. Aug. 23, 1968. Mr. Hartl is the President of Otter Tail Power Company.

Heckman, Robert. Interview by the author. Crookston, Minn., May 24, 1968.

Holes, Mrs. Bernard. Interview by Donald Berg. Hunter, N.D., July 15, 1966. Mrs. Holes, the daughter-in-law of James Holes, Sr., pioneer farmer in Cass County, was born in Norway in 1888.

Hollands, George. Interview by the author. Hickson, N.D., May 12, 1967. The son of pioneers who homesteaded in the Valley in 1872, Hollands was born in 1885 and resides on the home farm.

Hoppe, Mrs. August. Interview by the author. Comstock, Minn., May 23, 1968.

Hovde, Ole Olson. "A Family History of Mr. and Mrs. Ole Olson Hovde." A typed manuscript written in 1937 from material compiled earlier by Mrs. William Hewitt, a daughter of the Hovde's, born Oct. 15, 1872. Additional material was supplied by Ernest O. Nelson, grandson, born in 1890, and edited by Eva Hewitt, granddaughter of the Hovde's. NDIRS, File 850. In May, 1868, Ole Olson Hovde purchased a $50 ticket to America and boarded the *Emerald* with 100 other hopeful emigrants, including his fiance. For weeks prior to the journey, the Hovdes had been baking and drying flatbread made of pea, barley, oat, and rye meal. They filled a barrel three feet in diameter and six feet high, which was sufficient to feed several people. This bread lasted until they had settled in Dakota and at times it was the only food available. The trip from Tonsberg to Quebec took eleven weeks. Their passage ticket was paid through to Orfordville, Wisconsin (near Janesville), a Norwegian settlement where they could secure help until they found work. Mari Gulbranson, Hovde's fiance, journeyed with him to Orfordville where they saved money for two years in preparation for their marriage and trip to the Red River Valley, "for they had set their hearts upon a home in the newly opened Dakota Territory." Mari did housework in Beloit and Hovde worked on a farm for an Irishman. After the farm work was over, Hovde found a second job cutting cord wood. He could cut two cords a day at $.75 a cord. In the winter of 1868 and 1869, he lived in a converted box car with other immigrants. Mari and Ole were married May 1, 1871, and then left for the Red River Valley.

Howe, George, Jr. "The Complete Journal of School District No. 10, Harmony Township, Cass County, North Dakota." Casselton, N.D., Nov., 1877-1933.

Hubbard, Fay. Letter to the Reverend William Van Dycken, moderator Red River Presbytery. Fergus Falls, Minn., May 24, 1968.

Jones, Mrs. L. E. "Our Town in Early Days." Before 1936. A typed manuscript in the files of the Wilkin County Historical Society.

Krabbenhoft, E. F., Sr. Interview by the author. Sabin, Minn., Aug. 19, 1968. Mr. Krabbenhoft was born June 10, 1880.

Krabbenhoft, Hans. Interview by the author. Route 2, Moorhead, Minn., Sept. 20, 1967. Mr. Krabbenhoft, born in 1892 on a homestead near the South Branch of the Buffalo River, remembers the extensive flooding of that area in 1897.

Lamb, Mabel. Interview by the author. Barnesville, Minn., Aug. 5, 1969.

Larson, Elmer R. Interview by the author. Fargo, N.D., Aug. 10, 1968. Mr. Larson, President of Western Minnesota Steam Threshers Reunion, Inc., and an authority on early machinery, contributed information on the mechanical operations of steam engines.

Lee, Mrs. Victor. Interview by the author. Barnesville, Minn., Sept. 3, 1968. Mrs. Lee, the daughter of homesteaders in the Silver Lake area of Clay County, spoke of foods and household items.

Liebenow, Frank. Interview by the author. Chaffee, N.D., May 12, 1967. Mr. Liebenow was born in Cass County in 1883 and has spent his entire life in the immediate area.

McCarthy, John E. Interview by the author. Wheatland, N.D., May 18, 1968. Mr. McCarthy was born at Wheatland in 1888.

McCradie, Mrs. Elizabeth. Letter to the author. Aug. 16, 1967. Mrs. McCradie is the daughter-in-law of James McCradie who settled in Elm River Township, Traill County, in 1878.

McLellan, D. J., Jr. Letter to the author. June 13, 1968. Mr. McLellan is an associate extension agricultural engineer at North Dakota State University in Fargo.

McGuigan, Mrs. M. B. Interview by Donald Berg. Fargo, April 12, 1966. Mrs. McGuigan is the daughter of Franklin E. Kindred and the niece of C. F. Kindred, a director of the Northern Pacific Railroad and the founder of Brainerd, Minn.

McMahon, Mrs. Michael (Ellen). Interview by Leonard Sackett. Larimore, N.D., Aug. 17, 1954. A typed manuscript. Larimore, N.D., 1937. NDIRS, File 195. The McMahons homesteaded near Larimore in 1882.

Madsen, Iver A., Jr. Interview by the author. Wheatland, N.D., March 10, 1967. Iver Jr. was born in 1891, the son of Iver Madsen who settled in Wheatland in 1877. Iver Madsen, Sr. left Denmark in 1851 when Prussia first threatened to take over his home province of Holstein. After twelve years as a sailor, and eight years as a gold miner in Australia, he came to America in 1871 to continue his mining activities. However, he settled at Faribault, Minnesota, where he farmed until 1875 when he was hailed out and his $2,000 in savings from gold mining had been exhausted. Madsen came to the Valley and worked on the G. S. Barnes bonanza near Glyndon for two years while he searched for land. He found the land that he wanted on May 7, 1876, four miles from Wheatland, North Dakota, at Section 12-140-53, Cass County. When he returned the following year there was still no sign of life for miles around.

Mallinger, Mrs. Emma. Interview by the author. Barnesville, Minn., Aug. 5, 1969.

"Minutes of Session of the Deerhorn Presbyterian Church." Wilkin County, Minn., 1891-1968. The complete records of the church from formation to closing provided by Mrs. David Peet, Wolverton, Minn.

Moe, Lorraine. "Richland Lutheran Church." Christine, N.D., 1967. A typed manuscript in the files of the Red River Valley Historical Society.

Moll, Edith S. "Moorhead, Minnesota, Frontier Town, 1871-1915." Unpublished Master's Thesis, North Dakota Agricultural College, Fargo, N.D., 1957.

Morris, Melvin. Interview by the author. Wheatland, N.D., May 2, 1968.

Nelson, Norman A. Interview by the author. Rollag, Minn., May 1, 1968. Mr. Nelson, secretary of the Western Minnesota Steam Threshers Reunion, Inc., gave information on the living conditions and economics of pioneer life.

Nokken, O. G. "Peter P. Nokken Family." A typed history of one of the first families of rural Moorhead, Minn. The family still operates the farm that was homesteaded in 1871.

Olsen, Edgar I. Interview by Donald Berg. Harwood, N.D., July 10, 1966. Mr. Olsen was born at Hannaford, Sept. 29, 1889.

Olson, Mrs. Ann. Interview by the author. Crookston, Minn., Feb., 1966.

Olson, O. A. "Christmas Eve in Dakota Territory in the Eighties." See next entry.

―――. "Loves Labor Lost." (Poem). Mr. Olson, born in 1886, spent much of his life as a farm manager in charge of almost 100 farms, and had a broad view of the impact of the 1920's and 1930's on area farmers.

Opgrand, Mrs. Carl. Interview by the author. Halstad, Minn., July 2, 1969. Mrs. Opgrand, a lifetime resident of the area, was a rural school teacher for several years.

Opgrand, Miss Johanna. Interview by the author. Halstad, Minn., July 2, 1969. Miss Opgrand, born near Halstad in May, 1889, has spent her entire life in the area and worked as a rural school teacher and a store clerk.

Overby, Arthur. "David McCauley." A typed manuscript in the files of the Wilkin County Historical Society.

―――. Several interviews by the author. Wolverton, Minn., 1967-68. Mr. Overby, President of the Wilkin County Historical Society, is the son of the Andrew Overbys who homesteaded in 1883. He resides on the same farm.

―――. "Sod House Days in the Red River Valley: A Biography of Mrs. Andrew Overby." A typed manuscript in the files of the Wilkin County Historical Society.

Pazandek, Ferd A. Interviews by the author. Fullerton, N.D., Sept., 1964, and July, 1968. Mr. Pazandak and his brother were pioneers in horseless farming in North Dakota. He was born in 1883 and started farming for himself in 1906.

Peet, David. Interview by the author. Wolverton, Minn., Aug. 24, 1968.

Peet, Theodore. Interview by the author. Wolverton, Minn., May 20, 1968.

Pehrsson, Daniel F. Interview by the author. Buffalo, N.D., Nov. 30, 1966. The son of the Reverend Daniel Pehrsson, pioneer farmer and farmed near Buffalo, Pehrsson operated the original farm until his death in Jan., 1970.

Power, James B. "Letterbooks." Vols. I-XIV. NDIRS, File 309. This file contains about 7,000 letters of Power, one of the leading individuals in the Red River Land in the 1870's and 1890's.

Pratt, Mrs. Robert. Interview by Donald Berg. Fargo, N.D., July 14, 1966.

Probstfield, Randolph M. "Family Diary, 1859-1962." This day-by-day account of actual events of the Probstfield family was thoroughly done by Mr. Probstfield or by one of the members of his family in his absence, and was continued by the family after his death. Social, economic, personal, medical, climatic, and agricultural events are recorded. The complete diary consists of fifty volumes. A great bulk of the material used in this work comes from the diary years of 1859 through 1900. Probstfield was born at Coblenz, Germany, Nov. 9, 1832, and died at Moorhead, Minn., Sept. 11, 1911. Mrs. Catherine Probstfield was born at Louisville, Ohio, Nov. 4, 1839, and died at Moorhead, Dec. 18, 1899.

Pruett, Mrs. Fay Purdy. Interview by Donald Berg. Moorhead, Minn., July 21, 1966.

Rasmussen, Wayne D. "History of Mechanization of American Agriculture." A mimeographed copy supplied by the Research Service of the U.S. Dept. of Agriculture. n.d.

Reber, John. Letter to Arthur Overby. Foxhome, Minn., July 3, 1968. Mr. Reber, born in Wilkin County in 1883, was the son of an early surveyor in the area.

Reitan, Henry. Interview by the author. Halstad, Minn., July 2, 1969. Mr. Reitan was born in March, 1891, near Halstad, the son of one of the pioneer settlers in Norman County. Mr. Reitan as a young boy acquired some of the lumber from the superstructure of the *J. L. Grandin* for material for a tree house.

Rheder, Henning. Interview by the author. Comstock, Minn., Aug. 11, 1968.

Rendahl, Sena Amdahl. "Rendahl Family Records." Concordia College Library, Moorhead, Minn., 1955. A typed manuscript.

"Salem Lutheran Church." Horace, N.D., 1955. A typed history of church records. The Salem Church is the oldest Lutheran church still in service in the Fargo-Moorhead area.

Sands, Alfred. Interview by Donald Berg. Alvarado, Minn., July 18, 1966. Additional information found in NDIRS, File 5. Martin Sands, Alfred's father, came from Norway in 1869 at age fifteen and settled with his parents in Kandiyohi County, Minnesota.

In 1875 he moved to the Red River Valley where he could obtain prairie grass land for his livestock trading enterprise. For several years he sold livestock, which he secured from farmers in the Kandiyohi area, to his neighbors in the Valley. In a drive in 1878 he brought three saddle ponies, two mules, four oxen, and ninety head of cattle. He later established a meat market which he supplied with his own livestock. Martin Sands laid claim to three separate quarters of land and built a shanty on each quarter. He maintained his claim by sleeping in a different shanty each night. When his parents and brothers arrived in the area, they built one house on the line, over all three pieces of land. Father and mother slept in a room on their homestead and the brothers and their families slept in bedrooms on their quarter sections until final proof was established.

Schroeder, Ernest. Interview by the author. Glyndon, Minn., July 24, 1968. Mr. Schroeder is the son of Clay County's original potato king.

Schultz, Mrs. L. A. Letter and interview by the author. Chaffee, N. D., July 20, 1966. Mrs. Schultz was born at Leonard, Dakota Territory, Nov. 30, 1887.

Sillers, Mrs. D. H. Interview by the author. Moorhead, Minn., Aug. 3, 1969. Mrs. Sillers' mother was Cynthia Jones who taught rural school in Clay County for many years around 1900.

Simison, Dr. Carl. Interviews by the author. Barnesville, Minn., Dec. 15, 1967, and July 24, 1968.

Slotten, Russell, and Douglas Anderson. Interviews by the author. Fargo, N. D., Oct., 1968, and Jan. 10, 1969. Mr. Slotten and Mr. Anderson are public relations officers for Northern States Power Company.

Stafne, Ann. "Christine Hagen Stafne, Pioneering in the Red River Valley." Dept. of Agricultural Economics, North Dakota State University, Fargo, 1943. A typed manuscript. The Jens Hages (later changed to Hagen) cited religious and economic reasons for leaving Norway. Influenced by Mormon missionaries and disturbed by increasing taxes in Norway, Hage decided to emigrate in 1869. The Hagens (as they were now called) noted that the ships were crowded, unsanitary, and lacked necessary conveniences. To make conditions worse, most of the passengers were seasick. Upon arrival in America, the Hagen family went to Menomonee, Wisconsin, where Jens became a cabinet maker. Menomonee was filled with immigrants, most of whom worked for the lumber industry. Jens heard about the great opportunities in the Red River Valley and after three years as a cabinet maker went west to look for land. To be near friends, he purchased homestead rights from Sivert Hoel for $100. While he was in the process of moving his family from Wisconsin in 1873, a claim jumper settled on the land and had to be evicted. Hagen's farm was seven miles northwest of Fort Abercrombie along the Wild Rice River in a community of nine Norwegian families.

Syvertson, Sam. Interview by the author. Barnesville, Minn., Dec., 1968. Mr. Syvertson gave information on freight and passenger charges of the Great Northern Railroad, past and present.

Tenney Papers. NDIRS, Files 515 and 519.

Thortvedt, Levi. "The Early History of the Red River Valley." NDIRS, File 332. The Thortvedts were one of the early families to settle along the Buffalo River in Clay County in 1871.

Tweton, Mrs. Edwin. Interview by the author. Moorhead, Minn., July 28, 1968.

Vetter, Rev. Wendelyn. "A Brief History of German-Russian Migration Viewed in the Light of Land Tenure." Dept of Agricultural Economics, North Dakota State University, Fargo. A typed manuscript. 1952.

Ward, Lois. "North Star Presbyterian Church." Humboldt, Minn., 1967. A typed manuscript in the files of the Red River Historical Society.

Welsh, Donald. Dr. Welsh, professor of history at Valley City State College, is an authority on Pierre Wibaux, an early rancher and one of the first growers of alfalfa.

Woell, Mrs. Henry. Interview by the author. Casselton, N. D., May 18, 1968. Mrs. Woell was born near Casselton in 1884 and is the sister of the late Senator William Langer.

Wolverton Township Records. Wilkin County, Minn. These records are in the possession of Arthur Overby.

PRINTED MATERIAL

Alvarado Golden Jubilee, 1905-1955. Compiled by Alvarado Jubilee Committee. Alvarado, Minn., 1955.

Anglesburg, Eva K. *For Many Moods.* Bismarck, N. D., 1938.

Anderson, Arlo W. "Knut Hamsun's America," *Norwegian American Studies*, XXIII, ed. Carlton C. Qualey. Northfield, Minn., 1967, pp. 175-203.

Arnold, H. V. *The Early History of Inkster, North Dakota.* Larimore, N. D., 1916.

————. *The Early History of Ransom County: Including References to Sargent County, 1835-1883.* Larimore, N. D., 1918.

————. *History of Grand Forks County with Special Reference to the First Ten Years of Grand Forks City.* Larimore, N. D., 1900. Arnold wrote and published many well documented books on the early history. His great advantage was that he was a historian on the spot and because he was a newspaper publisher he had the mechanical facilities to produce the books.

Atkeson, Mary M. "Women in Farm Life and Rural Economy," *Women in the Modern World: The American Academy of Political and Social Sciences*, CXLIII (May, 1929), 188-190.

————. *The Women on the Farm.* New York, 1924.

Bailey, L. H. "Can I Make a Farm Pay?" *World's Work*, I (March, 1901), 548-551.

Becker, Carl. "Kansas," *America is West: An Anthology of Middlewestern Life and Literature*, ed. John T. Flanagan. Minneapolis, 1945, pp. 626-643.

Benton, Alva H. "Large Land Holdings in North Dakota," *The Journal of Land and Public Utility Economics*, I (Oct., 1925), 405-413.

Bidwell, Percy W. "Pioneer Agriculture: The Northeast," *Readings in Economic History of American Agriculture*, eds. Earl D. Ross and Louis B. Schmidt. New York, 1925, pp. 173-192.

Bill, Fred A. "Early Steamboating on the Red River," *North Dakota Historical Quarterly*, IX (January, 1942), 69-85.

Billington, Ray Allen. "How the Frontier Shaped the American Character," *American Heritage*, IX (April, 1958), 4-9, 86-89.

————. "Preface," *The Farmer's Frontier, 1865-1900*, Gilbert C. Fite. New York, 1966.

Blegen, Theodore C. *Norwegian Migration to America: The American Transition.* Northfield, Minn., 1940.

Bowsfield, Hartwell. "The United States and Red River Settlement," *Historical and Scientific Society of Manitoba Transactions*, Series III, No. 23 (1966-67), pp. 33-42.

Brewer, William H. "Agricultural Progress," *Harper's: The New Monthly Magazine*, L Dec., 1874-May, 1875), 880-889.

Briggs, Harold E. *Frontier of the Northwest: A History of the Upper Missouri Valley.* New York, 1950.

————. "Grasshopper Plagues and Early Dakota Agriculture, 1864-1876," *Agricultural History*, VIII (Jan., 1934), 51-63.

————. "The Great Dakota Boom, 1879-1886," *North Dakota Historical Quarterly*, IV (Jan., 1930), 78-108.

Burdick, Usher L. "Recollections and Reminiscences of Graham's Island," *North Dakota Historical Quarterly*, XVI (Jan., 1949), 5-30.

Callan, F. G. *A History of Richland County and the City of Wahpeton, North Dakota.* (Federal Writer's Project, W.P.A.) Wahpeton, 1937.

Carson, Gerald. *The Old County Store.* New York, 1954.

Cavileer, Charles. "The Red River Valley in 1851," *North Dakota History*, XII (Oct., 1945), 206-213.

Chestney, G. W. *The Red River of the North. (Federal Writer's Project, W.P.A.)* Breckenridge, Minn., 1939. In the files of the Wilkin County Historical Society.

The Challenge of the Prairie

Crofford, Mrs. H. E. "Pioneer Days in North Dakota: Ida C. Hall, A Pioneer Teacher of North Dakota," *North Dakota Historical Quarterly*, II (Jan., 1928), 129-137.

Dale, Edward Everett. *Frontier Ways*. Austin, Texas., 1959.

Dakota Farmer, Vols. I-V, 1881-1886. This farm magazine has excellent coverage of what has happened in agriculture in both Dakotas from 1881 to the present. It also carries articles of historical interest about the daily activities of farm families in both states.

Danhof, Clarence. "Farm Making Costs and the Safety Valve: 1850-60," *The Journal of Political Economy*, XLIX (June, 1941), 317-359.

———. "The Fencing Problem in the 1850's," *Agricultural History*, XVIII (Oct., 1944), 168-186.

Dewey, L. H. *The Russian Thistle: Its History as a Weed in the United States*. United States Department of Agriculture Bulletin No. 15. Washington, D. C., 1894.

Dick, Everett. *Vanguards of the Frontier: A Social History of the Northern Plains and Rocky Mountains from the Fur Traders to the Sod Busters*. Lincoln, 1941.

———. *The Sod House Frontier: 1854-1890*. New York, 1937. Everett Dick's books are well researched histories on the day-to-day life of the frontier's people.

Drache, Hiram M. "Boom Towns or Doomed Towns," *North Dakota Teacher*, XXXIX (Dec., 1959), 14-15, 36.

———. *The Day of the Bonanza: A History of Bonanza Farming in the Red River Valley of the North*. Fargo, N. D., 1964.

———. "The Economic Aspects of the Northern Pacific Railroad in North Dakota," *North Dakota History*, XXXIV (Fall, 1967), 320-372.

Eastman, Doris. "Pioneer Women—The Lonely Ones," *Fargo Forum*, Feb. 28, 1961, p. 25.

Elton, Emma Erickson. *Eglon Memories: A History of Eglon Township, Clay County, Minnesota*. Hawley, Minn., 1967.

———. *History of the Vaalhovd Family, 1857-1957*. Hawley, Minn., 1960. (Privately printed). Mrs. Elton was born at Hawley in 1875 and became an active historian at an early date. In 1857 the Erich Vaalhovd (later Erickson) family left Norway and eight weeks later docked at Quebec where the father was quarantined with typhoid. Because of the lack of funds, only Karen, the eldest daughter, remained with her father while the mother and six other children, ages 1 to 18, continued to Wisconsin where all but the 1 and 5 year old found work. After the father died, Karen went to Chicago and was never heard from again. After a few years in Wisconsin, the Vaalhovds moved to Allamakee County, Iowa, where the eldest son, Nels, established a farm. The family was unable to care for Christian, one of the younger children, so he was placed in a foster home. At this time the family name was changed to Erickson. The Ericksons farmed in Iowa until 1875 when they moved to Hawley with four other Norwegian families. The trip by covered wagon from the northeast corner of Iowa to Hawley took them three weeks. Emma Erickson, born in 1875 to the Nels Ericksons in their 14 x 20 foot frame house, became a homesteader herself when she filed a homestead claim in 1905 in the northwest corner of Williams County in extreme western North Dakota and made final proof by commuting in September, 1906. Her homestead shack was a single board building, 10 x 14 feet, covered with tar paper and banked with sod. Among her fellow homesteaders were a large number of females, some preachers, teachers, store clerks, newspaper men, a Negro, some college professors, and even a few farmers. Like most other homesteaders in that area, she had made the mistake of trying to make a living on too small a farm and was forced to return to Hawley in 1914.

Engelking, R. F., C. J. Heltemes, and Fred R. Taylor. *North Dakota Agricultural Statistics*. North Dakota Agricultural Experiment Station Bulletin No. 408 (Revised). Fargo, N. D., 1962.

Fargo Argus, Fargo Daily Argus, and *Fargo Weekly Argus*, 1879-1885; *Fargo Forum*, 1927-1968.

Fargo and Moorhead Directory, Vol. V. 1898-1899.

Fingal Enger Family History. Fargo, N. D., 1961. (Privately printed). Fingal Enger was born in Norway in 1846 and homesteaded in Steele County in 1872.

Fite, Gilbert. *The Farmer's Frontier, 1865-1890*. New York, 1966. Gilbert Fite has produced many books on agriculture and the frontier. *Farmer's Frontier* in some respects is a composite of his extensive background of material. It is one of the best single comprehensive studies of the western agrarian frontier.

Folwell, William Watts. *A History of Minnesota*, III. St. Paul, Minn., 1926.

Gannon, Clell G., and Russell Reid. "Natural History Notes on the Journals of Alexander Henry," *North Dakota Quarterly*, II (April, 1968), 168-200.

Gewalt, Chet. *Breckenridge: 100 Years of Progress*. Breckenridge, Minn., 1951.

Gill, W. R., and A. W. Cooper. "Tillage Tools," *Yearbook of Agriculture, 1962: After A Hundred Years*, ed. Alfred Stefferud. Washington, D. C., 1962, pp. 421-426.

Gillette, J. M. "North Dakota Weather and the Rural Economy," *North Dakota History*, XII (Jan.-April, 1945), 2, 5-98.

"Give the Farmer's Wife A Chance," *World's Work*, XL (Sept., 1920), 435-436.

Glaspell, Mrs. Kate Eldridge. "Incidents in the Life of a Pioneer," *North Dakota Historical Quarterly*, VIII (April, 1941), 184-190.

Gleanings in Bee Culture, XXII (Sept. 1, 1894), No. 17. Medina, Ohio. Ads from various pages.

Hamsun, Knut. *On Over Grown Paths*. New York, 1967.

———. "The Prairie," *The Living Age*, CCCX (Aug. 27, 1921), 549.

Hargrave, Joseph James. *Red River*. Montreal, 1871. Excellent early source by one who traveled through the region in the 1860's.

Haven, Gilbert. "Feathers Dropped from a Flying Wing," *Zion's Herald*, XLIX (Oct. 31, 1872), 518.

Haycraft, I. G. "1873-1877, The Grasshopper Plague," *With Various Voices, Recordings of North Star Life*, eds. Theodore C. Blegen and Philip D. Jordan. St. Paul, Minn., 1949, pp. 310-313.

Healy, W. J. *Women of Red River*. Winnipeg, 1923.

Hedges, J. B. "Colonization Activities of the Northern Paicfic," *Mississippi Valley Historical Review*, XIII (Dec., 1926), 314-321.

Hillsboro Banner Diamond Jubilee Edition. Hillsboro, N. D., June 28, 1956.

Hitchcock, A. P. "The Joys of Being a Farmer," *Country Life in America*, XX (July 1, 1911), 45-47.

Hobart, Charles A. "Pioneering in North Dakota," *North Dakota Historical Quarterly*, VII (July, 1933), 191-227.

———. "Pioneering in North Dakota," *North Dakota Historical Quarterly*, VIII (Jan., 1941), 14-131.

Holbrook, Stewart. *Machines of Plenty, Pioneering in American Agriculture*. New York, 1955.

Hope of the Prairie 1882-1927: 75th Anniversary Booklet. Hope Anniversary Committee. Fargo, N. D., 1957.

Huntington, Bill. *Both Feet in the Stirrups*. Billings, Montana, 1966.

Jarchow, Merrill E. "Farm Machinery in Frontier Minnesota," *Minnesota History Bulletin*, XXIII, No. 1, (1942), 316-327.

Johnson, Glenn E. "Here, There, Everywhere," *The Valley Times*, Moorhead, Minn., 1967-68. These articles carried very detailed information on a variety of topics relative to early days in the Fargo-Moorhead and Clay County area. The articles are in the files of the Clay County Historical Society of which Mr. Johnson is the president.

Johnson, Roy P. "Roy P. Johnson's Red River Valley; Indian Attacks in the Red River Valley," ed. Father Louis Pfaller, *Red River Valley Historian*, II (March, 1968). A reprint of a series from the *Fargo Forum*.

———. "Roy P. Johnson's Red River Valley: Stage Coaching Days Were a Colorful Era in Valley History," ed. Father Louis Pfaller, *Red River Valley Historian*, II (Autumn, 1968). A reprint of a series from the *Fargo Forum*.

———. "They Carried It All," *The Fargo Forum: Dakota Territorial Centennial, January 1881-December, 1885*. Feb. 28, 1961. Mr. Johnson, long-time staff member for the *Fargo Forum*, was one of the most active local historians for many years. He has articles on a wide variety of subjects and in most cases his stories were based on thoroughly documented research.

Krause, Herbert. *The Threshers.* New York, 1946.

Lamphere, George N. "A History of Wheat Raising in the Red River Valley," *Minnesota Historical Society, Collections*, X (Feb., 1905), 1-33.

Larimore, North Dakota, 1881, Diamond Jubilee. Larimore Diamond Jubilee Booklet Committee, Larimore, N. D., 1956.

Larsen, Hanna Astrup. *Knut Hamsun.* New York, 1922.

McLean, Harry F. "Presentation of the Statue of a Pioneer Family to the State of North Dakota," *North Dakota History*, XIV (Oct., 1947), 273-286.

McLure, W. Frank. "The Countryman Has the Better of It," *World's Work*, II (Oct., 1901), 1307-1311.

Matson, C. H. "A Giant Kansas Farm," *World's Work*, IV (July, 1902), 2327-2329.

Merck Veterinary Manual. Rahway, N. J., 1961.

Moorhead Independent, Holiday Supplement, Jan. 5, 1900. A booklet-type edition. Copies received from Virgil Tonsfeldt and James Wiedemann.

Morgan, Lewis Henry. *The Indian Journals 1859-62*, ed. Leslie A. White. Ann Arbor, Mich., 1959.

Morton, William L. *Manitoba: A History.* Toronto, 1967.

Munro, J. A. "Grasshopper Outbreaks in North Dakota," *North Dakota History*, XVI (July, 1949), 147-153.

Murray, Stanley Norman. *The Valley Comes of Age: A History of Agriculture in the Valley of the Red River of the North, 1812-1920.* Fargo, N. D., 1967. This book is a well documented and detailed account of Valley agriculture. It is likely to remain the definitive book on the subject for a long period. Murray knows the area intimately which helps make the book very valuable.

Nicollet, Joseph Nichols. *Report Intended to Illustrate a Map of the Hydrographical Basin of the Upper Mississippi River.* Washington, D. C., 1843.

"Old Settler's Deceased," *History of the Red River Valley, Past and Present*, I, Grand Forks, N. D., 1909, 133-184.

Ostenson, Thomas K. "Relationship of Real Estate Taxes to Land Values in North Dakota and Selected Counties," Department of Agricultural Economics, North Dakota Agricultural Experiment Station, North Dakota State University, Fargo, N. D., 1967.

Overby, Oscar R. *The Years in Retrospect.* Northfield, Minn., 1963. (Privately printed). Anne Overby, wife of Ole Overby and Oscar's mother, could never forget her mother's last words as she (Anne) departed for America in 1882. Anne's mother said, as she wiped her tears on a fresh new apron, "I would just as soon see you off to the cemetery." Ole Overby was a woodsman and had worked as a carpenter, mason, and blacksmith which proved helpful to him on the frontier. Neither Ole nor Anne had received any formal education in Norway and decided that their best hope for the future was in America. They prepared large amounts of food for their ocean journey, but, like others before them, found that long before they reached America the food had become unfit. The Overbys' initial destination was Motley, Minnesota, where Mrs. Overby gave birth to their first child. To save money, Overby walked the railroad track the 125 miles from Motley to Fargo where he begged for food until he obtained a job on the Northern Pacific working north from Valley City. Overby was teamed with an Irishman who did not want to work at their job of hauling dirt up the steep banks with a wheelbarrow. When the inspector noted their lack of progress, both were fired and left stranded on the open prairie—one grumbling in Irish and the other in Norwegian. Overby wandered to Wheatland where he joined a crew of sod busters but left them after a few days when they were unable to secure work. With knapsack, gun, and compass, he headed for Portland, Dakota, where he found a community of Norwegians who were happy to hear news from Norway. He eventually settled in the Sheyenne Valley about seven miles east of Cooperstown.

Pioneers: A Look Into the Past. Old Settler's Memorial Movement Association, Inc., Hillsboro, N. D., 1963.

Pinches, Harold E. "Revolution in Agriculture," *Yearbook of Agriculture, 1960: The Power to Produce*, ed. Alfred Stefferud. Washington, D. C., 1940, pp. 1-10.

Power, James B. "Bits of History Connected with the Early Days of the Northern Pacific Railway and the Organization of Its Land Department," *North Dakota State Historical Society, Collections*, III (1910), 337-349.

Pressly, Thomas J., and William H. Scofield. *Farm Real Estate Values in the United States By Counties 1850-1959*. Seattle, Wash., 1965.

Pyle, Joseph G. "James J. Hill," *Minnesota History Bulletin*, II (Feb., 1918), 295-323.

Qualey, Carlton C. "Pioneer Norwegian Settlement in North Dakota," *North Dakota Historical Quarterly*, V (Oct., 1930), 14-37.

The Record, Vols. I-V. Fargo, N. D., 1895-1899. An excellent periodical on local affairs.

"The Red River Carts, 1851," *With Various Voices, Recordings of North Star Life*, eds. Theodore C. Blegen and Philip D. Jordan. St. Paul, Minn., 1949.

Robinson, Elwyn B. *History of North Dakota*. Lincoln, 1966.

Rogin, Leo. "The Introduction of Farm Machinery in Its Relation to the Productivity of Labor in the Agriculture of the United States," *University of California Publications in Economics*, IX. Berkeley, 1931. An excellent and extremely thorough study on the subject of the impact of machinery on agriculture.

Ross, Alexander. *The Red River Settlement: Its Rise, Progress and Present State*. London, 1856.

Ross, Earle D. "Retardation in Farm Technology Before the Power Age." *Agricultural History*, XXX (Jan., 1956), 11-17.

Schell, Herbert S. "Official Immigration Activities of Dakota Territory," *North Dakota Historical Quarterly*, VII (Oct., 1932), 5-24.

Schmirler, Rev. A. A. A., and Page Community Committee. *Our Page 1882-1957*. Fargo, N. D., 1958. This is an excellent community history.

Semling, C. K., and John Turner. *A History of Clay and Norman Counties Minnesota*. Indianapolis, Ind., 1918.

Shannon, Fred A. "The Homestead Act and the Labor Surplus," *The American Historical Review*, XLI (July, 1936), 637-651.

"Significant Historical Events of North Dakota," *North Dakota Historical Quarterly*, IV (July, 1930), 277.

Smalley, E. V. "The Isolation of Life on Prairie Farms," *The Atlantic Monthly*, LXXII (Sept., 1893), 378-382.

Smith, Helena Huntington. "Pioneers in Petticoats," *American Heritage*, X (1959), 37-38, 101-102.

Spearman, Frank H. "The Great American Desert," *Harper's*, LXXVII (July, 1888), 232-245.

Spokesfield, Walter E. *The History of Wells County, North Dakota, and Its Pioneers*. Jamestown, N. D., 1928.

"State Geographic Board Report on North Dakota," *North Dakota Historical Quarterly*, II (Oct., 1927), 282-284.

Stevens, O. A. *Russian Thistle Life History and Growth*. North Dakota Agricultural Experiment Station Bulletin No. 326. Fargo, N. D., 1943.

Thompson, C. W. "The Movement of Wheat Growing: A Study of a Leading State," *The Quarterly Journal of Economics*, XVIII (1904), 570-584.

Thornton, W. B. "The Revolution by Farm Machinery," *World's Work*, VI (Aug., 1903), 3766-3779.

Torrison, Alfred. "Fisher's Landing, Minnesota," *North Dakota Historical Quarterly*, IX (Oct., 1941), 27-34.

The Truth About Wilkin County. Wilkin County Publicity Club. Breckenridge, Minn., 1910.

Valley Alert. Breckenridge, Minn., Sept. 5, 1968.

Valley Alert, Wilkin County Centennial 1868-1968. Breckenridge, Minn., July 18, 1968.

Visher, Stephen Sargent. *The Geography of South Dakota*. United States Geological Survey, Ca. 1915.

Walster, H. L. "North Dakota's War on the Russian Thistle," *The North Dakota Quarterly*, XXIV (Summer, 1956), 95-100.

Warkentin, John. "Mennonite Agricultural Settlements of Southern Manitoba," *The Geographical Review*, XLIX (July, 1959), 342-368.

Warren Sheaf. Warren, Minn., Dec., 1880-Feb., 1897; May 8, 1968.

Weber, Father Gerald; Mrs. Arnold J. Christopher, and Martin H. Lutter. "St. Francis Xavier Mission at Pembina: Advent of Christianity into the Upper Midwest," *Red River Valley Historian*, II (Autumn, 1968), 1-3, 31-34.

Webb, Walter Prescott. *The Great Plains*. Boston, Mass., 1931.

Wilkins, Robert P., and Wynona H. Wilkins. *God Giveth the Increase: The History of the Episcopal Church in North Dakota*. Fargo, N. D., 1959.

Woodward, Mary Dodge. *The Checkered Years*. Caldwell, Idaho, 1937.

Wright, Thomas C. *Otter Tail Power Company: From Its Origin Through 1954*. Fergus Falls, Minn., 1955. (Privately printed).

PUBLIC DOCUMENTS

Commissioner of Railroads Annual Report. Dakota Territory, 1886, 1888. State of North Dakota, 1890, 1896, 1901.

Historical Statistics of the United States from Colonial Times to 1957. United States Department of Commerce. Washington, D. C., pp. 289-290.

Minnesota Agricultural Statistics 1967. Minnesota Department of Agriculture and the United States Department of Agriculture. St. Paul, Minn., 1967.

Monthly Meteorological Report, 1876-1888. United States Weather Bureau, Fargo, N. D.

Statistical Abstract of the United States: 1965. United States Department of Commerce. Washington, D. C., p. 663.

Technical Bulletin No. 243. University of Minnesota Agricultural Experiment Station. St. Paul, Minn., 1

United States Weath. Bureau Official Records, 1889-1897. Moorhead and Fargo.

United States Weather Bureau Climatologist Chart, Aug. 21, 1967.

ST7XsDh18Z

der of May 26, 2021

y.   Item

The Challenge of the Prairie: Life and Times of Red River Pioneers
Drache, Hiram Dr. --- Paperback
0913163457
0913163457 9780913163450

turn or replace your item
t Amazon.com/returns

7XsDh18Z/-1 of 1-//MSP9-CART-A/next-1dc/0/0528-11:00/0528-00:09   SmartPacS

A gift for you

Hi Aunt Ardelle, I hope you enjoy this historical description of life on the plains in the Red River Valley as told by a professor at Concordia College. Love, Alan From Alan Krause

amazon Gift Receipt

Send a Thank You Note

You can learn more about your gift or start a return here too.

Scan using the Amazon app or visit
https://a.co/9JmxHSw

The Challenge of the Prairie: Life and Times of Red River Pioneers
Order ID: 114-6075416-4478660   Ordered on May 26, 2021

Index

Aaker, H. H., 283
Aal Lutheran Church, 254
Aarestads, 267
Abandoned house, for school, 303
Abercrombie, N.D., 13; early church, 254; farmers victimized, 88
Accidents, axe, 268; home, 271; horse, 139, 267; hunting, 266; well, 115
Adams, Ferdinand, land purchase, 311
Agassiz Literary Club, 209
Agriculture, United States Department of, fencing cost, 71; household lighting, 50; studies on power use, 94, 106
Agricultural revolution, 51, 55
Agricultural Society, 209
Aladdin lamps, 50
Alcohol, hot raw for diphtheria, 265; in medicine, 276 fn.; in patent medicine, 270 ff.
Alcoholism, a problem, 278
Alden Farm, certified seed, 317
Alexandria, Minn., 5, 6, 119; source of flour, 95; supply center, 21, 22
Alfalfa, introduced, 63
Alias, use of, 289
Alkali water, 116
Allen, Albert A., mayor of Jamestown, 154
Alliance, dances, 209; meeting Moorhead, 138
Alpenkraüter, German medicine, 270 ff., use of, 276 fn.
Alpha, 9
Alpholds-Basunen, 227
Altar and pulpit, cost of, 254; altar set, cost of, 254
Alternative income, 316-318
Altona, Manitoba, settlement, 18

Alvarado, Minn., 13, 160, 316; early school, 302
Amb, Fred, saloon, 281
Ambs Place, 280 (see saloon)
Amenia and Sharon Land Company, 52
Amenia, N.D., light plant, 52; strong temperance headquarters, 287
American, 236, 241; defined, 235
American Agriculturist, 228
Amidon, C. F., temperance leader, 287
Amundson, Ole, early settler, 22
Anderson, August, 275
Anderson, Mrs. Elizabeth Preston, 287 ff.
Anderson, John, 155
Anderson, Rev. Martin, 291
Anderson, Peter, 151
Andrus family, 235
Ankerfeldt, Edwin, first school, 303; prairie fire, 162
Ankerfeldt, Emil, 155; need to hunt, 216; social life, 222; storm of 1890, 155
Ankerfeldt, Mrs., isolated by storm, 155
Ankerfeldts, fishing, 78; hunting, 76
Animal problems, 86-87; sickness, 88-91
Anson Northup (also *Pioneer*), 5, 7, 11
Antelope Township, Scotch settlers, 235
Anti liquor bill, 291
Appendicitis, 263
Apples, 124
Apple trees, planted, 102 ff.
Appliances, household, 109
Appreciation, of land, 310 ff.
Arbuckle, Dr. C. W., 265
Argus, 226 (see *Fargo Forum*)
Aristocrats, 236 (see big farmers)
Arnold, H. V., 114
Arthur, N.D., 220; lights, 52

339

Rabbits, disease, 216, use of, 216
Raccoons, 76
Rahm, August, 202, 267
Railroad, rates, 14-15, 189, 217
Railroad coach, as a church, 249
Railroad fare, 18
Railroads, 11–15; for wood hauling, 111; problems, 228; stopped by fires, 164; source of income, 316
Rain, 172, 176 fn.
Raleigh Man, 128
Ransom County, 58, 65, 178
Rathskeller Over the Rhine, 280. See Saloon
R.E.A., 51
Reader, 306 ff.
Reaper, 182; self binding, 56
Reception house, immigrant, 23
The Record, 166
Red Lake River, 7, 159
Red River, 4, 5, 7, 70, 177, carts, 5; crooked stream, 9; drying up, 171; fish, 77; flooded, 159; freezes over, 148; high water, 11; hunting area, 216; low water, 11; stops grasshoppers, 165; supply of wood, 111
Red River Gazette, 226
Red River Land, 3
Red River Land Co., 227
Red River plain, 160
Red River Presbytery, 257
Red River Star, 228
Red River Trail, 135
Red River Valley, described, 74
Red River Valley Hail Insurance Co., 169
Red River Valley University (State School of Science), 298
Reflections, on pioneering, 28–30
Refrigeration, lack of, 93
Religious development, 248–252; education, 308; life in rural areas, 258
Remeley, F., 87
Rendahl, Sena, 104, 276 fn.
Reo, 144
Reynolds, N.D., 311
Rheumatism, 271
Rice, Jimmy, 123
Richland County, 178, 234, first settlers, 16
Richland County Globe, 227
Richland Lutheran Church, 254
Rich's Ferry, 137
Riel, Louis, 260
Ringsaker Lutheran Church, 258, 286
Ris gröd, 121
River crossings, early, 137

"Road agent," 128
Roads, Casselton to Buffalo, 144; condition of, 138, 144; in Cass Co., 144; first graded in Clay Co., 143
Robbers, 140; 87 ff.; at scholhouse, 304
Roberts Mill, 96
Roberts, T. M., 127
Rodgers, Rev. George, 23
Roen, Narve, 27, 64, 135
Roff, George, 90
Rolette, Joe, 25
Rolvaag, O. E., 238
Röme gröt, 120, 121, 262
Romness, Township, 214
Root beer, 95
Root cellar, 98
Root, William, 303
Rosholdt, Rev. T., 253
Rosser, Gen. Thomas R., 250
Rosser, Mrs. Betsy, 250
Rothsay, Minn., 144, early church, 253; flour mill, 96; jag wagon, 288
Rotary snow plow, 157
Rull, 121
Rum, 201
Runaway, with horses, 140
Russian thistle, 178
Rust, 178
Rustads, 280. See Saloon
Rural Free Delivery, 109, 127
Rural New Yorker, 69

Sabin, Minn., Brass Band, 211; flooded, 143; potato center, 317; school, 308; under water, 1888, 138
Sacks, to catch grasshoppers, 167
Saffron, 120
Saint Benedict, N.D., 233
Saint Cloud, Minn., 6
St. Francis Xavier Mission, 248, 295
St. Olaf College, 219
St. Paul, Minn., 4; hunters, 216
St. Paul, Pacific, Minneapolis Railroad, 162
St. Paul Pioneer Press, 228
St. Thomas Parish, 253
Salary, of ministers, 252 f.; teachers, 298 ff.
Salem Congregation, 254
Saleratus, 122
Saloon, business profits of, 278; number of, 279 ff.; opened at Page, 287; in Moorhead, 280
Sal Soda, 90
Salt, 4, 5; lack of; pork, 119, 121
Sam, Hop, 237
Sampson, Ella, 197